SHOW AND TELL

BY THE SAME AUTHOR

Biographies:
NOTES ON A COWARDLY LION: THE BIOGRAPHY OF BERT LAHR
PRICK UP YOUR EARS: THE BIOGRAPHY OF JOE ORTON
THE ORTON DIARIES (EDITOR)
COWARD: THE PLAYWRIGHT
DAME EDNA EVERAGE AND THE RISE OF WESTERN CIVILIZATION:
BACKSTAGE WITH BARRY HUMPHRIES
SINATRA: THE ARTIST AND THE MAN

Criticism:
A CASEBOOK ON HAROLD PINTER'S *THE HOMECOMING*
(EDITED WITH ANTHEA LAHR)
UP AGAINST THE FOURTH WALL
ACTING OUT AMERICA
ASTONISH ME
LIFE-SHOW (WITH JONATHAN PRICE)
AUTOMATIC VAUDEVILLE
LIGHT FANTASTIC: ADVENTURES IN THEATRE

Novels:
THE AUTOGRAPH HOUND
HOT TO TROT

Plays (Adaptations):
ACCIDENTAL DEATH OF AN ANARCHIST
DIARY OF A SOMEBODY
THE BLUEBIRD OF UNHAPPINESS
THE MANCHURIAN CANDIDATE

SHOW
AND TELL

NEW YORKER PROFILES

JOHN LAHR

BLOOMSBURY

First published in the United States in 2000 by
The Overlook Press, Peter Mayer Publishers, Inc.

First published in Great Britain 2001

The articles in this volume first appeared in *The New Yorker*

Woody Allen (December 9, 1996), David Mamet (November 17, 1997),
Frank Sinatra (November 3, 1997), Arthur Miller (January 25, 1999),
Liev Schreiber (December 13, 1999), Roseanne (July 17, 1995),
Irving Berlin (March 8, 1999), Wallace Shawn (April 15, 1998),
Eddie Izzard (April 6, 1998), Neil LaBute (July 5, 1999), Bob Hope (December 21, 1998),
Ingmar Bergman (May 31, 1999), Mike Nichols (February 21, 2000),
Bert Lahr (November 16, 1998), Mildred Lahr (May 13, 1996)

Bloomsbury Publishing Plc, 38 Soho Square, London W1D 3HB

ISBN 0 7475 5413 7

10 9 8 7 6 5 4 3 2 1

Printed in Great Britain by Clays Ltd, St Ives plc

To
Deb Garrison
&
Connie Booth

CONTENTS

SHOW AND TELL

INTRODUCTION

I REMEMBER IN 1962 standing in the wings of the Music Box Theatre on Broadway, where S. J. Perelman's "The Beauty Part" was doing brisk business, and watching my father, who was the show's star, get a laugh out of nothing. Later, walking back to the dressing room, I asked Dad how he knew the unpromising words were funny. "I listened to the audience, and they told me where the joke was," he said. It was a brilliant answer, which took me many years to fathom. Now I see that it was relevant not just to the business of comedy but also to the business of writing.

Listening with an alert ear, an informed mind, and an open heart is a large part of what I do these days for a living. It's a performance; it's also a delicate collaboration with the person I'm writing about, in much the same way that an actor and an audience inspire each other. Whether entertaining on the stage or on the page, for this particular game of show and tell to pay off, will and trust have to be part of the equation from both sides. These ingredients are hard-won; they can't be faked. The playwright Anna Deavere Smith, who acts out her research of contemporary Americans in brilliant cameos for her one-woman shows, told me: "There is also the issue of 'Am I worthy to hear them?' I like it that in some cases the dance that you have to do to get to the position of being allowed to listen is difficult." Of course, there is an element of seduction in the enterprise; but the encounter, at least for me, is based first on an empathy for the work, which then feeds a curiosity about the person who made it. This sense of connection—a form of love, I guess, but not a blind or a sentimental attachment—is what over time forges the agreement, draws out the subject, and, finally, allows the writer to ask the forbidden questions. The people profiled here are largely show people whom the public thinks it knows; they have a well-worked out social face, and so I have to listen hard to find that place in them which is not at ease and which their art defines and releases. Style, it seems to me, is metabolism. If you can find the pulse of the artist, you can find the pulse of the art. The whole purpose of the enterprise is to show how the life and the art intersect.

A Profile is a short exercise in biography—a tight form in which interview, anecdote, observation, description, and analysis are brought to bear on the public and the private self. The literary pedigree of the Profile can be traced from Plutarch to Dr. Johnson to Strachey; its popular modern reinvention is owed to *The New Yorker*, which set up shop in 1925 and which encouraged its reporters to get beyond ballyhoo to something more probing and ironic. Since then, with the wacky proliferation of media, the genre has been debased; even the word itself has been hijacked for all kinds of shallow and intrusive journalistic endeavors. There is no tabloid intention here. A full *New Yorker* profile, which nowadays runs on average to ten thousand words, takes about four months to research and to write; in my case, I usually amass about fifteen hundred pages of transcribed interviews, which form the backbone of the piece. In "The Journalist and the Murderer," my colleague Janet Malcolm argues controversially that the relationship of the journalist to his subjects is like that of an analyst to his patients. "They will tell their story to anyone who will listen to it, and the story will not be affected by the behavior or personality of the listener." She's not altogether wrong, but she's not exactly right, either. Here, for instance, David Mamet links his ear for dialogue to his fear of childhood abuse; Roseanne talks about comedy in terms of phallic aggression and her "psychic penis"; Mike Nichols discusses his director's obsession with control in terms of the particular powerlessness of his immigrant childhood; Ingmar Bergman connects the penetrating eye of his camera to his obsession with getting his standoffish mother's attention. These are all singular responses to singular questions.

Recently, it dawned on me that I am in the preservation business— preserving the memory of show-biz traditions, performances, players, and the conversation their art has with our times. The world that made these "cavorting hybrids" also made me, which is why I have included in a book about self-disclosure two portraits of my own family. My goal is to bring the reader as close to the person and the craft as I can. For me, there's a palpable thrill in this propinquity. It's a matter of some pride that I was the first writer to be given access to the inner sanctum of Roseanne's comedy team; or to be allowed to quote for the first time from Arthur Miller's notebooks for "Death of a Salesman" and to be taken by Miller himself to the cabin he built in the Connecticut woods to write his great play; or to sit next to Ingmar Bergman in seat No. 675 in the Upper Circle at the Royal National Theatre in Sweden, Stockholm, where as a boy he got his first glimpse of theatre and where he still comes between rehearsals to think about things.

Without *The New Yorker*'s support, and without the entrée its reputation provides, none of these profiles would have been possible. The past eight years at the magazine have been the happiest in my writing life. I owe a great debt of gratitude to both the magazine's former editor Tina Brown, who gave me a chance to play on such a big stage and to the encouragement and friendship of the present editor, David Remnick. Deborah Garrison, who now wields her red pencil for Alfred A. Knopf and Pantheon, edited all these pieces and made the doing of them something like joy. Her swiftness, her taste, her poet's ear for the right word, her sense of excellence, her faith in me and the work made the writing of these profiles an extraordinarily educational, exciting, and intimate experience. I am also grateful to the enthusiastic, hard-working panjandrums of Overlook Press—Peter Mayer and Tracy Carns—who have turned the fruits of this happy collaboration into a handsome book.

When I was a boy and already interested in words, I dreamed persistently of owning a magic pen. I would hold onto the pen (it was shiny and silver), and it would write like fury. Writing doesn't happen like that, of course; but sometimes, when I consider the accumulated intelligence of the magazine's editors, fact-checkers, readers, and colleagues who help to burnish my sentences and to present me to the world as the writer I always dreamed of being, it certainly feels just as magical and wonderful. To all those at *The New Yorker*—and you know who you are—a tip of my cloth cap.

J.L.
New York
March 9, 2000

WOODY ALLEN

THE IMPERFECTIONIST

IN THE TELEVISION ALCOVE of Woody Allen's book-lined and flower-filled Fifth Avenue duplex penthouse is a framed letter from Arthur Conan Doyle which mentions Houdini, the great escapologist. The letter was a paper-wedding-anniversary present from wife No. 2, the actress Louise Lasser, but to Allen its meaning is more than sentimental. Allen, who had a childhood fascination with magic—"To be able to perform a little miracle was such a heady feeling, something worth practicing endless hours for," he told me during a four-day conversation this fall—is also interested in great escapes, particularly his own. Like Broadway Danny Rose, Allen is "strictly pavement," and metropolitan to his marrow, but his airy apartment is a rustic cocoon: an open tiled fireplace, kerosene lamps, wicker baskets full of logs, polished pine floors, walls covered with Early American folk art. Even his writing room is not the unkempt, minimalist sump his movies might lead you to expect, but is dominated by a four-poster bed, under whose blue calico canopy he likes to sprawl and write, overseen on the bedside table by framed photographs of Cole Porter, Sidney Bechet, and Fyodor Dostoyevski—all, like him, technicians of distraction and delight.

When he is not closeted at home, Allen is locked away about twelve blocks south, manufacturing the illusion of himself at the Manhattan Film Center, which consists of a three-room editing suite at the far end of a dusky marble corridor on the ground floor of the former Beekman Hotel, on Park Avenue at Sixty-third Street. A large, low-ceilinged screening room, wallpapered in olive-green brushed velvet, with an olive-green carpet, and eight olive-green chairs pressed against one wall, serves Allen variously as audition hall, conference room, and clubhouse. At one end, behind a curtain, is a film screen; at the other end, on a little dais, is an old drab-green couch, whose left side, where Allen sits, has been worn through to its cotton lining.

At first, in this subterranean green-brown stillness, he is hard to take in. He is small, to be sure (he claims to be "tall" at five feet seven), and is dressed in his familiar unprepossessing tweed and corduroy, but there's a difference between the magician and his bag of tricks. Allen does not stammer. He is not uncertain of what he thinks. He is not full of jokes or bon mots, and when he is amused he is more likely to say "That's funny" than to smile. He is courteous but not biddable. He is a serious, somewhat morose person who rarely raises his voice, who listens carefully, and who, far from being a sad sack, runs his career and his business with admirable, single-minded efficiency.

Even when he was growing up, Allen was more formidable than he liked to show; the dissimulation of powerlessness appealed to him in the same way that the fantasy of being invisible gives a thrilling sense of power. "I didn't want to play Bogart," he says. "I didn't want to play John Wayne. I wanted to be the schnook. The guy with the glasses who doesn't get the girl, who can't get the girl but who's amusing." Allen admits that in fact he was never a nebbish, never that shlub in his classic standup routine who goes to an interfaith camp "where I was sadistically beaten by boys of all races and creeds." He was a good athlete at school (a medal winner in track, a lead-off hitter and second baseman in baseball, a schoolyard basketball player). And, contrary to his standup role as a social nudnik, Allen "wasn't a guy who was totally devoid of feminine companionship or couldn't get a date." In a sense, Allen's fiction has succeeded too well: the public won't divorce him from his film persona. "I'm not that iconic figure at all," he says. "I'm very different from that."

The real Allen holds himself in reserve. He is, like all great funny men, inconsolable; there is a boundary he draws around himself to protect himself and others from his sense of absence, which is palpable in his weak handshake, in the mildness of his voice, and in his subdued mien. Allen's antidote to anxiety is action: he saves his energy for the distraction of work, and his work ethic evolved early. "As an aspiring playwright in my late teens, I would meet some comedians, and I was taken by the fact that they all seemed to have a million distractions," he says. "I thought to myself, The guy who's gonna come out at the end of the poker game with the chips is the guy who just focusses and works." He adds, "You have to just work. You can't read your reviews. Just keep quiet. Don't get into arguments with anybody. Be polite, and do what you want to do, but keep working." Onscreen, Allen is a loser who makes much of his inadequacy; offscreen, he has created over the years the most wide-ranging œuvre in American entertainment. He is a standup-comedy star, the author of three volumes of classic *New Yorker* casuals and five plays (including two Broadway hits), an actor, and, of course, a writer-director of movies. His newest film, "Everyone Says I Love You," is a musical, and one of his most radiant works. His next film, "Deconstructing Harry," is already in production. This will bring the total of Allen's feature films to twenty-seven, which averages out to one a year since 1969, when he started making movies and mass-marketing his anxieties.

"I've never felt Truth was Beauty. Never," Allen says. "I've always felt that people can't take too much reality. I like being in Ingmar Bergman's world. Or in Louis Armstrong's world. Or in the world of the New York Knicks. Because it's not this world. You spend your whole life searching for a way out. You just get an overdose of reality, you know, and it's a terrible thing." He adds, "I'm always fighting against reality." Recently, however, reality got much uglier for Allen. In August of 1992, the news broke of his love affair with the twenty-one-year-old Soon-Yi Previn, one of the eleven children of his frequent collaborator and longtime companion Mia Farrow, with whom Allen has two adopted children—Moses, who is eighteen, and a daughter, Dylan, who is eleven—and one biological son, nine-year-old Satchel. Throughout the brutal war between him and Farrow, a scorched-earth campaign of unseemly primal betrayals on both sides which was played out in the tabloids in 1992 and 1993, Allen remained an omnipresent part of the culture's dreamtime. In the press, he was under siege; in his writing room, he was prolific. He finished "Husbands and Wives"; he wrote and directed "Bullets Over Broadway," "Manhattan Murder Mystery," and "Mighty Aphrodite"; he starred in a television version of his first Broadway hit, "Don't Drink the Water"; and he never missed a day—"not a single Monday"—of playing jazz at Michael's Pub. "He's *very* intransigent—in the best sense of the word," says the director

Sydney Pollack, who turned in a splendid acting performance as one of the self-deceived spouses in "Husbands and Wives." "For all the mild-man-neredness, the Mr. Peepers thing, I have always felt he was a very strong man." In the midst of his crisis, Allen didn't go completely underground. "He refuses to stay off the streets, no matter how many people recognize him," Pollack says. "It's a pain in the ass for him. But he needs to move around in life all the time." As Allen once joked, "I hate reality, but, you know, where else can you get a good steak dinner?"

In "Stardust Memories" (1980), the character played by Allen, a movie director named Sandy Bates, declared a moratorium on funny business. "I don't want to make funny movies anymore," Bates says. "I . . . you know, I don't feel funny. I—I look around the world, and all I see is human suf-fering." Allen had decided to serve up more serious fare to his moviegoing audience. He says, "I was gonna do films that had a harder edge, like 'Husbands and Wives.' If I wanted to make a film like 'Shadows and Fog,' I was not in any way going to live out my end of the contract with the audi-ence. I was gonna break that contract. I hoped that they would come with me, but they didn't." In an essay about Allen, the film critic Richard Schickel suggests that the audience left Allen, but Allen disagrees. "I left my audience is what really happened; they didn't leave me," he says. "They were as nice as could be. If I had kept making 'Manhattan' or 'Annie Hall'—the same kind of pictures—they were fully prepared to meet me halfway." But Allen defiantly refused. "Stardust Memories" made the point in its penultimate moment, when a disgruntled member of the audience, an old Jewish man, exits from the screening of a Sandy Bates movie. "From this he makes a living?" he says. "I like a melodrama, a musical comedy with a plot."

Now, sixteen years later, Allen has made that musical comedy with a plot and, incidentally, put a big deposit in the karmic bank. "Everyone Says I Love You" is a capriccio—Allen's wry version of an all-singing, all-danc-ing "champagne comedy," played out on the elegant avenues of New York, Paris, and Venice, starring Goldie Hawn, Alan Alda, Julia Roberts, Drew Barrymore, Tim Roth, and the old Ghost of Christmas Past himself. Here, in the world of pure money, Allen re-creates the sense of escapism which is his most vivid memory of moviegoing as a youngster in Brooklyn in the forties and fifties, "where no one's ever at a loss for the right phrase and everything comes out right at the end." Allen goes on, "After the double feature, you'd walk out again at four o'clock in the afternoon and suddenly the horns would be honking and the sun would be shining and it would be ninety degrees, and it wouldn't be Fredric March and Douglas Fairbanks, Jr. I personally felt I wanted to grow up, move into Manhattan, and live like that. I wanted to pop champagne corks and have a white telephone and trade ever-ready quips." The world of "Everyone Says I Love You"—where mannequins in shopwindows dance, where love almost always finds a way, where even the dead rise in ghostly chorus to sing "Enjoy Yourself (It's Later Than You Think)"—is meant to be an anodyne for both the audience and the author. "I had a pretty tough time for a year or two in there," Allen says, referring to his recent domestic troubles, which give urgency and poignancy to the film's bittersweet but unrepentant gaiety about lost love and new love. "His heart is opening," Goldie Hawn, who plays Woody's ex-wife in the movie, says; she compares him to "an armadillo" emerging from his protective carapace. Even Allen admits, "Perhaps in some way my relationship with Soon-Yi has had a salubrious effect. I'm willing to play more or be more playful." He says, "I thought, I want to enjoy myself. I want to hear those songs from over the decades that I loved so much. I want to see these people on Fifth Avenue and Park Avenue. It comes from what I wish the world was really like."

The lavish world of the musical denies emptiness and loss, but as a child growing up in Flatbush, Allen, who was born Allan Konigsberg, was visited early by what he once called "the bluebird of unhappiness." Allen has joked about his family's values being "God and carpeting"; what dominates his memories of his "lower-lower-middle-class" family is his warring, volatile parents, whose unhappy vibes "were there all the time as soon as I could understand anything." (He was the firstborn; his beloved sister, Letty Aronson, who is a co-executive producer of "Everyone Says I Love You," followed eight years later, in 1943.) "They were surviving. They were people of the Depression. They had no time for foolishness," he says of his parents, who were not so much hostile to him as indifferent.

The feeling was mutual. "I spent my time in my room," Allen says. "I never felt that either of my parents was amusing in the slightest way." He rarely used his parents as an audience for his magic tricks and never for his jokes. "That would have been like serving tennis balls into the ocean," he says. "I loved my parents. I do love them. But I had no interest in currying favor with them. I had other fish to fry at a very young age." (Martin and Nettie Konigsberg are now ninety-six and ninety, and live close to Allen. "I saw them this morning," he says. "It's the same thing. I'm sixty years old and I'll be standing in front of my parents now, I mean now, and they'll still say, 'Oh, come on, get a haircut. You look terrible.' " He adds, "They've stayed together out of spite.") By her own admission, Nettie was "very strict." "I remember you would hit me every day when I was a child," Allen is recorded saying to her in a documentary interview that is excerpted in Eric Lax's 1991 biography of Allen. His mother replies, in part, "I was very strict, which I regret. Because if I hadn't been that strict, you might have been a more, a not so impatient . . . you might have been a—what should I say? Not better. You're a good person. But, uh, maybe softer, maybe warmer."

"Everyone Says I Love You" reverses the gravity of Allen's past and acts out the importance of illusion to psychic survival. "In the end, we are earthbound," he says, explaining humor's ability to "defy all that pulls you down, that eventually pulls you all the way down." He goes on, "The comedian is always involved in that attempt somehow, through some artifice or trick, to get you airborne. Being able to suggest that something magical is possible, that something other than what you see with your eyes and your senses is possible, opens up a whole crack in the negative." "Everyone Says I Love You" does just that; and, by my lights, it belongs in the canon of Allen's best comic work: "The Purple Rose of Cairo" (one of his own favorites), "Broadway Danny Rose," "Annie Hall," "Hannah and Her Sisters." "Now, I'm gonna level with you," begins the narrator, a flirtatious seventeen-going-on-thirty-seven-year-old called D.J., which in this swank world is short for Djuna. "We are not the typical kind of family you'd find in a musical comedy. For one thing, we got dough. And we live right here on Park Avenue in a big apartment—a penthouse." On the contrary, the wealthy lawyer stepfather and his radical-chic wife with their household of bumptious and precocious kids, a gaga grandfather, and a

Prussian cook are exactly the elegant folderol you expect to find in a musical. Here, carrying the well-written story forward, is a shrewdly chosen selection of standards, including "Just You, Just Me," "My Baby Just Cares for Me," "I'm Thru with Love," and "Makin' Whoopee," all sung by the actors (except Drew Barrymore, who is dubbed). Allen, who says, "I never, ever sing, not even with my jazz band," here sings a few bars of "I'm Thru with Love"—an event that does for pessimism what Chaplin's speaking did for silence. "I've locked my heart / I'll keep my feelings there," Allen intones, in a stanza whose meanings speak beyond the film's moment. "I've stocked my heart / With icy frigidaire." Allen never looks into the camera as he delivers the words, but his cracked, reedy voice finds a perfect pitch for loss and isolation. "I used to tell Mia all the time that I wish everybody sang in life as in a musical," Allen says. "Because you get transported into a world that is a better world than the one I live in. There's a certain tenderness and affirmation."

Allen is naturally a fan of Chaplin, and Chaplin is honored in Allen's living room by a rare photograph from his vaudeville days. Like Allen, Chaplin created joy out of the morbidity of solitude; his Charlie, like Allen's Woody, was a metaphor for his era. Their behavior is informed by many similar qualities: both are self-educated, reclusive, melancholy, and meticulous; both are comic geniuses who give life without actually loving it. But the differences in their styles are instructive. Allen disagrees with the argument that silent comedy was harder to do because the comedians had to get laughs without the benefit of sound. "My contention has always been that silent films were easier because they were working with one simple thing—the visual," he says. "But once you got out of the visual with sound and it became less abstract and more realistic and you heard the comedian's words, guys like Keaton and Chaplin were not at all funny. It's much harder when you speak."

Allen tried speaking his words onstage for the first time in October, 1960, in a one-night audition at New York's Blue Angel. "I had unusual stage fright," Allen says. "I didn't have vomiting, but I couldn't eat all day long from the thought that at ten o'clock that night I was gonna go onstage." For the previous eight years, since he was seventeen, he had progressed rapidly from writing gossip-column gags for a press agency to writing sketch material with such masters of this arcane craft as Danny Simon, Larry Gelbart, and Mel Brooks. Originally, Allen seemed to just read his jokes to the audience. His manager at the time, Jack Rollins (who had discovered and managed, among others, Mike Nichols and Elaine May), recalls that he and his partner, Charles Joffe, who are now Allen's co-executive producers, "would howl with laughter" when Allen read his material. "He would be deadpan. It just broke us up." He adds, "The absence of shtick." Rollins convinced Allen that for the jokes to go over they had to be delivered with personality, and that required a perform-ance. "He had no—zero—experience as a performer," Rollins says. "He would recite his stuff like a child doing show-and-tell. It was mechanical, lifeless, bloodless, monotonous. But the material was brilliant."

In 1954, also at the Blue Angel, the nineteen-year-old Allen had been blown away by Mort Sahl and his conversational style. "It was the greatest thing I'd ever seen," Allen says. "People thought he was a great writer and not a great deliverer, but they're completely wrong. He was so skillful that you thought he was just talking."

Sahl created what Allen calls "the illusion of naturalness"; Allen creat-ed the illusion of haplessness. In his first night out, he stepped up to the microphone and, in his nasal voice, began to embellish on his short-lived student days at N.Y.U., where he'd actually earned an F in English and a C-minus in Motion Picture Production. "A lot of significant things have occurred in my private life that I thought we could go over tonight and, um, evaluate," he said. "I was a philosophy major. I took all the abstract philosophy courses in college like Truth and Beauty and Advanced Truth and Beauty and Intermediate Truth and Introduction to God. Death 101. I was thrown out of N.Y.U. my freshman year. I cheated on my metaphys-ical final in college. I looked within the soul of the boy sitting next to me."

Allen, who now talks about the art of joke writing in poetic terms— "You do it by ear, the same way that a poet needs a certain amount of syl-lables to make things happen right: the stammering, the repeating, the repetitions are all an instinctive attempt to get the right rhythm"—had discovered something in his low-key delivery. By a combination of bril-liance and good luck (what he calls "a shooter's bounce"), Allen had hit on a persona, much in the way that Chaplin had found Charlie when he put on the bowler and picked up the cane. "Keaton and Chaplin reflected an era where the anxieties and underlying vocabulary of people's longings were physical. It was a physical era. It was trains and machines," says Allen, whose stance onstage was physically almost frozen. "I came along after Freud, when the playing field had shifted to the psyche. It was interior. What was interesting to people suddenly was the psyche. They wanted to know what was going on in the mind." At the beginning of the century, Chaplin's kinetic tramp made a legend of dynamism; by its end, Allen's paralyzed Woody made a legend of defeat. "How can I find meaning in a finite universe, given my shirt and waist size?" he asked. Allen's jokes raised the promise of meaning, then flunked the task. A climate of retreat had asserted its hegemony over hope. The shrug had replaced the pratfall.

Allen kept up his burlesque nihilism in *The New Yorker* between 1966 and 1980 with twenty-eight casuals, which were collected into "Getting Even," "Without Feathers," and "Side Effects." One of his pieces, "The Kugelmass Episode," won the O. Henry Award for best short story in 1978. In these jeux d'esprit Allen indulged his philosophical frivolity ("Eternal nothingness is O.K. if you're dressed for it") and sent up a variety of literary genres, like diaries, in "Selections from the Allen Notebooks" ("Should I marry W? Not if she won't tell me the other letters in her name"), and pulp detective fiction, in "The Whore of Mensa":

> "I'm surprised you weren't stopped, walking into the hotel dressed like that," I said. "The house dick can usually spot an intellectual."
>
> "A five-spot cools him."
>
> "Shall we begin?" I said, motioning her to the couch.
>
> She lit a cigarette and got right to it. "I think we could start by approaching *Billy Budd* as Melville's justification of the ways of God to man, *n'est-ce pas?*"
>
> "Interestingly, though, not in a Miltonian sense." I was bluffing. I wanted to see if she'd go for it.
>
> "No. *Paradise Lost* lacked the substructure of pessimism." She did.

"When the contact is intimate between the mind and the emotions of the reader, you can just drop snowflakes," Allen says of the difference between jokes for the page and jokes for the stage. "The most gossamer things work. But when you're out there facing five hundred people, you've got to have a good joke line." Eventually, Allen stopped writing what he calls "little soufflés." "I did not want to look up after years and just have a number of collections of those kinds of things, like S. J. Perelman and Robert Benchley," he says. "If I was going to take the effort to write prose, then I should write a book, because I felt that a book would be more substantial and more worthwhile and more challenging."

In moviemaking, Allen has been writing books, but on film. He has found his bliss, and he has a very specific definition of the term. "Bliss comes from the success of denial," he says. "Moviemaking is an immense distraction, which is a godsend. If you weren't killing that time and you weren't distracted, you'd be sitting home confronting issues that you can't get second-act-curtain lines for." Allen exerts an almost occult control over his work. "I have control of everything, and I mean everything," Allen told me one afternoon in the crepuscular gloom of his screening room. "I can make any film I want to make. Any subject—comic, serious. I can cast who I want to cast. I can reshoot anything I want to as long as I stay in the budget. I control the ads, the trailers, the music."

This is another way in which Allen is like Chaplin: in the history of the American film industry he is the only comedian besides Chaplin to be allowed to control his product and to work as an artist. Chaplin owned an entire studio and employed a huge workforce that "stood in line, at attention" when he entered the studio gates, as a publicist for his operation once wrote. Allen, who doesn't have a real studio, and refuses such ceremony, has nonetheless engineered a way to be always in production. His dream deal evolved out of an early relationship with David Picker, the late Arthur Krim, and Eric Pleskow, the enlightened panjandrums of United Artists, whom Allen says he "was blessed by," and who had a hands-off policy during the making of movies like "Bananas," "Sleeper," and "Love and Death."

"It was a bit of an uphill fight," Pleskow says. "But overseas he became very important. Italy was the first foreign country where Woody became a big hit. Then it spread to France, and the Germans took him to heart as well. We developed a kind of rhythm. We could count on a film almost every year from him."When agents and industry executives questioned the wisdom of setting such a contractual precedent with Allen or tried to get a similar deal for their clients, Pleskow would tell them, "Look, if you bring me another Woody, who writes, directs, and acts, then we're talking about the same playing field." He goes on, "Woody was also able to get enormous casts for reasonable costs, because people want to work with him." In 1978, Krim and Pleskow left United Artists to form Orion Pictures, and Allen, after satisfying his U.A. obligations with "Manhattan" and "Stardust Memories," followed them there. Their laissez-faire policy continued from "A Midsummer Night's Sex Comedy" (1982) until they left Orion, in 1991. But Allen's carte-blanche arrangement still stands. His last three movies have been for Sweetland Films, a company of foreign investors, who retain foreign rights for themselves and allow Allen's friend and executive producer Jean Doumanian to sell the domestic rights to a distributor. Miramax took on "Bullets Over Broadway" (which cost sixteen million to make and grossed twenty and a half million worldwide), "Mighty Aphrodite" (which cost twelve million to make and grossed about eleven and a half million), and now "Everyone Says I Love You." "Woody has sacrificed great sums for his creative freedom, and he couldn't be happier about it," Sam Cohn, Allen's agent, says. In the old days, before Sweetland, Allen took union-scale wages for his services as writer, director, and actor, and his aggregate salary, according to Cohn, was "less than three hundred thousand dollars." He then got fifteen per cent of a film's gross, from the first dollar. If the film did well, he did well. ("Hannah and Her Sisters," for instance, which cost nine million dollars to make, grossed fifty-nine million worldwide.) In Allen's current deal with Sweetland, he gets a cash fee "in the very low seven figures," and then participates in the profits after Sweetland has recouped its money.

What would happen if he didn't completely control his product? I asked him. "I'd be gone," he said.

Allen sees his extraordinary artistic freedom as a mixed blessing. "You have no one to blame but yourself when you fail or when you do bad work," he explains. "I've often said, 'The only thing standing between me and greatness is me.' "Although Allen never revisits his films once he's finished them, he has a clear sense of their merits and limitations. "I would love to do a great film. I don't feel I've ever done a great film," he says, listing "The Bicycle Thief," "Rashomon," "Citizen Kane," and "Grand Illusion" as his standards of excellence. He adds, "I'm still in pursuit, and that pursuit keeps me going. If it happens, it'll happen by accident, because you can't pursue it head on." Indeed, the charm of work is its promise of forgetfulness, not of immortality. Allen's Herculean regimen—he sleeps seven hours a night, devotes one hour to the clarinet ("To maintain the low level that I play at, you have to practice every day"), and spends most of the remaining day at work—is awe-inspiring to those who know what an endurance test making a movie is. "I am both deeply depressed and exhilarated by what he does," Sydney Pollack says. "It gives me a *terrible* headache. If I'm *lucky*, in my wildest dreams I can make a picture every three years. I don't know how he does it." Of his prodigious output, Allen says, "It keeps you from the fear here and now." To a man like Allen, who is "hyperaware" of his finiteness, the medium of film offers certain exquisite properties. Movies not only stop time and kill time—they preserve time.

Comedies take Allen about a month to write, dramas about three months. Allen, who was practically writing before he could read, takes no pride in his facility. But he is unique among contemporary American filmmakers in having developed an uncanny ability to write complex, full-bodied female roles, and the actresses cast in Allen's films have won a disproportionate number of Academy Awards—Diane Keaton, Mira Sorvino, Dianne Wiest twice—and nominations (Jennifer Tilly and Judy Davis). "I was interested in women at a young age," Allen says. "When I was in kindergarten, I was trying to date them. I mean date them. I would ask them if I could buy them a soda or something." He goes on, "I remember in P.S. 99 they called my mother to school—this was in the fifth grade—and said, 'He's always in trouble with girls. That's all he thinks of.' "

"He loves women. He's not frightened of women. Thank God," says Barbara Hershey, who turned in a powerful performance in "Hannah and Her Sisters." Diane Keaton remembers being "crazy about him" at their first meeting, when she saw him standing on the stage of the theatre where she was auditioning for "Play It Again, Sam.""He could always get the girls, you know," says Keaton, who got the part and, for a while, Allen himself. (They stayed together for about three years.) "Girls have always liked him and had crushes on him because he's so funny and talented."

"It's more of an affinity with women," Dianne Wiest says. "There's some kind of relish, some kind of cherishing. It's complicated, really." She goes on, "He comes alive when he talks about Diane Keaton or when he talks about Soon-Yi. His whole affect changes. I've seen it with Keaton, especially. The way he listens to her. The way he makes fun of her. The way he has pride in her." (The teasing continues to this day. Recently, Allen called Keaton to leave a message on her answering machine. "I saw you on a television interview," he said. "The collagen is working.")

By his own admission, Allen has "gone to school" on the women in his life, and the particular intensity with which he takes them in——his habit of listening to and apprehending them——perhaps accounts for the fierce loyalty of his women friends. (Allen does have male friends, too: among them are the actor Tony Roberts, and the writers Marshall Brickman and Douglas McGrath.) Allen includes Wiest and Farrow in his gratitude when he says that the women he knows "have made major contributions" to his work. He adds, "I've been able to make a contribution to them, but they are there to make me look like a hero." Wiest claims that "no one else that I've ever worked with has demanded of me things that I was absolutely certain that I could not do," and she explains the genesis of her prima-donna role in "Bullets Over Broadway": "I called him and asked him for a job, basically. He is a very loyal, loyal friend to me. He said, 'Of course I'll write something for you.' When I got the script, I called him up and said, 'Who the hell were you thinking about when you wrote this? Because it wasn't me.' " But Allen knew, before Wiest did, that she possessed the right qualities, and he found a way to get them out of her. Sometimes the situation has been reversed: for instance, Mia Farrow's hard-edged, wig-wearing blonde in "Broadway Danny Rose" was not a type that Allen ever would have thought Farrow capable of, until, after observing Mrs. Rao, of the Italian restaurant Rao's, in New York, she said to him, "I'd love to play that kind of a woman."

"When I started writing professionally, I could never, ever write from the woman's point of view," Allen says. "It was when I met Keaton that I started. She has such a strong personality and so many original convictions." Keaton showed Allen how to appreciate the beauty of industrial landscapes, of old people's faces and their eccentricity. "I became interested in her and interested in her sisters and her mother as people," Allen says. "I felt I had a lot to learn from her. So I started to try and write things that gave her an opportunity to get out and do her thing." He adds, "It became fun for me to write from the female point of view. I had never done it before, so it was fresh. It also didn't carry with it the burden of a central comic persona that had to see everything the way a wit sees everything." "Annie Hall," for instance, celebrated Diane Keaton and memorialized her high style and her and Allen's high times. "There's no human that makes me laugh like Keaton," Allen says. "She took me over to meet her grannies. Her 'grammies,' that's what they were. She would say, 'Friday night, it's Grammy Keaton, and then I have to see Grammy Hall on Tuesday night.' She had me over to her house for Thanksgiving. I was sitting around with these grammies. I almost died. After dinner, they bring out a deck of cards and everybody plays penny poker. I'm sitting there with this enormous table of goyim playing penny poker. And they're all looking at me suspiciously, like I have a scheme to take them in the card game. It was a scene I eventually put into 'Annie Hall.' "

In his gleanings from the personalities of his female friends, Allen is aware of a curious sleight of hand that takes place. "I'll write something that I think is a true character," he says. "When you see it—if I've hit it—you think that I know more about the woman than I really know. It's an intuitive thing, from knowing the actress and knowing the character that I want to write for her. When it works, you can extrapolate truths from it, because it's inadvertent. If you write something from the heart, it's full of truths that you never had to cerebrally impose on it. Someone can look at it and say, 'Gosh, how can you know so much about this subject?' Well, you don't."

Casting is another area where Allen's method is "strictly instinctive." Over the years, his shrewd selection has proved to be the kiss of life to many a career. In "Everyone Says I Love You," for instance, Allen gives Goldie

Hawn an opportunity to be better and more varied onscreen than she's probably ever been. "I've never played a mother of so many children," Hawn, who has four children, says. "I've never been able to bring that wisdom—that connection to older children—to the screen."

The actual process of auditioning and casting people, however, is embarrassing to Allen. "Very often it approaches enormous awkwardness," he says, explaining, "I feel for these poor people." Over the years, according to his casting director, Juliet Taylor, Allen "has gotten socially more relaxed"; nowadays, he actually sees and "reads" the actors. There was a long time when he preferred not to hear them read. But Allen still keeps these encounters "embarrassingly quick"—just long enough to get "that first rush of what they are."

The Woody Allen casting call is something of a legend in the business. It is held at his screening room, and Allen, who rarely sits during an audition, usually tries to head the actors off on the threshold of the screening room before they can take up a beachhead and sink into a chair. Even prior to meeting Allen, they are primed by Taylor with a litany of caveats: "You shouldn't be offended," "He does this with everyone," "This can be very brief." Just how brief Allen demonstrates by going into his spiel: "We're doing this around September. There are a number of uncast roles. Juliet Taylor thought you might be right for one of them. I just wanted to see you. Just to take a look at you physically so I don't have to do this from photographs. We'll let you know about this. Thank you." By the clock, with pauses and a few cordial nods of the head, it's maybe thirty seconds. When Taylor and Allen were considering English actors like Sir Ian McKellen or Sir John Neville for parts in "Mighty Aphrodite," Taylor had to take Allen aside. "You have to let him sit down," she told him. "He's a knight." She adds, "Somebody else would come in who wasn't a knight but was very prominent. Woody would say, 'But they're not a knight. Why do I have to let them?' " Goldie Hawn, for her first meeting, swept into the screening room and, because of her star status, was given the couch. "She was beautiful, she was full of energy, she was great, she lit up the room," Allen says. "After the first ten seconds, I didn't have to have any more of her, that was enough." But not enough for Goldie. "I was just eating the air in the room, because he was saying nothing," says Hawn, who launched into an extensive, buoyant account of her travels. Allen cut her off with a joke. "Could you leave the room, so I could talk?" he said.

Allen is always looking for what he calls "thrill capacity." "Any artist— you see it very clearly in jazz musicians—comes out there, and what differentiates the great ones from the lesser ones is that they can thrill you with the turn of a phrase, a run, or the bending of a note. This is true of acting." He goes on, "You never know what Diane Keaton's going to do or what Dianne Wiest is going to do or what Marlon Brando's going to do. The same with Judy Davis. If you do ten takes with her she'll do it ten different ways."

Allen preserves a kind of authorial detachment from the actors; he stands apart from them, watching, judging, mulling, and then, like a novelist scrapping and recasting a chapter, he has been known to dismiss an actor and reshoot the scene. "He doesn't want to stand there and beg a performance out of you," Pollack says. "So he watches, and if it isn't working you're fired." (There have been a couple of dozen casualties over the years.) Allen also doesn't talk much to the actors. This can be disconcerting and demoralizing for the ensemble. Barbara Hershey, whose "favorite thing is to put my head together with the director and create the character," got no joy from Allen in "Hannah and Her Sisters." "I never wanted to tell her anything," Allen says of his laissez-faire approach. "I would tell her not to think about it. 'Just get out there. Do what you feel in the moment. Fight for your survival. If you're doing something wrong, I'll tell you about it.'" The method saves Allen a lot of time and boredom. "That would be tedious to me," he says. "To have actors come over, sit down, and to go over all that nonsense with them. You accept the part. When you read the script, I assume you have enough brains and common sense to know what you're getting into."

Many actors find the experience cold, but it is also freeing and—in Allen's hands, anyway—effective. Hawn likens Allen's directing style to good parenting. "We have a tendency with our own children to impose what we believe their life should be," she says. "We put in front of them all the do's and don'ts, shoulds and shouldn'ts. So we corral the spirit. Woody gives you the space to experiment with your creativity, to feel abandonment. Therefore, you start to discover what else you can do."

"Woody throws you into the Mixmaster and turns on the switch," Alan Alda, a veteran of three Allen films, says. "One of the things that happen is that the actors are so without their usual props—without the usual acting tricks that they can rely on—that they reach out to each other on-screen in an extraordinary way. You see wonderful relating in his movies. People really look like they're talking to each other. The other reason they look like they're talking to each other is that they really are listening, because they don't know what the other one's gonna say. They know the gist of it, but he seems to deliberately write it in a formal, uncolloquial way and asks you to make it colloquial. Most of the time he'll say, 'That sounds too much like a joke. Mess it up a little bit so it doesn't sound so much like a joke.' "

In "Everyone Says I Love You," there is a scene where Alda and his family argue over breakfast about family matters, for which, Alda says, "he did more directing there than in the entire first movie that I did with him." Allen himself uses the scene to illustrate his "typical way of directing." "It would be one master shot—everybody'd be in it," he says. "I'd get the actors together and tell them, 'These are the points that I need to make. I want to know that you're going to Le Cirque tonight, that the mother feels that she's championing the ex-con, and that the right-wing son is against her. I want that to come out.' " Allen goes on, "I just want the whole family to have breakfast and talk among themselves. So I say, 'Step on each other's lines. If you have a line that you want to be heard, fight to get it out. If you have exposition that's important, get it in somehow.' "

Allen is not easy on his actors, or on himself. "He's a sweet man, but he is not sweet when he's working," Wiest says. "Working with Woody is sweating blood, because he hears if you don't hit the notes. He's got great musicality. It's about hitting the notes. It's precision within the feeling. You've got to put the bead on the string, but before you even get to the string with Woody the bead has to be precisely round. It has to be great." Wiest, who in "Bullets Over Broadway" was made to descend a staircase about thirty times, knows Allen's look of displeasure—what she calls "a mild and gentlemanly disgust." She explains, "His head is tilted to one side. The left side of his mouth is up, the right side is down. His eyes are downcast. It's a thoughtful pose. But I know what's coming. I know it's not good for me." After the first day of shooting, Allen phoned Wiest. "You know, it's terrible. It's terrible!" Allen told her. "I told you so!" Wiest remembers telling him. "I think you should get somebody else." He said, "No, I think it's something to do with your voice. We'll reshoot it." Wiest, who has a high-pitched speaking voice, lowered it, and after the scene was reshot Allen said, "That's it." Wiest says, "That *was* it. That was the character. I'd be in the middle of a take and he'd go, 'Voice! Voice!' "

"It's just not good," he told Diane Keaton in the first week of shooting "Manhattan Murder Mystery." She explains, "He just will think of another way if it doesn't work. But if you're not cutting the mark, you're gone. It's not about friendship. It's not about anything. It's about the work." Allen does not regard his judgments as ruthless; in fact, he sees his lack of ruthlessness as a weakness. "I'm the opposite of a perfectionist. I'm an imperfectionist," he says. "I'm uncompromising with what I want to do with my work, but I'm not ruthless. I wish I were more ruthless. I feel that my work would be better if I could bring myself to express feelings of impatience or anger that I have but don't like to burden other people with." He goes on, "A more mature person would not go through that kind of mental anxiety. He would say, 'I'm sorry, we agreed that the costumes would all have red feathers on them and I'm not shooting unless they have red.' But I'll say, 'Well, all right, we'll do it this way.' "

Not always. On "September," Sam Shepard was granted permission to improvise a speech, and, according to Wiest, ended up talking about leaving Montana to go East to medical school. As Wiest and Allen were walking back to the dressing room, Allen turned to her. "Montana? Montana?" he said. "The word 'Montana' is gonna be in my movie?" It wasn't.

As a director, Allen gets what he wants, but when he gets in front of the camera he also—to some degree—must give the public what it wants. In "Everyone Says I Love You," Allen plays a typical Allen schlepper—a lovelorn American novelist living in Paris, called Joe Berlin. Joe's girlfriend has run off with his best friend, and he's suicidal. "I'm gonna kill myself," he says on a New York visit to his ex-wife, Steffi (Hawn), and her second husband (Alda). "I should go to Paris and jump off the Eiffel Tower. I'll be dead. You know, in fact, if I get the Concorde, I could be dead three hours earlier, which would be perfect. Or w-wait a minute. It—with the time change, I could be alive for six hours in New York but dead three hours in Paris. I could get things done, and I could also be dead." But on a trip to Venice with his daughter, D.J., he finds and wins the object of his desire—the married but unhappy Von (Julia Roberts). By the lucky coincidence of Allen's story, D.J. has eavesdropped after school on sessions conducted by her best friend's analyst mother, and Von is one of the regular patients; thus D.J. knows Von's intellectual passions (Titian), her problems (search for perfection), and how to manipulate her erogenous zones (blow gently between her shoulder blades). Joe, given all this advance intelligence, can't miss, and he doesn't. His uncanny powers are a deception, but Von sees him as a fantasy come true. "You know it's not that he's tall or handsome," Von tells her shrink. "But he's, um, magical."

Allen's art mediates between the need for illusion and the need to reach some accommodation with the real: Von leaves Joe—not because his magical-seeming con has been uncovered but because it has done its work too well. Her fantasy of perfection has been fulfilled; she is no longer tortured by the ideal and can accept the real. She decides to return to her marriage. Joe says, "Well, s-, but s-supposing I said to you that—that none of this was really true, that this is all a façade that I've been putting on. And I've been . . . playing this character just to . . . just to win you over, to get you to like me, make you happy?" Von counters, "I'd say you were crazy." Von can't accept the truth; Joe can't ever quite admit it. The moment demonstrates Allen's dilemma, which is that his strength is also his limitation: he's the spellbinder trapped by the success of his magic into a performance of someone he is not.

"The only hope any of us have is magic," Allen says. "If there turns out to be no magic—and this is simply it, it's simply physics—it's very sad." At the finale of "Everyone Says I Love You," he finds a way of expressing this longing for magical escape whose search dominates his films and his life. Joe, now abandoned by Von, takes his former wife, Steffi, away from a Paris Christmas costume ball and down to a spot by the Seine where, decades before, their romance began. Hawn and Allen are in evening dress, reminiscing. It's romantic stuff, but with regret just below the surface. As "I'm Thru with Love" strikes up, they start to dance—a Gene

Kelly moment in a Woody Allen body. "What is more ridiculous than a man singing or dancing, in a certain sense?" Allen asks. "It's the aspiration of your most intense feelings, musicalized. If you took the music away, it would look so silly. It's so vulnerable and so open." But the music is there, and so is the magic—in the form of special effects. As if levitating, Hawn glides weightless beside Allen, vaults over him, is lofted by one foot high into the air above him. Allen shows the audience the trick and at the same time plays it on them. Here, Allen, the overreacher, finds a way of expressing "that almost something"—a Romantic imminence of perfection, harmony, and transcendent grace. After the dance, they kiss; but, as Allen says, "the truth of the matter is, it isn't magic. You kiss her, and she goes back to her husband, and they go home."

Comedians are by nature enemies of boundaries. They live easier by the laws of joy which they create than by the laws of good behavior which society sets down. Their job description is to take liberties—something that the public applauds in art but abhors in life. Allen is not the only comic powerhouse to have come a cropper in this confusion of realms. Oscar Wilde was jailed, exiled, and ruined for flaunting sexual convention offstage as brazenly as his epigrams undermined social convention on it. Joe Orton was murdered in his bed for the sexual rapacity in private that made his comedies so successful in public. And Charlie Chaplin, throughout his career, consistently scandalized the American public, which called for his censure, his apology, even his deportation. Chaplin defied convention by wedding three teen-agers: he was twenty-nine when, in 1918, he married a seventeen-year-old actress; he was thirty-five when he married the already pregnant sixteen-year-old Lita Grey; and he was fifty-four when he walked down the aisle with the eighteen-year-old Oona O'Neill. He also fought—and lost on retrial, against all evidence to the contrary— a paternity suit brought by the twenty-five-year-old actress Joan Barry.

Near the end of "Everyone Says I Love You," at a costume ball where everyone is dressed as one of the Marx Brothers, the boy-crazy D.J. meets "a terrific guy—I mean, talk about sexy," and the camera angle widens to reveal that she, the daughter of Allen and his ex-wife in the movie, is dancing in the arms of a comedian, a Harpo Marx look-alike. The image echoes

Allen's own transgression with Soon-Yi. In a sense, the public knows too much and too little about Allen's domestic turmoil. The very source of Allen's comedy—his ability to compartmentalize anxiety and to escape his sense of absence by turning it into fun—is what he came up against in the brouhaha: his detachment, so often the source of his comic glory, became his grief. Even now, when he talks about Mia Farrow, it's the legal, not the emotional, aspect of the transgression which he acknowledges. "People think I fell in love with my daughter. They couldn't tell the difference between my real daughter and Soon-Yi Previn," Allen says. "People think I was married to Mia. I was never married to Mia. I never lived with Mia for one moment in my life. Mia lived across the Park and I lived here." He adds, "Mia spread the word that Soon-Yi was underage, that I had raped her, and that she was retarded. Now, she's twenty-six years old. She is in graduate school at Columbia." (In an affidavit, Allen pointed out to the judge that "Soon-Yi was as old as Ms. Farrow when Ms. Farrow first married.") Farrow has disagreed with Allen's characterization of her remarks, but doesn't Allen's explanation dodge the issue of his parental role in the Farrow ménage in any case? "Until Dylan was born, I had no contact or interest in any remote way with the children, none whatsoever," he says. "I lived my life. They lived their life. Mia and I went out and worked together and that was fine. The only reason I believe that we stayed together was because we achieved a kind of separate stasis. It was comfortable and very distant, I mean, very distant, uh, you know, in every way." Allen, one presumes, was present at the conception of their son.

"Artists are just like everybody else when it comes to moral questions and questions of human behavior," he says. "They're not entitled to any more leeway." But Allen, who has always gone his own way in art, has done the same in life—at a cost to himself, and sometimes, as he must know, to others. "He has great balls," Diane Keaton says, of the artistic gutsiness that also translates into Allen's behavior. "He's got balls to the floor." "Deconstructing Harry" was originally called "The Worst Man in the World"; in it Allen brazenly addresses what he perceives as the public's view of him. "I'm going right into the teeth of it," he says. "It's about a nasty, shallow, superficial, sexually obsessed guy. I'm sure everybody will think—I know this going in—they'll think it's me." When the furor first broke in the press, and Allen was accused by Farrow of abusing Dylan, his own view, he says, was "everybody's nuts. If it wasn't for a deeper pain in terms of children I thought that it was almost comical." He goes on, "The thing just kept snowballing and snowballing. People kept saying, 'This guy's career is finished.' I thought, You must be joking. My career can never be finished, because I will always write. Nobody can stop me. The stupidity of these allegations will fall by the wayside—if not in a week, in five weeks or ten, and of course eventually they did." After a fourteen-month investigation, which included a lie-detector test and a series of interviews at the Yale-New Haven Child Sexual Abuse Clinic, the Connecticut authorities terminated their investigation without filing charges against Allen. But he has still been tarred by the brush of child abuse.

"On many, many occasions, many occasions, over the phone and in person, Mia had said to me, 'You took my daughter, and I'm going to take yours,' " Allen told "60 Minutes" in 1992. (History is fable agreed upon, and, again, the two sides don't agree: Farrow denies ever having said this.) When the elevator door to Allen's penthouse opens, the first thing that meets the eye is pictures of the children, on the hallway wall, and when Allen walks into his writing room, he goes through Satchel's bedroom, past what looks like a life-size Tyrannosaurus rex standing guard over the bed. But the legal system has determined that it is not in Dylan's best interests to see her father, and Allen, whose supervised visits with Satchel are currently suspended by mutual agreement, has asked the court for more extensive visitation rights and is awaiting a decision. (Moses has chosen not to see Allen.) In the meantime, Mia has changed the children's names. Dylan is now called Eliza; Satchel was briefly Harmon and is now Seamus. "The children's best interests have not been served well at all," Allen says. "Murderers, dope addicts, people in prison—convicted people—are allowed to see their children. I wasn't even charged with anything, and I'm not allowed to see them." He adds, "I got a bad judge." Allen is thinking of turning the issue into a film. "We keep going to court, and every appeal is long and costly. I don't see the kid, and the kid doesn't see me. There's nothing I can really do about it legally, but I am going to do something about it publicly. I have a wonderful idea for a kind of documentary that's funny and sad and original. I will probably call it 'An Error in Judgment,' because they kept trying to pressure me into saying I made an error in judgment. I think there has been an error in judgment here, but it's been made by the judge."

Allen has no such qualms about his own decision. "I feel it's been one of the best relationships, if not the best, of my life," he says of Soon-Yi, who is thirty-five years Allen's junior, and whose presence is a reminder of life's bounty. "This was a poor girl who was an orphan in Korea, starving to death, eating a bar of soap for food and then throwing it up," Allen says (though he doesn't specifically credit Mia, who adopted Soon-Yi, with liberating her from all this). In his standup act, Allen used to joke that he was "breast-fed on falsies," and proper nourishment—emotional and otherwise—was an issue in his own childhood. "I always ate alone—lunch, breakfast, all meals. I never ate with my family," he says. "There were no books. There was no piano. I was never taken to a Broadway show or a museum in my entire childhood. Never." To this day, Allen needs constant stimulation. "When I go for a walk, I get a topic to think about, I never just go out casually," he says. "If I get into an elevator and I'm gonna go up more than three flights, or something, I'll buy a newspaper. I can't stand the unstimulatedness, because the anxiety sets in very quickly." Allen, who couldn't trust his family to meet his needs, fed himself. As he says in one of his evergreen lines, "I was the best I ever had."

This great joke admits Allen's loneliness in the kingdom of self, a loneliness that can be placated only by attainment—by the power to somehow redeem life and to see in the eyes of others the glow of the ideal. "Years ago," Allen told me, "I wanted to write this story where I would play a broken-down little magician in a cheap apartment or something. The girl downstairs would enter her apartment, and in some way she was going for some kind of psychological therapy. I would overhear her. I would follow her, then contrive to meet her and contrive to make her life what she wanted it to be."

Soon-Yi, it seems, has allowed Allen to live out this fantasy of omnipotence. "She gets a big kick out of all that I can provide for her, loves it. I love doing it for her," he says. "It's a wonderful relationship, because here's someone that I can really make happy and do things for and who appreciates it. There's just no hostility." In the eyes of the tabloids he is some kind of wolf in sheep's clothing, but to Allen "there's a genuine love between us." He says, "We underwent a crucible of intense terror tactics when this thing happened. The two of us were in the house. We'd be laughing that it seemed like the entire world was against us. Downstairs, we couldn't go out of the house because there were television trucks and paparazzi all over. The two of us would go up on the roof to get our fresh air for the day. We were housebound sometimes for a week. You know, it was quite romantic. She came through with flying colors for me. She stood by me in every way. She just wanted me to know that, whatever happened, she loved me." Soon-Yi now runs the house she has helped to redesign, and she and Allen have lived together for almost four years. In the den at the far-north end of their apartment, which overlooks the entire leafy expanse of Central Park, Allen has placed a gigantic refectory table, where Soon-Yi does her work: books, a computer, and papers are laid out as if at a banquet. It's life's banquet, which Allen himself, in his drivenness, can only peck at. His delight in providing for Soon-Yi is not unlike his description of doing a magic trick: "being able to do something that isn't of this routine, humdrum, cruel world." His reward is as simple as it is profound: to see his best self reflected in the accepting eyes of another. A similar chemistry is played out in his moviemaking. "There is that constant aspiration toward the magical moment," Allen says, "but in the end . . ." He stops and looks away. The sentence goes unfinished. The gloom of his mortality settles over him.

No one gets out of life alive; but the final surprise about Allen is that, for all his legendary negativity, he seems to enjoy his life and has worked hard at enjoyment. He "still gets a thrill" at the sense of blessing when, in the lush part of New York he inhabits ("the zone," he calls it), "I see those families take their kids to those private schools and their chauffeurs pulling up, and see the guys in tuxedos and the women coming down, and the doormen getting them cabs." It's the "champagne" world Allen dreamed of inhabiting in ice-cooled Brooklyn movie houses on the empty summer afternoons of his youth.

One Monday a few weeks after our conversation, Allen and I met again for dinner before going on to his gig at Michael's Pub, which has moved to the high-ceilinged elegance of the Parker Meridien, on West Fifty-seventh Street. Allen usually plays only the first set, and there's most always a line outside the room, so he enters the building from the rear and comes up through the kitchen just in time to go on. That night, he was facing a full house of about a hundred fans who were paying the twenty-five-dollar cover charge to hear the band but mostly to stare at him.

Allen plays the antiquated Albert-system clarinet used by his jazz heroes, players like Bechet, George Lewis, Johnny Dodds, and Albert Burbank. He has a Buffet clarinet, which he assembles at his table, in the rear of the room, facing the bandstand. "I don't think New Orleans jazz means much to anybody, but to a small few of us it's great," he says, fitting a Rico No. 5 reed onto his mouthpiece. What ravishes Allen about the music is the "warmth and simplicity" of it. "The more primitive the better for me. The enjoyment is more direct," he says. "The feeling is completely uncomplicated by any kind of cerebration. It's as simple as can be. Sometimes it's three chords. The guys who play it, who can really do it, make it so beautiful that it's astonishing."

Allen takes the stage. Here, wedged between a beefy banjoist and a crew-cut trumpeter, he goes through the band's repertoire and into a straight shot of joy. He plays almost the whole set with his eyes closed and his crossed left leg pumping like a piston. He claims to have a love for the music but "no gift," which isn't exactly true. What he lacks in breath he makes up for in vibrato. As the band swings into its program, which tonight includes "You Always Hurt the One You Love," "Seems Like Old Times," and "We Shall Not Be Moved," Allen's delicate fingers and his body warm to the task. He wriggles on his chair, rolling his shoulders and his head as he teases his croaky sound out of the clarinet. It's as if he were shedding skin, shaking free of his body and his woe.

Sometimes, in the early hours of the morning, Allen practices upstairs in his bedroom, staring out into the night. His treat is to put on a Bunk Johnson record and play in with the band. "I play with all the great players without having to meet them," he says. "To me it's like real. It's transporting. It's like being bathed in honey." In music, in film—in fact, in everything he does—Allen has created a fantasy world so potent that some of his most far-fetched dreams have come true. After all, as he says, Willie

Mays has flied out to him in a softball game at Dodger Stadium; he has played clarinet marching in New Orleans parades and at Preservation Hall; he has supped with Groucho and with S. J. Perelman. In his comic routines, Allen painted himself as the prince of pessimism: "I wish I had some kind of affirmative message to leave you with. I don't. Would you take two negative messages?" Yet he has certainly seized life with passion and with gratitude. "As you watch comedians with joy, or watch films with joy, it becomes metabolized and you pay it out," he says. "You're eating this food endlessly, endlessly. Then you look up and it's part of you." There is something poignant in Allen's avidity for delight. "If I were to close my eyes and imagine Woody," Diane Keaton says, "something I would keep with me is just the image of him watching 'Cries and Whispers.' Do you know what I'm saying? Him being swept away. I've seen it on his face. I've seen it. It's moved me. It makes me love him."

DAVID MAMET

FORTRESS MAMET

When I met David Mamet this summer, he made me the gift of a Boy Scout knife. On one side of the knife was the Scout motto: "Be prepared." The words, which invoke both prowess and paranoia, seemed to sum up the twin themes of Mamet's work, and of his guarded life. We were sitting in the back room of his headquarters, on the second floor of a two-story yellow clapboard building on Eliot Street in Cambridge, Massachusetts, at a table with a large Second World War poster hanging over it which read "Loose Talk Can Cost Lives! Keep It Under Your Stetson." There was no identifying name on the bell to the front door or on the office door. You had to feel your way along until you found Mamet hidden away, which is how it is with him. Mamet, who is masterly at communicating his meanings in public, is prickly in private. He is a small but powerfully built man; in the stillness of his presence and in the precision of his sentences, he exudes an imposing, specific gravity. "Fortress Mamet" is how Ed Koren, the cartoonist and Mamet's Vermont neighbor, refers to the emotional no-go area that Mamet creates around himself, and I was acutely aware of this hazardous moat as Mamet eased into a chair across the table from me, wearing his summer camouflage: a khaki baseball cap, khaki shorts, and a purple-and-brown Hawaiian shirt. Over the years, Mamet has adopted many fustian public disguises to counterpoint a personal style that Albert Takazauckas, the director of his first Off Broadway hit, "Sexual Perversity in Chicago," in 1976, characterizes as "blunt, blunt, blunt." He adds, "It's his lovely cover." As the star of Chicago's booming Off Loop theatre scene in the early seventies, Mamet affected Che's guerrilla look: fatigues, combat boots, a beret, and, for good measure, a cape. After his Pulitzer Prize for "Glengarry Glen Ross" (1984), his play about salesmen in a cutthroat real-estate competition,

Mamet assumed a Brechtian swagger: cigar, clear plastic eyeglass frames, and open collar, which consolidated in one iconic image the powerhouse and the proletarian. Now, in his mellow middle age, Mamet has forsworn the cigar and adopted the posture of rural gent: work boots, blue jeans, Pendleton shirt, and trimmed beard. In all these guises, the one constant is Mamet's crewcut, which dips like a tree line over the craggy promontory of his broad forehead and gives him an austere first appearance. "The crewcut . . . is an honest haircut," he has written. "It is the haircut of an honest, two-pair-of-jeans working man—a man from Chicago."

Mamet is certainly a workingman, even though, at a million and a half dollars a movie, he's far from a wage slave. He has written twenty-two plays, six collections of essays, two novels, and fourteen films, five of which he also directed. He belongs in the pantheon of this century's great dramatists; he has done for American theatre at the end of the century what his hero, the iconoclastic sociologist Thorstein Veblen, did for American sociology at the beginning: provide a devastating, often hilarious new idiom to dissect the follies of American life. Mamet's muscular imagination strips dialogue of literary nicety and robs plot of that naturalistic decoration which has progressively tamed theatre. His plays, though rooted in reality, are fables, whose uniqueness lies in their distinctive music—a terse, streamlined orchestration of thought, language, and character which draws viewers in and makes them work for meaning. No other American playwright, except perhaps Tennessee Williams, has ranged so widely. (Mamet is the only major American playwright ever to succeed as a screenwriter.) Three of his movies—"The Edge" (with Anthony Hopkins and Alec Baldwin), "Wag the Dog" (with Robert De Niro and Dustin Hoffman), and "The Spanish Prisoner" (with Steve Martin), which he also directed—are being released this year, which turns out, on November 30th, to be his fiftieth.

Mamet claims he doesn't lose his temper, but anger still defines him. "He's a coiled snake," his forty-six-year-old sister, the screenwriter Lynn Mamet, says. To those who have passed the test of loyalty, Mamet is an amusing, endearing, vigilant friend. "He was and continues to be one of the funniest and silliest people I've ever met," says the comedian Jonathan Katz, who has been Mamet's best friend since their days at Goddard

College, in Vermont, and with whom Mamet conceived the film "House of Games." "He was a master of disguises. We would have this running gag. Whenever one of us was meeting the other guy at the airport, we would be in disguise. One of my favorite disguises was when he was sitting in the airport with a paper bag on his head and smoke coming out of it. He was smoking a cigar under the paper bag." In public conversation, however, Mamet is courtly and wary; his style of discourse is not so much straight talk as Indian wrestling. He wrong-foots the listener with a curious brew of slang and erudition, mixing words like "ain't," "marvy," "jolly," "vouch-safe," "desuetude" in the same breath. There's a jaunty smile in these sentences, but a smile with cold teeth. "Oh, goody gumdrops," he said when I told him I'd be able to join him in Cabot, Vermont, where he owns a farmhouse and a hundred-acre parcel of rolling land. "Goody gumdrops from the gumdrop tree."

As I attempted to ask him unwelcome questions about his childhood, the presence of the Boy Scout knife on the table reminded me of the knife that the distraught ten-year-old John flashes in Mamet's autobiographical masterpiece "The Cryptogram"—a play about the betrayal of the boy by his parents. He is on the stairway looking down at the living room, where his mother, abandoned by his father and unable to meet his emotional needs, sits in the tortured last beat of the play. At whom, exactly, is the boy's murderous energy aimed, himself or others? His gesture foreshadows the life of the playwright, who learned to turn aggression into art: the knife became a pen. Knives are tools of creation as well as of destruction, and Mamet likes to whittle. His specialty is carving animal figures for his three daughters—Willa (fourteen) and Zosia (nine), both from his twelve-year marriage to the actress Lindsay Crouse, which ended in 1991; and Clara (three), from his marriage, in the same year, to the Scottish actress and singer Rebecca Pidgeon. The knife as an ambiguous symbol of penetration is the central metaphor of "Three Uses of the Knife," a collection of Mamet's lectures about theatre to be published later this year, in which he recounts an anecdote first told by the blues singer Huddie Ledbetter, better known as Leadbelly, who once said, "You take a knife, you use it to cut the bread, so you'll have strength to work; you use it to shave, so you'll look nice for your lover; on discovering her with another, you use it to cut out her lying heart." In its affecting irony, this progression illustrates for Mamet the essential elements of dramatic structure; it also demonstrates, he writes, "the attempt of the orderly, affronted mind to confront the awesome."

If Mamet felt affronted now, it was by my request that he turn back to the memory of his past. "My childhood, like many people's, was not a bundle of laughs. So what?" he said. "I always skip that part of the biography." After a while, he added, "This might help. There's a movie I'm hoping to do in the fall about making a movie. The female movie star is having a breakdown. She's crying. She says, 'I never had a childhood.' The director puts his arm around her. He says, 'I had one. It's no big deal.' "

Despite his disclaimer, the dominating themes of Mamet's work—the sense of not belonging, the imperative of speaking out, the betrayal by authority—evolve directly out of his childhood. He was the firstborn son of two handsome, highly intelligent, upwardly mobile first-generation Americans, Leonore (Lee) and Bernie Mamet, whose families were Ashkenazi Jews from Russia and Poland. "Are you an only child?" I asked Mamet when we first met, in 1983. "Yes," Mamet said, "except for my sister." "We lived in an emotional hurricane," says Lynn Mamet, the extrovert of the pair, who still speaks to her brother almost every day from her home on a scorched hillside canyon in Los Angeles. She adds, "We were safe for each other." Until their parents divorced bitterly, in 1958, when David was eleven and Lynn was eight, they lived on Euclid Avenue in Chicago's South Shore Highlands, in a capacious three-story red brick house that stood as a kind of totem to the Mamet family's self-invention. "My life was expunged of any tradition at all. Nothing old in the house. No color in the house," Mamet told me. "The virtues expounded were not creative but remedial: let's stop being Jewish, let's stop being poor." Lynn says, "There was a great deal of pressure for us to be the best Americans we could be. There was no room for us to make mistakes." She and her brother lived in fear of the ferocity of parental expectations—what Lynn calls "hoops of fire." "It was succeed or die," Mamet says.

Bernie Mamet, a tough labor lawyer who represented over three hundred unions, and once argued—and won—a case before the Supreme

Court, preached an exacting semantic gospel of precision, nuance, and observation. "The map is not the territory" was one of Bernie's mantras, which voiced his bedrock belief that nothing was all black or all white. He hectored his children to listen "with the inner ear," and, according to his second wife, Judy Mamet, played games with them to build up their powers of observation and memory. " 'Stickler' is a soft word for my father's attachment to the absolute necessity of expressing yourself correctly," Lynn Mamet says. "It's just that what was correct changed on a daily basis." In the crossfire of family conversation, David grew quickly into an agile sparring partner for his parents, and also learned to listen defensively. "From the earliest age, one had to think, be careful about what one was going to say, and also how the other person was going to respond," says Mamet, whose celebrated "ear for dialogue" evolved out of listening for danger. "In my family," he once said, "in the days prior to television, we liked to while away the evenings by making ourselves miserable, solely based on our ability to speak the language viciously."

Indeed, Mamet's prolific output and his compulsion to master skills (writing, directing, piano playing, sharpshooting) are a daily reiteration of competence in adulthood which seeks to redress a childhood whose litany was "You are not living up to your potential." Lee, who Mamet says "kind of created this wonderful persona of elegance," also had a short fuse and a sharp tongue. "You just didn't know where it was coming from—she could blow at any minute," Lynn says. "When they harvested the bipolar patch, she ripened first." To Lynn, Lee said, "If only I could have had a pretty daughter"; and, to David, "I love you but I don't like you." Lee had elusive verbal ways of parrying her children's demands, and this mystification, where what was being said wasn't what was meant, brought with it a sense of helplessness and frustration. Mamet demonstrates the shifting sand of this dynamic in "The Cryptogram," where John, the distressed young boy, can't make himself seen or heard by his self-involved mother, Donny. John is suicidal, and when he confesses his dark thoughts to her she seems to acknowledge them but then both literally and figuratively wanders away:

JOHN: Do you ever wish you could die? (*Pause.*) It's not such a bad feeling. Is it?

DONNY: I know that you're frightened. I know you are. But at some point, do you see . . . ? (*Pause. Exits.*) (*Offstage*) John, everyone has a story. Do you know that? In their lives. This is yours.

The boy's anxiety goes uncontained; throughout the play he is almost never touched or held. "They were not tactile," Lynn says of her parents. "If they were tactile, it was like being touched by a porcupine." Mamet is more forgiving: "They didn't have a clue," he says, explaining that Bernie and Lee had their children in their early twenties. Still, his portrayal of John's demoralized childhood and narcissistic mother connects to the notion of the "corrupt parent" that Mamet later outlined in one of his essays: "The corrupt parent says: 'If you wish to be protected you must withhold all judgment, powers of interpretation, and individual initiative. *I* will explain to you what things mean, and how to act in every situation'. " David himself was always in trouble for speaking up at home. "He would tilt at every fucking windmill," Lynn says. At such moments, his mother would say, "David, why must you *dramatize* everything?" "She said it to me as a *criticism*," Mamet told me. "I found out—it took me forty years to find out—that rhetorical questions are all accusations. They're very, very sneaky accusations."

Between his mother's mixed messages and his father's high standards, Mamet, who from an early age was a voracious reader but a wretched student, grew up believing he was stupid. "I was like the professor in 'Oleanna' "—his controversial play about a university professor accused by his pupil of sexual harassment—"who all his life had been told he was an idiot, so he behaved like one," Mamet says. "I just always assumed people assumed I was gonna come to a bad end." In "Jolly," an autobiographical one-act play that is part of three meditations on his past called "The Old Neighborhood," he addresses the psychological sleight of mind by which parents project their own inadequacy onto their children, as a grown up brother and sister sit talking about the sins of their parents:

BOB: . . . That's their way. That's their way. That's their swinish, selfish, *goddam* them. What *treachery* have they not done, in the name of . . .

JOLLY: . . . I know . . .

BOB: . . . of "honesty." God *damn* them. And always "telling"
us we . . .

JOLLY: . . . yes

BOB: . . . we were the bad ones.

In Mamet's family, the helpless collusion of children with their parents' sadism was acted out in good times as well as bad. In his essay "The
Rake" he recounts one such incident that took place after the family went
out to dinner. "My stepfather and mother would walk to the car, telling us
that they would pick us up," he writes. "We children would stand by the
restaurant entrance. They would drive up in the car, open the passenger
door, and wait until my sister and I had started to get in. Then they would
drive away. They would drive ten or fifteen feet and open the door again,
and we would walk up again, and they would drive away again." He continues, "They sometimes would drive around the block. But they would
always come back, and by that time the four of us would be laughing in
camaraderie and appreciation of what, I believe, was our only family joke."

In 1958, Lee married Bernie's law associate—a close family friend,
also named Bernie. She had moved out of the house with the kids, and they
ended up in Olympia Fields, on the outskirts of Chicago, which Mamet
called New South Hell. She didn't inform the children of her wedding
plans. "We'd been in Florida with my father," Lynn says. "We came home.
They said, 'How was your weekend?' We said, 'O.K. How was yours?'
They said, 'We got married.' David responded 'So what else is new?' and
went into the other room." He was profoundly distressed by his impulsive,
fist-pounding stepfather, who occasionally punched Lynn, and broke the
glass top of the kitchen table several times with his explosions of temper,
"so the table was associated in our minds with the notion of blood," Mamet
writes in "The Rake." His anxiety about this new "cobbled-together family" is powerfully evoked in his description of one afternoon in Olympia
Fields, when, as his sister remembers it, she came out to call him in to dinner while he was raking leaves. He hit Lynn in the face with the rake. "He
opened up the whole side of my face," Lynn, who still has a scar above her
lip from her brother's outburst, says. "If you could pick a single incident in

David's life which has constantly eviscerated him, it was possibly that act, which also explained a great deal to him internally. How he felt: his anger, his rage, his confusion, his life." But neither child—David out of guilt, Lynn "out of a desire to avert the terrible punishment she knew I would receive"—would fess up to Lee about what had happened. "My mother pressed us," Mamet writes. "She said that until one or the other answered, we would not go to the hospital; and so the family sat down to dinner, while my sister clutched a napkin to her face and the blood soaked the napkin and ran down onto her food, which she had to eat; and I also ate my food, and we cleared the table and went to the hospital." In a way, Mamet's iconoclasm as a writer is a means of understanding and of finding words for his fury. It also, he says, "stills two warring needs—the need to be accepted and the need to be revenged."

At the age of fifteen, after a series of blowups with his mother and stepfather, Mamet returned to Chicago to live with his father, on Lake Shore Drive. Although he was offered an airy, ample room, he chose to live in the maid's quarters near the back door, which made escape easy.

But Mamet could never escape his father. "Bernie Mamet was clearly the intense relationship of David's life, and there seems to be no aspect of the relationship of father to son that they did not explore to hell," says the director Gregory Mosher, who is Mamet's foremost interpreter and has collaborated with him on fifteen plays over the years. Mamet looked like his father; his skepticism and his savage view of entrepreneurial capitalism came from Bernie, who, according to Judy Mamet, regularly "railed against the inequities of commerce," and advised his son, "Don't trust an expert." Mamet remembers this theme being driven home in one of his father's early jokes: "A guy takes his son. He puts him on the mantelpiece, and to his son he says, 'Jump!' Kid says, 'Daddy, I'm frightened.' Father says, 'I'm your father. You kidding? Jump!' Kid jumps. Father steps back and the kid falls on the floor. Dad says, 'That's the first lesson. Don't trust anybody.' "

As a playwright and theorist, Mamet has adopted his father's advocate style of thinking against the system. "He was a winning lawyer. He believed in being smarter than the other guy and working harder than the other guy," says Mamet, who based the character of Jimmy Hoffa, in his

1991 film, on Bernie. "One of Dad's lines I put in the movie," Mamet says. "He said, 'Some people say that the client's gotta pay you to do your best. The client's not paying me to be best, the client's paying me to win.' "

Bernie, who had wanted to go on the stage himself as a young man, was deeply competitive even with his son. "He came to see 'American Buffalo,' " Mamet says. "He said, 'When are you going to chuck all this nonsense and go to law school?' " "He was a very hard man," says Sheila Welch, who observed them during the opening of "Edmond," in 1982, and later became the producer of Mamet's Atlantic Theatre Company. "He was very, very critical. I think he taunted Dave, almost like Mozart's father— you know, 'You have to be better'—but in a sense he secretly didn't want David to be better than him." For about four years in the eighties, the father and the son stopped talking to each other, but they made up after the birth of Mamet's second daughter, in time for Mamet to cast his father as a terrorist in his movie "Homicide." The occasion is memorialized in a photo of them on the set, in which Bernie sits slumped at a table in the foreground, wearing a leather jacket, and above him, dominating the frame, David stands on a radiator giving orders. On July 5, 1991, Mamet stood over his father for the last time, at his funeral. (Bernie had died of cancer, at the age of sixty-eight.) He spoke at the service; afterward, as is the custom in Jewish ceremonies, the mourners filed forward one by one to shovel a spadeful of dirt onto the casket from a huge mound of earth beside the grave. Mamet had his turn. But when the gravedigger picked up the shovel to finish the job, Mamet took the shovel back from him without a word and started to fill in the grave himself. It was a blistering summer day. After a while, he took off his jacket, and the wilted mourners watched for nearly forty minutes while he buried his father.

Mamet graduated from Goddard College, which he calls "sex camp," in 1969. By 1975, he was famous. His psychological makeup then, as now, was "essentially that of an unsure student who has finally discovered an idea in which he can believe, and who feels unless he clutches and dedicates himself to that idea, he will be lost." At sixteen, he had become a dogsbody and bit player at Bob Sickinger's innovative Hull House Theatre, in Chicago. "It was the first time in my confused young life that I had learned that work is love," he wrote later. He was by then well read in the literature of avant-garde drama, especially the plays of Harold Pinter. "It was stuff you heard in the street," he says. "It was the stuff you overheard in the taxicab. It wasn't writerly." He adds, "Pinter was sui generis. He was starting out with his vision of the world, and he was going to write it." (Pinter would later champion Mamet. "He sent me, unforgettably, 'Glengarry Glen Ross,' with a note saying 'There is something wrong with this play. What is it?' " Pinter recalls. "I wired him immediately. 'There is nothing wrong with this play. I'm giving it to the National.' ") Mamet began playwriting in his final year of college, after a summer vacation spent working as a busboy and odd-job man at Second City, Chicago's improvisational theatre, and watching comic players like Peter Boyle, Robert Klein, and David Steinberg; the quick cuts and blackouts of their revue format became part of Mamet's early punchy minimalism. "For the next ten years," he said, "none of my scenes lasted more than eight minutes."

Mamet had also taken off his junior year to study acting in New York with the renowned Sanford Meisner, at the Neighborhood Playhouse. Meisner believed that "every play is based upon the reality of doing," that "good acting comes from the heart," and that "there's no mentality in it." He urged his students to "fuck polite"; he devised the Word Repetition Game, in which two actors play off each other, each repeating exactly the words the other has just said, in order to bring out real emotion and impulsive shifts in behavior. Mamet wasn't chosen by Meisner to go on to the next year of classes, but when he began writing plays his distinctive fractured cadences and overlapping dialogue gradually transferred the rigors of the Word Repetition Game from the stage to the page. "I think the rhythm of his dialogue actually comes from the repetition exercises," says Scott Zigler, who has been a member of the Atlantic Theatre Company since its inception, in 1985, and who directed "The Old Neighborhood" on Broadway. "The rhythm is simply the rhythm of being in the moment." For instance, "Sexual Perversity in Chicago" begins:

> DANNY: So how'd you do last night?
> BERNIE: Are you kidding me?

DANNY: Yeah?

BERNIE: Are you fucking kidding me?

DANNY: Yeah?

BERNIE: Are you pulling my leg?

DANNY: So?

BERNIE: So tits out to here so.

But if it took Mamet a few years to absorb Meisner's teaching into his writing, it took him no time to incorporate Meisner's rogue ideas into what Mamet called his South Side Gypsy attitude. His senior-year project was his first completed play, "Camel"—a revue composed of thirty-four blackout bits based on "the more potent pieces in my journal." (It's a method that Mamet still uses, mining material from the daily ledgers he keeps.) He had never directed a play "in my whole sunlit lifetime," he wrote in the project notes. But, he went on, "I remembered that Acting is Doing. So I just started doing." Mamet had the chutzpah to charge fifty cents admission, a gesture that ruffled a lot of hippie feathers. "I wanted to communicate to the public at large that this was going to be no ordinary theatrical event," he wrote. Also, he added, "I felt like it." The last sentence of the project report served as Mamet's envoi to college life: "It's time for the actor to find another big rock to push up that long hill."

Everyone, including Mamet, conceded that he was not an actor. But in 1970, after undertaking various acting stints and odd jobs, Mamet found himself back in Vermont—this time teaching acting, first at Marlboro College and then, in 1971, at his progressive alma mater, which had no grades, no requirements, no tests. "So here comes Mamet dressed in tailored sailor pants, this tight shirt, with impeccably done hair. He walks like he's got a ramrod up his butt, and he just laid down the law," the actor William H. Macy, who is one of Mamet's closest friends, and who was nominated for an Academy Award last year for his performance in "Fargo," says of Mamet's arrival in class. "The first thing he said was 'If you're late, don't come in. If you're not prepared, don't do the class. If you want to learn to act, I'm the guy who can teach you. If you're not here for that, leave.' The class just looked at each other, going, 'Who is this fucking guy?' " Macy continues, "But he won us over. He was not egotistical in any way.

He just had this unshakable confidence." Mamet was in the habit of fining latecomers a dollar a minute and then burning their money. After about a year and a half of study, according to Macy, Mamet "walked in one day and said, 'I've written these plays.' It was 'Sexual Perversity in Chicago' "—a comedy about the vagaries of dating which, a few years later, would become Mamet's first hit. "In that incarnation," Macy goes on, "it was a bunch of blackouts—about twelve of them. A role for everyone. Who knew he even wrote?"

Mamet himself seems never to have doubted his playwriting ability. "I was just sure," he says. "I mean, how are you sure you got a fastball?" He adds, "Writing was something I could do. I figured, Well, if you fuck this up, you deserve everything that's gonna happen to you." When Mamet was about twenty-two, a friend sent a draft of "Sexual Perversity in Chicago" to Mike Nichols, who had recently made "Carnal Knowledge"; he said he'd have turned it into a movie right away except that he'd just made one like it. "I thought, Oh my God, these guys actually believe in me," Mamet says. "I better start working right now. I better have another play and another play after that." In 1972, he formed the St. Nicholas Company, in Vermont, with Macy and another of his students, Steven Schachter; in 1973, they shifted their base to Chicago, where, Mamet writes, "the air feels new, and all things still seem possible."

Mamet, who worked in the Windy City only between 1973 and 1977, is either Chicago's most famous New York playwright or New York's most famous Chicago playwright. "Chicago is very, very different from New York," he says. "In Chicago, you lived with your theatre company. The money that you made you shared. If you didn't work together, you starved. You weren't in it for an individual career." Chicago's earthiness extended to its pragmatic literary tradition, which carried with it "an intolerance for the purely ornamental." "Performance art—whatever the hell that may be—would have been completely foreign to Chicago, which is very meat and potatoes," Mamet says. "If it's a comedy it would be a good idea if it were funny." Mamet and his cohorts, who soon added the actress Patricia Cox to their founding group, lived by their wits. They helped fund their productions by giving acting classes. "We invented this myth of the Chicago theatre scene," says Gregory Mosher, who considers having bumped into Mamet in 1975 "the central fact of my life." "What made the Chicago theatre scene was that no one cared. The audience didn't care. They were profoundly indifferent to everything we did."

In those days, Mamet resided and wrote at the Lincoln Hotel. "His room was the size of a closet. He had no belongings. It was Spartan like you can't believe," Macy says. But "from the very first day I met him," a Chicago playwright, Alan Gross, recalled in the Chicago *Tribune* in 1982, "David told me he was an important American playwright. . . . He was completely self-encapsulated. He knew exactly what he wanted to do and what was expected of him; he had a great rap, a great act." According to the program note for the St. Nicholas's début production, the company was named for the patron saint of "mountebanks, prostitutes, and the demimonde." And Mamet had a bit of the mountebank in him. "He was very, very fast on his feet," the company's first literary manager, Jonathan Abarbanel, says, referring to what he calls Mamet's "intellectual Barnumism." Abarbanel once told the magazine *Chicago*, "He would be talking—'As Aristotle said, blah blah.' Or, 'I was rereading Kierkegaard the other day.' I remember saying, 'Aristotle never said that! You weren't reading Kierkegaard!' And he'd go, 'Sshhh! Don't tell anyone.' "

While Mamet waited tables, drove taxis, and cleaned offices to support his theatrical habit, he turned Chicago into a kind of raffish playground. "He always had very good luck with the ladies," Macy says. "Oh, man, smooth as silk." (One of Mamet's best come-ons—"Is anyone taking up an inordinate amount of your time these days?"—is memorialized in "Sexual Perversity in Chicago.") He explored the city's gritty corners, whose vernacular he savored and kept note of. Among his actor friends, Ed O'Neill had been a football star at Ohio University; Dennis Farina had been a policeman; and J.J. Johnston, a walking lexicon of underworld phrase and fable who was from the South Side, had been a bookie. Having been raised on high culture and hated it, Mamet was drawn to "people who don't institutionalize their thought."

"Dave got hit with the gangster bag early," Johnston, who recalls telling him about the old-time hoods, says. "These crooks, most of them, have pipe dreams. They can't do anything right. Like they say, these guys would fuck up a two-car funeral." Mamet, who has written a lot about criminals, including his screenplays for "The Untouchables," "Things Change," and an upcoming movie about Meyer Lansky, sometimes socialized with them and saw their pathos at first hand. "They're entrepreneurs," he says. "They speak their own language. Like many people engaged in violence, they're sentimental." He tried to talk his way into a daily North Side poker game of petty thieves, which was held in a junk shop owned by a fence called Kenny. "I came out several times, hung out, they didn't want to let me sit down," he says. "Then, one day, I wasn't there. They said, 'Where were you yesterday? We missed you.' I said I was teaching drama at Pontiac Correctional Center. It turned out later that many of them had done time at Pontiac. So they started calling me Teach, and they let me sit down on the game." It was out of this subterranean milieu that Mamet made his first masterpiece, "American Buffalo"—a tale of betrayal cloaked in the comedy of a botched heist, set in a Chicago junk shop. When he handed the script to Mosher, a stripling director just out of Juilliard who was in charge of the Chicago Goodman Theatre's Stage 2, Mosher told him he would read it over the weekend. "You don't need to read it," Mamet said. "Just do it." He paused, then added, "Tell you what. I'll put five grand in escrow, and if the play doesn't win the Pulitzer, keep the money."

Mamet didn't win that year's Pulitzer and never made good on the promise, but "American Buffalo" made his name. It was produced on Broadway in 1977, giving Mamet his first real payday; it was the beginning of his being able to make a living as a playwright. Though it was only his second full-length play, it was a great leap forward in his storytelling. As late as 1991, Mamet maintained that it was "the most structurally competent" of his plays. "It has the form of a classical tragedy," he said then. As he put it to me recently, "That's the only thing I ever really worked hard at in my life: plotting. Do it and do it, and do it again." He added, "I'm not looking for a feeling—I'm looking for an equation. Given the set of circumstances, what does it end up with? How is that inevitable? How is that surprising?"

What Mamet had excavated from the junk-shop poker games and captured in "American Buffalo" was the notion of a world and an idiom composed of waste. In the swagger of small talk he found a metaphor for the

spiritual attrition of American capitalism. His small-fry characters hilariously emulate the badinage of big business. "You know what is free enterprise," says Teach, the punk who kisses himself in on a plan to rob the coin
collection of a man who recently paid the junk-shop owner ninety dollars
for a nickel. "The freedom of the *Individual* . . . to Embark on any Fucking
Course that he sees fit . . . in order to secure his honest chance to make a
profit. . . . The country's *founded* on this, Don. You know this."

Mamet's rhythm gave the words and the pauses an unusual emotional
clout. "Dave's dialogue is a string of iambs, which can often be broken
down into fives," Mosher says. "For example, 'But all I ever ask (and I
would say this to her face) is only she remembers who is who and not to
go around with her or Gracie either with this attitude: The Past is Past, and
this is Now, and so Fuck You' is, I believe, twenty-seven iambs in a row."
Joe Mantegna, one of Mamet's favorite actors, talks about seeing Mamet
"tapping it out with his pen" while actors speak their lines. Sometimes
Mamet could be even more insistent. "He sits in the back of the house
going, 'Pick up, pick up, pick up!' " Mosher says.

In Mamet's plays, speech becomes the doing that reveals being; identity is dramatized as each character's struggle to speak his meaning. For
instance, Teach, who is full of big plans, can't think clearly. When he makes
his sensational entrance cursing "Fuckin' Ruthie," who has insulted him for
eating a piece of toast off her plate, we hear a syntax that reels backward
like his fearful, scrambled mind:

> Only (and I tell you this, Don). Only, and I'm not, I don't
> think, casting anything on anyone: from the mouth of a
> Southern bulldyke asshole ingrate of a vicious nowhere cunt
> can this trash come.

Over the years, so many people have written Mamet to complain
about the "language" in his plays that in the eighties he had a form letter
printed which read "Too bad, you big cry baby." Once, while talking on the
phone in the kitchen to the producer Fred Zollo, Mamet reached into the
refrigerator to help his daughter Willa get a Fudgsicle. "Oh, fuck," he said.
"Daddy, don't use that language," Willa laughed. Mamet replied, "That lan-

guage put that fuckin' Fudgsicle in your mouth." In his plays Mamet rel-
ishes slang for its impoverished poetry; it helps to create the sense of energy and of absence which his work dissects. In "Sexual Perversity" it's the
absence of self-awareness (" 'Cunt' won't do it," Deb says to the inchoate
Danny. " 'Fuck' won't do it. No more magic. . . . Tell me what you're *feeling*. Jerk"); in "American Buffalo" it's the absence of beauty and possibility
("There is nothing out there," Teach says after trashing the shop. "I fuck
myself"); in "Glengarry Glen Ross" it's the absence of community and
calm ("Fuck *you*. That's my message to you. Fuck you and kiss my ass,"
Shelly "the Machine" Levene crows at Williamson, the guy who gives out
the property leads, after making what he fondly thinks is a sale). Out of
the muck of ordinary speech—the curses, interruptions, asides, midsen-
tence breaks, and sudden accelerations—Mamet carefully weaves a tapes-
try of motifs which he sees as "counterpoint." "The beauty of the fugue
comes from the descant, from the counting," he says. "The melody line is
pretty damn simple. Anyone can write that." When he composes, Mamet
says, he doesn't picture the characters onstage; he hears them. "The
rhythms don't just unlock something in the character," he says. "They *are*
what's happening."

Until Mamet emerged, American commercial theatre was primarily a literary, naturalistic theatre, where words were a libretto for the actor's
emotions, and where the actor determined the rhythms. To be successful,
the author had to become invisible. But Mamet brought the author's voice
back onto the stage; his ideas about acting protect the author's voice at the
expense of the actor's invention. "The words are set and unchanging. Any
worth in them was put there by the author," he writes mischievously in
"True and False." "If you learn the words by rote, as if they were a phone
book, and let them come out of your mouth without your interpretation,
the audience will be well served." This is, to say the least, controversial.
"It's completely nuts," says the director Karel Reisz, whose films include
"Saturday Night and Sunday Morning" and "The French Lieutenant's
Woman." "In order to get what you want from the other actor, you have to
invent, color, invest it with your own feelings. I think the notion of separating words from actions is very odd; words are part of the action. It's the

reason why the shows he directs are so poor. The element of believability is not there; you have the sense of automata reciting the words."

Mamet, like Pinter or Beckett, is perhaps not the best interpreter of his own vision. ("The Cryptogram," for example, was given an excellent English production by Mosher which Mamet did not see, and was directed by Mamet, first in Cambridge and then in New York, without the same impact.) But once he had defined his voice he was determined to defend it. He even traded punches with the actor F. Murray Abraham during the New York production of "Sexual Perversity in Chicago" when Abraham rejected Mamet's tempo in his line readings. "He was like a man on a mission," says Fred Zollo, who met Mamet in those early years and went on to produce most of his major plays as well as many of his films. "I just wanted to be so far ahead," Mamet says. "I didn't want to look back and find somebody gaining on me. If I couldn't write a play, I'd write a movie or I'd write a poem or I'd direct something or I'd teach a class or write a book. I didn't care." He continues, "I ain't gonna go home."

In 1976, Mamet moved to New York, married into show-biz aristocracy—Lindsay Crouse was the daughter of Russel Crouse, who, with his partner Howard Lindsay, wrote such Broadway smash hits as "Life with Father" and "The Sound of Music"—and got down to work. During this period, he began supplementing his playwriting with screenwriting. He got his first assignment through Crouse, who was on her way to audition for Bob Rafelson's 1981 remake of "The Postman Always Rings Twice." He told her to tell Rafelson that "he was a fool if he didn't hire me to write the screenplay," he says. "I was kidding, but she did it." Rafelson called Mamet and asked why he should hire him. "I told him, 'Because I'll give you either a really good screenplay or a sincere apology.'" He also wrote "The Verdict," and by 1982 he was at work on "Glengarry Glen Ross," which had its début at London's National Theatre and then went on to become a huge hit on Broadway. Crouse, who starred in such films as "Slap Shot" and "Places in the Heart," for which she was nominated for an Oscar, "understood the joy and glamour of show biz," the playwright John Guare says, "and she had integrity." Guare remembers walking with her in Vermont: "She said to me, 'Just look at him. Do you realize that this man has made himself? He's been given no help.' I understood David's sense of will through her pride in it. She was so sublimely proud of him—until she wasn't." But in the years they were together Crouse was essential to him. "She saw herself as a creative partner, and in some ways she probably was," Sheila Welch says. She adds, "David wasn't very smooth socially. Lindsay had social graces. David learned how to present himself in the theatre world from her." Mamet was now properly seen as well as heard. "That's why I love the theatre," a character says in "Edmond." "Because what you must ask respect for is yourself." If he hadn't found the theatre, Mamet has said, "it's very likely I would have become a criminal—another profession that subsumes the outsider, or, perhaps more to the point, accepts people with a not very well formed ego and rewards the ability to improvise."

"Injury has given David enormous energy," Sidney Lumet, who directed "The Verdict," says. "I have no idea where it comes from, but there's a sense of 'I've been screwed.' A lot of the movies are very much about being had." In fact, all Mamet's movies, including the recent crop, and most of his major plays, are about betrayal. Many of them revolve around con artists, those picaresque urban hunter-gatherers who scour the postindustrial wasteland in search of both surplus and leisure, and around con games, which give his sense of betrayal a dramatic form. Mamet himself has performed a mentalism act at county fairs, and when he was in college he shilled for his friend Jonathan Katz, then a nationally ranked Ping-Pong champion. "We would stage a game for money between him and me, and I would let him win," Katz says. "He wouldn't give me a rematch. I'd get 'upset,' but some other guy would give me a rematch, having just seen me beaten by David playing badly." The magician and master card manipulator Ricky Jay says of Mamet, "He has what a hustler has. He has 'grift sense.' It's what makes his plays work." In "House of Games" (1987), the first movie that Mamet both wrote and directed, the con illustrates the dilemma of trust. "I 'used' you. I did. I'm *sorry*," Mike, the con man, says to his mark Ford, who has caught him out. "And you learned some *things* about yourself that you'd rather not know." He continues, "You say I Acted Atrociously. Yes. I did. I do it for a living." Writers do the same in the service of their story, but with this difference: their lies are like truth. Mamet sees a parallel to the con game in writing for the theatre. The con of performance is to rob the audience not of money but of its preconceived notions. "The trick is leaving out everything except the essential," Mamet explains. "As Bettelheim says in 'The Uses of Enchantment,' the more you leave out, the more we see ourselves in the picture, the more we project our own thoughts onto it."

The con trick has a still more abiding pull on Mamet's imagination: it reverses the parental situation. In the con, the public is put in the role of the helpless child, while the con artist is the parent who knows the game and controls all the rules and the information. The whole enterprise is an assertion of omnipotence and a refusal to admit helplessness, which speaks to something deep in Mamet's nature. At the finale of "House of Games," Mike is held at gunpoint by Ford, who has shot him twice. Ford says, "Beg me for your life." But Mike, a con man to the last, won't. He'd rather die than be infantilized and surrender his sense of autonomy. Ford shoots him again. "Thank you, sir, may I have another?" Mike says as Ford fires three more shots into him. In real life, Mamet also controls the rules of his game: he is the agent of all action, all answers, all interpretation. Even Mamet's instructions to actors, which demystify the notion of character ("There *is* no character. There are only lines upon a page"), are a way of insuring that the play's meaning and invention stay with him. "He controls the actors with an iron hand, in the rhythms and little quarter words and half words and stammers," Mike Nichols, who uses Mamet's work in his acting classes, says. "He says '*You vill do vhat I say!*' more than any writer that's ever written for the theatre, with the possible exceptions of Lillian Hellman and Pinter. For the actor to force his life through this iron control leads to such exciting things." It can also sometimes flatten and dehumanize performances, as it did Lindsay Crouse's in "House of Games." But as a film director Mamet has progressed from that static, unsure first effort, which one critic accurately observed was shot "like an Army training film," to the fluid, well-paced achievement of "The Spanish Prisoner," in which a con trick played on a credulous company man becomes a moral lesson about how the getting of wisdom equals the getting of skepticism.

About every eighteen months, Mamet likes to direct a movie. "When I'm making a movie, I'm just about as happy as I can be," he says. "I'm playing dollhouse with my best friends in the world." He oversees these occasions with patriarchal good humor and consideration. "He's an embarrassingly stand-up guy," the producer Art Linson says. "He expects nothing from people. So when somebody does something, the slightest gesture, he's truly moved." Every night after shooting, Mamet goes among the crew and thanks each member personally. His sets are exceptional for their congeniality. "I've had many happy movie experiences, but that one was right up there at the top," Steve Martin says about playing the heavy in "The Spanish Prisoner." Mamet keeps a joke reel of each film, which is to say a partial record of his practical jokes. On the first day of "The Spanish Prisoner," for instance, he laid out for the actress Felicity Huffman a Brünnhilde costume, complete with horned helmet. Once, during the shooting of "Oleanna," he asked William Macy to learn a new full-page speech on the spur of the moment and he put it on cue cards for the take. "I start the speech," Macy recalls. "I do the first card. I get to the second card, and it reads, 'But what do I know? I'm just a dumb towheaded cracker from Georgia. You know, when Dave first picked me out of the gutter. . . ' "

Of course, Mamet has less fun being a hired hand on other people's Hollywood projects. "Being a writer out there is like going into Hitler's Eagle's Nest with a great idea for a bar-mitzvah festival," he says. His streamlined screenplays, which have no embellishments or explanations, are not studio-executive-friendly. "They're dry sponges waiting for the water of performance," Sidney Lumet says. "And that's when they swell up to five thousand per cent." Mamet's script for "The Verdict" had been forgotten by the producers, who had spent more than a million dollars in development, but Lumet read Mamet's early version and said it was the one he wanted to shoot. Likewise, Paramount was indifferent to Linson's notion of going after Mamet to write "The Untouchables." A cartoon of their first meeting, in 1984, is pinned on the wall of Mamet's cabin, with Linson giving his pitch: "Dave, don't you think that the best career move for someone who'd just won the Pulitzer Prize would be to adapt 'The Untouchables' for a *shitload* of money?" Mamet's screenplay departed from the TV series, and, inevitably, the executives didn't like it. Nonetheless, when it was filmed by Brian De Palma it grossed over two hundred million dollars worldwide and gave Mamet considerable heat in the industry.

Actually, Mamet's minimalism and his notion of character suits screenwriting. He works up his story on file cards. "You know the movie's ready to be written when you can remember it," Mamet says. "When the progression of incidents is so clear that you no longer need the cards, then you're ready to write." He writes very fast. "He wrote the first draft of 'The Untouchables' in what seemed like ten days or less," Linson recalls. "He has occasionally turned a script in to me and said, 'Could you please sit on it for a couple of weeks? I don't want them to think it's this easy.' Dead true. Once Dave gets something, it just kind of writes itself." Rewriting Mamet is very difficult. "It looks like somebody put a patch on a pair of Levi's," Linson says, and, though Mamet will accept notes and supply rewrites, "there'll come a time where the gate comes down and it's '*No más.*' "

Mamet's talent and his inflexibility have given him something of a bad-boy reputation in Hollywood, whose folly he memorialized in "Speed-the-Plow." "I find that a smile and a hearty 'Fuck you' does the trick," he says of seeing off the intrusive suggestions of movie executives. Sometimes even his own producers get it in the neck. Mamet once handed Zollo a copy of "American Buffalo" to do as a movie. "Have you adapted it for the screen?" Zollo asked. "Adapted it?" said Mamet. "Have I fucking what? I'm going to adapt it right now for you." Mamet demanded the script back. "He crosses out 'A Play by David Mamet' and he writes 'A Screenplay by David Mamet,' " Zollo says. Mamet is fortified in his truculence by the lesson of his poker playing ("If you're smarter than the other guy, be smarter than the other guy") and by a favorite dictum of the English critic William Hazlitt, which he paraphrases as "Don't try to suck up or even be nice to your intellectual inferiors. They'll only hate you more for it." He adds, "Having read that makes my life a little bit easier." About two years ago, Bob Conte, of HBO, gave Zollo a few pages of notes to give to Mamet on his "Lansky" script, which is finally being produced this year. "Essentially, almost all of our notes concern the following issues: Chronology, Clarity, and Character (alliteration unintended)," Conte wrote. "Tell him to Suck My Dick," Mamet told Zollo. "Alliteration unintended."

Mamet's life as an uncompromising writer/director seems in direct contrast to—and is probably made possible by—the tranquillity of his surroundings. In Vermont, he lives in a converted farmhouse, originally built in 1805, that sits on the rise of a hill and looks down a sloping meadow onto a large beaver pond. There are deer, bear, and moose in the sur- rounding forests, where Mamet likes to walk and sometimes hunt—or, as he says, "take my gun for a walk." He never shoots anything. "My wife calls me the Deer Protection Association," he says. If he gets in his Land Rover, a gift from Linson for a week's rewrite, he can be at Goddard College in fifteen minutes; if he gets on his mountain bike, as he does with Rebecca several times a week to go into town for the mail, Cabot is less than four miles of hard pedalling away. Mamet's kingdom consists of the farmhouse, a red barn, and a cedar cabin whose shingled roof is tucked under the bough of a pine tree about a hundred and fifty yards from the house.

Onto this rough-hewn masculine landscape Rebecca Pidgeon has put her graceful mark: red, white, and pink hollyhocks press up against the fence posts; under the kitchen window, she has planted an array of herbs among rows of rhubarb, spinach, and lettuce, which Mamet looks upon with the kind of wonder that Jack had for the beanstalk. "After roses, it's all broccoli to me," he says. Mamet's admiration for his wife's competence and for her attentiveness to the world around her is transparent and touch- ing. "She's had a tremendous effect in anchoring him, in calming him down, in making him feel it's O.K. to be scared, it's O.K. to be upset, it's O.K. to fail," Lynn Mamet says. "There's nothing self-destructive about her. She's healthy. And I think it's allowed my brother to exhale for the first time in his life."

Mamet first laid eyes on Pidgeon, who is nineteen years younger than he is, at National Theatre rehearsals in London for a 1989 production of "Speed-the-Plow," in which she was playing the tenacious, idealistic secre- tary who almost succeeds in making the producing goniff do good. "He came up to her and said, 'You know, I always wanted to meet a girl like that,'" the actor Colin Stinton, who played opposite Pidgeon, recalls. "She blushed and was sort of flattered by it, I think." Pidgeon, who had her own rock band in addition to her acting career, was resourceful, straightfor- ward, and beautiful; and she didn't bore him. "You think she likes me?" Mamet badgered the painter Donald Sultan, with whom he had travelled to London. Sultan explains, "I said, 'Yeah, I think she likes you.' He said,

'What makes you think that?' I said, 'Well, every day for the last six months, every thought, every word, every action has been yours. How could she not like you?'" Pidgeon herself was surprised that she did. She says, "I had imagined him as this old, tall, very intellectual, cold, godlike kind of writer, and then I see this young, vibrant kind of street urchin. I thought, How could this be possible?" In the meantime, Mamet called his sister from London. "He said, 'I've found her,'" Lynn Mamet says. "He told me about her. I said, 'So, you'll marry her.' He went on for months, driving me crazy. 'She's in London, I'm here; she's got this career, I'm here; she's eleven, I'm here.' "

After a two-year long-distance courtship, they married; Mamet had found his bliss and a new mellowness. Zollo was surprised when Mamet agreed in 1994 to let him mount "The Cryptogram," which he had kept in his trunk since the late seventies because of its intensely personal material. "He felt safe in his life," Zollo says, by way of explanation. Pidgeon says, "We're extremely compatible. There's no 'I'm going off to be a genius and be troublesome and mysterious and worried.' We have a very peaceful life." Contentment seems to have opened Mamet up even in literary ways. "I think his women's writing has improved since his marriage to Rebecca," Lynn says—a statement borne out by the complex rewrite of the mother's role in "The Cryptogram," and by the corporate femme fatale in "The Spanish Prisoner," a part well played by Pidgeon. Lynn goes on, "I don't think David has written a lot for women because I don't think he's been around that many women to whom he wishes to listen, and therefore replicate their voices."

Rebecca and Clara go down through the meadow to hunt for frogs at the beaver pond, and Mamet heads for the cabin. "I've never been anything other than happy here," he says as we approach the porch, whose left side is piled high with firewood. In the winter, when it can get to forty below and the snow is deep, Mamet makes the trek in snowshoes. When he arrives, his ink is frozen, so he improvises a trivet out of pie plates, putting pencils under the ink bottle and warming it up on the black Glenwood's parlor stove that dominates the front half of the room. There is an exhilarating sense of containment and comfort here, where Mamet's cherished objects are arranged carefully around him: a canoe paddle with a beautifully painted pike on its blade hangs on the beam separating the writing area from the reading area; there's a dartboard, a skeet thrower, a collection of campaign buttons, a .58 muzzle-loader, a nine-pound medicine ball, and bookcases full of outdoor reading like "The Parker Gun Shooter's Bible Treasury" and "Black Powder Gun Digest." It's as if, instead of with the stove, Mamet were keeping himself warm with the things he loves. "Being a writer is all so ethereal that I think most of us tend to surround ourselves with tchotchkes so we can actually be sure we have a past," he says. "Or a life."

Mamet types with his back to the window on a blue Olympia manual typewriter, above which a kerosene lamp is suspended by a chain from a beam smudged black with smoke. The special calm of the place is in part the peace of having no electricity; it is also the peace of the activity that goes on there. Writing has always been Mamet's way of containing terror, or what he calls "mental vomit." "David's brain is a very busy place. It's very cluttered," Lynn Mamet says. "Writing's the only thing that stops the thinking, you know," Mamet says. "It stops all that terrible nonsense noise that's in there." In "The Edge," where the billionaire bookworm thinks himself out of the backwoods, Mamet quite literally shows the triumph of thought over terror. It's something that he clearly works hard at in his own life. Across the room, on a table in front of the sofa, his serious reading is laid out: D. W. Winnicott's "Thinking About Children"; a special Hebrew prayer about "the good wife," whose twenty-two verses are traditionally read by the husband to his wife on holy days; and Seneca's "Letters from a Stoic." Mamet has underlined only one passage in Seneca: "Each day . . . acquire something which will help you to face poverty, or death, and other ills as well."

When Mamet set out on his theatrical journey, the teachings of the Stoics emboldened him. "The stoical motto is 'What hinders you?' " he explains. "I'd like to be able to write clearer. 'What's stopping you?' I'd like to be able to figure a project out. 'What's stopping you?' I mean, let's say Sophocles took eighteen years to write 'Oedipus Rex.' It's not under your control how quickly you complete 'Oedipus Rex,' but it is under your control whether or not you give up." He adds, "It doesn't have to be calm and clear-eyed. You just have to not give up."

A heron lands on top of a sixty-foot tamarack tree that towers on the ridge above where Rebecca and Clara are starting back up the hill. Mamet studies it through the window, then walks over to his desk looking for his camera. Taped there is a blue file card with a snatch of dialogue on it, which I bend close to read. "Here, take it," Mamet says and hurries me into the bright day with his camera in hand. Clara and Rebecca are skipping up the path; Clara is clutching a heron's feather. Mamet darts around them trying to capture the scene. Clara drops her feather; Mamet stoops down to pick it up. Clara's hand touches the top of his bristly head. It's a fragile moment, whose mysterious joy sends him glancing up to see it reflected in his wife's eyes. In his high-school yearbook, to print beside his nerdy photograph, Mamet had chosen the quotation "And so make life and that vast forever one grand, sweet song." He seems somehow to have lived up to his early romantic plan, even if his song is a fierce, rueful, sometimes cruel one. Just how his talent and his life have come together so well seems, like all blessings, both miraculous and inexplicable. I glanced at the file card in my hand:

A) *Life*, maan . . .

B) . . . life.

A) It is so crazy—let me tell you: if you saw it in a movie, you would not believe it. You know why? BECAUSE IT HAS NO PLOT.

FRANK SINATRA

SINATRA'S SONG

To GET TO THE BUSTLE OF Manhattan from Hoboken, New Jersey, which is just across the Hudson River, takes about fifteen minutes by ferry; to forget the deadliness of the place has taken Frank Sinatra most of his lifetime. Sinatra was born in Hoboken, on December 12, 1915. In those days, from River Road, now called Sinatra Drive, you could see New York's crenellated skyline, rising like a bar graph of profits, and, if you walked to the dock's edge, the ass end of the Statue of Liberty. The vista was at once a thrill and a rebuke. As an adult, Sinatra often referred to his home town as a "sewer"; after 1947, when he was given the key to the city, he didn't return to it officially until 1985, when he received an honorary degree from Stevens Institute of Technology, an engineering school that his ambitious mother had wanted him to attend. Dolly Sinatra, who had an immigrant's faith in success, wanted her school-shy son to become some kind of powerful man. In time, of course, Sinatra seized more than power; he infiltrated the Western world's dream life. He is "the most imitated, most listened to, most recognized voice of the second half of the twentieth century," the New York disk jockey William B. Williams said in the fifties, tagging him forever with the epithet Chairman of the Board. Sinatra, whose tape-recorded voice was heard by the Apollo 12 astronauts as they orbited the moon, and whose two hundred and six CDs currently in print make him the most comprehensively digitally preserved music-maker in the history of recorded sound, refers to himself as the Top Wop. Even the Secret Service, which protected him when he produced Presidential inaugurals for both John F. Kennedy and Ronald Reagan and whenever he lunched with Nancy Reagan at the White House, spotted the sense of manifest destiny in Sinatra. Its code name for him was Napoleon.

Sinatra's life has been one long show of mastery over his Hoboken years, whose scars are harder to see than those on his neck, ear, and cheek from an agonizing forceps delivery that yanked the nearly thirteen-pound baby out of his twenty-one-year-old mother's diminutive body and prevented her from having other children. "His bravado, his bigness, the size of him in public life—it's part of him. But underneath there is something quite—I don't want to say 'sensitive,' because that's an understatement— underneath there is a delicate, fragile boy," his daughter Tina Sinatra told me recently. When he was a young man, Sinatra's expectations were woefully at odds with his abilities. He wanted to build bridges, but he'd spent only forty-seven fractious days in high school; he wanted to be a sportswriter, but he was a "deez, demz, and doz" guy; he loved music, but he couldn't read it, and was too impatient to learn an instrument. "The story of Sinatra, of me, of all kinds of people of our time is that they had to cross the bridge either from Jersey or from Brooklyn to Manhattan and have people say 'You fit,'" the writer Pete Hamill says. (Hamill is the son of Irish immigrants, and a high-school dropout, whom Sinatra once approached to write his biography.) He adds, "You went there to sort of say, 'Hey, this is mine, too.' "

As a solitary latchkey kid, Sinatra would often wander down to the Hoboken wharves, dangle his feet over the docks, and stare at the cityscape, trying to imagine a future. "He didn't dream," Tina Sinatra insists, of her father's often repeated account of those days. "He said, 'I'm gonna do it. I'm gonna get across this river. I'm gonna go there and make a name for myself.' " At Sinatra's back—far from the river, in the shadow of the New Jersey Palisades—were the working-class warrens that first-generation Italians like his parents were trying furiously to climb out of. Hoboken had large Irish and German populations; Italians were at the bottom of the pecking order. As a young man, Sinatra's father, Marty, boxed as a bantamweight under the name Marty O'Brien, in order to be allowed to compete. Dolly, who had strawberry-blond hair and blue eyes, sometimes passed herself off as Mrs. O'Brien, and when they opened a bar, during Prohibition, they called it Marty O'Brien's Bar.

Books have been written about Frank Sinatra's women, who were trophies to his success; but his squat, bespectacled mother—the outspoken daughter of a well-educated lithographer who had brought his family to Hoboken from Genoa—had more to do with his success than any of the countless babes with whom he was associated. Dolly spoke all local dialects of Italian as well as a gamy version of English, and she was a popular local political figure, a Democratic ward boss who could guarantee the Party machine at least five hundred votes at every election. She made things happen for others and for herself. Her son may have lacked for her attention when he was growing up (between the ages of six and twelve he was cared for during the day by his grandmother), but even in the midst of the Depression, Dolly made sure that her moody boy had a circle of friends, by providing him with a dapper, plentiful wardrobe, a 1929 Chrysler, and enough spending money to treat his cronies to sodas and movies. Sinatra's tenacity, drive, and cunning owe a lot to Dolly, who always had her eye on the main chance: in her time, she was both a midwife and an abortionist, a local politician and a Prohibition saloonkeeper. "She was the force!" Sinatra said. "My son is like me," Dolly said. "You cross him, he never forgets."

"I think he was partial to his dad," says Nancy Sinatra, Sr., who was married to Frank throughout the forties and is the mother of Nancy, Tina, and Frank, Jr. Sinatra's father was a quiet, passive man, while Dolly, a typical Italian *balabusta*, controlled the Sinatra household and had a stevedore's heart and mouth. "Son-of-a-bitch bastard" was her most common curse; she called Sinatra's sidekick, the saloonkeeper Jilly Rizzo, "fuckface" (as she did most everyone else); she nicknamed her youngest granddaughter, Tina, Little Shit. Among her grandchildren, Dolly favored Frank, Jr., whom she could idealize and pamper as she had her own son. "She always said to me and Nancy, 'When I'm dead, everything goes to Frankie. You girls get nothing,'" Tina Sinatra says. "She was a difficult woman." Even though Dolly spoiled the child, she didn't spare the rod. She kept a piece of wood the size of a billy club behind the bar at home. "When I would get out of hand, she would give me a rap with that little club; then she'd hug me to her breast," Sinatra told Hamill one night in the seventies as they discussed the singer's erstwhile biography in a Monte Carlo hotel room. Hamill adds, "Then Sinatra said, 'I married the same woman every time.' That's Ava. That's all the women. He had this mother who punished and hugged him, and they were all part of the same thing."

From the start, Sinatra embraced and bullied the world as his mother had embraced and bullied him. "All of Dolly's ambitious energy was thrust into him," Tina Sinatra says. One episode in Sinatra's youth bears witness to this. Dolly had prevailed upon her son's godfather and namesake, Frank Garrick, who was the circulation manager of the *Jersey Observer*, to get her son a job. Sinatra duly found work on the paper's delivery truck. When the *Observer*'s sportswriter died, Dolly got Sinatra to go back to Garrick and ask for the writing job. Sinatra arrived at the paper dressed for reporter's work, but Garrick was out; undeterred, Frank sat at the dead writer's empty desk and went through the motions of doing the job. When the editor asked Sinatra who he was, he answered that he was the new sportswriter and that Garrick had sent him. His lie was discovered when Garrick arrived, and his godfather was forced to fire him. "Oh, the temper and the words and the filthy names he called me. . . . Like he was going to kill me," Garrick told Kitty Kelley in "His Way," her unauthorized biography of Sinatra. "He called me every terrible name in the book and then he stormed out. He never said another word to me until fifty years later, after his mother died. She wrote me off, too, and even though we lived in the same town, she never said another word to me for the rest of her life."

Over the years, Dolly and her son also went through periods of not speaking. "Nancy, our mother, wasn't good enough," Tina Sinatra says. "Then, all of a sudden, she was good enough. When Ava was on the horizon, this was against God, how can he do this? But then the press turned in their favor. They became the Romeo and Juliet with his mother keeping them apart. Dolly changed her whole attitude. She always gave Dad a tough time." There was another Mexican standoff after Sinatra announced his engagement to his fourth and current wife, a former Las Vegas showgirl, Barbara Blakely Marx, whom he married in 1976. "I don't want no whore coming into this family," Dolly said. As Sinatra told Shirley MacLaine in her excellent memoir "My Lucky Stars," "She was a pisser, but she scared the shit outta me. Never knew what she'd hate that I'd do."

Dolly enjoyed singing, for example, especially at weddings and at political beer parties, but she didn't want her son to be a singer. The notion had first dawned on Sinatra when he was about eleven and was in his parents' bar, where there was a player piano in the front room. "Occasionally, one of the men in the bar would pick me up and put me on the piano. I'd sing along with the music on the roll," Sinatra said in a 1986 lecture he gave at Yale University. "One day, I got a nickel. I said, 'This is the racket.' I thought, It's wonderful to sing. . . . I never forgot it." Under pressure to make something of himself, Sinatra increasingly focussed on the one asset he was sure he possessed: his voice. "In my particular neighborhood in New Jersey, when I was a kid, boys became boxers or they worked in factories; and then the remaining group that I went around with were smitten by singing," Sinatra said during a 1980 radio broadcast. "We had a ukulele player, and we stood on the corners and sang songs." Sinatra liked to listen to Gene Austin, Rudy Vallee, Bing Crosby, Russ Columbo, and Bob Eberly—but of all of them he idolized Crosby, whose casual sailor's cap and pipe were props that Sinatra himself would soon adopt. As his ambition to sing grew, so did Dolly's hectoring. When she saw a photo of Crosby in her son's room, she threw a shoe at him and called him a "bum."

But when Dolly realized that she couldn't break her son's will she tried to empower it. She chipped in for the orchestrations Sinatra rented to local bands who, as part of the deal, took him along as singer; she bought him portable speakers and a microphone; she used her influence to help him hustle gigs at roadhouses, Democratic Party meetings, and night clubs. In 1935, still unemployed and living at home, Sinatra attached himself to a trio in nearby Englewood called the Three Flashes. "We took him along for one simple reason," said the trio's baritone, Fred Tamburro. "Frankie-boy had a car." When the Three Flashes—all Italian kids looking for a leg up—were asked to do some movie shorts for Major Bowes, whose radio "Amateur Hour" was the most successful show on the air, Sinatra wanted to sing with them; they turned him down. Dolly quickly intervened, and before long the Three Flashes became the Hoboken Four. On September 8, 1935, they appeared on the millionaire Major's show, singing the Mills Brothers hit "Shine." Sinatra's first words in public were at once pushy and playful; they got a laugh. "I'm Frank, Major," he said. "We're looking for jobs. How about it?" The Hoboken Four won that night, with forty thousand people calling in—the largest vote up to then in the show's history.

From that first moment, the public took Sinatra in with an affection-ate avidity that he could never call forth from his mother. "She always expected more of him," Nancy Sinatra, Sr., says. "It was never enough. For her, the cup was always half empty. It was difficult to please her." Her son, who moved her into palatial comfort in Rancho Mirage, California, after Marty died (she had a five-bedroom house, with a cook, a gardener, three maids, and security guards), could do no wrong and do no right. Dolly saw his success but never saw the person. "She thinks she's the big hit," Sinatra said in a 1975 television interview. "If she were here with us now and she wanted to say something about me, she'd refer to me as 'Frank Sinatra.' While I'm sitting here."

Beyond talent, beyond technique, the palpable but invisible power of every great star stems from the need to be seen and to be held in the imag-ination of the audience. This is especially true of Sinatra. The stillness, attention, and unequivocal adoration that were never there in Dolly were undeniable in the rapt enthusiasm of his listeners. "Thank you for letting me sing for you" was often Sinatra's exit line at the end of his concerts. In song, he was his best self, and he craved to see that goodness reflected in the adoring eyes of others. "His survival was his mother audience," MacLaine, who often toured with Sinatra, writes. "He desperately needed her to love him, appreciate him, acknowledge him, and never betray his trust. So he would cajole, manipulate, caress, admonish, scold and love her unconditionally until there was no difference between him and her. He and she had become one." Offstage, Sinatra was dubbed the Innkeeper by his friends, because of the largesse of his hospitality; onstage, he operated more or less the same way. He fed others to ensure that he got what he needed.

"Frank is a singer who comes along once in a lifetime, but why did he have to come in my lifetime?" Bing Crosby once joked. Sinatra's voice was smaller and lighter than Crosby's, but, as Whitney Balliett observed in *The NewYorker*, "his phrasing and immaculate sense of timing gave it a poise and stature Crosby's lacked." Sinatra's phenomenal impact, however, had to do

not just with musical timing but with the timing of the technology that sat-
urated the nation with his sound. As Henry Pleasants notes in "The Great
American Popular Singers," in 1930, only a decade before Sinatra made his
name, the reigning crooner, Rudy Vallee, threw away the megaphone that
had broadcast his sound and, by linking a borrowed NBC carbon microphone to amplifiers and several radios onstage, created a crude kind of
concert amplification. ("I sing with dick in my voice" is how the notoriously foulmouthed Vallee explained his appeal.) Because of the lack of
sophisticated miking technology, singers had had to sing in high ranges to
play the room and to be heard above jazz bands. The microphone changed
all this, bringing intimacy and articulation to the forefront of popular
singing and making possible a whole new expressive style, which relegat-
ed the belters of the previous era—Al Jolson, Sophie Tucker—to history.

Sinatra himself began by singing with a megaphone, but the microphone soon became his totem. "To Sinatra, a microphone is as real as a girl
waiting to be kissed," E. B. White once wrote. Sinatra said, "Many singers
never learned to use one. They never understood, and still don't, that a
microphone is their instrument." Gripping the stationary mike with both
hands and only occasionally moving it back and forth, he used it as a prop
in a kind of foreplay. "You don't crowd it, you must never jar an audience
with it. . . . You must know when to move away from the mike and when
to move back into it," he wrote in *Life*. He added, "It's like a geisha girl uses
her fan."

He also caught the wave of other sound innovations that were making
song a pervasive part of daily American life. By 1938, more than half of all
broadcast programs were recordings of popular music. In 1933, there
were twenty-five thousand jukeboxes in the land; by 1939, there were two
hundred and twenty-five thousand, and by 1942 four hundred thousand.
The car radio, which was introduced in 1923 and became a standard feature by 1934, completely transformed the automotive experience. Record
sales, which had dipped to $5.5 million in the depths of the Depression,
had rebounded by 1940 to $48.4 million, and by 1945, when Sinatra was
a household name, reached their all-time high of $109 million. Muzak,
which had been successfully tested in New York hotel lobbies and dining
rooms in 1934, had become a fact of industrial life by 1940 as America

geared up for war. By the time Sinatra emerged from his brief apprenticeship as a ballad singer with touring dance bands and attained the status of
solo act, the technology of enchantment was in place.

At first, Sinatra was more certain of his ability to enchant than was the
trumpeter Harry James, whose struggling band he toured with for six
months. "Well, what a voice!" the singer Connie Haines remembers James
telling the young Sinatra, when James called him over to their table at the
Rustic Cabin to offer Sinatra his first big break. "Then James said, 'We
gotta change that name.' Frank pushed his tie up and made a direct turn.
He says, 'You want the voice, you take the name.' " According to Earl
Wilson's 1976 biography of Sinatra, when Down Beat asked James the name
of his new singer, he replied, "Not so loud! The kid's name is Sinatra. He
considers himself the greatest vocalist in the business. Nobody ever heard
of him, he's never had a hit record, he looks like a wet mop. But he says
he's the greatest." James went on, "If he hears you compliment him, he'll
demand a raise tonight." Indeed, in January of 1940, Sinatra jumped ship
and joined Tommy Dorsey's band for a hundred dollars a week.

"You could almost feel the excitement coming up out of the crowds
when that kid stood up to sing," said Dorsey, whom Sinatra made the godfather of his firstborn child. "Remember, he was no matinée idol. He was
just a skinny kid with big ears. I used to stand there so amazed I'd almost
forget to take my own solos." In fact, the secret of Sinatra's vocal impact
lay primarily in his observations of Dorsey's trombone playing. "He would
take a musical phrase and play it all the way through seemingly without
breathing for eight, ten, maybe sixteen bars. How in the hell did he do
that?" Sinatra told his daughter Nancy in her book "Frank Sinatra: An
American Legend." "I used to sit behind him on the bandstand and watch,
trying to see him sneak a breath. But I never saw the bellows move in his
back. His jacket didn't even move. So I edged my chair around to the side
a little and peeked around to watch him. Finally, after a while, I discovered
that he had a 'sneak pinhole' in the corner of his mouth—not an actual
hole but a tiny place he left open where he was breathing. In the middle of
a phrase, while the tone was still being carried through the trombone, he'd
go 'shhh' and take a quick breath and play another four bars."

Sinatra began to "play" his voice like Dorsey's trombone. "I began swimming in public pools, taking laps under water and thinking song lyrics to myself as I swam holding my breath," Sinatra said. "Over six months or so, I began to develop and delineate a method of long phraseology. Instead of singing only two bars or four bars at a time—like most of the other guys around—I was able to sing six bars, and in some songs eight bars, without taking a visible or audible breath. That gave the melody a flowing, unbroken quality and that's what made me sound different." His sound astonished even the professionals. "After the first eight bars, I knew I was hearing something I'd never heard before," I was told by Jo Stafford, who had never seen or heard Sinatra before he walked onstage with her and the Pied Pipers for his début with Dorsey.

By 1941, the year before Sinatra went solo, *Billboard* had voted him the best male vocalist of the year. But the Sinatra phenomenon—what the press called Sinatrauma—began officially on December 30, 1942, at New York's Paramount Theatre, only three months after Sinatra made an acrimonious departure from Dorsey's band. "I hope you fall on your ass" was Dorsey's parting shot to Sinatra, who, with the help of his new agency, had engineered a cash buyout from his original contract, which had called for a total of forty-three per cent of Sinatra's lifetime earnings. He was now billed as the Extra Added Attraction to Benny Goodman and his Orchestra, and when he stepped onstage he walked into pandemonium. It was a watershed moment for him, and one that he had planned carefully, making sure that his press agent, George Evans, had primed the pump. "The dozen girls we hired to scream and swoon did exactly as we told them," Evans's partner, Jack Keller, said later. "But hundreds more we didn't hire screamed even louder."

Sinatra had fretted a long time about going solo. "The reason I wanted to leave Tommy's band was that Crosby was Number One, way up on top of the pile," he said during his Yale lecture. "In the open field, you might say, were some awfully good singers with the orchestras. Bob Eberly (with Jimmy Dorsey) was a fabulous vocalist. Mr. Como (with Ted Weems) is such a wonderful singer. I thought, If I don't make a move out of this and try to do it on my own soon, one of those guys will do it, and I'll have to fight all three of them to get a position." Sinatra was the first to break through, and his fabulous success proved to be the thin end of the wedge for the Big Band Era and the beginning of the Vocalist's Era. Within a month, his salary went crazy—from seven hundred and fifty dollars a week to twenty-five thousand—but not as crazy as his entranced fans. "Not since the days of Rudolph Valentino has American womanhood made such unabashed love to an entertainer," *Time* wrote. "Girls hid in his dressing rooms, in his hotel rooms, in the trunk of his car," Arnold Shaw wrote in his 1968 biography. "When it snowed, girls fought over his footprints, which some took home and stored in refrigerators." When Sinatra returned to the Paramount Theatre again, in October, 1944, the line began forming before dawn and soon swelled to approximately twenty thousand fans, packed six abreast. Many members of the audience for the first show wouldn't leave the theatre, and the frustrated crowd outside went berserk, in what became known as the Columbus Day Riot. Two hundred police, four hundred and twenty-one police reserves, twenty radio cars, and two emergency trucks were called in to control the rampaging, mostly teen-age girls.

Plato called songs "spells for souls for the creation of concord"; Sinatra's crooning was balm to a republic desolated by the economic losses of the Depression and heading for war. "The best way to describe crooning is 'Don't make waves,' " says the lyricist and musical director Saul Chaplin, who, along with his collaborator Sammy Cahn, wrote for Sinatra at the beginning of his career. "Sinatra's voice sings a straight line in a straight tone. There are no sudden louds or softs. The oscillation of the sound waves isn't wide." Sinatra—or Swoonatra, as he was dubbed—had another explanation for his appeal. "I was the boy in every corner drugstore, the boy who'd gone off to war," he said. Actually, a punctured eardrum made him ineligible for service but available for leading roles. It was another piece of extraordinary good timing. The old stars were in the service, and the new ones wouldn't emerge until the end of the decade: Sinatra had an open field on which to sing and dance. In 1945, he won a Special Award from the Academy for "The House I Live In," a progressive ten-minute short about racial tolerance, and Modern Screen voted him the year's most popular movie actor.

Of course, Sinatra's best acting was not on film but in song. "When I sing, I believe, I'm honest," he told *Playboy* in 1963. "An audience is like a broad. If you're indifferent, Endsville." Sinatra instinctively approached song as drama. "You begin to learn to use the lyrics of a song as a script, as a scene. I didn't know I was doing that at the time, but I was," he said years later on TV. "I try to transpose my thoughts about the song into a person who might be singing that to somebody else. He's making his case, in other words, for himself." Sinatra's scrawny frame (he had a twenty-nine-inch waist, weighed a hundred and thirty pounds, and stood about five feet ten), his high voice, and his shy smile made him a safe object for teen-agers to adore. He personified the longing he sang about. "I'll never thrill again to somebody new," he confided in "I'll Never Smile Again"; in "This Love of Mine," whose lyrics he co-wrote, his sexual torment overwhelmed him: "It's lonesome through the day / And oh! the night."

Sinatra didn't just sing a song; he made it his own. He brought a special urgency to his proprietorship. The songwriters he embraced, especially after he went solo—Cole Porter, Ira Gershwin, Johnny Mercer, Alec Wilder, E. Y. Harburg, Arthur Schwartz, Sammy Cahn, Jerome Kern, Lorenz Hart, Oscar Hammerstein—were the voices of the educated middle-class mainstream, whose sophisticated wordplay, diction, and syntax had an equipoise that contrasted with the social self-consciousness that so bedevilled Sinatra. According to Hamill, Sinatra built up his vocabulary doing crosswords, and in the seventies was reading Strunk and White's "Elements of Style" for help with grammar. His signed articles were ghost-written; he submitted to very few television interviews, and then only with friends like Arlene Francis or Aileen Mehle, in whose syndicated "Suzy" column he announced his first retirement, in 1971—people who he felt would protect him. But once he was inside the lyric, he had command of the language that he found paralyzing elsewhere. When he opened his mouth in song, he was calm; he was smooth; he was sensitive; he had no hint of the Hoboken streets in his pronunciation; what he called his "Sicilian temper" was filtered through the charm of lyrics and music into poetic passion. With other singers—Vic Damone, for instance, and Tony Bennett—you admired the technique; with Sinatra you admired the rendition. He presented the song like a landscape he'd restored, painting himself into the picture so masterfully that it was impossible to imagine it without him.

Sinatra's appropriations of the standards was also the acquisition of the manners of another class. "It's like stealing a Cadillac—except he's stealing George Gershwin," Hamill says. " 'You see what they got?' " Hamill says Sinatra said to him in the seventies as they watched Hamill's children walk around the gardens of Monte Carlo. " 'They can go to the best schools. They can walk in everywhere, and they will know when they walk in what to do.' I said, 'What do you mean?' He said, 'Anything. Simple stuff. What fork to pick up.' " Hamill adds, "It's no accident that Sinatra aspired in the music to grace. The ballads, in particular, have a grace to them that is really extraordinary. And that's about knowing what fork to pick up."

A decade after Sinatra's Paramount triumph, a headline in the *World Telegram & Sun* put what he came to call his Dark Ages into bold relief: "GONE ON FRANKIE IN '42; GONE IN '52." A new youngster, Johnnie Ray, had the nation's ear, and Sinatra's records no longer sold in their familiar quantities. "What do you think is happening?" he asked the columnist Earl Wilson. He added, "I'm not throwing in any sponge to Johnnie Ray!" Sinatra's career, his marriage, and his voice were showing visible signs of cracking under the pressure of his momentum, and the fans who had adored his crooning were not so adoring of his bad behavior, which they now read about regularly in the papers. In 1947, Sinatra had managed to get himself photographed with Lucky Luciano and other mobsters in Havana, thereby giving the syndicated columnist Robert Ruark a three-part field day. "SHAME, SINATRA!" was the first column's banner. Then, there was the issue of Sinatra's egalitarian political opinions, which let him in for Red-baiting by the right-wing press; he was labelled a Communist in the F.B.I. files. But of all Sinatra's sins the most unacceptable to the public were his unabashed extramarital exploits. According to press reports, he appeared to be making an almost heroic effort to bed the female population of an entire industry—as though he were hell-bent on proving himself through conquest as his career dipped. In the late forties and early fifties, he was frequently photographed with the objects of his desire, among them Marilyn Maxwell, Lana Turner, and, especially, Ava Gardner;

it was a list whose ranks would ultimately include Joan Crawford, Marlene Dietrich, Kim Novak, Lauren Bacall, Angie Dickinson, Gloria Vanderbilt, Natalie Wood, Marilyn Monroe, Sophia Loren, Judy Garland, and Juliet Prowse. "Sinatra's idea of paradise is a place where there are plenty of women and no newspapermen," remarked Humphrey Bogart, who was Sinatra's good friend and the model for his emerging "tough guy" persona. "He doesn't know it, but he'd be better off if it were the other way around."

Indeed, Sinatra, who had learned the importance of publicity from Dorsey, and had launched himself on the press with presidential lavishness in the forties (he bought the columnists dinners, jewelry, engraved Dunhill lighters), now lashed out at the journalists who were chronicling his decline. "To tell Louella Parsons to go fuck herself was quite a major thing in those days, when everybody was quivering," Sinatra's buddy Tony Curtis says. And Parsons wasn't the only writer to get a Sinatra jolt via Western Union. He also took on Westbrook Pegler, who had called him a "fellow traveller," and he struck the *Daily Mirror*'s reactionary columnist Lee Mortimer on the side of the head—a blow that landed Mortimer on the floor and Sinatra with an out-of-court settlement that cost him twenty-five thousand dollars. "He gave me a look," Sinatra said before lawyers sanitized his explanations. "It was one of those 'Who do you amount to?' looks. I followed him out. I hit him. I'm all mixed up."

The force of Sinatra's explosive unpredictability could be devastating. His close friend Leonora Hornblow says, "It's instant. It's uncontrollable. It's like a volcano. You want to run away. He's got lungs, mind you. When he yells, you hear it." Anyone who knew Sinatra well also knew what Sammy Cahn called "the blue-eyed ray"—the intense beam of romance or rage that Sinatra emitted. "That look he also locked into very young, like he did his conception of women," Shirley MacLaine says. "He sort of gave me that look which was a look between 'I'll protect you' and 'Do you want to have an affair?' You couldn't tell when one stopped and the other started." Lauren Bacall, too, felt the powerful manipulation of Sinatra's stare. "He would be looking at you as if you were It. Then he'd be laughin' and jokin' and he walked off by himself. No one was gonna tie him down," she says. "I think one of the reasons that he and I split——it was his doing, not mine—was that he felt he never could live up to the kind of a man and husband Bogie was. He knew it would never work, because he'd be cheating on me in five minutes—because that's what he did. That's about the Swingin' Guy. That's about 'It's quarter to three, there's no one in the place except you and me.'"

Sinatra's womanizing ultimately threatened to undermine what success he still had. In the late forties, George Evans told Earl Wilson at the Copacabana, "Frank is through. A year from now you won't hear anything about him." He added, "You know how much I've talked to him about the girls. The public knows about the trouble with Nancy, and the other dames, and it doesn't like him anymore."

The siren that lured Sinatra onto the rocks was Ava Gardner, who was, like him, a card-carrying romantic narcissist—someone as self-absorbed, impetuous, and powerful as he was. In her 1990 autobiography Gardner recalls Sinatra's coming over to her and her first husband, Mickey Rooney, at a Los Angeles night club with his celebrity smile at full candlepower: "He did the big grin and said 'Hey, why didn't I meet you before Mickey? Then I could have married you myself.'" She adds, "Frank Sinatra could be the sweetest, most charming man in the world when he was in the mood." And for a while he was. When they first got together, Gardner took him back to her little yellow house in Nichols Canyon. "Oh, God, it was magic," she writes. "And God Almighty, things did happen."

Gardner was Sinatra's match in brazenness and in sexual independence, and their relationship was tempestuous. "The problems were never in the bedroom," Gardner once said. "We were always great in bed. The trouble usually started on the way to the bidet." In New York, after one jealous argument, Sinatra called Gardner's adjacent suite. "I can't stand it anymore," he said. There was a gunshot. Gardner bolted into his room. Sinatra was lying face down, the smoking revolver still in his hand. "Frank! Frank!" Gardner screamed. Sinatra looked up. "Oh, hello," he said. He had shot the mattress.

Their affair, which the public followed as avidly as they did "Stella Dallas," finally destroyed Sinatra's marriage. On Valentine's Day of 1950, Nancy Sinatra petitioned for a legal separation. The press response was vitriolic, and shortly thereafter, on April 26th, at the Copacabana, Sinatra opened his mouth to sing and nothing came out. "It became so quiet, so intensely quiet in the club—they were like watching a man walk off a cliff," Sinatra's accompanist and conductor on that night, Skitch Henderson, recalled. "His face chalk white, Frank gasped something that sounded like 'good night' into the mike and raced off the floor, leaving the audience stunned." His throat had hemorrhaged, through stress and over-work. ("I didn't speak for forty days," he told Arlene Francis about his recovery. "For forty days I didn't say a single word.")

Sinatra married Gardner in 1951; they separated eleven months later. "I remember exactly when I made the decision to seek a divorce," Gardner writes. "It was the day the phone rang and Frank was on the other end, announcing that he was in bed with another woman. And he made it plain that if he was going to be constantly accused of infidelity when he was innocent, there had to come a time when he'd decided he might as well be guilty." In the short time that they were husband and wife, though, Gardner, whose star was in the ascendant, did what she could to bolster Sinatra's falling star. Her ten-year contract with M-G-M contained a clause stipulating that "at some time prior to the expiration of her contract, we will do a picture with her in which Frank Sinatra will also appear." Although they never worked together, Gardner interceded on Sinatra's behalf with Columbia's president, Harry Cohn, to help her husband land the part of Maggio in "From Here to Eternity." And Gardner, in her alco-holic, reclusive later years, was supported by Sinatra. Through their jeal-ous rages, their sexual betrayals, and their reconciliations, Sinatra and Gardner were sensational public fodder; their private hell was memorial-ized by him in the outstanding "I'm a Fool to Want You," which he co-wrote and recorded in 1951, apparently so overcome with feeling that he did it in one take and left the session:

> I'm a fool to want you
> I'm a fool to want you,
> To want a love that can't be true,
> A love that's there for others too. . . .

In the meantime, the public seemed indifferent to the old standards and avid for novelty. At Columbia Records, Mitch Miller, the powerful producer who found the mother lode of "Mule Train" and Frankie Laine, was trying to find a commercial avenue for Sinatra. Although Miller got Sinatra to do some up-tempo numbers, including the seminal "Birth of the Blues," in which Sinatra defines the swinging, hard-edged style of his middle years, he also persuaded Sinatra to record "Tennessee Newsboy," with washboard accompaniment, and "Mama Will Bark," with the zaftig Dagmar, and Donald Bain barking like a dog. ("The only good business it did was with dogs," Sinatra quipped, although the song got to No. 21 on the charts.) These recordings represent the nadir of Sinatra's musical career, but they were also a barometer of Columbia's mismanagement and Sinatra's rudderless desperation. Miller was the donkey on whom Sinatra pinned the tail of his decline. "You cannot force anyone to do a song. People don't understand this," Miller told Will Friedwald in "Sinatra!: The Song Is You." "Sinatra said I brought him all these shit songs, I forced him to do shit songs." Certainly Sinatra disliked Miller's control-room intrusions into his music-making. As Sinatra's regular drummer in those days, John Blowers, recounted to Friedwald, "All of a sudden one day finally, quietly, he looked at the control room and said 'Mitch, out'—and Frank always pointed his finger—and he said, 'Don't you ever come in. Don't you ever come into the studio when I'm recording again.' Mitch never came again. Frank wouldn't permit it." In Sinatra's final months at Columbia, his song selections seemed to be a message to his producer: "There's Something Missing," "Don't Ever Be Afraid to Go," and "Why Try to Change Me Now?" Years later, Miller caught up with Sinatra in Las Vegas, and went to shake his hand, seeking a kind of reconciliation. "Fuck you," Sinatra said. "Keep walking."

The losses piled up. In 1949, M-G-M let Sinatra go. In 1950, George Evans died, at the age of forty-eight. In 1952, "Meet Danny Wilson" flopped, and Universal refused to renew Sinatra's option for a second film; he was dropped by Columbia Records; CBS cancelled "The Frank Sinatra Show"; and he was released by his theatrical agency. "I was in trouble. I was busted, and I must say that I lost a great deal of faith in human nature because a lot of friends I had in those days disappeared," Sinatra recalled at his Yale lecture. "I did lie down for a while and had some large bar bills for about a year." Then, he explained, "I said, 'O.K., holiday's over, Charlie. Let's go back to work.' "

But who would hire him? When his new agent, Sam Weisbord, called Alan Livingston, the A. & R. man at Capitol Records, and asked if he would sign up Sinatra, Livingston said yes. "You would?" Weisbrod replied. Livingston explains, "I'm quoting him verbatim. I said, 'Yes.' He said, 'You would?' I mean, for an agent to react that way!" In 1953, Livingston, who later signed the Band and the Beatles, signed Sinatra to a one-year contract with six one-year options and a five-per-cent royalty. "Frank Sinatra was totally down and out. I mean he was gone. In addition, his voice was kind of gone," Livingston says. "At the time I signed Frank, we had our national sales meeting. There were around a hundred and fifty salesmen, branch managers, regional managers there. I would play them upcoming records. I'd tell them about new artists. I said, 'I want to tell you this: we've just signed Frank Sinatra.' The whole place went 'Ooh'—like 'Oh, God, what are you doing to us?' They were just so unhappy about it." Livingston adds, "I remember my response. I said, 'Look, he's the greatest singer I've ever heard. He's in trouble, and he hasn't done anything for a long time. All I know how to deal with in my job is talent. This is talent.' "

At Capitol, Sinatra began to pull out of his skid. His songs seemed to announce it. On April 30, 1953, teamed with a brilliant new thirty-two-year-old arranger, Nelson Riddle, whom Livingston had suggested, Sinatra cut "I've Got the World on a String" and "Don't Worry 'Bout Me." "Sinatra was elated by the sound," Ed O'Brien and Robert Wilson write in "Sinatra 101: The 101 Best Recordings and the Stories Behind Them." "During the playbacks that evening, Sinatra made the rounds in the studio, gleefully slapping the backs of musicians and technicians, and telling many of them that he was back."

Then, in August, "From Here to Eternity" was released, and Sinatra was reborn for sure. "By getting stomped to death in that movie, he did a public penance," Mitch Miller told Friedwald. "You can chart it. From the day the movie came out, his records began to sell." Sinatra was thirty-eight when he received the Academy Award for Best Supporting Actor in the film. He gave up his psychiatrist and took up permanent residence in his success; by 1954, the Sinatra-Riddle partnership had produced the first hit single he'd made in seven years, "Young At Heart," which went to No. 2 on the charts.

Sinatra now had a public history of troubles and new triumphs to take on the road, and his songs were increasingly viewed by his audience and by him as a kind of autobiography: "All or Nothing at All"—the gamble on his talent; "I'm a Fool to Want You"—unrequited love of Ava; and now "I've Got the World on a String"—his comeback. But the new Sinatra was not the gentle boy balladeer of the forties. Fragility had gone from his voice, to be replaced by a virile adult's sense of happiness and hurt. "It was Ava who did that, who taught him how to sing a torch song," Nelson Riddle said. "That's how he learned. She was the greatest love of his life and he lost her." As Sinatra put it, "You have to scrape bottom to appreciate life and start living again." In the forties, his vocal experiments had to do primarily with smoothness; in the fifties, he discovered syncopation, and the new swagger of his voice broadcast the cocky sense of possibility which was America's mood as well as his own. In "Taking a Chance on Love," which he recorded on April 19, 1954, he sang, "Now I prove again / That I can make life move again / *Mmm*—I'm in a groove again / Takin' a chance on love."

The phenomenon of Sinatra as a crooner and playboy had somewhat obscured the public perception of him as a musician. But Riddle's arrangements, which were not overly busy, showed off Sinatra's musicianship to sensational advantage, and left room for him to act his new part as Swinger. "The man himself somehow draws everything out of you," Riddle told Jonathan Schwartz on WNEW in the early eighties. "And I always felt that my rather placid disposition had a beneficial effect on him." Together, they created the classic Sinatra sound—as luck would have it, just when technology produced both high fidelity and the long-playing record. "Never before had there been an opportunity for a popular singer to express emotions at an extended length," Schwartz says. As many as sixteen songs could be held by the twelve-inch L.P., and this allowed Sinatra to use song in a novelistic way, turning each track into a kind of chapter, which built and counterpointed moods to illuminate a larger theme. In their seminal L.P.s—"In the Wee Small Hours," "Frank Sinatra Sings for Only the Lonely," "Songs for Swingin' Lovers!," and "A Swingin' Affair!"— Sinatra and Riddle came up with the first concept albums. Between April, 1958, and April, 1966, Sinatra had no *Billboard* Top Ten singles, but he had twenty Top Ten albums. "Only the Lonely," which came out in 1958, stayed on the charts for a hundred and twenty weeks; the 1959 follow-up album, "Come Dance with Me," remained for a hundred and forty weeks.

From his earliest Dorsey days, Sinatra had understood the importance of arrangers. "When the arranger would run down the orchestration, he would hear where the figures were, and when he sang the song he would arrange to clear it so those figures came through," Saul Chaplin, who watched Sinatra adapt to Dorsey's orchestrations, says. "He'd drop a note which he could have held because he knew the over-all is what counts, not just his voice alone." In performance, Sinatra often honored this division of labor by announcing the arranger and the songwriter of a number before he sang it. With Riddle, he was patient and precise about what he wanted. "When you hear a Frank Sinatra album, it's the product of Frank Sinatra's head," Riddle told Schwartz. "He was always very coherent about what he wanted—where the crescendi should take place, where the diminuendos, the tempi, naturally the key. Sometimes it became almost painful in discussing an album of twelve or fourteen songs. It was a very precise, tense atmosphere. I would practically blow my stack because we'd take almost an hour on each piece. Then human nature would set in after five or six or seven or eight of those. He'd get tired. He'd say, 'Do what you want with the rest.' That would be the end of the thing, and we were both, I think, somewhat relieved."

The result Riddle achieved in "I've Got You Under My Skin" was, he said, "a sort of a cornerstone recording for both him and me." The arrangement starts with a comfortable, loping rhythm that Riddle called "the heartbeat rhythm" ("Sinatra's tempo is the tempo of the heartbeat," he said) and then sets up a marvellous instrumental tension around Sinatra's voice. Riddle always found little licks—certain spicy, nearly out-of-key notes—that would tease the key, and added the glue of "sustaining strings" almost subliminally to the rhythm and woodwind sections. At the instrumental breaks in the songs, Riddle gave solo voices to oboes, muted trumpets, piccolos, bassoons; in "I've Got You Under My Skin," it was to Milt Bernhart's trombone, which whipped up the excitement until Sinatra joined the song again and brought it back to the heartbeat rhythm where it had begun. Sinatra had wanted an extended crescendo; Riddle provided one that was longer than had ever been heard in an organized arrangement.

The song won a fans' poll as the all-time-favorite Sinatra recording; it "changed American popular music, and that is not overstating the case," Schwartz says. "Nothing was the same after that specific arrangement and also the sound of the 'Songs for Swingin' Lovers!' album itself." Sinatra had found his groove. His singing in this period was more than a sound; it was an attitude. He gave us words, postures, rhythms—a sense that sex and life were going to be a a big "wowie," as he sang in "Me and My Shadow." The postwar party had begun, and while the fifties were stalled in normalcy, Sinatra had about him a whiff of the libertine. His style—the thin, sensitive line of his look and of his singing—had the immanence of the hip combined with the articulateness of the traditional, to which all of us preppy white boys could relate. We dressed Sinatra, doing up our paisley Brooks Brothers ties into Windsor knots. We talked Sinatra: "Charlies" for breasts, "gas" for fun, "bird" for pecker, the suffix "-ville" added to as many words as we could work into our new patter. We wanted to go to the party, and it seemed that Sinatra had always been there.

After the humiliations of his decline, nothing so moved Sinatra as the spectacle of himself as a powerhouse: big talent, big guys around him, big bucks behind him, big connections to the mainstream and to underworld power. "He used his success in film, in singing, and in business to pump up the persona of untouchable," Tony Curtis says. "Notice I don't bring up the Mafia. He in himself was his own godfather. He ran his own family and his friends like that. Untouchable."

Before his comeback, Sinatra had survived hand to mouth, primarily on borrowed money; after it, he laid the groundwork for an empire. Sinatra, who lives in Beverly Hills but who once kept homes in New York and London as well, ruled over his kingdom in his heyday primarily from his compound in Rancho Mirage, which grew over the years into a kind of metaphor of his aggrandizement, with a helipad, a swimming pool, tennis courts, a screening room, and a state-of-the-art kitchen with full twenty-four-hour service. The compound also boasted two two-bedroom guest-houses, each with his-and-hers bathrooms and, in "the Kennedy room," a red White House hotline telephone that was originally installed for an aborted visit by J.F.K., in 1962. (Much to Sinatra's rage, the President, on orders from Bobby Kennedy to distance himself from Sinatra and his Mafia connections, stayed instead with Bing Crosby, in nearby Palm Desert.)

Sinatra's lavish entertaining bespoke not just a man of talent but a man of property. He owned nine per cent of the Sands Hotel in Las Vegas, which he turned almost single-handedly into an entertainment mecca; he became vice-president of the corporation, and earned a hundred thousand dollars for each week he performed, until falling out with the hotel, in 1967. For a time in the sixties, he also owned fifty per cent of the Cal-Neva Lodge in Lake Tahoe. In those days, buttons began to appear with Sinatra's face on them, bearing the motto "IT'S SINATRA'S WORLD, WE JUST LIVE IN IT." And so it seemed. Sinatra also acquired large interests in a small charter airline, a music-publishing house, radio stations, restaurants, and real estate. He formed Essex Productions and received as part of his fee twenty-five per cent of "Pal Joey"; another Sinatra company received the same percentage for "The Joker Is Wild," in which he starred.

By the end of the decade, Sinatra had earned so much money for Capitol that he wanted his own label. He proposed a fifty-fifty split with Capitol, who would distribute—a deal that was unheard-of in those days but is common now. When Capitol refused, Sinatra formed his own record company, Reprise Records; he pronounced it with a long "i," as in "reprisal." "Fuck you! Fuck your company!" Sinatra shouted over the phone to Alan Livingston when Livingston tried to reach a last-minute agreement with him. Livingston recalls, "Frank said, 'I'm going to destroy that round building. I'll tear it down.' " Although Sinatra was forced to make four more albums for Capitol, Capitol continued after he was gone to make Sinatra albums from unreleased recordings and sell them at cut prices. "The market was flooded with our Sinatra albums," Livingston says. "Reprise got killed. Nobody was taking their product. Then Jack Warner came in and bailed Sinatra out." (Sinatra sold two-thirds of Reprise to Warner Bros. in 1963, for more than three million dollars' capital gain.)

Onstage, Sinatra was in control of his world and beyond hurt. Offstage, he was fearful and somewhat paranoid. His paternal advice to Nancy was "Be aware. Be aware of everything around you." Wealth brought him a liberating sense of control over life. "I remember we were on a plane flying from Las Vegas to Palm Springs," Aileen Mehle says of a trip she took with Sinatra in the early sixties. "He had paper bags full of, I think, hundred-dollar bills. Loaded. Hundreds of thousands. He upended the bags in the middle of the plane and started throwing the money up in the air. Talk about playful! He said, 'I'm celebrating, because for the first time I have a million dollars cash in the bank that I don't give a damn what I'm going to do with.'"

Among his friends, Sinatra has always been known for impulsive, awesome acts of generosity—those grand gestures that Sicilians call *la bella figura*. "I always felt I could call and say, 'Frank, I'm in trouble. I need a hundred thousand dollars,'" Jo Stafford says. Sinatra once sent his friend the actor George Raft, who was under indictment for federal-income-tax evasion, a signed blank check with a note saying "To use if you need it." When Phil Silvers' partner Rags Ragland died just before they were to open the Copacabana, in 1946, Sinatra flew across the country to surprise the comedian and play straight man. "When someone was down on his luck, Frank was like the Marines. He was there," I was told by the late actress-turned-psychotherapist Ruth Conte, the former wife of the actor Richard (Nick) Conte, who was part of Sinatra's circle in the fifties. "When Nick left me, Frank called me. 'How ya doin', baby.' A kindness that was also an assertion of power. It was so reassuring to him to be able to use it."

Indeed, Sinatra's compulsion to assuage his friends' anxieties was a way of keeping his own at bay. "You sometimes feel like you want to run away from him," Burt Lancaster said. "Because if you say to Frank, 'I'm having a problem,' it becomes his problem. And sometimes maybe you'd like to try and work it out yourself." Sinatra's need to protect made him an extraordinary but contradictory friend. "If you helped him more than he helped you, the friendship was doomed because the balance he wanted had been tipped," MacLaine writes. "He was a happy man when he was able to come to my rescue. 'Oh, I just wish someone would try to hurt you so I could kill them for you,' he'd say."

Inevitably, Sinatra had trouble acknowledging the generosity of his friends and colleagues. "He just isn't built to give out compliments," Riddle has said of him. After Sinatra got an Academy Award, he said, "I did it all myself"; once, in a shouting match with a press agent who had the temerity to suggest that Sinatra was dependent on the public, Sinatra shot back, "I am not! I have talent and I am dependent only on myself!" This separation of himself from others, which accounts for his arrogance, also accounts for the special quality of loneliness in his singing. "He understood loneliness better than any other person of his generation," Hamill says. "I mean a certain kind of urban loneliness." But what Sinatra evokes is not strictly urban. It is a very particular American loneliness—that of the self adrift in its pursuit of the destiny of "me," and thrown back onto the solitude of its own restless heart.

As a singer, of course, Sinatra could be all-giving and all-conquering all the time. The cocked hat, the open collar, the backward glance with the raincoat slung over the shoulder, the body leaning back with arms wide open in song—these images of perfect individualism dominated the albums of the fifties. Sinatra was flying high. "Come fly with me! / Let's fly! / Let's fly away!" he commanded the world. But these lyrics also hint at Sinatra's escape into success—into an empyrean where no one could touch or judge him: "Up there! Where the air is rarefied / We'll just glide, starry-eyed." Sinatra retreated into his own deluxe isolation; instead of intimacy he offered the audience bits of his legendary public story. Some of his songs invoked his family ("Tina," "Nancy with the Laughin' Face"); in "Me and My Shadow" he referred to his saloonkeeping philosophes Jilly Rizzo and Toots Shor. Sinatra stood before an audience as a person who had caroused with killers and kings. He'd been married to the most beautiful woman in the world. He had won and lost and now won again. All this made him more interesting as a performer than anything he sang. Sinatra's best songs of the period—"All the Way," "Call Me Irresponsible," and especially "Come Fly with Me"—were written by Sammy Cahn, who had roomed with Sinatra, travelled with Sinatra, and lived a lot of Sinatra's story with him. The material *was* Sinatra. "Sammy's words fit my mouth the best," he told the producer George Schlatter.

But lyrics, like everything else, could suffer from Sinatra's egotism. "Ira Gershwin hated that Sinatra took 'A Foggy Day' and sang 'I viewed the morning with much alarm,' " the singer Michael Feinstein, who was for a long time Gershwin's assistant, says. "The lyric is 'I viewed the morning with alarm.' It drove Gershwin crazy, because he felt the word 'much' weakened what he originally wrote." Leonora Hornblow tells of an evening at actor Clifton Webb's when Cole Porter was present: "Frank fiddled with the lyrics. I think it was 'I Get a Kick Out of You'—you know, 'You give me a boot.' Cole got up and walked out. Cole had perfect manners. For him to do that while somebody was singing was like stripping his clothes off." Sinatra revered Porter (he leased Porter's apartment at the Waldorf Towers), but he also thought Porter "a snob," whereas Cahn wrote lyrics that had Sinatra's common touch. Cahn spoke and wrote in the same demotic, tough-talking, breezy manner ("Hey there, cutes, put on your Basie boots"). "Sammy saw himself as Frank," his widow, Tita Cahn, says. "Frank without the voice, without the looks." And Cahn played a large part in building the image of the loosey-goosey, unpredictable ring-a-ding guy. He and the composer Jimmy Van Heusen were commissioned by Sinatra to write a song using Sinatra's catchphrase for his first Reprise album, which was called, not surprisingly, "Ring-a-Ding-Ding!" The phrase—like Shakespeare's "Hey nonny nonny"—thumbed its nose at meanings and sincerity. Sinatra's songs of this period—the late fifties and early sixties—however beautifully rendered, don't express the truth of his hurt or the exhilaration of his innocence. "Ring-a-Ding-Ding!," for instance, is a slick piece of emotional coasting. It substitutes pop romance for Sinatra's real-life, orgiastic refusal to suffer:

> Life is dull, it's nothing but one big lull,
> Then presto! You "do a skull" and find that you're reeling,
> She sighs, and you're feeling like a toy on a string,
> And your heart goes ring-a-ding-ding! Ring-a-ding-ding!

Drink played a large part in Sinatra's ring-a-ding arrogance. "Frank Sinatra is, in the most dramatic and classical sense, an alcoholic," Jonathan Schwartz says. "There's a grandiosity, a fury, a self-pity, a night viciousness." He adds, "He made drinking an asset. He made it romantic." In the fifties, foreshadowing the performing indulgences of the sixties, Sinatra began bringing a tumbler of Scotch and a pack of cigarettes onstage. "Nobody's ever done that before or since, have they?" the author and renowned teacher of dramatic singing David Craig says. "Abusing himself like no singer in history." It was another way for Sinatra to flaunt his invincibility. "He's trying to demean his gift," Tony Curtis says. "He just wants to show you—like a juggler or a guy who works the tightrope, he goes up there with a drink in his hand and a cigarette butt—that he can still do it."

"If you can use some exotic booze / There's a bar in far Bombay," Cahn wrote memorably in "Come Fly with Me"; he also provided the Rat Pack with the ensemble hymn "Mr. Booze" in the movie "Robin and the Seven Hoods." Cahn had Sinatra's number, and he found a discreet way of turning Sinatra's quixotic lapses to public advantage. "Call me irresponsible," he wrote. "Call me unreliable, / Throw in undependable too." He understood that Sinatra's bad behavior was romantic in song; in life, he saw it differently. Tita Cahn recalls, "Sammy used to say that Frank was a man who kept putting the dream to the test, pushing it too far, hoping that someone would hit him and he'd be awakened. But nobody did. The dream wouldn't go away."

"Frank created this romantic figure he wanted to be," Lauren Bacall says. "There was something about him that was a little unreal. I think he fantasized a bit." She continues, "He was away singing at some club, and he would call me and say, 'I'm coming home tonight. I want you to be at the house when I get there.' I—jerk—thought, How glamorous. I'd get in my car, drive up to his house. I'd be standing there by myself, then suddenly *in he'd walk*. Oh, God, what a great moment! Then just as easily that night he could throw me out. He was capable of that kind of change." When news of Sinatra's engagement to Bacall was leaked to the press by her agent and Sinatra's friend Irving (Swifty) Lazar in 1958, Sinatra immediately dropped her. Years later, when he was seeing Mia Farrow, Bacall met him and chatted warmly with him at a party given by Lazar. "Frank never mentioned to me that he knew that Lazar had been responsible for the press, never said a word to me about it," Bacall says. "Swifty was sitting at another table across the room. Before Sinatra left, he got up and walked over to Lazar's table. He put his hands on the tablecloth and pulled the fucking tablecloth off the table—all the glasses, the plates, everything fell on the floor. He said, 'And you're the one who's responsible for what happened between us!' He turned around and walked out."

Sinatra, whom Peter Lawford called "the lovable land mine," was at once cursed and blessed by this notoriously thin skin. His hypersensitivity made him both hell on a short fuse and more sensitive to emotion in a lyric. Sinatra seemed compelled to discharge any unsettling feeling as quickly as possible. "It's not something I do deliberately. I can't help myself," he told *Playboy*. "If the song is a lament about the loss of love, I get an ache in my gut. I feel the loss and I cry out the loneliness." Song, like rage, had the ability to put Sinatra "beside himself"; and, like song, his fury served as a kind of antidepressant. "He never gave you the reality," Curtis says of Sinatra's singing persona. "I saw dissatisfaction, an anger, a frustration from that immigrant background of his." Even backstage in Las Vegas, when Sinatra walked off after a successful gig, Curtis noticed that Sinatra's face "was drawn and ready for a fight." Curtis says, "When he got up onstage, he seemed to say, 'Fuck you, motherfuckers. Sit quiet. I'll show you something.' That was part of the kick."

"The façade of being macho and strong grew as his career grew," says Nancy Sinatra, Sr. "He became part of that image. He was never quite that at all, believe me." But Sinatra was pleased with his reputation for toughness. When Al Capp mythologized him as Danny Tempest in the cartoon strip "Li'l Abner," Sinatra thanked him. "He believes in punishment. He's a bully," says Jonathan Schwartz, who for more than a decade has played nothing but the Chairman of the Board on his "Sinatra Saturday" program, and was forced to take a three-month "sabbatical" from WNEW after he called the final third of Sinatra's 1980 "Trilogy" album "a mess of narcissism." In "My Way," the anthem of Sinatra's later years, which Sinatra came to dislike, he sang, "The record shows I took the blows / And did it my way." Actually, the record shows that other people took the blows. In 1967, after his credit was stopped at the Sands in Vegas, Sinatra exacted retribution by signing a contract with Caesar's Palace and then going on a tear at the Sands: threatening dealers, driving a golf cart through a plate-glass window, breaking furniture and trying to set it alight, and finally confronting the executive vice-president, Carl Cohen. "I'll bury you, you son-of-a-bitch motherfucker," he told Cohen, whereupon Cohen removed the caps from Sinatra's front teeth. (Sinatra later laughed it off. "Never punch a Jew in the desert," he said.) "I think the rage might have been a double rage," Pete Hamill says of Sinatra's wild outbursts. "A rage against the object of his anger and a rage against himself in some way, for losing his temper and letting this classy façade crumble so easily."

As Sinatra's power grew over the years and he became a kind of law unto himself, he dealt with conflict by withdrawing the favor of his presence from people. After dropping Bacall, Sinatra encountered her by chance in Palm Springs. "He looked at me as if I were the wall. It was so terrifying. I have never had that experience before or since," she says. Friends were banished sometimes for a week, sometimes forever. Phil Silvers was cut off in the fifties after CBS programmed "The Phil Silvers Show" opposite ABC's "The Frank Sinatra Show." "You had to go Fridays, huh?" Sinatra said, and stopped speaking to Silvers for sixteen years. Peter Lawford bit the dust twice—initially when he was Ava Gardner's first date after her divorce from Sinatra. "He threatened to kill me and then didn't speak to me for five years," says Lawford, who was struck off again, after the Kennedys' postelection snub of Sinatra's Rancho Mirage estate, simply because he was married to J.F.K.'s sister Patricia. In 1959, when Sammy Davis, Jr., complained about Sinatra to a Chicago journalist, saying, "I don't care if you are the most talented person in the world. It doesn't give you the right to step on people and treat them rotten," he spent a couple of months in purgatory, and was returned to the fold only after he offered a public apology for his outburst.

The atmosphere of intimidation that surrounded Sinatra was reflected in the jokes of the Vegas comedians. Shecky Greene: "Frank Sinatra once saved my life. I was jumped by a bunch of guys in the parking lot and they were hitting me and beating me with blackjacks when Frank walked over and said, 'That's enough, boys.' " Don Rickles: "C'mon, Frank, be yourself. Hit somebody." Jackie Mason doesn't know what he did to offend Sinatra, but while he was playing the Aladdin Hotel in the early eighties, Sinatra came onstage after Mason's set and began berating him. "'The jerk-off rabbi.' 'Who the fuck is he?' This, that, 'Fuck him,' " Mason says. "I don't even know what happened. All I know is that a couple of weeks later, I opened the door of a car—ping!—a fist came in and busted me in the nose and before I could open my eyes he disappeared. I asked a lot of wise guys. They didn't *say* it was Sinatra. In my heart of hearts, I think it must have come from Sinatra." Even if Sinatra's menace wasn't verifiable, it was part of his aura—a rough justice underlined by his friendship with punks and presidents.

The most powerful among Sinatra's powerful friends was, of course, John F. Kennedy, for whom he acted as both fund-raiser and pander. The fun-loving Kennedy, whom Sinatra nicknamed Chicky Boy, enjoyed carousing with Sinatra's star-studded cronies; Sinatra repaid the honor of the association by calling his clique the Jack Pack, for a brief time, and even introduced Kennedy to one of his girlfriends, Judith Campbell. Sinatra got to visit Hyannis Port, to travel in the President's private plane, and to cruise with the President on the Honey Fitz; he escorted Jackie Kennedy, who didn't want him in the White House, to the inaugural gala he'd organized.

If Kennedy's high rank confirmed the brightness of Sinatra's star, the darkness of Sinatra's past was confirmed by the wise guys he was drawn to. Over the years, Sinatra rubbed shoulders with a gallery of hoodlums: Willie Moretti, Joe Fischetti, Lucky Luciano, Carlo Gambino, and, especially, Sam Giancana, who was the head of the Chicago mob in the fifties, and who called Sinatra the Canary. Part of Sinatra's freewheeling impudence came from the wisdom of the underclass—the knowledge that crime was free enterprise turned upside down and that there was a slim difference between being a killer and making a killing. "If what you do is honest and you make it, you're a hero," Sinatra said. "If what you do is crooked and you make it, you're a bum. Me—I grabbed a song." Sinatra walked a thin line between respectability and rapacity. He had learned the manners of the ruling class, and he owned all their pleasures; what the mobsters offered him was the flip side—their lack of propriety. They lived the darkness that Sinatra's bright public persona could only hint at in song. "He was in awe of them," Bacall says. "He thought they were fabulous."

Onstage, where the association gave Sinatra an aroma of toughness and menace, he sometimes joked about the wise guys; offstage, he was loath to talk. When Hamill first raised the touchy issue of the mobsters with Sinatra, Sinatra said only, "If I talk about some of those other guys, someone might come knockin' at my fuckin' door." But he later went on, "I spent a lot of time working in saloons. . . . I was a kid. . . . They paid you, and the checks didn't bounce. I didn't meet any Nobel Prize winners in saloons. But if Francis of Assisi was a singer and worked in saloons, he would've met the same guys."

A nineteen-page Justice Department memorandum prepared in 1962 suggests that Sinatra had contact with about ten major hoodlums, some of whom had his unlisted number. As a result, Sinatra has become, in Hamill's words, "the most investigated American performer since John Wilkes Booth." The press wanted to see corruption in Sinatra's connection to the Mob, although none has ever been proved; in any case, it's not cash but comfort that the Mob really offered Sinatra. In the company of these violent men, he was not judged for his own violent nature; in the context of their ignorance, his lack of education didn't matter. He could drop the carapace of sophistication and embrace his shadow.

The epigraph to one of his daughter's books about him quotes Sinatra as saying, "Maybe there might be value to a firefly, or an instant-long Roman candle." Sinatra's voice, as he well knows, put a lasting glow on six decades of American life and three generations of fans. Sinatra stumped for F.D.R., who invited him to the White House; he was still around to sing at the inaugural gala of Ronald and Nancy Reagan. His was a voice for all political seasons. In the forties, with "The Song Is You," "All or Nothing at All," and "I'll Never Smile Again," he tranquillized the nation; in the fifties boom, he was the slaphappy sound of good times ("Young at Heart," "Come Fly with Me," "Oh! Look at Me Now!"); in the sixties, he ushered in the optimism of the Kennedy era with "All the Way," "The Best Is Yet to Come," and "High Hopes"; and even into the eighties Sinatra was singing the tune of the smug, self-aggrandizing Reagan years with "My Way."

Over all those decades, Sinatra continually struggled to make his sound current. In the sixties, for example, under his own banner at Reprise, he produced a few great albums; at the same time, almost imperceptibly, as popular musical tastes underwent a seismic shift, Sinatra's records began to deteriorate into pickup albums—collections of singles, like "That's Life" and, a particularly lazy effort, "Sinatra's Sinatra," in which he just rerecorded his Capitol songs. (This prompted Jonathan Schwartz to joke, "Reprise Records, which Sinatra said stood for 'to play and play again,' really stood for 'to record and record again.' ") Times were changing, and Sinatra had to work to stay fresh. He tried bossa nova with the Brazilian Antonio Carlos Jobim; he mined the jazz seam in collaborations with Duke Ellington and Count Basie, which led to his touring with the Basie band and recording three albums with Basie, including the thrilling live album "Sinatra at the Sands." By the mid-sixties, however, with the advent of the Beatles and the British invasion, radio stations had been colonized by rock and roll. One night, waiting to go on in Las Vegas, Sinatra looked at the audience and said to Jimmy Van Heusen, beside him, "Look at that. Why won't they buy the records?" "Of course, they were buying the records by the million," says Schwartz, to whom Van Heusen told the story. "What he really was saying was 'Why don't I have hit singles?' "

Sinatra did have a few brief moments of singles glory in the sixties: "Strangers in the Night," "That's Life," "My Way," and "Something Stupid," with his daughter Nancy, which went to No. 1 in the charts in 1967 and became Sinatra's first gold single. He had long berated rock as "a rancid-smelling aphrodisiac," but now he tried to cross over and included in his repertoire works by Neil Sedaka, Joni Mitchell, Paul Simon, Stevie Wonder, and the Beatles. "Most of the rock songs Sinatra recorded came out dreadfully," the music critic John Rockwell writes in "Sinatra." "With stiff vocal phrasing and, worse, hopelessly anachronistic instrumental arrangements." He was completely out of synch with the spirit of Mitchell's "Both Sides Now"; he made a hash of Simon's "Mrs. Robinson"; and, although he finally got a good arrangement in a second version of George Harrison's "Something," he introduced the song for a long time as having been written by John Lennon and Paul McCartney.

He retired briefly in 1971, but by 1973, in response to thirty thousand fan letters and to his own agitated heart, he was back in the studio, and soon afterward he was on the road again. He returned with a new toupee and a gutsy new repertoire. Instead of falling back on his standards, Sinatra learned difficult new songs: "Winners," "You Will Be My Music," "There Used to Be a Ballpark," "Noah," "Dream Away," and "Send in the Clowns." His phrasing was more staccato now, and the bands filled in the spaces. But he had kept faith with his public, and they with him. In 1975, Sinatra took a full-page ad in the L.A. *Times*, reading, "IT WAS A VERY GOOD YEAR: COUN-TRIES: 8; CITIES: 30; ATTENDANCE: 483,261; TOTAL PERFORMANCES: 140; GROSS: $7,817,473." Sinatra still had some big innings left: the self-con-gratulatory best-selling "Trilogy" (1980), and the two multi-platinum "Duets" albums (1993–94), where he sang with contemporary pop stars like Barbra Streisand, Jimmy Buffet, Carly Simon, and Stevie Wonder. Sinatra was still reaching out for a new audience, and he found it, even if the product was well below his high standard. "I'm a belter now, baby," he was heard to tell the crowd in the late eighties. The last big notes he hit were in "New York, New York." Schwartz says, "By the eighties, Sinatra was singing knuckleballs."

At Caesar's Palace, sometime in the early eighties, Shirley MacLaine caught Sinatra's show. "I don't know what was bugging him," she told me, describing the evening's first set. "The magic wasn't there. He marked it. He couldn't wait to get out." Afterward, at dinner, Sinatra asked what she thought, and she gave him her version of a pep talk. "Frank, you really ought to remember how you got so many of us through a Second World War, and a New Deal, and gave us an education in music," she said. "Please don't just mark it, because it disrespects everything you meant to the whole country. You might seem to some like a ruin but to most of us that ruin is a monument." MacLaine adds, "His eyes just . . . It was like nobody had said that to him in a long time."

In the early nineties, Sinatra began forgetting lyrics. "He'd apologize to the audience," his pianist Bill Miller says. "They'd say, 'Hey, Frank we don't care.' And they don't. They want to see *him*." Miller goes on, "Then he had second thoughts. You'd see him shaking his head as if to say, 'I don't want them feeling sorry for me.'"

Sinatra's work is his legend; his legend is his work. Not surprisingly, he has eschewed autobiography or an official biography. "There's too much about my life I'm not proud of," he says. Inevitably, as children of the famous must, Sinatra's offspring all claimed their absent father by sustaining some part of his legacy. "You have to do it well," Nancy says. "You can't let people piss on it." She has written two elegantly produced books that are encomiums to the old man; Tina has produced a five-hour TV miniseries of his life story; and Frankie, Jr., who conducted Sinatra's orchestra, released a CD, "As I Remember It," in 1996, with new orchestrations of Sinatra standards. Sinatra's story is hard to keep ideal, filled, as it is, with brigands and barbarity. But as long as he was able Sinatra kept on doing the only kind of penance he knew: singing.

In New York, on Sinatra's eightieth birthday, the Empire State Building glowed blue for Ole Blue Eyes; on television two days later, Frank and Barbara Sinatra sat like the Sun King and his consort at a front-row table, while behind them L.A.'s Shrine Auditorium was packed to its chandeliers with the rich and famous in evening dress, attending a televised homage to Sinatra and his career. One by one, the grandees of American popular culture came forward to hymn his praises. The first to serenade him was Bruce Springsteen—one New Jersey Boss to another. "My first recollection of Frank's voice was coming out of a jukebox in a dark bar on a Sunday afternoon, when my mother and I went searching for my father," Springsteen said before launching into "Angel Eyes." "And I remember she said, 'Listen to that, that's Frank Sinatra. He's from New Jersey.' It was a voice filled with bad attitude, life, beauty, excitement, a nasty sense of freedom, sex, and a sad knowledge of the ways of the world. Every song seemed to have as its postscript 'And if you don't like it, here's a punch in the kisser.' " Springsteen continued, "But it was the deep blueness of Frank's voice that affected me the most, and, while his music became synonymous with black tie, good life, the best booze, women, sophistication, his blues voice was always the sound of hard luck and men late at night with the last ten dollars in their pockets trying to figure a way out. On behalf of all New Jersey, Frank, I want to say, 'Hail, brother, you sang out our soul.'"

Springsteen had met Sinatra for the first time a few months before
that, at Sinatra's house in Beverly Hills. After supper, the guests gathered
around the piano to sing. Among them were Bob Dylan, Steve Lawrence,
Eydie Gormé, the singer Patti Scialfa (who is Springsteen's wife), the producers George Schlatter and Mace Neufeld, and Tita Cahn. "You could feel
Frank—you know when a thoroughbred is sort of wired up and is ready
to race," Tita Cahn says. They harmonized for a while, and then someone
suggested one of Sammy Cahn's early hits with Sinatra, "Guess I'll Hang
My Tears Out to Dry." The group launched in:

> When I want rain,
> I get sunny weather;
> I'm just as blue as the sky,
> Since love is gone,
> Can't pull myself together.
> Guess I'll hang my tears out to dry.

"Hold it!" Sinatra interrupted. "You know I sing solo."
He finished the song alone.

ARTHUR MILLER

MAKING WILLY LOMAN

O<small>N A CRISP APRIL WEEKEND</small> in 1948, Arthur Miller, then only thirty-three and enjoying the first flush of fame after the Broadway success the previous year of "All My Sons," waved goodbye to his first wife, Mary, and their two young kids, in Brooklyn, and set off for Roxbury, Connecticut, where he intended to build a cabin on a hillock just behind a Colonial house he had recently purchased for the family, which stood at the aptly named crossroads of Tophet (another name for Hell) and Gold Mine. "It was a purely instinctive act," Miller, who long ago traded up from that first forty-four-acre property to a four-hundred-acre spread on Painter Hill, a few miles down the road, told me recently. "I had never built a building in my life."

Miller had a play in mind, too; his impulse for the cabin was "to sit in the middle of it, and shut the door, and let things happen." All Miller knew about his new play was that it would be centered on a travelling salesman who would die at the end and that two of the lines were "Willy?" "It's all right. I came back"—words that to Miller spoke "the whole disaster in a nutshell." He says, "I mean, imagine a salesman who can't get past Yonkers. It's the end of the world. It's like an actor saying 'It's all right. I can't speak'. " As he worked away on his cabin, he repeated the play's two lines like a kind of mantra. "I kept saying, 'As soon as I get the roof on and the windows in, I'm gonna start this thing,' " he recalls. "And indeed I started on a morning in spring. Everything was starting to bud. Beautiful weather."

Miller had fashioned a desk out of an old door. As he sat down to it his tools and nails were still stashed in a corner of the studio, which was as yet unpainted and smelled of raw wood. "I started in the morning, went through the day, then had dinner, and then I went back there and worked till—I don't know—one or two o'clock in the morning," he says. "It sort of unveiled itself. I was the stenographer. I could hear them. I could hear them, literally." When Miller finally lay down to sleep that first night, he realized he'd been crying. "My eyes still burned and my throat was sore from talking it all out and shouting and laughing," he later wrote in his autobiography, "Timebends." In one day, he had produced, almost intact, the first act of "Death of a Salesman," which has since sold about eleven million copies, making it probably the most successful modern play ever published. The show, which is being put on somewhere in the world almost every day of the year, celebrates its fiftieth anniversary next month with a Broadway revival from Chicago's Goodman Theatre, directed by Robert Falls and starring Brian Dennehey as the fanatical and frazzled drummer Willy Loman.

"He didn't write 'Death of a Salesman'; he *released* it," the play's original director, Elia Kazan, said in his autobiography, "A Life." "It was there inside him, stored up waiting to be turned loose." To Miller, there was a "dream's quality in my memory of the writing and the day or two that followed its completion." In his notebook for "Death of a Salesman"—a sixty-six-page document chronicling the play's creation, which is kept with his papers at the University of Texas at Austin—he wrote, "He who understands everything about his subject cannot write it. I write as much to discover as to explain." After that first day of inspiration, it took Miller six weeks to call forth the second act and to make Willy remember enough "so he would kill himself." The form of the play—where past and present coalesce in a lyrical dramatic arc—was one that Miller felt he'd been "searching for since the beginning of my writing life." "Death of a Salesman" seems to spill out of Willy's panic-stricken, protean imagination, and not out of a playwright's detached viewpoint. "The play is written from the sidewalk instead of from a skyscraper," Miller says of its first-person urgency. But, ironically, it was from the deck of a skyscraper that Miller contemplated beginning his drama, in a kind of Shakespearean foreshadowing of Willy's suicidal delirium. The notebook's first entry reads:

> Scene 1—Atop Empire State. 2 guards. "Who will die today? It's that kind of day. . . fog, and poor visibility. They like to jump into a cloud. Who will it be today?"

As Miller navigated his way through the rush of characters and plot ideas, the notebook acted as ballast. "In every scene remember his size, ugliness," Miller reminds himself about Loman on its second page. "Remember his own attitude. Remember *pity*." He analyzes his characters' motives. "Willy wants his sons to destroy his failure," he writes, and on a later page, "Willy resents Linda's unbroken, patient forgiveness (knowing there must be great hidden hatred for him in her heart)." In Miller's notebook, characters emerge sound and fully formed. For instance, of Willy's idealized elder son, Biff, who is a lost soul fallen from his high-school glory and full of hate for his father, he writes, "Biff is travelled, oppressed by guilt of failure, of not making money although a kind of indolence pleases him: an easygoing way of life. . . . Truthfully, Biff is not really bright enough to make a businessman. *Wants everything too fast*." Miller also talks to himself about the emotional stakes and the trajectory of scenes:

> Have it happen that Willy's life is in Biff's hands—aside from Biff succeeding. There is Willy's guilt to Biff re: The Woman. But is that retrievable? There is Biff's disdain for Willy's character, his false aims, his pretense and these Biff cannot finally give up or alter. Discover the link between Biff's work views and his anti-work feelings.

Although the notebook begins with a series of choppy asides and outlines, it soon becomes an expansive, exact handwritten log of Miller's contact with his inner voices. For instance, it reveals the development of Charley, Loman's benevolent next-door neighbor, whose laconic evenhandedness was, in Miller's eyes, partly a projection of his own father. Charley speaks poignantly to Biff at Willy's graveside ("Nobody dast blame this man"); what appears in the last scene as a taut and memorable nine-line speech, a kind of eulogy, was mined from words (here indicated in italics) that were part of a much longer improvisation in the notebook:

> A salesman doesn't build anything, *he don't put a bolt to a nut or a seed in the ground*. A man who doesn't build anything must be liked. He must he cheerful on bad days. Even calami-

ties mustn't break through. Cause one thing, he has got to be
liked. *He don't tell you the law or give you medicine.* So there's no
rock bottom to your life. All you know is that on good days
or bad, you gotta come in cheerful. No calamity must be
permitted to break through, Cause one thing, always, you're
a man who's gotta be believed. You're way out there *riding on
a smile and a shoeshine. And when they start not smilin' back*, the
sky falls in. *And then you get a couple of spots on your hat, and
you're finished. Cause there's no rock bottom to your life.*

Here, as in all his notes for the play, Miller's passion and his flow are
apparent in the surprising absence of cross-outs; the pages exude a startling alertness. He is listening not just to the voices of his characters but
to the charmed country silence around him, which seems to define his
creative state of grace:

> Roxbury—At night the insects softly thumping the screens
> like a blind man pushing with his fingers in the dark. . . . The
> crickets, frogs, whippoorwills altogether, a scream from the
> breast of the earth when everyone is gone. The evening sky,
> faded gray, like the sea pressing up against the windows, or an
> opaque gray screen. (Through which someone is looking in at
> me?)

On a bright-blue December afternoon last year, Miller, now eighty-three,
returned to the cabin with his third wife, the photographer Inge Morath.
Although she has lived with Miller for more than three decades, only one
mile away from the "Salesman" studio, she had never seen the place. "The
main house was occupied by people I didn't know. They were sort of engineer people. Very antipathetic," Miller said, swinging his red Volkswagen
into the driveway of the new, friendly writer-owners. In a tan windbreak-
er and a baseball cap, he looked as rough-hewn and handy as any local
farmer. (The dining-room tables and chairs in his current, cluttered 1782
farmhouse are Miller's handiwork, produced in his carpentry workshop.)

After a cursory inspection of his old home, Miller, who is six feet three and stoops a little now, set off toward the cabin, up a steep hump that sits a few hundred paces from the back of the house. "In those days, I didn't think this hill was quite as steep," he said.

The cabin, a white clapboard construction in somewhat urgent need of a new coat of paint, stood just over the top of the rise, facing west, toward a thicket of birch trees and a field. "Oh, it will last as long as it's painted," Miller said, inspecting what he had wrought. "See, if a building has a sound roof, that's it, you'll keep it."

"I didn't know it was so tiny," Morath said. She snapped off a few photos, then waved her husband into the foreground for a picture before we all crowded into what proved to be a single high-ceilinged room. Except for a newly installed fluorescent light and some red linoleum that had been fitted over the floorboards, what Miller saw was what he'd built. He stepped outside to see if the cabin had been wired for electricity. (It had.) He inspected the three cinder blocks on which it was securely perched against the side of the hill. "I did the concrete," he recalled. Leaving, he turned to take a last look. "I learned a lot doing it," he said. "The big problem was getting the rafters of the roof up there alone. I finally built it on the ground and then swung them up." He added, "It's a bit like playwriting, you know. You get to a certain point, you gotta squeeze your way out of it."

Where does the alchemy of a great play begin? The seeds of "Death of a Salesman" were planted decades before Miller stepped into his cabin. "Selling was in the air through my boyhood," says Miller, whose father, Isidore, was the salesman-turned-owner of the Miltex Coat and Suit Company, which was a thriving enough business to provide the family with a spacious apartment on 110th Street in Harlem, a country bungalow, and a limousine and driver. "The whole idea of selling successfully was very important." Just as Miller was entering his teens, however, his father's business was wiped out by the Depression. Isidore's response was silence and sleep ("My father had trouble staying awake"); his son's response was anger. "I had never raised my voice against my father, nor did he against me, then or ever," wrote Miller, who had to postpone going to college for

two years—until 1934—because "nobody was in possession of the fare."
"As I knew perfectly well, it was not he who angered me, only his failure
to cope with his fortune's collapse," Miller went on in his autobiography.
"Thus I had two fathers, the real one and the metaphoric, and the latter I
resented because he did not know how to win out over the general collapse."

"Death of a Salesman" is a lightning rod both for a father's bewilder-
ment ("What's the secret?" Willy asks various characters) and for a son's
fury at parental powerlessness ("You fake! You phoney little fake!" Biff tells
Willy when they finally square off, in Act II). After the play's success,
Miller's mother, Augusta, found an early manuscript called "In
Memoriam," a forgotten autobiographical fragment that Miller had written when he was about seventeen. The piece, which was published in *The
New Yorker* in 1995, is about a Miltex salesman called Schoenzeit, who had
once asked Miller for subway fare when Miller was helping him carry sam-
ples to an uptown buyer. The real Schoenzeit killed himself the next day
by throwing himself in front of the El train; the character's "dejected
soul"—a case of exhaustion masquerading as gaiety—is the first sighting
of what would become Willy Loman. "His emotions were displayed at the
wrong times always, and he knew when to laugh," Miller wrote. In 1952,
Miller, rummaging through his papers, found a 1937 notebook in which
he had made embryonic sketches of Willy, Biff, and Willy's second son,
Happy. "It was the same family," he says of the twenty pages of realistic dialogue. "But I was unable in that straightforward, realistic form to contain
what I thought of as the man's poetry—that is, the zigzag shots of his
mind." He adds, "I just blotted it out."

Every masterpiece is a story of accident and accomplishment. Of all
the historical and personal forces that fed the making of "Death of a
Salesman," none was more important than a moment in 1947 when
Miller's uncle Manny Newman accosted him in the lobby of the Colonial
Theatre in Boston after a matinée of "All My Sons." "People regarded him
as a kind of strange, completely untruthful personality," Miller says of
Newman, a salesman and a notorious fabulist, who within the year would
commit suicide. "I thought of him as a kind of wonderful inventor. There
was something in him which was terribly moving, because his suffering

was right on his skin, you see. He was the ultimate climber up the ladder who was constantly being stepped on by those climbing past him. My empathy for him was immense. I mean, how could he possibly have succeeded? There was no way." According to Miller, Newman was "cute and ugly, a bantam with a lisp. Very charming." He and his family, including two sons, Abby and Buddy, lived modestly in Brooklyn. "It was a house without irony, trembling with resolutions and shouts of victories that had not yet taken place but surely would tomorrow," Miller recalled in "Timebends." Newman was fiercely, wackily competitive; even when Miller was a child, in the few hours he spent in Newman's presence his uncle drew him into some kind of imaginary contest "which never stopped in his mind." Miller, who was somewhat ungainly as a boy, was often compared unfavorably with his cousins, and whenever he visited them, he said, "I always had to expect some kind of insinuation of my entire life's probable failure."

When Newman approached Miller after that matinée, he had not seen his nephew for more than a decade. He had tears in his eyes, but, instead of complimenting the playwright, he told Miller, "Buddy is doing very well." Miller says now, "He had simply picked up the conversation from fifteen years before. That element of competitiveness—his son competing with me—was so alive in his head that there was no gate to keep it from his mouth. He was living in two places at the same time." Miller continues, "So everything is in the present. For him to say 'Buddy is doing very well'—there are no boundaries. It's all now. It's all now. And that to me was wonderful."

At the time, Miller was absorbed in the tryout of "All My Sons" and had "not the slightest interest in writing about a salesman." Until "All My Sons," Miller's plays had not been naturalistic in style; he had "resolved to write a play that could be put on," and had "put two years into 'All My Sons' to be sure that I believed every page of it." But Miller found naturalism, with its chronological exposition, "not sensuous enough" as a style; he began to imagine a kind of play where, as in Greek drama, issues were confronted head-on, and where the transitions between scenes were pointed rather than disguised. The success of "All My Sons" emboldened him. "I could now move into unknown territory," Miller says. "And that unknown territory was basically that we're thinking on several planes at the same time. I wanted to find a way to try to make everything happen at once." In his introduction to the fiftieth-anniversary edition of "Death of a Salesman," Miller writes, "The play had to move forward not by following a narrow discreet line, but as a phalanx." He continues, "There was no model I could adapt for this play, no past history for the kind of work I felt it could become." The notebook for the play shows Miller formulating a philosophy for the kind of Cubist stage pictures that would become his new style:

> Life is formless—its interconnections are cancelled by laps- es of time, by events occurring in separate places, by the hia- tus of memory. We live in the world made by man and the past. Art suggests or makes the interconnection palpable. Form is the tension of these interconnections: man with man, man with the past and present environment. The drama at its best is a mass experience of this tension.

At first, the Manny Newman encounter inspired in Miller only the intimation of a new, slashing sense of dramatic form. The play's structure is embedded in the structure of Loman's turbulent mind, which, Miller says, destroys the boundaries between then and now. As a result, "there are no flashbacks, strictly speaking, in 'Death of a Salesman,' " he says. "It's always moving forward." In this way, Miller jettisoned what he calls "the daylight continuity" of naturalism for the more fluid dark logic of dreams. "In a dream you don't have transitional material," Miller says. "The dream starts where it starts to mean something." He continues, "I wanted to start every scene at the last possible instant, no matter where that instant hap- pened to be." He picked up a copy of his play and read me its first beats: " 'Willy?' 'It's all right. I came back.' 'Why? What happened? Did something happen, Willy?' 'No, nothing happened.' " He added, "We're into the thing in three lines." His new structure jump-started both the scenes and the stage language, whose intensity Miller called "emergency speech"—an "unashamedly open" idiom that replaced "the crabbed dramatic hints and pretexts of the natural." Willy dies without a secret; the play's structure, with its crosscutting between heightened moments, encouraged the idea of revelation. The audience response that Miller wanted to incite, he said, "was not 'What happens next and why?' so much as 'Oh, God, of course.' "

When, early in 1948, Miller visited his cousin Abby Newman to talk about the blighted life of his late father, Miller himself had just such an epiphany. Newman told Miller, "He wanted a business for us. So we could all work together. A business for the boys." Miller, who repeated Newman's words in the play, wrote in his autobiography, "This conventional, mundane wish was a shot of electricity that switched all the random iron filings in my mind in one direction. A hopelessly distracted Manny was transformed into a man with a purpose: he had been trying to make a gift that would crown all those striving years; all those lies he told, all his imaginings and crazy exaggerations, even the almost military discipline he had laid on his boys, were in this instant given form and point. I suddenly understood him with my very blood."

Willy Loman is a salesman, but we're never told what product he lugs around in his two large sample cases. Once, a theatregoer buttonholed Miller and put the question to him: "What's he selling? You never say what he's selling." Miller quipped, "Well, himself. That's who's in the valise." Miller adds, "You sell yourself. You sell the goods. You become the commodity." Willy's house echoes with exhortations to his two floundering sons about the presentation of self ("The man who creates personal interest is the man who gets ahead. Be liked and you will never want") and the imperialism of self ("Lick the world. You guys together could absolutely lick the civilized world"). In his notebook Miller writes, "Willy longs to take off, be great," and "Willy wants his boys prepared for any life. 'Nobody will laugh at them—take advantage. They'll be big men.' It's the big men who command respect." In Willy's frenzied and exhausted attempt to claim himself, Miller had stumbled onto a metaphor for a postwar society's eagerness to pursue its self-interest after years of postponed life. In Willy's desperate appetite for success and in the brutal dicta offered by his rich brother Ben ("Never fight fair with a stranger, boy. You'll never get out of the jungle that way"), "Death of a Salesman" caught the spirit of self-aggrandizement being fed by what Miller calls "the biggest boom in

the history of the world." Americans had struggled through the
Depression, then fought a world war to keep the nation's democratic
dream alive; that dream was, broadly speaking, a dream of self-realization.
America, with its ideal of freedom, challenged its citizens to see how far
they could go in a lifetime—"to end up big," as Willy says. (In the play,
Ben, whom Willy looks to for answers—the notebook points to him as
"the visible evidence of what the boys can do and be. Superior family"—is
literally the predatory imperialist who at seventeen walked into the
African jungle and emerged four years later as a millionaire.) Miller was
not the first to dramatize the barbarity of American individualism; but, in
a shift that signalled the changing cultural mood, he was the first to stage
this spiritual battle of attrition as a journey to the interior of the American
psyche. "In a certain sense, Willy is all the voices," Miller said later. In fact,
"The Inside of His Head" was Miller's first title for the play; he also briefly
toyed with the idea of having the proscenium designed in the shape of a
head and having the action take place inside it.

In the economic upheavals of the thirties, social realism reflected the
country's mood; plays held a mirror up to the external world, not an
internal one. But in the postwar boom Tennessee Williams's "The Glass
Menagerie" (1945) and "A Streetcar Named Desire" (1947), written in
what Williams called his "personal lyricism," suddenly found an audience
and struck a deep new chord in American life. The plays were subjective,
poetic, symbolic; they made a myth of the self, not of social remedies.
Indeed, the name "Willy Loman" was not intended by Miller as a sort of
socioeconomic indicator ("low man"). Miller took it from a chilling
moment in Fritz Lang's film "The Testament of Dr. Mabuse" (1933) when,
after a long and terrifying stakeout, a disgraced detective who thinks he
can redeem himself by exposing a gang of forgers is pursued and duped by
them. The chase ends with the detective on the phone to his former boss
("Lohmann? Help me, for God's sake! Lohmann!"); when we see him
next, he is in an asylum, gowned and frightened and shouting into an invisible phone ("Lohmann? Lohmann? Lohmann?"). "What the name really
meant to me was a terrified man calling into the void for help that will
never come," Miller said.

Willy Loman's particular terror goes to the core of American individualism, in which the reputable self and the issue of wealth are hopelessly tangled. "A man can't go out the way he came in," Willy says to Ben. "A man has got to add up to something." Willy, who, at sixty, has no job, no money, no loyalty from his boys, is sensationally lacking in assets and in their social corollary—a sense of blessing. "He envies those who are blessed; he feels unblessed, but he's striving for it," Miller says. Although Willy's wife, Linda, famously says of him that "attention must be paid," he feels invisible to the world. "I'm not noticed," he says. Later, Linda confides to the boys, "For five weeks he's been on straight commission, like a beginner, an unknown!" As Miller puts it now, "The whole idea of people failing with us is that they can no longer be loved. You haven't created a persona which people will pay for, see, experience, or come close to. It's almost like death. You have a deathly touch. People who succeed are loved because they exude some magical formula for fending off destruction, fending off death." He continues, "It's the most brutal way of looking at life that one can imagine, because it discards anyone who does not measure up. It wants to destroy them. It's been going on since the Puritan times. You are beyond the blessing of God. You're beyond the reach of God. That God rewards those who deserve it. It's a moral condemnation that goes on. You don't want to be near this failure."

"Death of a Salesman" was the first play to dramatize this punishing—and particularly American—interplay of panic and achievement. Before "Salesman," Eugene O'Neill's "The Iceman Cometh" (1946) raised the issue in the eerie calm of Harry Hope's bar, whose sodden habitués have retreated from competitiveness into a perverse contentment; as one of the characters says, "No one here has to worry about where they're going next, because there is no farther they can go." But in Willy Loman, Miller was able to bring both the desperation and the aspiration of American life together in one character.

Willy is afflicted by the notion of winning—what Brecht called "the black addiction of the brain." He cheats at cards; he encourages his boys to seek every advantage. Victory haunts him and his feckless sons. In a scene from the notebook, Biff and Happy tell Willy of their plan to go into business. "Step on it, boys, there ain't a minute to lose," Willy tells them, but their souls are strangled by their father's heroic dreams, which hang over them like some sort of spiritual kudzu. In another notebook entry, Biff rounds fiercely on Willy: "I don't care if you live or die. You think I'm mad at you because of the Woman, don't you? I am, but I'm madder because you botched up my life, because I can't tear you out of my heart, because I keep trying to make good, be something for you, to succeed for you."

In dramatizing the fantasy of competition, Miller's play was the first to dissect cultural envy in action—that process of invidious comparison which drives society forward but also drives it crazy. "You lose your life to it!" Miller says of the envy that feeds Willy's restlessness. "It's the ultimate outer-directional emotion. In other words, I am doing this not because it's flowing from me but because it's flowing against him." He goes on, "You're living in a mirror. It's a life of reflections. Emptiness. Emptiness. Emptiness. Hard to go to sleep at night. And hard to wake up." In his mind, Willy is competing with his brother Ben; with Dave Singleman, a successful old salesman who could make a living "without ever leaving his room" and who died a placid, accomplished death on a train to Boston; with his neighbor Charley, who owns his own business; and with Charley's successful lawyer son, Bernard. "Where's Willy in all this?" Miller asks. "He's competed himself to death. He's not existing anymore, or hardly."

In his notebook Miller wrote, "It is the combination of guilt (of failure), hate, and love—all in conflict that he resolves by 'accomplishing' a 20,000 dollar death." In death, Willy is worth more than in life. His suicide is the ultimate expression of his confusion of success with love and also of his belief in winning at all costs. As a father, he overlooked Biff's small childhood acts of larceny—taking sand from a building site, stealing basketballs, getting the answers for tests from the nerdy, studious Bernard—and Biff has continued his habit into adulthood, out of a combination of envy and revenge. A notebook citation reads, "It is necessary to (1) reveal to Willy that Biff stole to queer himself, and did it to hurt Willy," and "(2) And that he did it because of the Woman and all the disillusionment it implied." In the final version of the play, Biff, admitting in passing that he spent three months in a Kansas City jail for lifting a suit, tells Willy, "I stole myself out of every good job since high school!" At first, Miller saw the twenty thousand dollars of insurance money as cash to put Biff on the straight and narrow. " 'My boy's a thief—with 20,000 he'd stop it,' " he wrote in the notebook. Instead, Willy's suicide—the final show of force and fraud, in keeping with his demented competitive fantasies—is pitched on a more grandiose and perverse note. In an early draft of the terrific penultimate scene, where Biff exposes Willy and calls it quits with him and his dream, there is this exchange:

> BIFF (to him): What the hell do you want from me? What do you want from me?
> WILLY: —Greatness—
> BIFF: No—

In Miller's final draft, Willy, who will not accept his son's confession of thievery, takes Biff's greatness as a given as he visualizes his own suicide. "Can you imagine that magnificence with twenty thousand dollars in his pocket?" he says to Ben. He adds, "Imagine? When the mail comes he'll be ahead of Bernard again." When he goes to his death, Willy, in his mind, is on a football field with Biff, and full of vindictive triumph ("When you hit, hit low and hit hard, because it's important, boy"). "He dies sending his son through the goalposts," Miller says. "He dies moving." Miller pauses. "I think now that Kazan had it right from the beginning. He said, 'It's a love story.'"

On the last page of his notebook, Miller scribbled a short speech to give to the original cast after its members had read the play in galleys: "I want you all to know now that the cannons are quiet that this production has been the most gratifying I have known. I believe you are the finest ever gathered for any play and I am exceedingly proud and gratified not only for myself but for the American theatre." (The original cast included Lee J. Cobb as Willy, with Mildred Dunnock, Arthur Kennedy, and Cameron Mitchell.) In its passage to greatness, "Death of a Salesman" was enhanced enormously by the poetic set design of Jo Mielziner, who created a series of platforms, with Willy's house as a haunting omnipresent background. However, as Elia Kazan pointed out in his autobiography, "The stage direction in the original manuscript that Art gave me to read directly after he'd finished it does not mention a home as a scenic element. It reads, 'A pin-point travelling spot lights a small area on stage left. The Salesman is revealed. He takes out his keys and opens an invisible door.' " Kazan continues, "It was a play waiting for a directorial solution." It got it. "Death of a Salesman" also got its share of bad suggestions. Kazan's then wife, Molly Day Thacher, who was a playreader for the Group Theatre and had some influence over Kazan, tried to get Miller, as he remembers it, "to cut out Uncle Ben, all the memory scenes, and simply make it a realistic little narrative." And the co-producer, Kermit Bloomgarden, nervous of a play with "Death" in its title, took a poll among theatregoers which asked, "Would you go to see a play called 'Death of a Salesman'?" Nobody would. "They had a list of about fifteen titles," Miller says. "One was 'Free and Clear.' I'll never forget that."

In the intervening half century, the surface of American life has changed, but its mad competitiveness hasn't. "I'm not aware of any change in the way people look at this play," Miller says, but he admits that Willy's complaints about loyalty from the head office ring strange to contemporary ears. "Workers now—not just workers but management—know that nobody will have much pity for them." Last year, in a poll taken by the Royal National Theatre of eight hundred English theatre professionals, Miller was voted the greatest contemporary playwright; but in America, where in some quarters he's seen as a kind of Jeremiah, Miller is not accorded quite the same honor. He ascribes his decline in popularity to the erosion of the "unified audience" that came with the rise of the avant-garde in the early sixties. "The only theatre available to a playwright in the late forties was Broadway," Miller writes in the fiftieth-anniversary edition of "Salesman." "That theatre had one single audience . . . catering to very different levels of age, culture, education, and intellectual sophistication." He continues, "One result of this mix was the ideal, if not frequent fulfill-ment, of a kind of play that would be complete rather than fragmentary, an emotional rather than an intellectual experience, a play basically of heart with its ulterior moral gesture integrated with action rather than rhetoric. In fact, it was a Shakespearean ideal, a theatre for anyone with an understanding of English and perhaps some common sense."

But there was nothing Shakespearean in the response to "that damned disturbing play," as Kazan called it, on the night of its début, February 10, 1949, in Philadelphia. "The curtain came down and nothing happened," Miller says. "People sat there a good two or three minutes, then somebody stood up with his coat. Several men—I didn't see women doing this—were helpless. They were sitting there with handkerchiefs over their faces. It was like a funeral." He continues, "I didn't know whether the show was dead or alive. The cast was back there wondering what had happened. Nobody'd pulled the curtain up. Finally, someone thought to applaud, and then the house came apart."

LIEV SCHREIBER

FRESH PRINCE

In 1997, the director Tony Goldwyn was casting "A Walk on the Moon" and he was stuck for an actor to play Marty—the cuckolded blue-collar husband who is more intelligent than his circumstances would indicate—when he got a call from one of his producers, Dustin Hoffman. "There's this kid I'm working with," Hoffman told Goldwyn. "You gotta see him. He's special. He reminds me of me when I was his age." The actor in question was Liev Schreiber, who was on location with Hoffman in "Sphere." Schreiber, who got the job, and turned in one of his subtlest performances to date, is thirty-two and has been out of Yale School of Drama for only seven years. He has so far appeared in twenty-five films and sixteen stage plays. His is not a face familiar from gossip columns or talk shows; but he has a way of impressing the grandees of his craft.

"He has a kind of wisdom about human contradictions that is beyond his years," Hoffman says, comparing Schreiber with his peers in the new generation of actors. "He's very perceptive. He watches and observes, and he's amused by what he observes. It's an intrinsic part of him to transform what he sees into some kind of irony." For the American première of Harold Pinter's "Moonlight," the veteran British film and theatre director Karel Reisz hired Schreiber to play Jake, the older of two brothers, who defends himself against his father's dying messages through a series of private mocking games. "Dazzling," Reisz says was his thought after Schreiber's audition. "This boy can do anything. He's a mixture of urbane and rough. With that mixture, you can cook up a lot of meals."

Schreiber is the fetching transvestite in "Mixed Nuts"; the dithering nerd in "Walking and Talking"; the pretentious, humiliated would-be novelist in "Daytrippers"; one of the slashers in "Scream 2"; and the tattooed kidnapper in "Ransom." Last month, he was the young Orson Welles in HBO's "RKO 281," a bio-pic about the making of "Citizen Kane." This month, as if answering the plea at the end of the Times review of his 1998 performance in "Cymbeline"—"more Shakespeare, Mr. Schreiber"—he makes the leap from character actor to leading man: he is playing Hamlet in Andrei Serban's new production, at the Public Theatre.

On a bright November day, Schreiber scurried, ten minutes late, into a Serban rehearsal. "Sorry," he said, taking his seat in the semicircle around the handsome Romanian director, who was wearing chinos and a T-shirt and wire-rimmed glasses. Serban looked up briefly. "Never again," he said to Schreiber, and then continued analyzing Rosencrantz and Guildenstern. "They're like K.G.B. police dogs sniffing around," he said.

Schreiber and Serban have a creatively contentious relationship. "We fight well," Schreiber says. "He explodes the play and makes me take risks. He takes the play away from me." Serban sees Schreiber as a weird hybrid of the classical and the experimental actor. "Any time he tries a monologue, he will resist my idea, which is always to be different," Serban told me later. "He's continuously fighting, resisting, because there's a very classical actor in him. The classical actor is fighting the one that wants to break the rules. Something in him wants to break the rules to find other rules."

In this production, which veers from the visual grotesque to transparent realism, Serban combines various theatrical styles—a mélange of Brechtian artifice and the fairground stylization of Meyerhold—in order to break down conventional expectations and let an audience reëxperience the play. Serban's "Hamlet" begins with the ghost onstage, along with the smoke machine that's producing the ghostly vapors; placards with the faces of other great stage Hamlets are paraded around when Hamlet is lecturing the players about how to perform; he wears a pig's mask and plays the flute when he tests Ophelia's truthfulness. ("He should be played like a Zen master in madness," Serban told his actors. "We should not be worried for him.") Serban's protean approach is intended to mirror the play's central issue of seeming versus being with a style that is equally elusive. "It's so slippery," says Serban. "Everybody's a director of 'Hamlet,' everybody knows how 'Hamlet' should be done. It may be deeply controversial, but it will not be boring for one second."

Schreiber, who has an intelligent, round face, with pudgy cheeks and a somewhat weak chin—not the angular heroic outline of conventional leading men—is just right for Serban's atypical Hamlet. At six feet three, he has the muscular athleticism of a tight end, the position he played at Brooklyn Tech, where he was the captain of both the junior varsity and the varsity teams in the early eighties. ("I was really quite committed to hitting people," he says.) Serban sees the Prince of Denmark as "a big man with Prometheus-like qualities. It's somebody who cannot live with compromise. A positive version of the Misanthrope. The standards of his quest are so high he cannot fit into the world."

In the scene they ran through that morning, Hamlet has disposed of Polonius's body under the stairs ("Safely stow'd"). Dressed in a blood-stained butcher's apron, Schreiber popped up and down around the stage like a Grand Guignol jack-in-the-box, wielding a prop butcher knife and taunting the courtiers. At one point, he improvised cutting off his own finger, and this, after a good laugh from the assembled company, instantly became part of his character. "He's this volcano of a man who's clowning, who's sensitive, who's intelligent," Serban says of Schreiber. "Suddenly he does something like an animal, something that is so dangerous and so fresh."

All afternoon, Schreiber was happy playing the giddy goat, but at a rehearsal a week later, pressed for time at a run-through and balking at the rationale for wearing the pig's mask in the Ophelia scene, Schreiber had a real knockdown fight with Serban, and stormed out. "He just wouldn't do it with the mask," Serban said when he called me the next day to talk about what happened. "Then we both started to scream at each other. Finally, he did it, but it was humiliating for me and for him, because he had to just do it and shut up. Then, when he did the scene in the afternoon, in the run-through, although he was not at all sure that I was right, he did it with such candid innocence. It was fantastic." He adds, "Liev is uncorrupted in his feelings. He has lived life as a tough kid and has been bruised by life, and yet what he retained, which is remarkable, is a certain purity."

Schreiber lives about a two-minute walk from the Public, in a large south-facing one-bedroom apartment that looks out onto the Lower East Side, where he grew up in dingier circumstances. He bought the apartment two and a half years ago, but he has logged in only six months there. The place, like the man, feels in transition. The large main room, which is dominated by a whitewashed fireplace and a behemoth TV, tries to be adult, but the bric-a-brac of Schreiber's youth is everywhere: diplomas on the wall, fencing trophies on the mantel, a mountain bike propped in the hall.

Schreiber is about Hamlet's age, and he sees the Prince's concerns—even issues of family betrayal and personal humiliation—as part of a shared journey. The totems of his own spiritual quest are mixed with the childhood memorabilia around him: a gold Buddha sits stoically on the window ledge; Shakespeare glossaries and concordances clutter the glass dining-room table; on the kitchen counter is a collection of Shakespeare's sonnets; Shakespeare's influences—Seneca and Montaigne—are on the coffee table. Hamlet may be the most observed of all observers, but for him, and for Schreiber, growth lies in refusing the definitions of others. "The death of Hamlet's father creates a crisis for him—an identity crisis," Schreiber says. "He removes himself from the position of seeing himself through other people's eyes—Hamlet the Dane, Prince of Denmark, loved of Ophelia, the analytical whiz kid of Wittenberg, doted on by his mother. He tries to really understand what they're seeing and how much truth is in it."

The questions the play raises—What is real? What is truth? What is the difference between seeming and being?—are questions that Schreiber is trying to answer in his life and career. He started analysis a year ago and is just coming to see his profession as a form of spiritual inquiry and not merely as an exercise in narcissism and money-making. "This is the beginning of something different for me. A huge step," Schreiber says. "Hamlet's the biggest thing that's ever happened to me. I need to address my life the way that Hamlet addresses his."

Schreiber still answers to his infant nickname of Huggy. His father, Tell, who taught acting, came from a wealthy society family; he graduated from Dartmouth and was a wrestling and football star and an aspiring actor. His mother, Heather, who was born into a Brooklyn working-class household of Jewish Communists, is a highly cultured eccentric, with a firm knowledge of classical music and Russian literature (Liev is named after Tolstoy). But for many years she had a shaky grip on reality. "I was kind of strange," she says. "I think I liked silence and not being connected to the world." Heather, who has lived for the past fifteen years in an ashram in Virginia, was seven years older than her husband when they took up with each other in the mid-sixties, and was already the mother of three sons. When Heather was twelve, her own mother was lobotomized. As a result, Tell says, "Heather was a mother almost by compulsion. A somewhat peculiar mother, but I think a good mother." According to Tell, at the beginning of their marriage, in San Francisco, Heather had a bad experience on LSD and subsequently, over the next four years, was repeatedly admitted to hospitals and underwent therapy. The family moved to a ten-acre farm in British Columbia, which Tell thought would be "therapeutic." But, feeling herself held captive and threatened by Tell with being put in a mental institution, Heather bolted. As Tell pursued his AWOL wife, Liev and his mother were trailed by private detectives in various states; when he was three, he was kidnapped by his father from an upstate New York commune where Heather had decamped. By the time Liev was four, he was living with her on the fourth floor of a dilapidated walkup at First Avenue and First Street (his half brothers from her first marriage were parked with their father in a duplex on Central Park West), and he was the object of a fierce custody battle, which bankrupted his beloved maternal grandfather, Alex Milgram. (Milgram was the significant male of Schreiber's youth. He played the cello and owned Renoir etchings, and made his living by delivering meat to restaurants.)

Even in a strict geographical sense, Schreiber grew up in a sort of no man's land: the Hasidic community lay to the south, the Polish and Ukrainian communities to the north; to the east were Puerto Ricans; the Bowery lay to the west. According to his mother, Liev "was the only white kid on the block." "I spent an awful lot of time in the window," says Schreiber, who was a walking projection of Heather's hippie-Hindu fantasy: she dressed him in yoga shirts, overalls, and sneakers from the A. & P., which were "very, very uncool" among his Puerto Rican peers. "There was a pretty deep sense of shame," Schreiber told me. Until he was ten, Liev was forced by his mother to wear his blond hair down to his shoulders. "I looked like a girl," Schreiber says.

"I can't imagine how I could have been so stupid," Heather says of those days, when she was supporting them by driving a cab and making papier-mâché puppets. "I loved his hair. He looked like an angel and acted like a devil. Ladies would come over, and they would fawn over him. He would say things like 'Fuck you, lady.' He was a horrible kid, really horrible, but he looked exquisite."

"I took a kind of a beating," Schreiber says. "I was one of those 'Can I play?' kids, whom people didn't want in the group. They would run away from me. And when I did get to participate I was kind of awkward and hyper. I would go into my head a lot. I was very good at making up stories."

Schreiber's isolation and humiliation were compounded by his mother's apartment—a railroad flat, with a bathtub in the kitchen, that had no hot water, no electricity, no beds, no chairs, no tables. "Heather was a garbage-picker," Schreiber says. She and her son sat on boxes and slept on mattresses on the floor, both in the same room. A gutted piano leaned up against one wall. The apartment was lit by candles stuck into the bricks. "I loved poverty," says Heather. "I thought rich people were kind of stupid. I know that sounds insane. I thought it was bohemian and romantic. I was really kind of silly. It was fun, but probably not for him."

Although Liev says he "fought her like crazy"—boycotting dance and piano lessons, refusing to read, doing poorly at school—he was also an accessory to Heather's wacky regime: he ate vegetarian, took the Hindu names of Sivadas and Ayappa, meditated, and attended only black-and-white movies. ("You can imagine the resentment that I felt when I saw my first color movie, which was 'Star Wars,' in 1977," Schreiber says.) "Once, he brought a little boy to the house, but the boy had to go home," Heather recalls. "He didn't like to be in the dark. Huggy found all this mortifying. Why couldn't we be just regular straight folks who wore polyester? Why couldn't we just eat Thomas' English Muffins? He was very anti-me. In the second grade, they asked the children to write biographies of themselves. He wrote that he lived in this terrible situation with his mother, who was an alcoholic prostitute. The teachers felt terribly sorry for him. They would give him all sorts of things to eat that I didn't approve of—like peanut-butter-and-jelly sandwiches."

According to Heather, probably because she cast him in an adult role, Schreiber as a boy "didn't see any difference between adults and children. He hit two teachers." Their relationship was—and is—stormy but intimate. "My temper is incredible with my mother," says Schreiber, who, like all dutiful sons, pays a high emotional price for his faithfulness. "He's very protective of me, and very nasty," Heather says. "He'll yell at me, 'Oh! It's all about you! It's all about you!' He thinks I'm very self-centered. I think I'm self-centered, but compared to other people? Nah, I'm a bargain." She goes on, "He says I don't deserve any credit. He always says that. 'Neither you nor Tell.' He thinks we're both losers. I just think it's amusing. Because he so doesn't get it."

To a large extent, Schreiber's professional shape-shifting and his uncanny instinct for isolating the frightened, frail, goofy parts of his characters are a result of being forced to adapt to his mother's eccentricities. It's both his grief and his gift. Schreiber, who in his newly acquired psychotherapeutic lingo refers to himself as "an empathic personality," learned early to be sensitive to the needs of others and to decipher their motivation. "I could understand anybody," he says. "I was incredibly good at analyzing behavior. I knew what people were after. I loved to give them what they wanted. I loved to live up to expectations."

Once, at Yale, Schreiber was asked to perform an autobiography in movement. He played a child holding his mother's hand. "He just held the hand up high walking in a circle," his Yale movement teacher and friend Wesley Fata says. "Slowly that hand came down to where he became the adult and the parent became the child." Although Heather was compassionate, imaginative, and resourceful—and she encouraged those qualities in her son (she bought him a motorcycle at sixteen, to promote fearlessness)—she had some paranoid episodes in those years. "She would think that there were demons in the house," Schreiber says. He became her champion and protector. It was an impossible position, at once empowering and undermining. Heather saw him as her "miracle boy." "Not a day passed but she figured out three times to say, 'You're brilliant,'" Tell

Schreiber recalls. "Oh, my God, it was insufferable." The message that Schreiber received from his mother and learned to transmit back to her was "We are king. We are two fish in a bowl. The rest of the world will never understand us."

Between the ages of eight and thirteen, Schreiber stole things. "Anything," he says. "Money, mostly." The rationale was that he needed money to "buy sneakers and be like the other kids." But in stealing he was also acting out his anger at being a kind of psychological hostage to what he calls his mother's "daffy bliss." He pinched coins from his grandfather's laundry-change bowl, and he stole from the Integral Yoga Institute, where Heather worked, which eventually got her "in a lot of trouble." Having memorized the combination to the institute's safe, Schreiber shinnied three floors down a drainpipe, climbed in the window, and cracked the safe. "I was role-playing," he says. "The whole cat-burglar thing was 'To Catch a Thief.' It wasn't real money. It didn't belong to anybody. It was a movie. If I could be daring enough to go down the side of this building and get in her office, that money was mine." Over a period of years— Schreiber stole at judicious intervals—he took about five thousand dollars. He bought Polaroid cameras and meals for the kids in his neighborhood. But it didn't bring him closer to anyone. "Just made them think I was weirder," he says. At the age of eight, with some of his stolen money he treated himself to a helicopter ride around Manhattan. "I recently asked him, 'How did you do that?' " Heather says. "He said, 'Well, I told the pilot that my dad was just up the street and he was coming in a minute.' Then after a while—this is so creative!—he went to get his dad. He came back and said, 'My dad's busy. He can't come, but he gave me the money and said you should take me.' " She adds, "He was a wonderful con artist."

It took the institute a number of years to figure out who the thief was. When he was caught, at the age of twelve, Schreiber was packed off for a few lonely semesters to an ashram school in Pomfret, Connecticut. He took care of ponies and studied religion and philosophy, which, when he returned to junior high school at New York's I.S. 70, only qualified him for seeming "weird again." "He wasn't cool," says the TV actress Nadia Dajani, who was at I.S. 70 with Schreiber and still teases him about being a "hoodlum." "If you were in Catholic school, and you wanted to date a rebel, then you dated Huggy. But otherwise, no." She adds, "He was just a street punk from my neighborhood. He could have ended up like all these other idiots that we grew up with. In jail. I think Huggy was headed for that."

What turned things around for Schreiber was a football injury—a fractured ankle—at Brooklyn Tech, in 1984, which ended his sports career and led to his theatrical one. At the time, Heather approached Tell to pay for a good surgeon. He was happy to be invited back into his son's life; he paid for the doctor and also for private school. Liev ended up downtown at the exclusive Friends Seminary. Having learned how to be a ballplayer and a homeboy at Brooklyn Tech, he was now thrown in with the children of the upper-middle class, whom he'd been taught since childhood to despise. When he played Nick Bottom in the school production of "A Midsummer Night's Dream"—"I made a complete ass out of myself in the best way"—he found not just popularity but also his calling. Acting replaced stolen money as Schreiber's social currency; it provided a full, articulated sense of humor, true pathos, and a mask for admitting his fears. Schreiber considers the characters in plays his "peers": "Hamlet. Nick Bottom. Suddenly, there were people who were like me, who had been shamed worse than I had ever been shamed. Suddenly I could create a context for my life through characters. People would appreciate me through my characters, which validated my own experience. Plus at the same time—this is even more important to me—validated their experience."

This commonality was brought home to Schreiber in his first solo performance, at the age of eighteen, at Hampshire College, where he got his B.A. He was doing scenes from Eric Bogosian's "Drinking in America." Schreiber has a video of himself strutting and fuming in a startlingly assured streetwise imitation of "a total maniac that I hung out with," he says. "The monologues were all very hostile, very harsh. I was sort of saying, 'You think you know me, you bunch of rich kids from Hampshire College. This is where I come from.' " To Schreiber's amazement, the audience loved it. "I realized that we had a common bond," he says. "And the recognition of that bond was incredibly comforting, because I was afraid for a very long time that I had no bond." He adds, "It's very encouraging to know that your journey—as painful as it may be or as confusing as it may be—is not that different from the guy you're sitting across from. The more bizarre it gets, the more painful it gets, the more people seem to embrace it."

In mid-November, at a private screening of "RKO 281" at the Sutton Theatre, the head of HBO, Jeff Bewkes, called out the names of the distinguished cast members—including Brenda Blethyn, James Cromwell, and Roy Scheider—and asked them to stand. When he got to Schreiber, he said, "Finally, an actor of great range and talent, who will soon portray another quirky guy, Hamlet." Later, at the Waldorf, where HBO was throwing a party, Schreiber, dressed in a sharp designer jacket with a gray tie and a black shirt, cupped a Martini glass in both hands and assessed his performance as the boy genius Orson Welles. "It's complex. It's ambiguous, but it's human. That's the most you can hope for," he said.

Schreiber's career has been unusual for the ease with which he's moved between independent films, big-budget Hollywood films, TV films, and theatre. "I don't know that I want to be an actor for the rest of my life," he says. He is developing films to produce and perhaps direct, among them an adaptation of "The Merchant of Venice," for Dustin Hoffman. He has a deep, serious understanding of his craft. On the Orson Welles film, for instance, in many scenes he persuaded the director to use reaction shots instead of lines. "When he doesn't speak is when the truth kind of seeps out of him," Schreiber says. "That's what I'm interested in trying to find. The inexpressible. What's behind a guy who is twenty-four years old and has been thought a genius since he was eight."

I asked Schreiber what he thought *was* behind Welles. He answered without missing a beat. "A tremendous amount of deep, deep fear and insecurity," he said. "And a desire to know who he was—hoping that somehow by working he was going to define himself."

ROSEANNE

QUEENDOM COME

Once upon a time, in 1985, Johnny Carson introduced the freshest new comic voice on the Los Angeles comedy-club scene, a thirty-two-year-old Denver housewife, to his "Tonight Show" audience. Backstage, before going on, the comedienne opened a letter she'd written to herself years before, when she'd imagined this moment of triumph. Part of it said, "This is the beginning of your life, for She who is and is not yet." Then Carson said , "Please welcome Roseanne Barr!" and the nation took its first look at the radical feminist disguised as a faux naïf who would become an iconoclast the like of which had never been seen before on TV. She was a bulky five feet four, in flats and black slacks, with a gardenia corsage pinned to her black-and-orange jacket. She chewed gum as she smiled. She gave a girlish little wave of her left hand, and in a voice as affectless as her salute said, "Oh, hi. I been married thirteen years, and lemme tell you, it's a thrill to be out of the house. I never get out of the house. I stay home all the time. I never do anything fun 'cause I'm a housewife. I hate the word 'housewife.' I prefer to be called 'domestic goddess.' "

The laughs during her monologue were often longer than the jokes. "Do you guys like that guy Stephen King that writes those really scary books?" she asked the audience. "Well, now he has come out with the scariest book he ever, ever wrote. It is *so* scary. It's about a husband with a mind of his own." On video, the audience's shock is audible: there is a gasp, then applause, then cheering. Roseanne laughs along with the viewers. "Oh, don't get tense, ladies. It's just a fantasy. It could never really happen." It had taken Roseanne five years to perfect the six minutes of material and the ungrammatical jazz of her delivery, which steered her début expertly to its final punch. "Still, stuff bugs me," she said. "This bugs me the worst. That's when the husband thinks that the wife knows where everything is, huh? Like they think the uterus is a tracking device. He comes in: 'Hey, Roseanne! Roseanne! Do we have any Cheetos left?' Like he can't go over and lift up that sofa cushion himself."

From that moment, Roseanne was out of the house and into the fantasy life of the nation; her very presence was a provocation. Her body (she sometimes tipped the scales at more than two hundred pounds) and her unladylike talk made her America's bourgeois nightmare come to comic life. "Roseanne," the show she minted from the strong, bright part of her splintered personality, has been beamed around the world on prime-time television since 1988 and is going into its eighth—and probably final-year. The onetime waitress, who was working for a dollar and a half an hour plus tips in Denver when she began doing her standup act, now earns a little more than a million dollars for each of the twenty-five episodes she does in a season. Her production company, Full Moon & High Tide, negotiated a deal with ABC to produce up to four series. Roseanne figures that by the end of the century she should be worth around a billion dollars. On being asked in public recently about her stature as the most powerful woman in American entertainment, Roseanne feigned modesty and said, "What about Oprah?" In private, though, during a week I spent with her in L.A. this spring, Roseanne contended, "I'm way more up there than Oprah. I have commitments for solid pay-or-play series; and nobody—no man or woman—has that. Just me." Roseanne also has a screenwriting deal with Miramax. She won the fierce competition for the rights to co-produce (with Warner Bros.) an American version of Jennifer Saunders' hugely successful British sitcom "Absolutely Fabulous." She is refining contract arrangements to co-produce "Planet Hollywood Squares," a weekly version of the famous quiz show, and a late-night comedy show. And within three years Roseanne's Big Food Diner, which she started in Eldon, Iowa, during her interlude with husband No. 2, the comedian Tom Arnold, will be expanded to a string of diners across America. (They will feature "the real food that everybody likes," from her own calorie-crammed recipes.) Finally, Roseanne is planning to start a line of clothing for large women and has already made some of the designs. "Very simple and tailored things," she says. "No big swans and shit like that on them."

Commercial success has allowed Roseanne to win for herself, her comedy, and her feminist agenda what had previously been allowed only to a handful of great American funnymen, such as Charlie Chaplin and Woody Allen: the control of her product. Most comedians are hostile sharpshooters loudly proclaiming their innocence, but Roseanne has got where she is by biting the hands that have fed her—family, feminism, and Hollywood. She simply can't see a boundary without crossing it. Her divorces, her disputed history as an abused child, her public excesses—what she calls those "Prozac moments," as when she botched the singing of "The Star-Spangled Banner" at a baseball game—have fed the tabloids and sometimes obscured her gift. Roseanne has the rare markings of a true renegade comic spirit. Recently, two months before her third marriage—to her twenty-eight-year-old bodyguard/driver, Ben Thomas—she showed off the scar of her in-vitro pregnancy on the David Letterman show. The scar made news; but, in a way, the gesture was much more than a prank. The comic's job is to bare wounds to a world that won't admit its own. "The hollow and full run together," Roseanne has written of her paradoxical nature; and the genuine zany has no choice but to express this dividedness as a way of mastering it. "I am an overweight overachiever with a few dandy compulsive-obsessive disorders and a little problem with self-mutilation," she writes in a 1994 autobiography, "My Lives." "Like vampires and night creatures, we wander the earth, alone, haunted, not owning a body, just temporarily inhabiting one. Crazy all the way."

Roseanne holds nothing back: whatever emotion overtakes her, she expresses. "I'm pure id," she says. When *TV Guide* said that the current season of "Roseanne" lacked "the touch of Tom Arnold" (Arnold had been the show's co-executive producer), Roseanne called up the "Tonight Show" and got Jay Leno to cut his monologue short so she could rebut the remarks. "I've had the Tom Arnold touch, and, let me tell you, what he lacked in size he made up for in speed," she told the nation. To the charge of falling ratings, she fumed, "Did it ever occur to anybody that it was simply because of complications with my in-vitro fertilization and doctors ordering me to lay on my back for twelve weeks of my pregnancy and that during those times *I wasn't even on the show?*" Roseanne was in fine and fearless fury. "O.K., well I think what they're really mad about is that I'm a woman calling the shots; and that I was a waitress; and that I was a maid; and I never went past the ninth grade, and I *still* do a better show than any of them. And I just want to say now I'm back in full force and I've even fired the head writer who in my absence let my show go to hell. And it felt so great to fire yet another overpaid, undertalented man that the press cannot wait to give credit for *my* work. So in conclusion I would like to say that anybody who has a problem with that can kiss my ass!" At this point, Leno tried politely to approach Roseanne and segue into the next part of the show. "I'm not done! I'm not done!" she said, pushing him away and turning back to Mr. and Mrs. America. "And after that," she said, "they can kiss my baby's ass, too!" It was great television, and an exemplary lesson in Roseanne's roaring high dudgeon: If you can't stand the heat, stay out of her face.

Rage is Roseanne's ozone. She exudes it. She creates it. "It isn't a choice," Roseanne says. "You don't decide 'I'm going to be offensive or do something that upsets people.' It just happens." When Roseanne addressed the National Association of College Broadcasters not long ago, she began by saying, "Some of you have absolutely no talent and don't know what you're doing at all, have no point of view, and don't care. I predict that you're the ones who will be successful." The broadcasting wanna-bes laughed. Roseanne, as usual, was making the unacceptable irresistible. Because of the sexual politics of previous eras, the comediennes to whom Roseanne sees herself linked—Mae West, Judy Holliday, Lucille Ball—got their way by cunning indirection. But Roseanne prefers the head butt to the bon mot. She can rumble. Matt Berry, a standup comedian who performed with Roseanne in the Denver clubs and now works as a writer on her show, remembers the time that fifty bikers and their girlfriends came to a gig. "She used to have a line in her act where she goes, 'I really hate bikers. You know, they all got tobacco juice in their beards. They piss on the side of the road. And the men are even worse!' " he says. "She walks out. Sees all these bikers. Big, burly guys. She looks at the comics in the back. 'Should I do it?' We're yelling, 'Do it!' She did it. They fuckin' loved her. They went nuts."

Roseanne has reclaimed for female comedy the phallic aggression which is traditionally associated with male humor, whose totem, the Fool's sceptre, is actually the penis. Even Roseanne's physical posture—she has discarded the apologetic feminine stance onstage, and plants her feet firmly apart—suggests phallic power, which is, she insists, "really womb power that men stole." "A man standing with his legs apart is impersonating a woman," Roseanne explains, assuming the erect birth posture. "Men all have womb envy. We don't have penis envy." She goes on, "My psychic penis is way larger than any man's. My attitude is, I have a vagina and therefore I have the bigger penis." Roseanne stated her position most succinctly in her rough-and-tumble standup days, when, she says, "I was the filthiest act ever. I would do anything." She'd end her set by saying, "People say to me, 'You're not very feminine.' Well, they can *suck my dick*."

In her comedy, Roseanne is unrelenting, which translates in psychological terms as inconsolable. Laughter is her revenge on a childhood she characterizes as a "roiling nightmare of Dickensian struggle." Roseanne was born in 1952, into a poor Jewish family living among Mormons in Salt Lake City. She remembers praying "either make me retarded or make me a Mormon," and explains, "They all seemed so happy; they didn't see the ugliness I did." Roseanne's grandmother Bobbe Mary lost all her relatives in the Nazi concentration camps, and ran an apartment house for survivors of the Holocaust; Roseanne remembers that her mother, who was born in Utah, lived in constant fear of being exterminated. "Her hobbies," Roseanne writes, "were being a credit to her race and hiding in the basement." This is not comic hyperbole. "Our mother would say, 'They'll come for us,'" Roseanne says. "I remember her taking us down to the basement if someone just came and knocked on the door. I really, truly believed that if anybody found out we were Jewish they would kill us." But, she says, "I knew Jews were allowed to live safely in New York." This knowledge came from "The Ed Sullivan Show" and the Jewish comedians on it. "It was like Radio Free America," she says. "I loved them all—Totie Fields, Jack Carter, Buddy Hackett. But the comedian who really moved me was Richard Pryor. I knew that he was inside the stereotype and fighting against it, that he was going to blow it up from the inside. I got that immediately. I thought, By God, I'm going to do the same thing being a woman."

All the oppression and self-loathing that male authority perpetrates against women seem to have coalesced, one way or another, in her. She claims to have twenty-one separate personalities, and four years ago went public with the accusation that her parents abused her (which they deny). According to family lore, as an infant Roseanne screamed so frantically and jammed her fist in her mouth so consistently that she rubbed the skin off her nose and had to be put in a tiny restraining jacket. At sixteen, after she was hit by a car (her head was impaled on the hood ornament), she was institutionalized for a year, and when she got out she often had a recurring nightmare that she could not wake up. "I was horrified that people would think I was dead and bury me alive," Roseanne says. She also turned her fury recklessly on herself—cutting herself, burning herself, and abusing her body by alternately starving and gorging it. Nonetheless, in the midst of a chaotic family atmosphere Roseanne learned that the way to survive was to be fierce and funny. Her father, whom she characterizes in her books as a bully and a slob, had grown up wanting to be a comedian. "So I just kind of grew a part of me that was very aggressive in a comedic way," Roseanne says. "Because if I was to dare to be aggressive and it wasn't funny, I would be hurt badly. But if it was funny he would laugh. It was really weird." Laughter became both a seduction and a defense—a way for Roseanne to call attention to herself and to create a buffer of space around herself. "He taught me that comedy was mightier than the pen *and* the sword," Roseanne says. "We would always have contests, showdowns, and I would always win. Even if it was anti-male, anti-him, he would say, 'Good one.' "

In 1971, when she was eighteen, Roseanne had an illegitimate daughter, Brandi ("My father spat at me; he *spat* at me!"), whom she gave up for adoption and with whom she was reunited a few years ago. (Brandi now works on Roseanne's show.) That same year, Roseanne left home and met her first husband, Bill Pentland, who was a motel night clerk in Georgetown, Colorado, where Roseanne was prep cooking and washing dishes in a restaurant. By the time she was twenty-six she was caring for three children under the age of four (Jessica, 1975; Jennifer, 1976; and Jake, 1978) in a house that occupied six hundred square feet. As she later joked, "I breed well in captivity."

In reality, she didn't. She worked variously as a window dresser, a maid, a waitress, and a prostitute, and gradually began to write comedy. Roseanne calls her emergence a "slow dawning." "I aspired to be Gertrude Stein, or Dylan Thomas, or some poetess tragically and forlornly trying to scrape some piece of misery off the sole of my soul and write some touching little fat girl shit about it," she wrote in her first book, "Roseanne: My Life as a Woman" (1989), "until . . . I heard Lord Buckley, and Lenny Bruce, and understood the jazz of words alone." In 1980, when Roseanne went to work as a cocktail waitress at Bennigan's, which became known to the regulars as Rosie's, she found her arena. "I'd go, 'That's six bucks for the drinks, another three bucks for me to take them off the tray and give them to ya,' " she says. "I'd shortchange 'em. Eat food off their plates. They always laughed. This one guy goes, 'Well, Roseanne, do you know anybody that is married and does not want to get divorced and wants to fool around with somebody else who is married, who has a lot of money, who likes to have a lot of sex and be taken care of?' And I go, 'Well, yeah. Your wife.' " At Bennigan's, Roseanne "felt like a star"; and, more important, she was at liberty. From eight at night to two in the morning, she worked the room, fending off the male come-ons with "the meanest comebacks imaginable." It was at Bennigan's that Roseanne first learned of the Comedy Works, a club where aspiring comics could test their material. "That's when it hit me that the place was invented only for me to go and do it," she says. "I always knew. Totally always. That I was gonna be a comic and I was gonna have my own show and I was gonna be as rich as Bill Cosby." To Pentland (who is now on good terms with Roseanne; last year he had a walk-on part in her show), Roseanne's almost messianic sense of her calling was "like somebody saying they're gonna win the lottery." He made her a mike stand from a screwdriver and a broom handle so she could practice her delivery in their living room; but he was skeptical. "I was happy to see her get a hobby that fulfilled her," he says. "My sense of it at that time was that Roseanne wanted to be more than a performer—she wanted to be a political voice."

As Roseanne writes, "I began to tell the truth about my life—because I couldn't tell the truth off the stage. And very quickly, the world began to blow apart." The first time Roseanne went onstage and pronounced her rebellion—what she calls "a huge, cosmic 'NO' "—she felt "chilled and free and redeemed. I had decided to Stand Up." Roseanne took her new-found freedom to the outer limits. She had one gig as an m.c. at a strip club. "I had a woman partner," Roseanne says, speaking of a cohort named Susan Bublitz. "Me and her would go on there and of course we'd see the strippers downstairs afterwards. I swear one had a flattop under her wig. Puts on muscle shirt, sweatpants, Nikes. A butch cat. Me and Susan were onstage one night. I thought it was hilarious. I go, 'We'd like to do our impressions of the strippers for ya.' All these drunk fuckers are goin' 'Take it off!' So we start makin' out. And I go, 'Don't you know these women are fuckin' dykes, and they hate you?' On Friday and Saturday nights at midnight, they made me and Susan eat bananas. Then they'd have the guys in the audience vote on which one of us was the winner. I'd just take the banana, peel it, and eat it. Susan'd be like—I'd watch her—doing the whole thing. She won every night. And I'd go, 'Fuck you. *I* swallowed!' "

Roseanne had also begun working at the radical Woman to Woman bookstore (where, she says, she kept men out with a baseball bat), reading in women's history, and lecturing on feminist ethics. She recalls one lecture on pornography that she gave with a black woman in Wyoming, when the local feminists didn't want to hear Roseanne's class analysis and she and her partner were "sort of run out of there on a rail." "They were kind of O.K. when it was about oppression of women," she says. "But when we talked about women as oppressors of other races, they didn't want to hear it."

Roseanne carried the ideological battles at the bookstore into her private war over comedy. "I used to always get up and go, 'Why are we talking to women who go to college and learn how to talk like men? Go talk to the women on welfare, if you want a fuckin' grassroots movement,' " she says. In a letter to a lesbian comedienne whose act disgusted her, she wrote:

> I'm going all over this town with stories about what my life experience as a woman has been. I performed at a lesbian coffeehouse and received the stunned oxen look from all of the women/womyn/chicks there. . . . I'm going to be a comic,

and I'm gonna talk about what I know, and . . . I have a place
and a reason for being in this movement. Deal with me. The
subtle bigotry I feel from lesbians (not all of them) infuriates
me. If some comic can stand up and tell about growing up
Catholic, or Jewish or Wasp, then I can tell my story about
growing up straight. . . . Besides the fact that I'm married to
a man, and have children, I'm the most radical woman in this
town, dig it, and your heterophobia is boring. Separate your
issues. If this is a woman's movement then it's only dealing
with about 10% of the world's women. . . . I am one of the
other 90%—deal with that. Aside from your het bigotry, you
also have the attitude of otherness with black and Jewish
women. Deal with it. You don't let me do my shit in front of
you, and the boys don't let me do it for them. What a movement.

"The act didn't work well at the beginning," Roseanne says of finding
her female comic voice in those early days, but she did have her inspired
moments. "I remember Lenny Bruce said Jackie Kennedy was climbing
out of the limo in Dallas to save her own ass. That's Lenny, the archetypal
male comic. My joke was: I'm a woman and I know that was never, never
true. She wasn't climbing out to save her own ass. She sees her husband's
brains sliding down the back of the car, and she's going out there because
she's trying to clean up the mess!" That particular joke was a turning point
for Roseanne. She told it in a jazz club, and there was shocked recognition
in the laughter she got. "I knew right then that I had hooked into exactly
what I see and what I feel and the way to use language to express it,"
Roseanne says. Nothing now was sacred, not even the sisterhood. "I don't
know why lesbians hate men," she used to joke. "They don't have to fuck
them."

During her academic feminist phase, Roseanne also did a bit about
breast feeding: "Contrary to popular belief, breasts are not on our body to
sell stereos and cars; they're to feed children." The second time she performed it at the Comedy Works, a woman in the first row picked up her
chair and turned it so that her back was to Roseanne. "I just snapped,"

Roseanne says. "That was when I believed in this sisterhood-feminist shit and didn't know what the real world was about. I go, 'What are you doing!' I left my text. 'Are you trying to tell your husband, "Don't worry. I'll still blow you. I won't listen to that big bad woman"?' And then I got silence. They banned me. They wouldn't let me work at the club anymore." Undaunted, she organized a protest of feminist comediennes in Boulder called Take Back the Mike and was finally reinstated without having to change her act. The victory taught Roseanne one basic maneuver of comic attack: "Don't keep secrets. Tell on 'em. Because they're weak, they can't live in the light of day."

Looking back on that difficult period now, Roseanne says, "I had to make a choice between being radical and being mainstream. I made a conscious decision that I was never going to talk that academic feminist language again. It's all about white male élitist horseshit. So I went back to the way people I grew up with, the people like me, talk. And why wouldn't we be heard? I just talk louder, and I'm heard. I'm also discredited a lot." Roseanne's rejection of manners and clean language is both a critique of and a revenge on the decorum of patriarchy, which assures that women collude in their own destruction. "I love the word 'fuck,' " she says. "It's a verb, a noun, everything, and it's just infused with intense feeling and passion, you know, negative and positive. And women aren't supposed to say it, so I try to say it as much as I can." She goes on, "When I was a teen-ager, my mother had this book called 'Fascinating Womanhood.' I opened it to a page that said, 'Watch your little girl and see how she gets her way with your husband. She snaps her head and shakes her curls. You need to emulate that. You do that if you want your way with your husband.' So he'll buy ya a friggin' toaster! I was just freaked out by it. My mother's havin' a meeting once a week with these ladies, and they talk about doin' this shit. It was so ugly, so horrible, and I'm like 'I'm never gonna get married.' One chapter was called 'Domestic Goddess': you know, you cook for him, you clean for him, you're his fuckin' slave, and you're supposed to do it all with a smile. And I just remember sitting there over breakfast with my sister and the whole thing came crashing together."

Like Chaplin discovering his bowler hat and cane, when Roseanne found the character of Domestic Goddess she found her idiom and her popularity. The first time she did the new act, in Kansas City, she got a standing ovation. Lois Bromfield, a comedienne who performed with Roseanne in the early days and has become a writer on Roseanne's show, explains, "She hit that nerve of the woman in the Midwest whom nobody spoke to. They'd had no one to relate to—not for a long time."

Roseanne's studio is just over the leafy foothills of Coldwater Canyon and Laurel Canyon, which wind down from fashionable Beverly Hills into the smoggy lumpen sprawl of the Valley. Here, only walking distance from her soundstage, in Studio City, is the America Roseanne speaks for: McDonald's, Winchell's doughnuts, Blockbuster Video, and Du-Par's Restaurant ("Breakfast Served All Day"), where waitresses stand on sore feet and make wisecracks, the way Roseanne herself once did.

At nine o'clock on a Monday morning, the cast and crew straggle in, and about ten minutes before the first reading of this week's script is to begin, Roseanne's stretch limo slinks into view. Her driver, who calls her Boss, opens the door for her. She is dressed in a denim skirt and pea-green hiking boots with cleated rubber soles, topped incongruously with frilly white socks. "Jesus Christ, I'm tired," she says as she emerges.

Although Roseanne is pregnant with the son she has decided to name simply Buck ("He's too macho to have a middle name"), her face and her presence have no lustre. Without eyeliner, lipstick, and blusher, which are applied only on taping days, Roseanne's definition is muted and vague. Her face has little mobility. In fact, despite her obvious intelligence and authority, there is something cadaverous about Roseanne, a deadness that only rage and laughter can banish. (She seems to love combat precisely because it makes her feel more alive.) The most cursory encounter with Roseanne and the climate of free-floating anxiety and hate in which she operates gives credence to her claims of child abuse. Something has been murdered in her; and this is palpable in the flatness of her voice, the slouch of her body, the quicksilver shifts of mood from bombast to gloom, the timidity and detachment behind her eyes. Over the last few years, Roseanne has undergone some well-publicized cosmetic operations: the breasts she used to joke about ("Actually, I only have one breast. I just part it down the middle") have been reduced; she's had a stomach tuck and a nose job. ("My face was so bad," she said. "Every time I looked in the mirror, I looked like my dad, and I couldn't stand it.") But, despite all these changes, nothing can erase the evidence of her soul's unease.

Inside the cavernous soundstage, the sets of the show are spread around like rooms in a behemoth doll's house. A table has been set up in the middle of the studio for the show's director, Gail Mancuso; the current head writer, Eric Gilliland; and members of the cast, who trickle in from the kitchen, where coffee, doughnuts, and smoked salmon are on tap. Behind the table, a number of director's chairs have been lined up for the writers, who mill around holding copies of the new show—"The Blaming of the Shrew," by Lawrence Broch. This episode of "Roseanne" is something of a rarity, because it was written solo instead of group-written, or "gang-banged"—the writers' term for the collaborative process in which the scenes are divided among teams of writers. Still, the group has been polishing Broch's work for a week prior to this first reading. Behind the writers' chairs is an entire bank of tarpaulined theatre seats that will hold the audience when the show is taped on Thursday, but today they seat only me and the parents of Ashley Johnson, a precocious and talented eleven-year-old who is to play Lisa, the "shrew" of the piece, with whom D.J., Roseanne's fictional son, is to have his first date.

Roseanne pulls up a chair between John Goodman, who plays her husband, Dan Conner, and Laurie Metcalf, who plays her neurotic fictional sister, Jackie. Ranged around the table are Michael Fishman (D.J.), Michael O'Keefe (Jackie's reticent husband, Fred), Johnny Galecki (the erstwhile boyfriend of Roseanne's younger fictional daughter, Darlene; Darlene herself—the hilarious Sara Gilbert—is at Yale, where she is an art major), and Ellen DeGeneres, who is making a guest appearance on this episode, as an inept therapist trying to give marriage guidance to Jackie and Fred.

Roseanne remembers the first time she took a seat at a production read-through, before she'd wrested control of her show from the producers. "They had, like, extras and the crew people sitting at the far end of the table, and the stars up at the other end of the table," she recalls. "I remember walking in and going, 'Oh, Jesus Christ! Everything in the men's world is exactly like the Army. Everything's militaristic. Rank.' I thought, How am I gonna do it? I was really into being an anarchist then. So I sat at the end with the crew guys. The producers were so pissed! But I wanted to make the statement that this show wasn't about corporate America, it wasn't about corporate thinking, it was about people, the American people."

Now Roseanne greets the assembled table with "Happy Purim," and everyone laughs. To Roseanne, the calm here is the calm of a battlefield after the bodies have been removed. "Everybody's banned," she says. "And they have been since the third show. Banned." That is, the network is banned; the advertisers are banned; even the owners of the show, Carsey-Werner, are banned from Roseanne's space. According to Marcy Carsey— who, along with her partner, Tom Werner, has produced "The Cosby Show," "Cybill," and "Grace Under Fire"—Roseanne walked off the show "five or six times" during the first thirteen episodes. Carsey prefers to think of their absence from Roseanne's set as a choice rather than a requirement. "We made a judgment; I don't know if it was right or not," Carsey says. "We thought that part of the thing Roseanne was doing was acting out against authority, which she saw as us. So we thought—like the good parents we are sometimes—that when somebody is acting out like that you stay away for a while. We talked to the writers, went over stories, edited rough cuts. We just weren't on the set."

Part of the battle between Roseanne and her producers has been about the ownership of the show. Although Roseanne may own the show's success, she does not completely own its origins. In 1987, Roseanne had craftily designed her first HBO special as a kind of pilot to present her trailer-trash character to the networks, even briefly going into a backstage double-wide to deal with her beer-swilling couch potato of a husband and her bumptious kids. Roseanne wanted to create a TV sitcom around her domestic-goddess character, and her agents had her taking meetings all over town. Meanwhile, quite independently, Carsey-Werner was developing a show about a working mother. "We were looking for the outrageous voice that could be the center of the show," Carsey says. "We pitched it to Roseanne. But the fact is that that show was in development. She was cast in the role, and she brought a lot to the role."

Roseanne, however, is her own greatest creation, and the imperialism of her fame extends to the show, which she sees as incontrovertibly hers.

She wanted to run it her way. Martin Luther announced his revolution by nailing ninety-five theses to the church door; Roseanne announced hers by posting a one-page broadsheet, which is now framed in the makeup room of her trailer, on her dressing-room door. She prophesied that the show would be a hit (it went to No. 1 after the ninth episode), and the document served notice on the company to behave or be gone. It said,

> THESE ARE THE PEOPLE WHO ARE GOING TO BE FIRED IF THEY'RE NOT NICE TO ME. PEOPLE WHO *I* AM BOSS OF——EVERYBODY 'CAUSE *I* GOT MY OWN TV SHOW. ALL PRODUCERS, ALL WRITERS, ALL SUBJECT TO CHANGE.

Below was a long list that Roseanne had graded and, she says, continued to grade every week. Those in her good graces got a check by their names; those in bad odor got "applicable" written beside theirs. Some, who were on probation, got "not applicable as yet."

Seven years on, Roseanne finds this memento of those embattled early days "hilarious." She still has skirmishes with her writers, but the worst one was the first. In the inaugural script for the show, written by Matt Williams, a former producer-writer on "Cosby" who is credited as the creator of "Roseanne" (and who refused to be interviewed for this article), Roseanne was the passive second banana. "The sister was my character," Roseanne says. "And I was like June Cleaver: 'And then what happened, darling?' "

Roseanne claims that the producers were going behind her back to Goodman and Metcalf to suggest they do the show without her, and says she was shocked that Williams had demoted her defiant character to a feed. "We had a war from Day One," she says. "He goes, 'Well, I don't think people will like you.' And I go, 'Well, if they don't like me, why did I get this show?' " The show was then called "Life and Stuff," and that was another point of loud contention. "I go, 'What are you tellin' me? It's called "Life and Stuff"? Kiss my ass! It's called "Roseanne." ' He just went insane, and I went insane, too." Roseanne kept rewriting Williams's scripts. She recalls one of their shouting matches at the ABC offices, when Williams tipped over a table: "He goes, 'I'm not your fucking scribe! I write what's meaningful to me! I'm a fuckin' writer! I'm an artist!' And I'd be like, 'Well, not on this show, by God. You're gonna write what I tell you to write.' " Roseanne characterizes her fury as "so strong I could've sucked out his will to live with my nostrils." Williams and Roseanne crossed their Rubicon, which she describes in "My Lives," on the fourth episode. In a love scene with John Goodman, Roseanne refused to say, "Well, you're my equal in bed, but that's it."

"That is not a woman's voice," Roseanne said. "And I'm not gonna say it."

"You will say it as written," Williams replied.

What followed was one of the high-water marks in the annals of entertainment intransigence: Roseanne's infamous sit-in—or, rather, bed-in. "I said, 'When this show goes to No. 1, you're fuckin' outta here.' I didn't have anything. They had fifteen lawyers. They come stand around me: 'Say the line, Roseanne, as written.' I say, 'No, I'm not gonna fuckin' say it.' It was so horrible." Pentland, who had quit his thirty-thousand-dollar-a-year job with the post office after Roseanne's success, was at home minding their three kids when Roseanne's SOS came from the studio. "It was like talking to someone in a bunker over a military telephone," Pentland says. "Carsey-Werner's attorneys were down there saying, 'You're in breach of contract. You're going to lose the show.' We renewed our faith in that call. We'd lived broke, and we could do it again if we had to. We decided that if we let them win she would lose control of everything she'd been working for. Once they couldn't bluff, they lost their ability to intimidate her. It was kind of like the Cuban missile crisis, when Dean Rusk said, 'The other guy blinked.' From that moment on, she had control of the show and made it into a much better product."

Roseanne's neurotic TV family was the first one to put America in contact with something resembling real life in the working-class world—a place where children are difficult, parents have real emotional and financial problems, and there's a discrepancy between what American society promises and what it delivers. The message of "Roseanne" flies in the face of the vision of consumer contentment conjured by the show's advertisers, who currently cough up about a quarter of a million dollars per thirty seconds to be on during her show, the fourth-highest rate on ABC (after the Super Bowl, the Academy Awards, and "Home Improvement").

"Working-class people have to work really, really hard for just the smallest thing, so they're stronger," Roseanne says. "They're more into God, more into community, more into family than middle-class people are. Totally. Middle-class people are fearful of losing. So everything is about a fear of loss. When everything's based on money, everything's for sale, including their integrity and their morals." Over the years, the Conners' struggles have provided Roseanne and her writers with opportunities to discuss racism, unemployment, lesbianism, abortion, aging, and masturbation, among many other issues. ("On my show, I'm the boss," Roseanne said in a special episode that brought her together with many of the famous TV moms of earlier eras; "and Father Knows Squat.") In the story that the actors are reading today, D.J. is in thrall to Lisa, a pint-size bundle of assertiveness who is Roseanne in miniature. Lisa calls D.J. "doofus," complains about her corsage for the dance, and generally rules the roost. Dan doesn't like seeing D.J. bossed around; Roseanne, of course, loves it. "If a boy is pushing a girl around, he's trying to keep her *down*," Roseanne explains to Dan. "But if a girl is pushing a boy around, she's trying to elevate herself. Can't you see that? Boys bullying girls is a step backwards. But girls bullying boys—now, that's the future." D.J. and Lisa skip school, go to Chicago, and are brought home by Dan, who then enlists Roseanne both to punish D.J. for his truancy and to offer some sound parental advice about equality in relationships. Meanwhile, in the subplot, Jackie and Fred are in therapy, discussing their relationship.

As the episode is read—and read well—by the cast, the writers cheer the script on. There is nothing more ravishing to a writer than to hear words sweated out in private get laughs in public. It's like planning a party and hoping that it turns into a blast; the anxiety is that a good time won't be had by all. Here "all" means Roseanne. A dip in the collective response at the first reading might cause Roseanne to draw a haphazard line through a speech or a page—a gesture that in a nanosecond may wipe out a good part of a writer's weekly work. So the writers' non-stop heehawing—a kind of laughter that combines exhaustion, hopefulness, and fear—is to an outsider's ear slightly frantic and unreal. Sometimes an actor gives the words an unexpected spin, and then the tension momentarily collapses. The room is suddenly gleeful, hooting it up, thrilled by the promise of the writers' collective mischief. Today, Roseanne is enjoying things—especially Ashley Johnson's no-nonsense Lisa, who clocks all the different haircuts of the Conner men standing by the door and says, "Man, who gets drunk and cuts this family's hair?" And later, when Jackie gets on her high horse and says to Roseanne, "I'm just waiting to hear you say 'You may be right, Jackie,' " Roseanne's comeback, the writers agree, is a "classic Roseanne line": "Yeah, and I'm waiting for chocolate air." The phrase brings the house down and earns the kind of look from Roseanne that the writers are always watching for—that wide-eyed twinkle that says nothing short of nuclear attack will make her part with the words.

After the reading, the writers amble back to their warrens in Building 3, some four hundred yards away from the studio, while Roseanne and Gail Mancuso get to work on the therapist scene. After a couple of passes at it, DeGeneres looks over at Roseanne and says, "I'm completely mirroring Jackie's emotions, which I think is so wrong for a shrink."

"I hate headshrinkers so much," Roseanne says. That statement leads to a discussion of psychiatrists' fees. DeGeneres says hers is ninety dollars an hour. "Is that what they cost?" Roseanne asks, taking a sudden detour down memory lane. "Mine was three-fifty. It was about that good. My first one, I remember, used to fall asleep. While we were all talkin'. Community mental-health association. My little sister was only about six, and she didn't want to be involved in the family therapy. She brought her toothbrush and knitting. She'd sit there and knit and then take her toothbrush out and rub it on the wall. Every one of us would do something to signal that we weren't interested. We had the cheesiest."

But Roseanne's subsequent therapy has brought her some measure of understanding. In "My Lives" she challenges the notion, promoted by her family in various interviews, that the abuse in her household was just ordinary family horseplay. (Roseanne claims that her sisters were both abused, too; they deny it.) Roseanne writes, "Everyone's Dad sticks his hand down his daughters' pants, squeezes their tits, their ass, their legs. *Every* twelve-year-old gets photographed with a movie camera by her father while she's in the tub. . . . *All* fathers talk sexually all the time to their daughters, don't they? *All* mothers hold pillows over their children's faces until they black out or pretend to, and stare at their children with hatred-edged eyes. There were no boundaries." Roseanne remembers watching her parents being interviewed on "60 Minutes": "They said they didn't molest their children. They were a family of fanny pinchers. . . . What they were saying was—and this is exactly how it was in my childhood—We're gonna pinch your fannies as much as we want even if it makes you horrifically uncomfortable and scared and destroys everything in you." She goes on, "That's how they think. They're trying to use the semantics of language to cover up what they do, which is why I'm so into naming things. It's not 'fanny-pinching'—it's naked ass-grabbing. There's a big fuckin' difference."

Roseanne's parents, Helen and Jerry Barr, have not been in contact with Roseanne except by lawyer since her public statement about their child abuse. Roseanne now says she is "at peace" with herself about it. In 1987, in her first HBO special, Roseanne thanked her parents for letting their children "say whatever we wanted as long as it was funny." In one "Roseanne" episode, there is a moving moment when her father has died, and Roseanne is left alone beside his coffin at the funeral home. Roseanne takes out a piece of paper on which she has written her last goodbye, which turns out to be an indictment. "O.K.—I'm angry at you for lying to me my whole life," she says. "I'm angry that I didn't ever know who you really were. I'm mad that when I was a kid you ignored me and when you did give me any attention it was usually violent. I'm mad that you left us alone with a crazy mother. I'm mad that because of you I grew up distrustful of men and I couldn't even trust my own husband for the first five years we were married." Roseanne concludes, "So, Dad, I'm forgiving you, just because I need to move on with my life. And I forgive myself for being so damn angry." She lifts the lid of the coffin, places her list of grievances inside, and, at the door, turns back and says, "Thank you for your humor. I love you. G'bye." The speech, which Roseanne says she wrote, sums up the blessings and the barbarity of the Barr family. But the scene also demonstrates how Roseanne negotiates her survival. She literally deposits her grievances with someone else and walks away. In life, she does the same thing. Instead of being persecuted, Roseanne persecutes; instead of being shamed, she attacks; instead of being annihilated, she annihilates.

Roseanne recalls that her first family target was her uncle Sherman, who used to denigrate her grandmother's cooking while scarfing it. "I'd say things to my uncle like 'Well, if you don't like the soup, why do you eat five bowls of it?' " she says. "He'd laugh. My mother would laugh—until one day he got mad and said, 'You've got a smart mouth, little girl.' And I said, 'Well, yeah, but just because you can't answer me.' You know, the way kids do. My grandmother turned around and said, 'Shut up. You have to respect him. He's your elder.' And I remember this huge catharsis in my head, like 'Oh, well, women aren't supposed to defend themselves against men. There's always some sort of threat if you do.' And I just thought about that forever and ever. I always understood that the women in my family were not assuming any of the power that was inherently theirs. They apologized for it. It always appalled me, and it still appalls me." But in those days if Roseanne wasn't venting her aggression in jokes, she couldn't express anger or deal with problematic situations at home except in a cartoonish play voice. "I always defined it as a play voice till I went into therapy and found out it's a person," Roseanne says, of the personality she calls Cindy, who is, she says, "probably the person who most saved my life." Roseanne goes on, "One time I was hosting 'Saturday Night Live.' I wanted to do a sketch with Cindy in it, 'cause I was getting real brave and I'd been in therapy for a couple of years and I thought I would be able to handle it. So I allowed her to come through, and the other actors were real scared, 'cause you can sort of tell it's not a character. It's a person."

At the end of the DeGeneres scene, Roseanne settles into a leather armchair perched on a wooden trolley and calls over some of her assistants, pointing in the direction of the Conners' kitchen. "Girls," she says, "pull me over there." The sight of Roseanne being lugged across the studio strikes everybody, including Roseanne, as amusing. "This is the port-a-throne," she says. She passes the time between setups talking with the crew, hankering out loud for Swensen's Sticky Chewy Chocolate ice cream, and casting a beady eye over the script of each scene after it has been rehearsed. Roseanne's line "In this family we solve our own problems. No psychiatrists. No therapists . . . no pediatricians" is sent back to the Big Room for more work. "If I don't get it, the public won't get it. I'm dumber than they are," she says. And the line at the end of Act I also displeases her. D.J. has been grounded after being AWOL with Lisa in Chicago. "You like him going with Lisa," Dan needles Roseanne, in the act's final beat. "And if it doesn't work out with her, I hear Squeaky Fromme is up for parole soon." Goodman gets a laugh from the crew, but Roseanne thinks the reference is passé. She says, "We're gonna dump that. I need a better line."

"Are there any great women criminals anymore?" Goodman asks.

"Yeah, me," Roseanne says.

Roseanne sidles up to the script supervisor, Hayden Ghaffary, whose job it is to relay Roseanne's notes directly to the head writer, in the Big Room, and tosses the script on the lectern. "Act II, Scene 2," Roseanne says to her. "I want it beat everywhere. It's sappy shit." In sitcom slang, "beat" means to better a line, which is what the writers, working in teams, spend most of their waking hours trying to do. Their private term for this enterprise is "feeding the monster."

Roseanne employs more writers for her show than are employed on any other sitcom, and she mixes standup comics in with TV writers, to give the comics on-the-job training in commercial storytelling. This "comedy college" consists of a relatively young, morose group made up mostly of men. The actors keep a cordial distance from them; the burnout rate here is high, and the brass are loath to fraternize with the enlisted men. (Eight of the twenty-four writers assembled for the run-through will not return for Roseanne's eighth season.) "I have six kids," says Dave Raether, a veteran of three seasons. "I have dinner with my family maybe once every three weeks." But the compensation for the fourteen-hour days is a king's ransom. Even a mid-level writer who stays for a few years will have made his million, or close to it; and the head writer, Eric Gilliland, who is thirty-two, will make two and a half million dollars this year, whether he finishes the season or not.

At noon, when the writers are summoned from their compound to take their first look at the episode on its feet, they follow the show from set to set. All the while, of course, they laugh. Beside me, William Lucas Walker, an executive story editor, is watching Roseanne closely and mak-

ing marks in his script. A wavy line means that a joke needs work; a small
check means a titter; a large check means a boff, or big laugh; and an "R"
means Roseanne laughed. ("Here's how you can tell if it's funny," Roseanne
explained later. "If I say it and nobody laughs, it's not funny.") For the writers, every day is a war of attrition, but when a big joke stays in, like one
that Walker got into the pot-smoking episode—where Dan, in a wave of
sixties nostalgia, recalls the slogan "Today is the first day of the rest of your
life," and Roseanne says, "Who ever knew it was going to be such a long,
bad day?"—the battle seems worth the effort. "If I write a play," Walker
explains, "thirty million people aren't going to laugh at a joke I wrote."

Once the run-through is over, a sudden entropy envelops the place.
Roseanne disappears into her trailer for meetings, and without her gravi-
tational pull the studio loses its sense of agitation and fun. The actors go
home; the writers drift back to their offices, complaining about cuts. "The
show's O.K.," says Walker, beckoning to one of the writers. "But it'll be a
lot stronger by Thursday." Danny Zuker approaches, dressed in shorts, his
shirttail dangling underneath a jean jacket. Walker introduces him to me
as the Mel Brooks of the staff.

"I can't believe you guys can laugh all week at the stuff you've written," I say.

"It's easy once you sell your soul," Zuker says.

At nine-thirty on Tuesday morning, Ghaffary is on the phone to Gilliland,
who is in the writers' main building. The actors are called for ten, but it's
clear from the urgency in Ghaffary's voice that Roseanne is already on the
premises. "There was a slight logic problem, and Roseanne found a way to
fix it," Ghaffary says. "Page twelve. Before D.J. and Lisa leave. She's cut
everything after that speech until page fifteen. She wants some sort of conflict before they exit, and she would like that before the run-through. In
an hour."

"I need a rewrite!"

Roseanne's voice precedes her, and, like her body, it takes up space.
She looms into view wearing a black beret and a turquoise T-shirt that says
"It Must Be Venus Envy." "Roseanne is just an explosion," says the writer
Lois Bromfield. The male writers may privately curse Roseanne's abrasive

blasts, but the women on the staff are thrilled by them. "If she threw scripts at people and called the head writer 'boy'—all things I've seen her do—and she was wrong, Roseanne would be insane," Bromfield says. "But here's the incredible part. She's almost always right." Roseanne's concern of the moment is a short trailer-park scene, for an episode that is to be taped along with "The Blaming of the Shrew" on Thursday. Roseanne has donated a walk-on part for a charity auction, and, paying fifteen hundred dollars for the privilege, Sharon Stone has bought it. "Can we get a rewrite?" Roseanne asks Ghaffary, and then grabs the phone from her to speak directly to Gilliland. "Did you hear all this stuff about the rules she's got?" Roseanne says about Stone's Thursday schedule. "It's unbelievable. She'll be here at one-thirty to acclimate. Two hours for makeup. Can you dig that? And she wants a tight pink beautician's outfit. Two hours for makeup! I said, 'Just tell her to get up out of bed and come down. That's what she should look like.' Is that hilarious? Do you love that? So, we won't be able to start the show till seven-thirty."

Later, inside the tidy calm of her trailer, Roseanne's persona softens. There is a punch-in lock on her trailer door, a bodyguard outside talking on the limousine's car phone. "For me, as a woman, the only place on earth that's ever existed that I don't feel all the male oppression is just inside my little office," she says. Roseanne, the star and executive producer of her show, puts her job description this way: "I'm a real good editor. I just edit down to get to the jokes quicker. You'll notice that yesterday I did a lot of general editing; today I started on the jokes. I always make sure that everybody else has their jokes, and then, on Wednesday, I do mine. My jokes." Roseanne has always written jokes. "It's like automatic writing. It's all unconscious. Comedy's about the unconscious," she says. "If you can tap into that. It's only about four or five times a year that I can do that." But the gruelling production schedule can't wait for Roseanne's unconscious to kick in, and therefore she needs writers. This haunts and infuriates her, and makes for an uneasy alliance with the help. Earlier in the morning, as I stood watching Roseanne rehearse, a writer, unknown to me and asking for anonymity, whispered, "She doesn't write the show. She never has written the show. In general, when she does decide to participate, like this week, because you're here, she's the source of very bad ideas that the writers have to circumnavigate to make the show any good at all."

Roseanne dismisses this kind of vitriol as typical male folderol. "They're so horrified of their mothers' power that they have to spend their whole life diminishing it," she says. In any case, the argument about creative ownership of the show is academic: Roseanne owns the mill and the charisma. And she treats the writers as extensions of herself. "I give them a big speech in the beginning," Roseanne says, and, without much coaxing, launches into it: "The world is run by women, contrary to what you believe—especially the family, especially the working-class family. These women that we're doing the show about, they make no compromises. They don't kowtow to men like middle-class women do." But Roseanne says it's hard to find men or women who can write about a working-class milieu. "This is the best group I've ever had," she says. "But, by virtue of the fact that they're male, they can only write what they've seen about women. So I try to get women in here, and they can't do it, either. In order to get power in Hollywood, or anywhere in the world, they've had to emulate men. They sound like male voices. The thing that's always missing in the stuff they write for me is the anarchy and the fight. They don't get it. Because they're so fucking damaged—if you want the bottom line—that they cannot see a woman as anything but a big, loving, nurturer sex thing. I see it in their work. When I get tougher with them, I get back castration and mutilation jokes. I'm like, 'Now I have to go back there and baby these fuckers along to get a decent joke out of them that has a woman's point of view.' " She goes on, "I had to find a place where they loved me as well as feared me. It's like being Big Mama. I always have to have my tit out for every fuckin' one of 'em, you know. I resent it. It's a big drain."

Roseanne's notion of mothering includes the knowledge that "they like to be spanked." And although Roseanne claims that her tongue-lashings are "an act"—part of the negotiating skills she's had to learn to get the best work from her writers—they also express her very real ambivalence. Kevin Abbott, one of the show's senior producer-writers, who will not be back next year, recalls how Roseanne spoke to the writers in March, at the first reading after Rob Ulin was deposed and Gilliland was promoted to replace him: "She starts off, 'I just want to say for all of you who don't know—Rob is dead; Eric is doing a great job. I'm really happy right now. And if I don't like the next one, I'll fire you, too. No, no, I don't mean that . . . I'm just sayin'. . .' She'd say something nice and immediately undercut it with something vicious. The writers were just staring at her with no idea of how to react. 'I really wanted to say something nice,' she said. 'But I just can't. It all just keeps coming out mean.' At one point, somebody laughed, and she turned and said, 'Don't laugh unless I tell you to!' So then there's a dead silence. Finally, Matt Berry goes, 'Can we laugh now?' She has a real love-hate relationship with writers. She really resents whatever they bring her."

Part of Roseanne's behavior can be explained by the comic's natural competitiveness. "I can't ever let anybody be funnier than me," she says. "I guess 'cause of my father, or something in my childhood. I just feel like this is war." But Roseanne's ferocity may come down to something else. "They frighten me," she says of the writers, comparing herself to a lion tamer. "I always have my whip. If I didn't have my whip and my chair in front of me, I wouldn't go into that goddam cage. They scare the shit out of me. I'm not lying. And not just men. Women scare me, too, especially the women that are out here. They don't even know that everything they're doing is against themselves."

Today, a young woman writer is ushered into the trailer to be interviewed by Roseanne, and Roseanne is cordial but reserved. The writer seems genuinely awed to be in Roseanne's presence, but rallies to roll her credits: "Uncle Buck," "Out All Night," "Pride & Joy." Roseanne cuts in to ask if she has children. No, she says, but her sister does, and they're darling. Roseanne asks when she could start, saying, "I do need women on the show. I especially need women committed to doin' the stuff that women really do." She suggests that the writer do a few scenes for the show, and then there is some flimflammery about writing commitments: the writer doesn't have the time just now, but she promises something within a few weeks, and leaves. The interview has lasted perhaps five minutes. Afterward, as Roseanne is herding me toward the door, she says, "See, that's what happens. Almost uniformly, always what happens with women. They come to interview for the job, but they don't want the job. They tell you they're not going to do it by saying what she said. Then you're real nice to them so they don't sell a story about you to the *Enquirer*." Roseanne laughs, and adds, "When I realized that I couldn't find any women writers, I went to my women friends who were comics, who'd got pretty well beaten down in the comedy clubs tryin' to say things as women. I got 'em, and I go, 'I want you to say the worst shit you always wanted to say. Send me stuff that just shocks me and scares me every single day and I'll tone it down.' That's how I got 'Absolutely Fabulous.' I'm using these women comics. They're just awesome." (The pilot, written by Jennifer Saunders and Roseanne, with Lois Bromfield, Ruby Wax, and Cynthia Mort, is being completed as we speak.)

At the door, she says, "Women like the one I just interviewed and most of the women I see don't have any ambition. They're satisfied if two or three of their jokes get into a show. Anyone who shows up and wants to stick her neck out and take the shit that comes from that, man, I'd take them in a second. It pisses me off, because when I was home with my three kids, and I was going to do standup, I'd get up and sit in a closet with a flashlight on, 'cause my husband was asleep, to write the shit I had to write. And so do a lot of women have to do that." She opens the trailer door to the glare of the afternoon. "So, if you just don't have the time right now," she says, "fuck you."

Over at the writers' compound, Dave Raether sits at his computer trying to focus the wandering minds of his comic team, who are sprawled on sofas in one of the joke rooms. A former journalist from Minnesota, Raether is the only one here who isn't a standup comedian. Matt Berry, Allan Stephan, Ed Yeager, and even Bromfield, the room's missing ingredient, who is off polishing the "AbFab" pilot, were all veterans of comedy-club circuits, and old publicity photographs of their standup selves are the only decorations on the walls. To describe the group's method of comic creation as "improvisation" doesn't do the process justice. It's more like throwing food at a wall and whatever sticks is what stays in the script. At this particular moment, the room is trying to find words for an exchange between Jackie and Roseanne about therapy.

"Is there anything about the therapist?" Raether asks. "How nice she was? How fucked up she was? Is there something that the therapist did that's funny?"

"Something about the room," says Yeager, a trim man with thinning hair who was with Roseanne in her Denver days. " 'You think that office was designed to make you feel comfortable.' "

" 'Very much like this kitchen,' "Yeager says.

" 'They must have the same designer,' " Stephan says.

" 'Must have the same designer,' " Raether repeats, turning back to his computer. "That's a good setup. O.K. Let's get some more jokes out of that."

As the afternoon wears on, Raether focusses his team on the last of their jokes to beat, where Roseanne and Dan try to talk to D.J. about being led around by Lisa. He reads the group in: " 'Well, what your mom means is, we know why you keep going out with her.' D.J.: ' 'Cause she tells me to.' " Raether looks up. "He's under her spell," he says.

" 'I put him under a spell,' " Stephan says. " 'She casts her spell. . . .' 'Dominating little bitch' won't work, will it?"

The room laughs, and Raether says, "That's sort of the joke. She's the sorcerer."

" 'Check his pupils, Dan. See if they're dilated.' "

" 'We need an exorcist.' "

" 'Check his balls.' "

" 'We need an exorcist.' " Raether laughs. "Good."

"Suddenly we're comin' alive here," Matt Berry says.

"How many have we got, Dave?" Stephan asks.

"Four," Raether says.

Stephan presses on. " 'And I thought they broke the mold with me,' " he says.

"Is there a twist?" Raether asks. "A different way of saying it? Roseanne fucks up the saying, makes it bigger."

"Wait a minute,"Yeager says. " 'After I was made, they broke the mold.' "

" 'Apparently they fixed my broken mold,' " Raether says.

"There you go," Stephan says. "Go for it."

"I'd try it," Matt Berry says. "What the hell. If they don't get it . . ."

It's time to pitch to the Big Room.

The Big Room houses a well-polished table and three senior producer-writers, who, by this hour in the afternoon, have lost some of their shine. Gilliland, whose shoulder-length hair and square-rimmed glasses make him a dead ringer for Mike in "Doonesbury," is slumped in the middle of the table with his head on the script, and Miriam Trogdon, a supervising producer, sits across from him with a row of empty Evian bottles lined up in front of her; at the end of the table is Kevin Abbott. Outside, palm fronds rustle in the bright day; inside, the Big Room has the crepuscular gloom of a writer's den. An amanuensis types every agreed-upon new joke into a portable computer, and the revision is instantaneously projected above him on a TV monitor.

"When I go in to pitch, I just enjoy it so much," Raether told me. "It's like performing. You know you're always going to get laughs." Raether takes a black leather swivel chair near Abbott, and the rest of his group belly up to the big table. They are beating the line "The whole time at the therapist's office, Fred just sat there like a bump on a log." Raether's first option draws a dead silence; undaunted, he launches into his second: "Roseanne says, 'Well, maybe you should have sent him to a tree surgeon.' "

"Oh, my God," says Gilliland.

Raether looks up from his pages. "We knew that one wouldn't—"

Gilliland cuts in, "I appreciate the joke of it."

Raether tries another: " 'Fred just sat there like a deer in headlights.' 'Well, all I can say, Jackie, is buckle up and hit the gas.' "

After a few more options, Gilliland stops him. "O.K. Those are good offers. We got enough here. We'll take the deer-in-headlights joke."

Next is the broken mold joke, which earns a "very funny" from Gilliland. The team is excused; another cadre enters. "Pitchy-poo," says Trogdon, and the process resumes. Afterward, the Big Room continues its weeding. There are setups to be clarified, lines to be cut. Gilliland is a patient man with a baby face and a permanently forlorn look. His idea of a good time is to listen to a Cubs game and read the paper in his garden on his day off. "The big trick in writing is to keep Roseanne herself separate from Roseanne Conner," Gilliland says. "I think Roseanne is more daunting. Roseanne Conner is more lovable—strong but wise, good, fair, and just."

On a break, Gilliland goes into the writers' snack room, which has shelves overflowing with M&M's, Pop-Tarts, Raisinets, Twix, and Starburst, and an icebox full of soda—enough sugar to keep the writers in orbit for weeks. A producer and her ten-year-old daughter come in, and the little girl ogles the candy like Pinocchio at the fair. She makes a bee-line for the M&M's. "She thinks this is life," her mother says.

"If this isn't life," Gilliland says, "I'm screwed."

"Wednesday is a low-energy day, because the actors don't want to give out before a performance," says Raether, standing outside the bungalow where he and his posse are taking a break from the morning's rewrites. "Usually, on Wednesday, the Big Room is working on next week's script."

"The Big Room," Berry says. "The power that goes on there is almost addictive."

"Yeah," Raether says. "Because you're around very interesting people. Five or six standups for fourteen hours a day. Really, really funny."

Bill Walker leans out a window near the Big Room. "She just yelled she wants a hundred jokes per page!" he shouts. The doors of the other bungalows open. "Ten jokes per comic per scene!" The words are repeated and passed on, and then the writers, like firemen responding to a station-house alarm, emerge from their rooms. They know the drill. They head for the main office and cluster around a TV monitor that is hooked up to the soundstage and trained on Roseanne. Big Mama is watching them, and she is not pleased. "I want it in an hour," Roseanne growls into the camera's eye. On second thought, she wants them front and center at Stage 2: "Now!"

Later, the standups are asked to Roseanne's trailer to pitch their options directly to her. "I guess it's like going to the principal's office," Roseanne says. "But they're excited. That's why I brought 'em down and let 'em sit there for two hours before they went into my room. I have to baby them along; and when you baby 'em along you get good things."

When the writers emerge forty minutes later, Raether says, "As I'm walking to the trailer, I'm thinking, This is the worst person in the world. But afterward I'm thinking, She's a riot. What a fun person. She started laughing at the glazed-ham joke. She could not stop laughing."

"Jackie accuses Roseanne of being bossy," Berry explains. "And her comeback is 'Bossy! Is a farmer who turns a pig into a glazed ham bossy?' "

"She's laughing," Raether says. "We're all laughing. It just seemed like the funniest possible joke."

"That's the way it should be," Stephan says. "You have her immediate reaction. It's a better system than her sending notes and notes coming back to her. That way, she never sees the choices."

"She worked on words with us," Berry says. "We had a great time."

On the day of the taping, everything broadcasts Roseanne's sovereignty. Each friend or special guest who enters the studio is tagged with a royal-blue wristband saying "Roseanne" and "Void if removed from wrist." A dozen or so stony-faced enforcers in suits rim the playing area and Roseanne's dressing room. Although Roseanne is easy with the actors during rehearsals and perky with DeGeneres and Stone for their photo opportunities together, there is nothing rollicking or accessible about her today. "Before I perform, I cast a circle—a magic circle—around myself," she says. Its mojo is palpable. She gives no eye contact, makes no gestures of acknowledgment, moves to her own beat. With one exception: when Stephan arrives, Roseanne recounts the morning's victory over a reporter, explaining, "I said to him, 'It's way better around here since we got rid of His Highness King Shit' "—Tom Arnold. "And then he asks, 'Are you upset that they're moving you to Wednesdays at eight?' And I go, 'They can move it to eight, they can move it to nine, or they can shove it up their ass for all I care. I'm getting paid the same.' I loved it. It was real fun. I got some great lines off about Rob gettin' fired. He goes, 'Did you bring in somebody else?' 'Nope,' I go. 'This is a blue-collar show. We fire from the top, not like white-collar shows, where they fire from the bottom.' "

About half an hour before showtime, the audience files in and the writers assemble near a soundproof booth just above the bleachers. They have their own monitor to watch. Broch, the original author of the episode, is there with his fiancée; Berry brings his two towheaded children; Walker arrives with a friend. Renee Kurtz, an ABC executive, and Raether, Abbott, Trogdon, and the others all cram into the booth, too.

The opening of the show sails along on wave after wave of laughter. In Roseanne's fourteen speeches there are eleven jokes, and all of them score. "I liked that scene," Raether says, applauding. "Especially my work." But in the next scene, when Dan and Roseanne argue about whether D.J. should be allowed to go to the lake with Lisa, Raether can be heard bleating, "Aaargh!" Roseanne has muffed a joke and won't reshoot it. "Screw it," she says. "It's gone." The audience cheers Roseanne's outburst, but inside the booth the writers seethe.

"Another brilliant, well-thought-out editorial decision," says Abbott from the back.

But soon there's joy in the room again as the audience howls at DeGeneres's psychotherapist scene.

"She's trimmed some stuff out of here," Abbott says.

Miriam Trogdon looks at him. "Who did?"

"Who do you think?"

The big charge for the writers in the second act is watching Roseanne's glazed-ham joke bomb.

"We worked on her all day trying to take that thing away from her," says Tim Doyle, another producer-writer.

"She picked *that* one?" Trogdon asks.

But all is forgiven when Roseanne makes the line about "chocolate air" sing. The audience rocks with laughter, and someone says to Trogdon, who coined it, "That's a great line. Major."

"I love hearing the writers in the room—'That's mine.' 'That's mine,' " Renee Kurtz says.

"At home, I say it for nearly all the jokes," Berry says. "My daughter goes, 'Daddy, how do I know which ones are yours?' I say, 'The ones that you're laughing at, those are mine. The others are Danny Zuker's.' "

At the post mortem in the writers' booth, Broch is hugged by his fiancée, Berry is hugged by his daughter, and Walker hugs his script. "She can make anything work," he says. "She can make a straight line funny. Just her behavior."

Roseanne moves briefly among the cast and crew, then unceremoniously disappears. The comic fireworks that the writers have planned all week are a kind of Roman candle that dazzles and dies too soon. Some of them wander over to the Canyon Restaurant's bar to savor their victories and mourn their losses before they begin to climb next week's mountain.

"You hate all the intimidation and all the mental games she puts you through," Abbott says. "But I will say one thing. The reason the show's been good over the years is because the writers are afraid to bring crap to the table. You watch the head writers go, 'We got to get something better here.' They're afraid to bring a joke that's anything less than the best you can get." He goes on, "When I leave at the end of the year, I'm really going to be sad. It will be kind of closing the door on a piece of television history. She's one of a kind."

"All I do is read about serial killers," Roseanne says four days later, seated in the parlor of her Brentwood Hills house, a huge Alpine-Tudor-style chalet. (She has essentially turned this house over to her kids; she and Ben Thomas live in a smaller, adjacent white brick house.) "Every book I have is about serial killers and abnormal psychology. That's where I get my comedy." She glances up at a gallery overlooking the parlor. With its dark wood beams and mottled light filtering through the surrounding trees, the room has a shadowy, brooding aura that fits Roseanne's mood. She continues, "When everything is corrupt and filthy and brutal and psychotic, you will be, too. And that will be considered normal. That's what I find funny. The things that are normal are horrific and horrifying to me."

By her own admission, Roseanne has a "criminal mentality." She says, "If I hadn't found comedy, I'd probably be out killing people." When her jokes score, she says, they "kill." And she prefers to be called "killer bitch" rather than "feminist." Roseanne says, "It's like this: I gave birth to ya, and I can take ya out, too. I think that's what makes me a bit different from other women. Because I'll beat the shit out of them, and not just verbally. I'm not opposed to violence. In fact, I think it's great. I think women should be more violent, kill more of their husbands. I like the fight. If people are comin' at you, you don't just sit there and lay down and go, 'Oh, bless you.' That's not in the human arsenal. To say that women should do that is to say women aren't human."

The warrior spectacle that Roseanne makes of herself in Hollywood, she explains, is meant to call into question the supremacy of middle-class liberal women like Jodie Foster, Susan Sarandon, and Meryl Streep, all of whom Roseanne considers "talented and fuckin' deluded." She says, "They don't have any subtext to anything they say. They're all just upset about salaries, or something that feminism was about twenty-five years ago. They're rewarded for making the women's movement appear to be lost in time. And they don't even know it. I want them to shut the fuck up and get out of the way of the real women that are doin' something. I'd like to see 'em go down to goddam South Central and talk to those women. Let's hear what they have to say about violence in America. Let's not hear from Jodie Foster, for chrissake!" Roseanne continues, "These type of women are just translators. And they are, in effect, castrated females—excuse me, but that's what they are. They're just too middle-class white." Once Roseanne reaches a certain threshold of anger, her mood lifts; her voice and body become animated. "Jodie Foster," Roseanne says, her eyes aglitter. "I hate everything she stands for, and everyone gathered around her to help her stand for it. It's a big fat fuckin' lie. Let's not be who we are. Let's hide behind our art. ('Nell' . . . I gotta do 'Nell' onstage sometime.) Let's oppress everybody who is exactly like us. Make it even harder for them to be who they are. In her fuckin' Armani with her tits hangin' out. And constantly rewarded and rewarded. And by who? The power structure that she totally speaks for."

For a Carnegie Hall appearance Roseanne plans to do next February, she wants to open with a screen image of Streep, Foster, and Sarandon which dissolves into her singing "Streetwalker Blues." She giggles at the thought of it. "It's a horrible song," she says, and, naturally, begins to sing:

> I've got nipples on my titties
> Big around as both my thumbs
> I've got somethin' between my legs
> That makes a dead man come.

The script for the new act is a neatly typed pile of ideas, which is stashed in a large mahogany desk in the main house. Roseanne has another office and another big desk in an outbuilding on the premises. Both are calm, well-ordered spaces, dominated by tanks of exotic tropical fish.

Roseanne will take six months to write and refine the material. She pulls out a page and reads, "It's not like in fairy tales; most guys are pigs. Like where the prince kisses the princess and she wakes up. Hey, in real life most guys, even if she didn't wake up, they'd still fuck her." Roseanne laughs. "It's so mean. I like it when it's mean," she says. "You want to get people moved or pissed, or something. Feel something. I like it when guys scream back at me, 'Bullshit, Roseanne!' "

Maybe because her lawyer will soon be arriving to discuss fallout from her divorce, or maybe because her rant against the actresses has tapped into Roseanne's bottomless reservoir of anger, she pulls out a section called "Tom Arnold." "I'm on a gag order. I can't say nothin' about him," she says, and fixes me with a glance. "But I can tell jokes." She sits down in her upholstered swivel chair. "Like this one: When you get married, all you hear is 'I'm the man. I wear the pants. I'm the man, I'll make all the decisions.' Yeah—till the divorce. 'What am I gonna do? How will I survive? I have to live the way I was accustomed.' How much do you need to have a shitty studio apartment with orange shag carpet that smells like piss, man? How much do you need for that? To have shelves made out of bricks you stole, and beer and pizza in your fridge? How much do you need to keep your stale water in your bong? That's what you were accustomed to, man. Fuck you, get a job. How're you gonna live? Just like before. Like a fuckin' pig. Sell stories to the *Enquirer*, like you used to. Put on your fuckin' Iowa sweatshirt and get fuckin' to it."

Later, in her other office, part of which is now an art studio, Roseanne pulls a big cardboard box out of a cupboard and sits cross-legged on the floor to pick through the flotsam and jetsam of fifteen years of hectic life: jottings on menus and in manuscript, "Roseanne" scripts and character sketches, and feminist feuilletons like "Big Mama Rag," "Celtic Healing Goddesses," and "Points of Unity"—the last a detailed document Roseanne wrote for the Woman to Woman bookstore. One of her earliest joke ideas, with "Write this up as a big story" scrawled across it, goes like this: "Boys like a good listener. Boys like to win at games. Boys like to think they're smarter than you. Boys don't respect a girl who gives in to them, so you go around practicing virginal behavior: being docile, being quiet, a gracious loser. But that's only till you get a man. Then you must start being the real you, if you ever were, and spend all your time trying to change him from someone who'd want to live with a stupid loser with no sex drive." Roseanne chuckles to herself as she reads.

"That's a hard thing to say."

"Yeah," she says. "But it's true."

Roseanne fishes out the mimeographed program she wrote for her comedy protest Take Back the Mike. Her bio reads, "Roseanne Barr—Person of Ceremonies: an adorably angry/vicious comic, wife of ten years, mother of three, affectionately referred to as 'castrating bitch' by many male colleagues." Pages of scribbled notions from the early eighties are churned up, a kind of grab bag of griefs being willed into good times:

- I have a song in my heart: Schubert's death waltz.
- My husband's given me the best years of his life. '76 and '77.
- I undress to motivational tapes.
- If you can't say something nice, I would probably like you.
- "Dance as though you're making love." "You mean you want me to go off and dance alone."

Roseanne rummages for a while, then pushes herself up and finds a chair. "While I'm alive on this earth, I'm going to create my own reality," she says. "I'm not gonna fit it around me. I'm not gonna cut myself anymore to fit theirs. That's in all things I do, including my language."

After next year, when "Roseanne" goes off the air, she will be at large. "I know I have bigger things to do besides this," she says. She has joked about running for president. ("We need new blood in the White House—every twenty-eight days.") Her millions, as she says, "don't make me vote any different, they don't make me dress any better," but they do give her clout. She has a ten-year plan: she sees herself as a children's-rights advocate, and she is talking about setting up a foundation. "I feel that because I got all this I'm supposed to do that," she says. "That's the tradeoff." She also fancies herself a TV mogul. Roseanne plans to either own a network or align herself with one, to program shows that "only empower women." She tells me, "It may appear like a pipe dream now, but you should keep the quote for when I do own a network, and then you can say I said so in '95."

Whatever happens, Roseanne's greatest achievement has been her own salvation. "*God, freeze the family hands, lips, the thousand diseases of us this time, in this generation,*" she prays at the end of "My Lives." "*Spare me my grandchildren—as you have spared me.*" When I ask Roseanne why she wants another child, she says, "I want to keep doing it until I get it a hundred per-cent right." She feels she has destroyed the neurotic family pattern that made her who she is. And if that has indeed come to pass, then the bless-ings of her life and her laughter have been engineered by the same fierce principle: without a killing, no feast. Roseanne stares at the battered card-board box. "It's amazing that I got away with it, isn't it?" she says.

IRVING BERLIN

REVOLUTIONARY RAG

A<small>T</small> W<small>OODLAWN</small> C<small>EMETERY</small>, in the Bronx, there is a small American flag staked in the greensward above Irving Berlin's gravestone. A flag in this setting usually signifies war dead, but Berlin, who died in 1989, at the age of a hundred and one, was not a soldier. His work—eight hundred and ninety-nine copyrighted songs— was another kind of service to his country. In his slangy, syncopated viva- ciousness, the songwriter, who changed his name from Israel Baline when his first song, "Marie from Sunny Italy," was published, in 1907, hymned the joys of the modern republic: the manners, the fashions, and the expec- tations of the masses from whom he'd emerged, having arrived from Siberia in 1893, at the age of five. "I'm writing American music," Berlin boasted in 1915, after "Alexander's Ragtime Band," which had taken him eighteen minutes to write, became the biggest-selling song in the history of the music industry up to that time; it sold a million copies in seven months in 1911, and helped its wunderkind composer, at twenty-one, earn a hundred thousand dollars after just three years at his craft. Berlin went on to say, "The reason American composers have done nothing high- ly significant is because they won't write American music. . . . So they write imitation European music which doesn't mean anything."

Berlin's jaunty songs caught the impertinence of the New World. As early as 1913, according to Laurence Bergreen's 1990 biography of him, they were honored at a Friars' Club roast by his mentor, the great Broadway showman George M. Cohan, as "music you don't have to dress up to listen to." With "Watch Your Step" (1914), billed as a "ragtime opera," Berlin was the first composer to straddle Tin Pan Alley and Broadway, and he was the only one ever to have a Broadway theatre—the Music Box—built solely to perform his work. His best effort, "Annie Get

Your Gun" (1946), is being revived on Broadway, with Bernadette Peters as the sassy sharpshooter Annie Oakley. The show produced eight standards—more than any other Broadway musical in history.

Over his lifetime, Berlin had four hundred and fifty-one hit songs; two hundred and eighty-two of them were in the Top Ten, and thirty-five made it to No. 1. Until the twenties, when people spoke of "jazz" they were more than likely speaking of ragtime, which Berlin was largely responsible for popularizing. He wrote lyrics as well as music, and the opening of "Alexander's Ragtime Band"—"Come on and hear! Come on and hear!"—was, like many of his early hits ("Everybody's Doin' It Now," "Call Me Up Some Rainy Afternoon"), an invitation to act, to taste the liberty of a society increasingly on the move. As Ian Whitcomb notes, in "Irving Berlin and Ragtime America," sometimes even a single word—like "Hurrah!" in Berlin's hit "My Wife Has Gone to the Country (Hurrah! Hurrah!)"—worked the same trick. "That lone word gave the whole idea of the song in one quick wallop," Berlin said. "It invited the roomful to join in the hilarious shout."

Since Berlin had risen from the masses, he understood the masses, and wanted a mass communication. "The mob is always right," he once told the *Times*. "There are darned few good songs which have not been whistled or sung by the crowd." Between 1900—the year Berlin's father, a cantor in the Old World and a poultry inspector in the New World, died—and 1910, nine million immigrants came to America. Berlin's lyric gift was forged in this new racial crucible; his early catalogue included songs called "Oh, How That German Could Love," "Colored Romeo," and "Latins Know How."

"The real American has not yet arrived," a character in Israel Zangwill's 1908 hit play, "The Melting Pot," said. "He will be the fusion of all races." Popular song was the first expression of this fusion: by bringing the culture of outsiders—the spice of their voices and their music—into the mainstream, song served as a powerful agent and chronicler of change. In a time before radio, when only a few of the nation's newspapers crossed state lines, Berlin's songs were everywhere, corrupting listeners with the pleasure of ethnic idiom and stories—Yiddle with his Fiddle, Alexander with his Band, and the nice Jewish girl in "Sadie Salome, Go Home," who leaves home to become a famous actress, only to be discovered by her boyfriend, Moses, as a stripper ("Oy, oy, oy, oy, where is your clothes? / You better go and get your dresses, / Everyone's got the op'ra glasses"). "The average U.S. citizen was perfectly epitomized in Berlin's music," Jerome Kern told Alexander Woollcott, who wrote the first book on Berlin, in 1925. "Both the typical Yankee and the Berlin tune had humor, originality, pace and popularity and both were wide awake."

Berlin saw the syncopated beat—the "ragged metre" he mythologized in song—as a correlative for the nation's tension and momentum. "All the old rhythm is gone and in its place is heard the hum of an engine, the whirr of wheels, the explosion of an exhaust," he told the *Times* in 1924. "The leisurely songs that men hummed to the clatter of horses' hoofs do not fit into this new rhythm. . . . The new age demands new music for new action." Speed also defined Berlin, who was as wiry and as streamlined as a whippet. "I used to think he was like quicksilver. Moving fast. Now you see him, now you don't," says Berlin's eldest daughter, Mary Ellin Barrett, who is the author of a memoir about him. "But when you saw him the experience was extremely intense. He was there with you. If you were talking to him, he would focus, even if it was only for a few minutes." Berlin was perhaps most focussed on the relation of song to the social fabric: he understood its subliminal impact ("It influences everybody, whether they know it or not") and its role in creating America's landscape of promise. He wrote, "What care I who cares for the world's affairs / As long as I can sing its popular songs?"

Indeed, many of Berlin's songs became—and remain—emblematic of the great ceremonial constructs of American public life, among them war (the First World War: "Oh! How I Hate to Get Up in the Morning"; the Second World War: "God Bless America," "This Is the Army, Mr. Jones"), Christmas ("White Christmas"), Easter ("Easter Parade"), Broadway ("There's No Business Like Show Business"). Berlin, who won the Congressional Medal of Honor in 1945, contributed to the political fortunes of a fellow Tin Pan Alley tunesmith, the flamboyant New York Mayor Jimmy Walker ("It's a Walk-In for Walker"), and he produced presidential campaign songs for Al Smith and Dwight Eisenhower, whose "I Like Ike" campaign song was a rewritten Berlin number. Once, during the Vietnam

War, the lyricist E.Y. Harburg, who shared Fifth Avenue offices with Berlin but not his political viewpoint (Harburg was an avowed left-winger), tweaked Berlin by suggesting that he rewrite "God Bless America" and call it "God Help America." Berlin tweaked him back with a heartfelt stanza:

> Martha's Vineyard, dear old ASCAP
> And a flat near Central Park
> God bless America
> When things are dark
> God bless America
> My Noah's Ark.

The blessings of America were not immediately apparent to the Baline family, who lived during Irving's childhood in four dank rooms on Cherry Street, in New York's Lower East Side. The neighborhood, with its estimated two hundred and ninety thousand people per square mile, dwarfed Dickens's London for density; it was, as Harold Evans writes in "The American Century," "perhaps the worst slum in the history of the Western world." Berlin, the youngest of eight children, didn't talk much about the impoverishment of his early life. "At a certain deep level he was impenetrable," Mary Ellin Barrett says. "He would let out things to you, but you had to be very fast to catch them. He did not repeat himself." She continues, "When I was a little fresh kid, I'd say, 'What was it like being poor, Daddy?' And he'd say, 'Poor? What is poor? I was never cold. I always had enough to eat.' He actually said, 'You are what you know; and it was all I knew.'"

At the age of thirteen, Berlin, "sick with a sense of worthlessness" at not being able to contribute to the family commonweal, left home and, as he put it, "went on the bum." "He tried to get a job on the docks," Linda Emmet, his second daughter, told me. "He was so small and so slight that he didn't have the muscles for it. He said, 'You know, I always knew that I had to follow a line, and it would've been easy to cross the line and do something that was not totally honest.' He never did. He had this real moral rectitude." She added, "He could be selfish; he could be reclusive;

but he was always a just man." In 1901, with a poor education and no skills, Berlin was merely a runaway with nothing to fall back on but his raspy tenor voice. Singing was the line of least resistance, and it was legal. A bed in a flophouse cost fifteen cents; if he couldn't hustle enough money busking in saloons, he would sleep on a park bench. Song, which Berlin called "a heart raiser and worry banisher," manufactured the blue skies he would later invoke. He sang on street corners; he sang as a song-plugger and as a "plant" at Tony Pastor's; he sang briefly in the chorus of a Broadway show and as a singing waiter in a Chinatown watering hole called the Pelham Café—a gig that went on until six in the morning.

"Part of Berlin's genius was that he was open to so much," says the musical-theatre historian Robert Kimball, who, with Emmet, is co-editing "The Complete Lyrics of Irving Berlin." "He was responsive to everything around him. He began as a parodist because he listened so well." As a singing waiter, Berlin hustled extra change by improvising risqué lyrics to the popular tunes of the day. "He honestly absorbs the vibrations emanating from the people, the manners, and the life of his time," Jerome Kern told Woollcott. "And in turn gives these impressions back to the world simplified, clarified, glorified." Berlin's ability to take the pulse of his public was developed at the Pelham Café. Philip Furia, in his fascinating new biography, "Irving Berlin: A Life in Song," quotes Jubal Sweet, another Pelham employee, recalling how Berlin worked the room: "Now a singing waiter couldn't be stooping over every time a coin hit the floor. Spoil his song like—see? No, he'd keep moving around easy, singing all the time, every time a nickel would drop he'd put his toe on it and kick it or nurse it to a certain spot. When he was done, he had all the jack in a pile."

From the beginning, Berlin kept his eye on both the music and the money. Although he made only thirty-seven cents in royalties from "Marie from Sunny Italy," he seized his opportunity. His career seemed to incarnate the advice given in a guidebook to immigrants on how to survive in America: "Do not take a moment's rest. Run." Between 1907 and 1914, he published a hundred and ninety songs. "Sometimes I turn out four or five songs a night, so you can imagine how many bad ones I write," he told Woollcott. Among his nine rules for writing popular songs, which included "heart interest" and "open vowels" for euphony, by far the most important one was the last: "Work and *work* and then WORK." "I gather ideas, and then I usually work them out between eight at night and five in the morning," he said. If he had to work during the day, he pulled down the shades and composed by artificial light. "I sweat blood between three and six A.M. many mornings, and when the drops that fall off my forehead hit the paper, they're notes," he told the magazine *Theatre*. Over the decades, the pace changed but not the pattern. Furia quotes Moss Hart, who collaborated with Berlin on several revues and on the musical "Miss Liberty" (1949): "Writing a show with Irving Berlin is tantamount to entering a monastery. You live it, breathe it, eat it and were it not for the fact that he allows you no sleep at all, I should say sleep it."

From the outset, Berlin was acknowledged to be a phenomenon. The New York *World* hailed him as "The Man Who Is Making the Country Hum"; his Tin Pan Alley fraternity sung his prowess with ditties like "Izzy Get Busy, Write Another Ragtime Song"; in 1919, he set up his own publishing company, to exploit the copyrights on his music. But Berlin was an improbable prodigy. He couldn't read or write music, and played only the black keys on the piano, in the key of F-sharp. "The key of C is for people who study music," he said in a 1948 interview. "The fact that I compose only in F-sharp gave me certain harmonies that other writers missed, because they knew more about music." He used a transposing piano, equipped with a lever under the keyboard which allowed him to hear his tunes in any of the other major or minor keys. Berlin, who had an uncanny ear, couldn't call out from his fingers what he heard in his head; his remedy was to hire a series of musical secretaries to explore his songs' chording possibilities and write them down. In "The Gershwins," a book of lyrics and reminiscences which Kimball wrote with Alfred Simon, Berlin describes what happened in 1919 when George Gershwin applied for the job. After notating Berlin's "That Revolutionary Rag," he played Berlin some of his own stuff. "What the hell do you want to work for somebody else for?" Berlin told him.

Berlin's awareness of his limitations led to ingenious solutions. "In my ignorance of the laws of music, I have often broken all the laws," he said in 1915. "The result was an original twist." He continued, "Also, in that my vocabulary being somewhat limited through lack of education, it follows that my lyrics are simple." In 1924, when he met Ellin Mackay, a pedigreed, sophisticated writer, then twenty-one—she later became his second wife (Berlin's first wife died of typhoid fever after their honeymoon to Cuba, in 1912)—she said to him, "Oh, Mr. Berlin, I do so like your song 'What Shall I Do?' "The song was "What'll I Do?"; Berlin pointed out the contraction, and added, "Where grammar is concerned, I can always use a little help."

He had a kind of genius for poeticizing the colloquial. For instance, in the song "Snooky-Ookums" (1913) he teased the notion of lovers' baby talk: "She's his jelly elly roll / He's her sugey ugar bowl." In Berlin's hands, ordinary locutions like "they say it's wonderful," "let's have another cup of coffee," "say it isn't so" became powerful romantic occasions. As he explained in a 1954 interview, " 'Easy to sing, easy to say, easy to remember and applicable to everyday events' is a good rule for a phrase." Berlin, who was a member in good standing of the witty Algonquin Round Table, worked on his vocabulary, and made a serious study of Alexander Pope and his supple use of the heroic couplet. He found cunning ways to get interior rhymes into a thirty-two-bar song. In "Puttin' on the Ritz," the play of high-low diction is set against a rhythm that Alec Wilder, in his classic study "American Popular Song," calls "probably the most complex and provocative I have come upon":

> Come let's mix where Rockefellers
> Walk with sticks or "um-ber-el-las"
> In their mitts—puttin' on the ritz.

But the real power of Berlin's songs is their exquisite pleasure in simple things, whether dancing cheek to cheek ("Heaven / I'm in heaven") or dressing up in top hat, white tie, and tails ("I'm dudein' up my shirt front, / Puttin' in the shirt studs, / Polishin' my nails"). Berlin's phonics could make his sense of wonder-the exclamatory "Oh!"—echo like a cheer through the wordplay of his apparently simple rhymes:

> There's no business

Like show business
Like no business
I know.

"Song and sorrow are playmates," Berlin once said. In his life, he knew more than enough about sorrow. He was a private, moody man, who in his later years became reclusive and rebarbative. His first memory was of watching from the roadside as his home in Russia was burned to the ground. He lost his homeland at five, his father at twelve, his family at thirteen, his first wife at twenty-four, his infant son at forty, and a good part of his fortune in the stock-market crash at forty-one. The pressure of songwriting kept him busy and hid his depression from him, but he could never successfully banish it. Over his long career, Berlin was immobilized at least twice—from 1930 to 1932, and from 1957 to 1962—by periods of anxiety. "I developed the damnedest feeling of inferiority," he said of the episode in the early thirties, an era that, besides the crash, saw the emergence of sophisticated musical challengers like the Gershwins and Rodgers and Hart. "I got so I called in anybody to listen to my songs—stockroom boys, secretaries. One blink of the eye and I was stuck." Although much has been made of Berlin's ear, his eye was also crucial to his sensibility. He needed to see the spell of a song working on the faces of his listeners—to see his music, and himself, being taken in. Once, while he was writing for the Marx Brothers musical "The Cocoanuts" (1929), he woke up the show's director, George S. Kaufman, at 2 A.M. to sing him his newest number, "Always." Kaufman later recalled, "I was presumptuous enough then to question Irving's first line, 'I'll be loving you always.' Always was a long time for romance. I suggested therefore that the opening line might be a little more in accord with reality—something like 'I'll be loving you Thursday.' " Berlin dropped the song from the show. "When he sings right in your face, he's reading you, studying you for your reaction," Joshua Logan, the original director of "Annie Get Your Gun," wrote in his autobiography. "If one blinked too often or one's eyes glazed for a second, Irving was apt to put the song away."

At other times, a song could so stun auditors that Berlin misread their silence as indifference, which is what happened with "There's No Business Like Show Business." "Irving, what's the matter, you left out the finale," Logan said to him at the end of the first day of rehearsals, after Berlin had played through the score again, minus that number. Berlin said, "I didn't like the way you reacted this morning. It didn't register." Logan wrote, "It wasn't petulance. He meant it. I was astounded. I asked him what he'd done with the lead sheet, and he shrugged and said he'd put it away in his files somewhere, and I said, 'Irving! Get it out of those files.' He argued with me, but I kept on insisting, until finally he gave in and went out to his secretary and asked her to dig it out of the files, and do you believe this—they couldn't find it?" Logan continued, "Eventually, thank heaven, they came up with his original lead sheet. There wasn't even a copy."

"Annie Get Your Gun" was what Berlin called a "situation show." Of Berlin's twenty-one stage productions, fourteen were revues, where the star was the song rather than the story. But Rodgers and Hammerstein had recently weighed in with "Oklahoma" (1943); Harburg and Arlen had done "Bloomer Girl" (1944). "Annie Get Your Gun" was Berlin's entry into this postwar fascination with the folkloric, and it gave him a way of asserting, as the show does, that "anything you can do I can do better." It was "just a kind of fresh wind in him," Mary Ellin Barrett says. "The freedom of the war over. Wanting to prove himself yet another time." The musical was not Berlin's idea, or, originally, even his assignment. He stepped in after Jerome Kern's sudden death, in 1945, and while he dithered for twelve days about whether to do the show he produced five songs, including "There's No Business Like Show Business" and "Doin' What Comes Naturally." In the end, Berlin came up with the entire score in two months; the delightful "Anything You Can Do" was written in the fifteen minutes between when Berlin discussed the concept with Josh Logan at a rehearsal and when Logan got back to his apartment, twelve blocks away. "'Hello, Josh—this is Irving. What do you think of this?' And then he sang the whole damned first chorus," Logan recalled. In what Alec Wilder calls a "near perfect" score, Berlin, with a "curious absence of ego," established the folksy wit of Annie Oakley: "You don't have to go to a private school / Not to turn up your bustle to a stubborn mule."

As Annie, the brassy Ethel Merman could pick off a song's high notes and key words just as surely as her character could hit clay pigeons. "With all due respect to the Gershwins and Cole, Irving gave me range, allowing me a kind of vulnerability I'd been missing in girls like 'Nails' Duquesne, Blossom Hart, and Hattie Maloney," she wrote in her autobiography. But Merman as Annie was neither believably vulnerable nor innocent—not that it mattered. She was a sensational smart-mouth who never related as well to the people onstage with her as to the people in the audience. At a recent preview of the new version of "Annie Get Your Gun," when the production was struggling to make Berlin's numbers land for the fetching Bernadette Peters, who *is* believably vulnerable, the way they'd landed in the noisy Merman editions, Stephen Sondheim approached the show's award-winning librettist, Peter Stone. "Steve said, 'Stop pushing for it,' " Stone told me. " 'Irving Berlin didn't write for smash finishes. He wrote gentle. He's very simple and straightforward. It was Merman who got the encores and the splash finishes.' "

In the last fifty years, theatregoers' expectations of musicals have changed: they demand story, not just standards. The history of "Annie Get Your Gun," whose songs are evergreen but whose book is not, bears out this change in public taste. The musical, which originally ran for more than eleven hundred performances, has never quite achieved its proper place in the Broadway pantheon. Part of the show's problem is the unwitting but breathtaking racism in the characterization of Native Americans. "Just like Battle Axe, Hatchet Face, Eagle Nose, / Like Those Indians, I'm an Indian too / A Sioux," Annie sings in the original, and, while the song is funny, its implications are not. At a recent panel discussion, Stone debunked Broadway purists who wanted to see the show performed as it was originally written, asking how they'd like to hear somebody onstage sing "I'm a Hebrew too / A Jew—ooo—ooo." Of course, "I'm an Indian Too" has been cut from the new version, and where the Native Americans were once the butt of the show's jokes they're now the agents of them. Native Americans are cleverly used as part of Buffalo Bill's travelling Wild West Show, and are also woven into a resuscitated romantic subplot—changes that completely remove the script's bad odor.

But the larger stumbling block for any "Annie Get Your Gun" produc-

tion is its dramatic construction. The challenge for Stone and for the director, Graciela Daniele—one that to my mind they've solved elegantly—has
been to make the songs emerge naturally from the tender simplicity of
Annie's passion for the sharpshooting headliner, Frank Butler (Tom
Wopat). Daniele has worked to deepen the lovers' tempestuous relationship, and Stone has found a concept for the show which makes its spirit of
innocence acceptable to a nineties audience. Now the story of Annie and
Frank Butler is a play put on by Buffalo Bill and his troupe. "The frame-
work removes it once from us, so that *we're* not making it simple—Buffalo
Bill is making it simple," Stone says. "It's something they would not forgive
us for but would forgive him for, because that's the business he's in." This
adjustment releases all kinds of emotional and visual energy into the show:
the cowboy band is onstage; the tent and the klieg lights are erected before
our eyes; the scenes are called out by the actors, who are all part of Buffalo
Bill's multiracial troupe of travelling players. Here "There's No Business
Like Show Business" is not an incidental show-biz anthem sung by a trio in
the middle of a musical but the defining opening number, which rouses the
troupe to start staging Annie and Frank's saga.

"Berlin was making the book take hard left and right turns to accom-
modate the songs," Stone says. "If you're gonna do them again, you've got
to smooth that part out." The great ballad "They Say It's Wonderful"—a
conditional love song of the kind pioneered by Rodgers and Hammerstein
in numbers like "People Will Say We're In Love," to raise the issue of love
in the first act, before it was possible for the characters to actually be in
love—has been shifted almost to the end of Act I. "They weren't ready to
sing it yet," Stone says. Likewise, Berlin's score originally had Frank's
beautiful ballad "The Girl That I Marry" followed immediately after his exit
by Annie's famous "You Can't Get a Man with a Gun." "It was as if you just
suddenly turned the page and a page was missing," Stone says. "So what I
did was have her sing a chorus of what he has just sung, changing it to 'the
girl that he marries.' She sings this thing and *then* sees her gun. She comes
back to reality. She's been in a reverie. That is, she can dream about it, but
she isn't gonna get him. Because a girl with a gun doesn't get anybody."
Even the disputed "I'm an Indian Too" was unconvincingly positioned at
the end of Act I, just after Annie had been jilted by Frank Butler. "I would

have taken 'Indian' out even if it hadn't been racist," Stone says. "She can't be funny there. She's just lost her man."

The finale of the new "Annie Get Your Gun" is "Old Fashioned Wedding"— a song that, as it happens, originally sounded a musical finale of a different sort. Written in 1966, on the occasion of Ethel Merman's revival of the show at Lincoln Center (a sensational performance, which I saw), it was Berlin's last great flourish. It was also the final showstopping fling of the traditional musical, to which joy and idealism would soon become alien. With her clarion swagger and a voice that could pass as young even if the fifty-eight-year-old star could not, Merman sang:

> I wanna wedding surrounded by diamonds in platinum.
> A big reception at the Waldorf with champagne and caviar.
> I wanna wedding like the Vanderbilts have,
> Everything big, not small.
> If I can't have that kind of a wedding,
> I don't wanna get married at all.

The adamancy of "Old Fashioned Wedding" foreshadowed Berlin's own intransigence about the changes in musical fashion which came into being with the Vietnam War. The center of American life—and the American musical that mythologized it—was collapsing. "Count your blessings," Berlin counselled in song; but the society now nightly counted body bags. Inevitably, this disillusionment was registered in popular song, and there was some irony in Berlin's position. His music, as the critic Gilbert Seldes wrote, in "The Seven Lively Arts," had "torn to rags the sentimentality of the song which preceded it." He continued, "What makes the first rag period important was its intense gaiety, its naivete, its tireless curiosity about itself, its unconscious destruction of the old ballad form and the patter song." Sixty years later, it was Berlin who was being dispossessed. "You don't have to stop yourself," he said in a 1962 radio interview, about writing songs. "The people who have to listen to your songs tell you to stop." He told Robert Kimball, "It was time for me to close up shop."

Berlin's last public appearance was in 1973, when he sang "God Bless

America" at a White House dinner for returning P.O.W.s. Then, in keeping with his favorite family mottos—"Take it in your stride" and "Don't count on it"—Berlin retired his genius. He wrote songs now and then for private occasions but not for publication. From his town house in Beekman Place, he kept track—increasingly by phone—of his business interests and his friends: Harold Arlen; Stanley Adams, the head of ASCAP; the writer Ed Jablonski. Once, according to Jablonski's forthcoming biography of Berlin, a depressed Arlen, who had just turned seventy-two, and who usually wrote Berlin an annual birthday song, complained to his friend of having "shot his wad." Berlin, his eighty-eight years notwithstanding, wrote back:

> A nightingale looked up to God
> And said, "Dear God, I've shot my wad,
> No longer can I do my thing,
> Dear God, no longer can I sing."
> And he replied, "Don't be a schmuck,
> No nightingale has had such luck,
> Your songs have built a golden nest
> For Stanley Adams and the rest.
> They're praying for the moment when
> You get off your ass and sing again."

WALLACE SHAWN

THE DANGLING MAN

THE PLAYWRIGHT AND ACTOR
Wallace Shawn was eating soup not long ago in a coffee shop on the Upper
East Side, with his friend and early champion the novelist Renata Adler,
when a group of young women surrounded the table. "They spied us
through the window, obviously riveted by Wally. Then they came inside,"
Adler recalls. " 'Aren't you—Oh, my God! Weren't you in "The Princess
Bride"?' 'And "Clueless"?' another one said. 'I loved "Clueless." Wait till I
tell my sister!' " Shawn admits that he finds such attention "very, very
strange—even weird and disturbing." When I interviewed him recently,
he told me, "People sometimes literally define me, and even embrace me,
for something, in a certain way, that I don't think of as being the main
thing I do. They say, 'Hey! You're the guy who was in "The Princess Bride"!'
And quite frequently I might be walking down the street thinking, Who
the hell am I?"

Shawn made his film début in 1979 as a sight gag in Woody Allen's
"Manhattan," where he was cast as the partly bald homunculus who is cat-
nip to Diane Keaton, and since then he has appeared as a character actor
in forty-one movies, co-written one cult film, "My Dinner with André,"
and starred as the eponymous hero in another, "Vanya on 42nd Street." But
all this—and Shawn's charming, clownish public persona—has obscured
his larger talent as one of American theatre's finest prose stylists and most
subversive playwrights. Even the *International Who's Who 1995–96* lists
Shawn's "stage appearances"—"Aunt Dan and Lemon," "Marie and Bruce,"
and "The Fever"—without noting that Shawn in fact *wrote* those excellent
plays. Although Shawn's work has recently been the subject of a critical
study, "Writing Wrongs," by W. D. King, and his plays have been staged at
the most distinguished theatres in England and throughout Europe, he

admits, "My plays are not actually performed in my own land." He adds, "It's very, very hard for your arrow to hit the target here. I'm not that discussed. That's why I'm going to England."

Shawn's newest play, "The Designated Mourner," débuts in London at the Royal National Theatre on April 24th.* It is directed by David Hare and stars, among others, Mike Nichols, who has been lured back to the stage, where he first made his name, by what he calls the "strange combination of glamour and horror" with which Shawn writes about the present.

"The Designated Mourner" is a kind of ghost story. The narrator, Jack (played by Nichols), who once married into an élite literary coterie within which he was merely a hanger-on, survives an authoritarian clampdown after an uprising of the underprivileged. He finds that he is the only remaining witness to the otherwise extinct highbrow community. His famous writer father-in-law, Howard (David de Keyser), and his ex-wife, Judy (Miranda Richardson), are conjured up, along with the pleasures and the problems that follow when a "very special little world has died." In a series of exquisite crosscut monologues, there emerges a vivid picture of patrician sensibility and snobbery, and of the reprisals that Jack blithely refers to as "the disembowelling of the overbowelled." Jack asks the audience, "I mean, are you with me here? Am I going too fast?" and then describes the underclass: "We're talking about people who have no resources—none at all—no *money*, you could say. . . . They just *don't like* us. They don't like us." Jack and his listeners share that chilling moment in the evolution of mankind when "everyone on earth who could read John Donne was now dead," and Shawn charts Jack's downward trajectory from erstwhile highbrow to militant lowbrow. He has survived by the willed failure of his imagination: he consigns Donne to the trash heap and embraces his attackers' disdain for any kind of individual excellence. It's not just the past that's dead; it's Jack's soul. His search for comfort and for escape from the anger that envy inspires brings him and us, almost without realizing it, face to face with the death of culture.

In Shawn's work, the stage is stripped of most of its comforting dramaturgical devices—no plot, no set, no action—so the audience has nothing but the actor, the words, and its own moral compass to steer by. "My plays are really about the audience," he says. "The main character is you."

*In May 2000, four years after the National production, Shawn teamed up with André Gregory to do a radically different and equally powerful American stage version—set in the dilapidated top floors of a derelict men's club—in which Shawn himself played the main character.

His plays are a trap for consciousness and conscience. "I'm just too ambitious, really, to feel that it's enough to provide a little distraction for the few people who see my plays," says Shawn, who left college with "every intention of becoming a diplomat" who would "make some difference in the world." Shawn, himself the son of great privilege—his father was the late William Shawn, the renowned editor of *The New Yorker* from 1952 to 1987—is hard on his privileged audience. "I mean, the American upper class doesn't primarily need to be soothed and comforted," he explains, "although, like everybody else in the world, that's what they would like. That's not what *I* provide for them because I feel that they're too soothed and comforted already." "There's nothing more fun than scaring the shit out of an audience," Mike Nichols says. "And I think 'The Designated Mourner' really scares the shit out of an audience." The event has already generated a lot of excitement, and has all the markings of a theatrical breakthrough. "I decidedly lose my underdog status with this production," Shawn says. "It's being done in a way that anyone in the world would envy."

Being both an underdog and an object of envy is a contradiction that Shawn embodies in his person. "A human being happens to be an unprotected little wriggling creature," he writes in his one-man show, "The Fever." "A little raw creature without a shell or a hide or even any fur, just thrown out onto the earth like an eye that's been pulled from its socket, like a shucked oyster that's trying to crawl along the ground. We need to build our own shells." Shawn's whimsical public shell is rock solid. Although he claims not to understand stage sets, his droopy, comic silhouette provides a distracting backdrop for his own contradictory nature. He is at once arrogant and modest, inept and cunning, dithering and bold, selfless and ambitious, well mannered and radical, materialistic and spiritual. In his dark turtlenecks, his woodsy jackets, and his sensible rubber-soled shoes, Shawn is a kind of rumpled, walking Lands' End catalogue. He is small, about five feet four. He is bald, with distinctive patches of side hair, which in the early seventies gave him the air of a mad professor. He has a lisp, which slightly deflates his seriousness, and when he's intellectually treading water he punctuates a conversation with declarations ("Well, uh," "Gee," "That's . . . just . . . incredible") that in his mouth, onscreen and off, become a fetching comic decoy for his acid thoughts, like the trout fly that hides the fishhook. Shawn's often parodied voice is halting and high-pitched, conveying a reflective tentativeness. "The difficulty with saying 'I love you,' " he once said to the director André Gregory, "is that it presupposes that you know who 'I' is and that you know who 'you' is." (Even his answering machine won't promise a quick reply: "Unfortunately, your message may be answered only after a long interval.") But Shawn's round, pug-nosed, sweet face, which screws itself into various noncommittal moods of bafflement, is the final, risible touch. Shawn presents himself as the opposite of predatory. He disguises himself as a fumbling, somewhat timid schlub: not someone streamlined for the brightness of day but, rather, an almost invisible night creature, like a slow loris, which survives in the jungle by playing dead.

Shawn's prose, like his persona, hides its seriousness behind a kind of semantic shuffling that disarms and attacks at the same time. "My style as a human being is to indulge people who need to escape," he has said. "Yet I insist on confronting them as a playwright. It's quite embarrassing, it's quite unpleasant, it's quite awkward." Shawn has learned that in order to make people swallow the barb of insight, he and his characters have to play the worm. In "The Fever" Shawn compares himself to a water bug ("It's waiting, squatting, deciding which way to move"), and in "My Dinner with André" the Wally character recalls his life as a dog. "I was just treated, uh, in the nicest sense of the word, like a dog," he says of feeling invisible when he was starting out in New York, in the late sixties, as a Latin teacher at the Day School. "I mean, I literally lived like a dog. I mean, you know, I would be at a party where there would be all these great personalities, and the idea that I could participate in things in any way except to sort of pad through on all fours and sort of lick people's trousers was just inconceivable."

In real life, however, Shawn has had access to almost everyone. He could get the script of "My Dinner with André" to Louis Malle within days of its completion and have Malle accept it immediately; he could invoke Henry Kissinger in "Aunt Dan and Lemon" and then lunch with him at the Four Seasons to discuss it; he could imagine Mike Nichols' inflections while writing "The Designated Mourner" and then call up Nichols when it was completed and get him to read the play—at Richard Avedon's apartment, where Shawn and Gregory had sometimes gone to write their movie. Shawn has been plugged into this network of attainment throughout his life: his Kirkland House group at Harvard included the sons of the presidents of the American Bar Association and the Federal Reserve Bank; his sidekick at Oxford was the film director Terrence Malick; and his longtime companion is the distinguished short-story writer Deborah Eisenberg. This is not to undervalue Shawn's talent or his accomplishments but to put his work in the context of the spiritual contradictions it addresses—the battle he sees in the world between privilege and neglect. Shawn's plays are critiques of American individualism as observed from its airless empyrean.

Although Shawn claims to feel sometimes like "an aristocrat in the seventeenth century," he lives more like a peasant. He has no television. He has no computer. He has no fax machine or microwave. One of his frequent retreats is at an undisclosed address above a laundry somewhere outside the chic boundaries of Manhattan. "I don't believe in habits or routines. I try not to have them," he says, and what he does for most of his day is also his secret. "You can say," Shawn told me, "that even the people who know him best honestly don't know what the fuck he does all day long." This seems to be true. André Gregory, who has directed three of Shawn's plays and considers him "one of my closest friends in the world," isn't quite sure where Shawn works. "I think he has an office down in the Village somewhere," Gregory says. (Some of the actors from his "Vanya" company once followed Shawn in the subway to try to see where he worked.) "The truth is I move around a lot," Shawn, who is almost always lugging a large satchel, says. "There's a kind of wandering-minstrel thing going on." Shawn won't discuss his writing routine ("I think it's bad luck"), and characterizes much of his day-to-day activity as sort of molelike, "doing little things." He also spends as much time as possible travelling in poor countries, which he sees as a form of corrective behavior. "In the face of enormous suffering," he told me, "humorous detachment is too grotesque even for me." He spent his first year out of college in India, and has subsequently "hung out" in Mexico, Guatemala, Nicaragua, and El Salvador, and in Poland and

Czechoslovakia, before and after their revolutions.

Shawn lives the way he does for a reason: nothing about him betrays the privilege of his education, the almost occult power of his family's literary connections, or the tenacity of his ambition, all of which might call down upon him hostile, envious attack. "A lot of his behavior is display that precludes attack," Renata Adler says. In fact, Shawn, who admits he's actually "a very arrogant and vain person," preëmpts envy by constantly spoiling any picture of his own distinction. "Wally had this persona when he arrived at Harvard, at seventeen," says Jacob Brackman, a college friend who wrote for *The New Yorker* before becoming a screenwriter; his film "The King of Marvin Gardens" used Shawn as the model for its hero, Jason Stabler (Jack Nicholson), whom Brackman describes as "this little underground man who sort of saw everything and had it all nailed down but was keeping you at arm's length all the time." Brackman adds, "In many ways, Wally was like a little Mr. Shawn, who was the biggest fumbler in the world. Wally's fumbling was completely from his dad. He was very polite and very stylized: he was telling you that he's just a miserable little worm." In Shawn's career as a character actor, no single performance has been more enduring than his presentation of himself, a cunning role-reversal of fortune. "He looks like a born victim—a not very well-dressed victim," the *Guardian* wrote in 1982, referring to Shawn's sartorial eccentricity of wrapping himself up in his black-and-white Magdalen College scarf in May.

Shawn was wearing that signature scarf when I first met him, in the early seventies. He appeared at my doorstep in Manhattan (sent at the suggestion of André Gregory), and was bearing six of his plays, entitled, unceremoniously, one through six. "I want you to read these," Shawn said. "But I don't want to know what you think." The gambit was typical of how Shawn wrong-foots life: a combination of frankness and imperiousness, dished up with po'-faced innocence. I recognized instantly that his modesty was the cover for an adamantine will; I sensed the familiar combination of power and panic which is the birthmark of a famous pedigree. We were both sons of cultural royalty: his father was a king of high culture, mine of low culture. We'd both lived on Manhattan's Upper East Side, attended Ivy League colleges, done postgraduate work at Oxford, gone into theatre. (The karma continued into adulthood when, in 1987, Wally played a jokey version of me in the film of my biography of Joe Orton, "Prick Up Your Ears.") The world we grew up in was a wonderful but worrying place, because there seemed to be no loss in it. We were equipped for pleasure but not for life. In "The Fever" Shawn describes our kind of cosseted childhood: "My friends and I were the delicate, precious, breakable children, and we always knew it. We knew it because of the way we were wrapped—because of the soft underwear laid out on our beds, soft socks to protect our feet." Part of this atmosphere was what Shawn calls "the unique element to what each of our fathers did," which increased the sense of separation from others and lent an undiscussable yet unswerving conviction that went well beyond the word "entitlement."

"I grew up expecting great things of myself," Shawn says, and the awed eyes of the world reflected his manifest destiny back to him. "From day one, the teachers at school expected great accomplishment and were interested." The fact that he was William Shawn's son was "a little bit of glamour in their day—it attracted them." He adds, "I didn't realize why they were grovelling at my feet, and it made me a very self-confident person until the age of forty, when I sort of figured it out—when I had a bit of a crisis of confidence." Shawn refers to the blessings of his life as "the voluptuous field that was given to me." He and his younger brother, the composer Allen Shawn, performed musical puppet shows and sketches, as many kids do for family friends, but in his family the shows were about Horace, the dynastic decline of China, "Paradise Lost," and Wittgenstein, and the friends were people like Naomi Bliven, Philip Hamburger, Whitney Balliett, and Janet Flanner. (These and other assorted literati would turn up at the family's occasional buffet suppers.) He went to the Dalton School, where in fifth grade he wrote and performed in a play about the death of Socrates. He played Socrates. ("It was a philosophical play, not that different from the plays I have written subsequently," Shawn says.) At school, he vied with Chevy Chase for the title of class clown. Chase was then, as he is now, a noisy entrepreneur of slapstick, while Shawn, who was reading "Ulysses" at fifteen in order to discuss James Joyce with the writer Joseph Mitchell, radiated a kind of lèse-majesté. He expounded on the uselessness of literature and tried to coax his classmates into not doing their Latin homework. In his own adolescent eyes, he had already become a kind of dandy of detachment.

"*The New Yorker* was not really like Eustace Tilley looking at the butterfly through a monocle," Shawn says. "But in some ways the son of *The New Yorker* is like that." He continues, "I have a certain coolness, which maybe someone who didn't like me would call coldness. A certain detachment. I'm not always totally in the moment. There's usually a certain amount of observing going on on my part. It's a habit I formed early. A teacher in high school said to me, 'You know, Wally, people were not actually put on the earth just to amuse you.' " Shawn, who bears a physical resemblance to his father, also acquired his father's byzantine quality of containment, and, from the beginning, theatre offered release from his self-consciousness. "When I was twelve, I saw 'The Iceman Cometh,' " says Shawn, who by thirteen had read the Random House collection of nine O'Neill plays. "My parents would have died rather than see 'The Iceman Cometh,' but Bruce and Naomi Bliven took me to see it. It had an overwhelming influence on me." The next year, he saw "Long Day's Journey Into Night" twice. "I remember the intensity of watching and doing plays, the intense seriousness contrasted to the shallow life of being a twelve-year-old with somewhat silly preoccupations," he says. "My life was placid on the surface. Somehow, when I encountered Eugene O'Neill I immediately thought, Yes, this man is really telling the truth. I had that double identity that I still have today. Some people think of me as a clown, but my natural bent is to deal with heavier issues of life and death, torment and tragedy."

The dissimulation in Shawn's persona and his interest in thinking against his privilege are ways of shouldering the weight of his regal birthright. "Well, I mean, it is defensive, but what can we do?" he said to me. "I can't wipe the stain of all that off me. I was treated like a little prince. I mean, that goes very deep. I was raised with the absolute understanding that I was a very special little being. A little king." Shawn mythologized the contradiction neatly in the opening speech of "My Dinner with André," where the down-at-heels version of Wally "trudges" uptown to eat with André, the glamorous experimental stage director. "When I was ten years old, I was rich," Wally's voice-over says. "I was an aristocrat, riding around in taxis, surrounded by comfort, and all I thought about was art and music. Now I'm thirty-six, and all I think about is money."

The joke is typical of the game of three-card monte that Shawn plays with his background. It's true that life as a playwright proved a far greater struggle for Shawn than he had first imagined. "My expectation was always that I would be immediately received and immediately respected," he says. But Shawn was reinventing the theatre to suit his own idiosyncratic attitudes and abilities. During his time at Oxford, he entered a playwriting competition. He didn't win, but he was hooked. In New York, a number of his Harvard classmates—Brackman, Hendrik Hertzberg, Tony Hiss, George Trow, and Jonathan Schell—were being brought onto *The New Yorker* as staff writers. Schell, in fact (in what must have been a complicated Oedipal drama for Wally, since Schell had been his roommate at both Putney and Harvard), was being groomed by Mr. Shawn as his successor. But while Wally's friends were becoming hot literary items in the big shop-window of the magazine, he was supporting his playwriting habit with a series of improbable jobs: shipping clerk, Xerox-machine operator, garment-district porter. "I thought that was cruel," Philip Hamburger says of Mr. Shawn's nonemployment of his son. "It didn't strike me as displaying the sublime sensitivity that Shawn was supposed to possess." Now the younger Shawn makes a show of sweet reasonableness about his exclusion from the halls of literary power. "If you want to be a writer, it's dangerous to have a job," he says. "My own father was an example. He wanted to be a writer. He ended up getting a job, and his life followed the direction of the job." Back then, Wally was forced to follow his own quirky, unconventional path. He told me he'd "sold stock in himself"—his way of rationalizing a twenty-five-hundred-dollar loan he took from a consortium of friends in the sixties, in order to go off and write his plays. (To this day, the investors receive a small yearly check.)

He spent months watching rehearsals of the Manhattan Project in order to write a modern version of "Peer Gynt" (which he ended up abandoning), and then delivered a cauterizing satire about a seventies cocktail party, called "Our Late Night" (1972). This was his professional début—a wild, foulmouthed foreshadowing of the yuppie free-for-all of the eighties, in which the actors explore, in graphic terms, the sexual facts of their inner lives. It was produced at the Public Theatre in 1975, and even Joseph

Papp, never fulsome about his employees, noted, "Wally is a very rare species. He is a dangerous writer." Gregory, who directed the play, recalls, "The dance critic John Gruen came to a preview and said it was the most dangerous night in the theatre since the opening of Nijinsky's 'L'Après-Midi d'un Faune.' Somebody tried to hit an actor. People would scream 'Shut up!' and 'Stop it!' It was very scary in the audience. I think what they were offended by was their own shadow—that Wally was seeing something under the surface of Americans."

Shawn certainly didn't foresee the row that erupted in the House of Lords when "A Thought in Three Parts" (1975)—three short plays that focussed on aspects of sexuality, including masturbation—was produced in London, by Max Stafford-Clark and the Joint Stock Company. Lord Nugent of Guilford, quoting from a *Daily Telegraph* review that called the play "as likely to give offence as anything I have ever seen in the theatre," called on the Government to "protect the public against this sort of pollution"; the Attorney General considered prosecution for obscenity; the Charity Commissioners threatened an investigation of Joint Stock's grant; tabloids were inundated with mail from the left and the right; and for a tense forty-eight hours Shawn actually feared deportation. In 1985, at the Royal Court in London, the début production of "Aunt Dan and Lemon," which explores Shawn's contention that "a perfectly decent person can turn into a monster perfectly easily" and, incidentally, foresaw the resurgence of anti-Semitism in the nineties, was booed and heckled by some members of the opening-night audience, who mistook the false logic of Lemon's proto-Nazi conclusions for Shawn's own.

"My characters are much wilder than me," Shawn told the *Times* in 1980. "I'm really a buttoned-up little creep." He explained to me, "I don't know a hell of a lot about real life, to put it mildly. That isn't my strong suit, a knowledge of life. Obviously, my weak point in school was sports. I was brought up in that Jewish tradition where the man is a reader of books and does nothing physical. B. H. Barry will never have a job choreographing a fight in one of my plays. If I think, What do I actually understand, appreciate, and know how to deal with?, it would probably be sitting in a chair and talking. I do have some grasp of that."

Shawn expressed this reflective side of himself—and courted a new kind of attack—in his last production, "The Fever," which he has described as "some kind of human exhortation which is meant to arouse thought and action, not appreciation or enjoyment." (It was his father's favorite of his plays.) In 1990, he performed the show in the homes of friends, turning himself into a kind of Marxist Ancient Mariner, and putting his cultural guilt and his despairing sense of self literally under the audience's nose. "There was a certain point in my life—in my early forties—where an awareness of my own position in the world created a kind of permanent unease and pain," Shawn told me. In the monologue, the Wally character describes shivering and vomiting in a tropical hotel bathroom as he meditates on the contradictions of the killing fields outside his window and his own deluxe life, and on the sin of separation, which ensures the poor's perpetual enslavement. "The Fever," Shawn says, was a way, in the form of a play, of "trying to speak to people and to say something I genuinely believed about myself, them, and the world that we actually live in." Shawn's home delivery was a way of "taking it off the cultural menu of entertainment" and of keeping the play from being turned into an art object. (I saw an exhilarating performance of it in his London hotel room.) When Shawn finally did put the play on the stage, at various New York venues, in late 1990 and 1991, he dispensed with the paraphernalia of commercial theatre in his most minimalist setup to date: no program, no dressing room, no costume, no curtain call. In Europe, "The Fever" was respectfully received; in New York, it was mugged. "A musty radical chic stunt destined to be parodied," Frank Rich wrote in the *Times*, and, without discussing the issues raised in Shawn's spiritual quandary, he swatted it away with such ferocity that the play—and the chance of Shawn's ideas' having wider debate—was stopped dead. In Germany he received more than twenty-five productions; in America there was just a handful. "I was absolutely sort of destroyed by his review," Shawn told me, in his bob-and-weave manner.

Now, five years later, Shawn's vision of the havoc of injustice has been reimagined in a more ambiguous, more oblique story. "And the poor, don't forget," he wrote in "The Fever." "They live on their rage. They eat rage. They want to rise up and finish us, wipe us off the earth as soon as they can." In "The Designated Mourner," a repressive state has arisen to prevent them from doing just that. The play brings together in one metaphor the fear of envious attack and the appeasing defensive maneuvers around which Shawn's whole social persona is organized: it is Shawn's "A Modest Proposal." Through Jack, he is demonstrating the systematic devaluation of the self in modern life as an adaptation to envy, which finally leads to the dumbing of society.

Jack is a projection of Shawn's fears—what he has no wish to be but what he sees our distracted society becoming. "As long as I preserve my loyalty to my childhood training, I will never know what it is to be truly comfortable," Shawn has written of growing up in the moral climate of a liberal household. "I feel a fantastic need to tear that training out of my heart once and for all so that I can finally begin to enjoy the life that is spread out before me like a feast." Shawn can't, which is his struggle and his peculiar genius. He lives with the contradiction of his continuous unease. "What is my role on the planet?" he says. "Is it just to consume and be a parasite and a happy hedonist?" At one point in "The Fever," he contemplates divesting himself of everything and resolving the dilemma of what he calls "being an overdog from the point of view of class analysis." He writes, "I could perfectly well put an end to the whole elaborate performance. If people are starving, give them food. If I have more than others, share what I have until I have no more than they do. Live simply. Give up everything. Become poor myself."

The flip side of Shawn's impulse toward abdication is Jack's self-abnegation. Instead of becoming poor, Jack impoverishes his own nature. Shawn wants to shrink the separation between himself and others—that distance which American individualism makes glorious. Jack just wants to shrink. Referring to John Donne at the finale, Jack says, "The rememberers were gone, and I was forgetting: forgetting his name, forgetting him, and forgetting all the ones who remembered him."

Shawn is alone among American playwrights in challenging the prestige of individualism. "A good deal of what Jack says about the self, I agree with," Shawn says, and adds that he finds the obsession with "the character called 'I' completely ludicrous." Certainly Jack has good sport with the notion of "I"—"this strange little thing that everyone has, this odd, tiny organ which the surgeons can't touch"—and with his own inner dialogue, his "idiotic arpeggios of self-approbation." Shawn steers the character not toward selflessness but toward emptiness, which brings a new, barbarous sense of power. In his so-called "Experiments in Privacy," Jack records episodes of shitting on books and pissing on poetry; he binges on television, tabloids, and pornography, and practices mindlessness. "Perhaps I could learn how to pass more easily from one moment to the next, the way the monkey, our ancestor, shifts so easily along from branch to branch as he follows the high road through the forest at night," Jack says, willing himself *down* the evolutionary ladder. "Let me learn how to repose in the quiet shade of a nice square of chocolate, a nice slice of cake."

In Shawn's unblinking prophecy, civilization dies not with a bang or a whimper but with a sneer and a sigh of pleasure. Shawn has survived his parents and his pedigree but not his guilt at upper-class comfort. "We need solace, we need consolation, we need nice food, we need nice things to wear, we need beautiful paintings, movies, plays, drives in the country, bottles of wine," he writes in "The Fever." "There's never *enough* solace, never *enough* consolation." His is a battle of conscience and contradiction in which there is no truce. "I know what I'm taking out of the world," Shawn told me. "What am I putting back? Am I putting something back in that is of value? I wouldn't be the one who knows."

EDDIE IZZARD

THE IZZARD KING

O<small>N AN UNSEASONABLY</small>
warm February afternoon in Toronto, the British comedian Eddie Izzard,
dressed in a blue Lycra "rave shirt," took out a Psion organizer from his
backpack, pecked at the keyboard with a finger whose nail was haphaz-
ardly varnished a deep purple, and scrolled through some comic notions
that over the next few months will probably find themselves worked into
the crazy flow of his new act:

- The Grim Reaper has been around since the dawn of
time. Scythes however were only invented after the Iron Age.
Before that did the Grim Reaper just have a club? A Grim
Clubber?
- Talk about bees and their wily ways / Do speech as an
Australian who thinks he's President of Austria because he's
dyslexic.
- What's the point of being in the Merchant Navy? Lots of
discipline and no guns or fancy uniform. Typical thing they
must say would be, "I want to take potatoes to dangerous
places."

Izzard was in Toronto on the second stop of his "Dress to Kill" tour,
which would go on to the U.S. Comedy Arts Festival in Aspen and then to
New York's Westbeth Theatre Center, where it's now playing. At thirty-six,
he is something of a cult figure in England, and is the first comedy act to
make the difficult passage across the Atlantic since Dudley Moore and
Peter Cook achieved it, in the early seventies. But Izzard, who has a mop
of highlighted blond hair and a short, stocky body, considers himself "a

very lazy person with huge drive," which is why he fakes himself out by doing so many comedy gigs, West End acting assignments (the world pre-mière of David Mamet's "The Cryptogram," Marlowe's "Edward II"), and now screen roles (this year, he can be seen playing opposite Sean Connery in "The Avengers"). He says, "Even my standup is designed for the laziest way of doing standup. I don't write it. I just go on stage and go." For him, it's an out-of-mind experience. "My mouth and my mind are not in con-trol of me," he says. "I'm not driving; I just let go." In "Dress to Kill," his nonsense manages to touch on the space program, James I, the Gunpowder Plot, established versus pagan religions, sci-fi movies, astron-omy, anthropology, and computers, to name but a few topics. Izzard's imaginative high-wire act, a kind of standup equivalent of skydiving ("It feels like flying around in the air, just swooping and diving, being on top of it"), is tense, and games are more fun when they are tense. To the Monty Python veteran John Cleese, who has called Izzard "the funniest man in England," the prospect of performing this kind of theatrical free fall "is more or less like being taken away by the Gestapo into a dark room."

Izzard, for his part, grew up listening to the Pythons and has commit-ted many of their routines to memory; he and a friend used to recite vari-ations of the "Four Yorkshiremen" sketch, to pass the dead time in chem-istry class. ("We never had a house. We lived in one corridor." "Oh, we used to dream of a corridor. We lived in a shoebox in the middle of the road.") But, unlike the Pythons, who went from university into theatre and television, he is a college dropout who got his comedy experience as a street performer, and became a masterly purveyor of what in the trade is called "comedy bollocks"—or, as he explains his particular brand, "take highbrow stuff, well researched, then talk shit about it." In his busking days (he worked as part of a double act in London for about four years before briefly going solo on the street, in 1987), he "learned to be able to talk and talk and talk and just not stop." He ad-libbed to audiences as he performed a water-evaporation trick, escaped from a woolly jumper while hand-cuffed and riding a unicycle, and engaged in heavy-duty sword fighting. ("Our deaths for your entertainment" was the shill.) Izzard still improvis-es and expands his comedy material with his public. When an idea regis-ters—he calls this "hitting funny"—he makes a mental note and adjusts the moment when he relives it the next night. No contemporary comedian is more adroit at calling the audience into play—something he learned to do in those early street days, when he had to work hard to "get an audience together." He used to set out a series of tea cozies in the shape of various animals. "They were very visual. People would look at them and think something was going to happen to them," he says. "I'd take ages to put them out. I wouldn't do anything with them, except this one thing where I'd say, 'This is a boomerang hippopotamus. Wherever I throw it, it will come back.' " He would then throw the hippo tea cozy outside the ring of spectators. "I'd repeat, 'Wherever I throw it, the hippopotamus always comes back,' " he says. "By this time, somebody got the hang of it and chucked it back. 'I told you it always comes back!' I could always get it through to people." He adds, "If they play with me, it makes it work, and everyone's happy."

Izzard does not tell gags; he does not have a written "routine"; he rarely invades his own privacy for material; he does not attack the audience, or, conversely, try to "dig it up," as comedians say ("Who here is from. . . ?"). "I just want to fuck around, take the audience one way, then back up on it," he says, likening the madcap mosaic of mind which he delivers to channel surfing. In "Dress to Kill," for instance, he goes into a riff about the stiffness of British movies between the thirties and the fifties ("Darling, I'm off to the war." "Oh, don't go, darling, it's so noisy") and observes that all the regional characters and even the working classes seem to speak in the Received Pronunciation of the upper orders. ("I must go, darling," he says in plummy tones. "It's my duty as a Cockney man. As a man of Cockney persuasion. I was born within five inches of Bow Bells. Ding dong, ding dong.") And that leads him to an imitation of Dick Van Dyke's mangled Cockney in "Mary Poppins." "He's dead, you know," Izzard says about Van Dyke, bursting the bubble of laughter. Then he shakes his head. "No, he's not." He pauses and continues, "He is. . . No. . . He is. . . No." At each volte-face, which he delivers with either a dour shake of the head or a smile, the audience's energy switches back and forth between worry and delight.

Izzard has about him the whiff of comic greatness but none of the presenting symptoms of most inspired funnymen. He is not morose, or aggressive, or chronically insecure. "He's always been a good bloke," says the director Stephen Daldry, who was directing plays at Sheffield University when Izzard, after being kicked out of his first-year accounting course, was hanging around the Student Union and developing such alternative epics as "Fringe Flung Lunch," "Sherlock Holmes Sings Country," and "World War II: The Sequel," which he ultimately took to the Edinburgh Festival. Daldry adds, "There's never been any edge to him."

But there is one thing that sets Izzard apart. He is a transvestite. He sees himself not as "trapped" in a man's body but as a male lesbian, "happily cohabiting." He's not polemical about it. "I'm not saying anyone else needs to do this," he explains. "I'm just saying this is me. If you don't like it you can piss off, 'cause this is my life." In the opening minutes of "Dress to Kill," he laughs the issue off the stage. "I'm a male transvestite, and I fancy women," he says. "I don't know why. I'm open for fancying men, but I can't get my head around that. Which makes me think it's a genetic thing. No particular choice there." He goes on, "So, male tomboy. . . That's really where I am. Running. Jumping. Climbing trees. Then putting on makeup when I was up there."

When Izzard is offstage, during the day, only his painted nails signal his bias; at night, his eyeliner, makeup foundation, and lipstick hardly draw attention to him as he strides out of the hotel in civilian clothes toward the Harbourfront Centre, where he's playing. Onstage, however, his costume is a glamorous Jean-Paul Gaultier "mandarin smock," black polyvinyl pants, and leather boots with blocky two-inch-high heels, which give him a kind of streamlined, raffish, almost Restoration look. "I've got this whole thing that in fact there are no transvestites," he says, seated in full regalia in the drab dressing room. "If women aren't transvestite when they wear all of men's clothes—flat shoes, men's jackets, no makeup, short hair— well, there's no bloody line." He adds, "They can have the option. Now I have the option. I have carved that for myself. I consider myself my own role model."

Izzard, who lives in a semi-detached Notting Hill Gate house, where he socializes with a wide range of female and male friends, has been aware of his predilection for women's clothes since the age of five. (He describes his two biggest passions as "soccer and makeup.") His father, John, says, "I remember his mother telling me Eddie dressed up in her clothes as a small child. It didn't worry either of us." He adds, "You didn't do the discipline bit with Eddie. He had to be far more gently handled than his brother." At fifteen, Izzard was caught stealing lipstick; he claimed that it was for a French girlfriend. He didn't come out as a transvestite until he was twenty-three. "It scared the shit out of me," he says. "Way off the scale. I kept thinking, Why am I doing this? What is driving it? I had to lie in darkened rooms with the curtains closed and spend time getting into my head where my head didn't want to go. Your mind builds up brick walls. And I had to tear them down."

Around 1985, he joined a transvestite-transsexual support group in Islington. At first, when he was trying to pass for a woman, he took the name Susan, and studied female mannerisms and walks. But Izzard's looks were "too blokey"; after a while, he asked the group to stop calling him Susan. "I thought, No, I'm Eddie. I'm gonna be Eddie. I'm just gonna go out and be me."

His "boyish-girlish" tomboy look gradually evolved, and he learned to challenge the eyes of others with calmness. He has often recounted an incident "where I had one guy trying to beat me up and another trying to get my autograph. One was yelling, 'You gay twat!' and his friend was saying, 'Wow! You're Eddie Izzard.' And I'm saying, 'No, I'm not a gay twat. I'm a transvestite. Get your slander correct.' "

"All I've got to do is to exist in a brave way," Izzard says, and his comedy allows him to accomplish this elegantly. In fact, even though he has a few jokes about it, his otherness is quite forgotten within minutes of his taking the stage. Like the camouflage of a species that has successfully adapted to its environment, Izzard's look blends imperceptibly with his laughter.

Izzard doesn't come onstage as if shot from a gun. He sort of shambles out, pitched slightly forward in his high-heeled boots, with his blue eyes shining and his shoulders in a sailor's nonchalant roll. He once began his act by making strange guttural sounds, and he still does a lot of preliminary "uhm"ing and "ah"ing, a technique his fellow-comedians call "Eddying." He stands slightly pigeon-toed, bending a bit at the knees—a loosey-goosey correlative for the millennial confusions about mind and body.

On the night I saw the Toronto show, Izzard was cooking. He was acting out his meditation on the discovery of random dinosaur bones ("How were these dinosaurs dying? Were they going 'I'm near death. I'll be leaving an arm over there. A jawbone over there. My bum in a hedge-ha-ha, that'll fuck off the paleontologists'?") when a statuesque young woman walked slowly down the aisle and came to the lip of the stage while he was in full swing. She held out a beer and a pint glass. "I got you a beer," she said.

"You got me a beer?"

"You looked thirsty." She poured the beer out slowly.

"There's a thing called timing," Izzard said. By now the auditorium was roaring.

"You can drink it later." She pushed the beer toward him.

"All right. All right," he said, moving the beer upstage. "Thank you." He turned back to the audience. "You don't get that in Shakespeare, do you? Alas, poor Yorick. I knew him, Horatio. We, uh, we had a beer together." Then, pivoting from one side of the stage to the other, Izzard started to dispute himself. "'You never fucking knew me.' 'I did!' " Somebody called out for him to drink the beer. "Not now," he said. "Not now. Later I can drink a beer."

"Go ahead," a woman called up from the first row.

"Well, no, it's not a beer show: 'Eddie Izzard Drinks a Beer.' "

"It's Canada! Enjoy it!" the woman shouted. Izzard demurred.

"Then pass it over here," she said. Izzard brought the beer center stage. "You have to come and get it if you want it," he said, shifting down to a sexy register. "If you're brave enough to come up here."

On occasions when he is interrupted and has to talk to an audience, his brain, he says, is "almost like a split screen," on which he can play and "work things out at the same time." Once, at the opening of his show "Definite Article," in London, a button of his jacket popped off. Someone threw a sewing kit on the stage, and Izzard, talking all the while, threaded a needle and sewed on the button. "If I'd failed to sew it on, that would have been seen as a real psychological failure," he explains. "I thought, As long as I sew it on, I'm fine, I can't really lose. I needed to keep the energy going." On this night, with the beer as with the button, Izzard, feeling the imperative of the audience's collective will, picked up the glass and chugged down the beer in one gulp.

Izzard's special way of playing is, he says, "a childlike thing that I locked in after six, which is when my mother died and which I wanted to keep hold of." He adds, "There's a kid there that comes in and plays onstage." His company, Ella Communications, is named after Dorothy Ella Izzard, who died of cancer at the age of forty-one. (Izzard was born in Yemen; the family was relocated to Bangor, in Northern Ireland; and after Dorothy's death her husband, who was an accountant for British Petroleum and rose to be chief auditor, settled at Bexhill-on-Sea.) Izzard has very few clear memories of his mother, who was a nurse and midwife and was devoted to Eddie and his older brother. "She was very understanding. I remember I would demand glasses of water and cups of milky coffee in the middle of the night. She'd get up and make them," he says. "She was great, and I didn't want her to go away." In fact, Izzard didn't know that his mother was dying. "I just thought she was ill and would get better," he says. "Then you come home one day, and she isn't there, and you don't see her ever again." Izzard's transvestism is a way of keeping his mother in mind. According to Stephen Grosz, an American psychoanalyst living in England, who has worked with transvestites, "There's an underlying belief that the mother has everything; and so by becoming the mother you've then lost all need, all want." Izzard stands before an audience as both man and woman, father and mother. As he jokes, "I'd be the perfect one-parent family."

But in reality the death of his mother virtually shattered the family: the boys were sent away to a series of boarding schools. The first school, St. John's, was in Porthcawl, Wales. "It had caning and no sweets," says Izzard, who sang "Jingle Bells" to himself to go to sleep at night. "I found chewing gum in a hedge and cleaned it up and ate that." He adds, "It was a lot of crying." At boarding school, he says, "I learned to close down emotionally." Later, as a teen-ager, when he discovered he could chip in funny words to complete his chemistry teacher's slow sentences ("My hit rate was one in five"), he found a way to banish gravity; he also found a public ("I became popular"). He says, "I think it links up with Mum. She suddenly disappeared. All this big-hearted affection disappears. It's an affection-replacement thing."

Izzard, who was sixteen when he decided to become a performer, thinks that performing for love is a good trade-off. "You do have to give. You can't just stand there and they give it to you," he says. "You go out and you perform your heart out." There is a kind of fierceness in his focus on an audience. "They gotta commit, big time," he says, choosing his verb carefully. "Or just bugger off." The primary appeal of his act is "to make myself laugh," he says. "The second one is to make them laugh." Izzard's laughter engineers a kind of emotional equipoise in him—it's about having all the information and yet not really knowing anything. His humor, he explains, "is informed but not informed." He's aware that in life, as he puts it, "shit happens. There is no answer." This is reflected in his act, where history begins in earnest and ends in fiasco: "Easter. There's a ceremony. It's got a pagan ceremony just sitting underneath it. Easter. Tough time for Jesus. Not a happy lad. All the disciples there saying, 'He's dead. Our leader is dead. How will we remember this day?'. . . 'Well, uh, I was thinking chocolate eggs. That could work.' 'Wrapped up in crinkly paper?' 'Yes, and you can put more chocolate inside when you open it up. A second amount of chocolate is inside!' 'Very good, Zebedee.' (One of them's called Zebedee.) 'Yes, that's it! And a bunny rabbit shall give it out. A bunny rabbit! With big ears, for the bunny rabbit will be the symbol. For when the ears are down and out, it is a cross.'"

A gentle snow was falling when I rolled into Aspen around dusk, a week after Izzard's Toronto gig. The town was full of city folks who were spending the week listening to comedians and honoring the giants of the craft, including Larry Gelbart, the cast of "Cheers," and the cast of "Monty Python's Flying Circus," whom HBO had flown over to be reunited on stage for the first time in almost two decades, in a show taped at the Wheeler Opera House, a local Victorian theatre. At night, the silence of the mountain world and the snow-silted frontier storefronts that had been turned into designer boutiques gave the place a dreamy sense of unreality. Izzard, who had spent most of the day snow-boarding and had banged his head, also seemed a bit dazed, but not from his fall. Almost the first words out of his mouth were "I've just been asked to do something at the top of the Python show. I can't believe it. I'm talking to Michael Palin about the Huguenots. I'm going with Palin and Terry Jones and Eric Idle to Steve Martin's one-act plays. I can't really take it in."

He was at the Python rehearsal promptly at two-forty-five the next afternoon, his backpack crammed with ski clothes for a gag that the Pythons were cooking up. The Flying Circus team, including the pony-tailed Terry Gilliam (the American cartoonist who has since become a director) and a mock urn containing the "ashes" of the late funnyman Graham Chapman, were already up onstage and seated in a row of lounge chairs like so many smiling trophies. A scrum of TV technicians, talking continually into headsets, surrounded the troupe, who kept up a show of professional jollity while lights and furniture were being adjusted around them. Izzard was standing in the aisle admiring the spectacle when a func-tionary came up to him and told him he'd just won the festival's Amstel Light jury prize for best one-person show. Izzard turned the moment into a little comedy. ("I've never won anything, really," he lied. "I'm casually bitter about it, but in a very relaxed way.") Then, tentatively, he joined the hubbub, moving across the stage to the far right, where John Cleese, the grandee of the group, was sitting and inhaling oxygen as an antidote to the thin Colorado air. At the sight of Izzard, Cleese put down his mask, hauled his famously gangly six-foot-five torso to its feet, and sort of beckoned Eddie into his outstretched arms. On royal occasions, such moments of conferring honor are called "elevation," but the embrace of the Old Turk and the Young Turk seemed to confirm the Pythons as much in their power as it did Izzard in his. "They've decided to give me an award for being British," Izzard told Cleese, who laughed. "You've got one for being British, too."

"Eddie, I'm English, in case you hadn't noticed."

"Well, I'm Yemenese, really."

"A Yemeni comic. I'd forgotten that."

Cleese quickly got down to business, suggesting that Izzard come onstage as an impostor at the opening of their segment—that he insinuate himself among the Pythons and start answering out of turn when the interviewer, the comedian Robert Klein, began questioning them. "We come on without you the first time. There's one too few chairs. We then go off, and then come back on slightly chaotically. You should come on at that point. In-ski up, you see what I mean. With your own chair. You should put it down and sit there. After we begin, you answer. Make up any fucking rubbish you like. Then we come over and unmask you and tell you to piss off. We'd like you to go down the stairs there." Cleese pointed to the carpeted red stairs that led into the auditorium and down the aisle.

Once the issue of Izzard's costume was resolved—"We had a bad idea," Cleese admitted, after everyone agreed that to put Izzard in ski clothes would give away the gag too early—they got down to just what Izzard would say when Klein opened the discussion by asking the Pythons how the group first met. "I'll just take it," Izzard said. " 'I met John on a train and Michael was the ticket-taker. Terry was doing a train robbery down the other end with Eric.' " Cleese wheezed with laughter and took another slug of oxygen.

The Pythons and Izzard were ordered into the wings to practice their entrance. The crepuscular gloom seemed to liberate a bit of boyish excitement in the cluster of Merry-Andrews. "So I'll be the nutter fan who's trying to break in," Izzard said. "I'll just try walking in behind everybody." Cleese was telling Gilliam to go on first, and Palin was dibbing last. "I've gotta work out a Last-Going-On Performance. Get a laugh early," he said. Jones giggled. Gilliam groused. Idle mumbled to no one in particular, "This is an improv. This is a Python improv."

After deciding on their entrance, they practiced Izzard's exit. "We'll let you go on a bit longer," Jones said.

"If I get into it," Izzard said.

"We'll play it off the audience," Cleese called out as Izzard started to improvise the "Four Yorkshiremen." The Pythons stood watching Izzard carry on, their eyes as bright with delight as his. Afterward, he slumped back into a chair between Gilliam and Cleese. "Not exactly what I thought I'd be doing yesterday morning," he said to Cleese. "Being in Aspen. Being with you guys. Doing this." As he left the rehearsal, he said, "If I get too overawed, I'm fucked. I've just got to go on like I was at college again. And they were at college. And fuck about."

On the night, Izzard showed no sign of nerves. He strolled from dressing room to dressing room chatting up his idols before showtime. When Izzard was a student at Sheffield, he had once interviewed Palin for the university paper; now he and Palin were standing in the corridor talking about how you handle hecklers. " 'Say something funny' or 'Boring' are the two worst ones that you can get," Izzard said. " 'You're a cunt' is fine." He expounded on his street technique of "positivizing" negative situations: "If someone says, 'You cunt bastard,' you say, 'Absolutely. I'm king of cunts. I am the absolute cunt of all time. I was trying to be a cunt bastard and you noticed it.' You embrace it and take it to you; and you repeat it over and over again until you sort of take it away from being a problem. You've made it part of your space."

As they waited to go on, Izzard stood with Palin, Jones, and Gilliam, watching a television monitor of a clip of Palin with Connie Booth, singing "The Lumberjack Song"—an old Python macho sendup, where the lumberjack wants to be a transvestite. "I've always thought I should do that song and spin it around," Izzard said. " 'I'm a transvestite but I want to be a lumberjack.' "

On the TV screen, Izzard's moment was well handled but brief. He managed to raise his quota of laughs and, in the process, to get pelted on the shoulder by Terry Gilliam with a well-thrown bread roll. But Izzard really hit funny that night in his own show, talking about the singer Engelbert Humperdinck. "How did he get his name? Were they all sitting in an office saying, 'Look, we're going to call you Bingelbert Hempledonk.' 'What about Binglebert Humperdonk?' 'I was thinking Geldebert Hingledunk.' 'Nah.' 'What about Hinglebert Enkledonk.' 'I've got a list—Geldebert Hingledunk. Hinglebert Enkledonk. Or Engelbert Humperdinck.' 'That's it!' "

In his dressing room later, Izzard mulled over the joke. "My instincts tell me that I need to play more on things around 'Engelbert.' I need to go 'Senglebert Bunderkink or Dinglebert Dingadonk. Engelbert Humperdinck. That's the one!'" he said. "I'm not quite sure I know. When it comes out of my mouth, I'll know, I'll feel it's right."

The next time I saw Izzard was on the small stage of the Westbeth Theatre, in New York. He was talking about Guy Fawkes and how he was "hung, drawn, and quartered." At the word "hung," Izzard tilted his neck and mimed a noose around it. At "drawn," he stepped back and pretended to sketch Fawkes.

"No, that's not it," a man shouted from the audience.

Izzard's eyes twinkled as he peered into the murky room. "Have you only just worked out that that's the first lie I've told you all night?" he said. "As it happens, there's a constant lying that goes on through the whole show." Instinctively, Izzard did a little of his "positivizing." He put his hands on his hips and rolled his eyes to the ceiling, imagining the man's bad review of the show. " 'The lies that were said in that room,' " he said. " 'I wanted to go out for a good night of realism.' "

NEIL LABUTE

A TOUCH OF BAD

ONCE UPON A TIME IN THE
early nineties, in the irony-free zone of Off Off Broadway, the writer and
director Neil LaBute sat onstage doing triple duty as an actor in his bar-
room play, "Filthy Talk for Troubled Times: Scenes of Intolerance." One of
the barflies was in the middle of a riff about AIDS and about her fear of
infection—"I say, put them all in a fucking pot and boil them . . . just as a
precaution"—when a member of the audience sitting right up front shouted, "Kill the playwright!" LaBute, who is thirty-eight and whose wiry
black hair and pug nose give him the look of a large, amiable hedgehog,
says his first thought was "to get to the exit, to lead the crowd out to safety"; another part of him was thrilled, because "people were listening
enough to go out of their way to make a response." The angry patron
stayed for the rest of the play, which is a testament to LaBute's good writing and to his canny view of theatre and film as "a contact sport," which
"should be the most of whatever it is—the most joy, the most terror."

LaBute, whose first play-turned-film, "In the Company of Men"
(1997), made his name and also earned him the sobriquet "the angriest
white male," courts provocation not for the sake of shock but to make an
audience think against its own received opinions. His production company is mischievously called Contemptible Entertainment; his work is cruel,
dark, and often very funny. "In the Company of Men" is about two corporate eager beavers—the venomous Chad and his sidekick, Howard—who
conspire to find a vulnerable woman, woo her, and then hurt her. "It's a
simple story," LaBute wrote in the introduction to the published screenplay. "Boys meet girl, boys crush girl, boys giggle." "Your Friends and
Neighbors" (1998), adapted from his play "Lepers," is a sexual merry-go-
round among friends. Together, the two films are a kind of "Rake's

Progress," and LaBute's model for them is Restoration comedy, which, as
he explained to me when we met in Hollywood this spring, "gets down to
the dirt of the way we live with each other and treat each other." He pays
homage to his source in "Your Friends and Neighbors" when, during a
rehearsal of Wycherley's "The Country Wife," the drama professor and
sleazy sexual predator, Jerry (Ben Stiller), sitting in the auditorium in
periwig and frock coat, explains to his cuckolded best friend, Barry
(Aaron Eckhart), why he bedded his wife:

> JERRY: . . . I just feel . . . Fuck, I don't know how to put this,
> I just feel . . .
> BARRY: "Bad"?
> JERRY: "Bad." Exactly! Bad.
> BARRY: I mean, my wife . . .
> JERRY: I'm sorry.
> BARRY: The same hotel room even.
> JERRY: I am sorry.
> BARRY: Yeah . . .
> JERRY: But I . . . I mean, I still feel . . .
> BARRY: . . . "Bad."
> JERRY: Right. "Bad."

The moral and emotional nonchalance of LaBute's characters echoes
the amorality and privilege of the Restoration fops, who, LaBute has said,
are "well-to-do people with time on their hands who go around hurting
each other, doing things that are pretty unpleasant, just because the opportunity presents itself." The original court entertainments emphasized the
notion of appearance versus authenticity. "Behind that great sense of costume—the wigs and makeup—there was a sense that all was well, even
while bugs were crawling in the wigs and the physical self was falling
apart," LaBute said. "There was still the sense that it was better to look
good than to feel good." LaBute's contemporary fops have no authentic
self to hide: they are all façade. He links this to the nineties obsession with
style and with the insistence on appearance as reality. "There's a huge sense
in the nineties of 'I can become anything I want as long as I present it tena-

ciously enough.' Clinton would be a fair example."

LaBute, who calls himself "a part-time moralist," is a practicing Mormon; he converted to the faith in the early eighties, before he married Lisa Gore, a psychotherapist who is deeply involved with the Church of the Latter-Day Saints. The Mormon obsession with moral improvement and with "pretending nothing bad happens," as he says, accounts in large part for LaBute's relish of transgression. The absence of surface detail in his films—"In the Company of Men" takes place in a nameless city and at a nameless corporation where nameless executive tasks are performed—allows the viewer to focus on the psychological aspects of the piece: the casual cruelties we commit, the ways in which we displace our anger. "Neil always wants you to personalize his work," says the actor Aaron Eckhart, who starred in both "In the Company of Men" and "Your Friends and Neighbors," and has a part in the forthcoming "Nurse Betty," LaBute's first mainstream Hollywood movie and the only one of his films that he has not written. "He wants you to say, 'I'm that person' or 'I have done that.' "

For the same reasons, in his stage work LaBute favors the black box—the unadorned proscenium—and the confines of the monologue. His versatility in this form is shown to brilliant and unsettling effect in a trio of short pieces collectively called "Bash." Here, in one of the pieces—a tandem monologue entitled "A Gaggle of Saints: A Remembrance of Hatred and Longing"—a soon-to-be-married college couple recount a road trip to New York City with a few Mormon college friends for a party at the Plaza. During the day's long trajectory of good times, the guys find themselves attacking a homosexual in a Central Park latrine:

> Tim leans into him one more time, takes a little run at it, smashing his foot against the bridge of this man's nose and I see it give way. Just pick up and move to the other side of his face. Wow. And then it's silence. Not a sound. And for the first time, we look over at Dave. . . . What's he thinking? And right then, as if to answer us through revelation . . . he grabs up the nearest trash can, big wire mesh thing, raises it above his head as he whispers, "Fag." I'll never forget that . . . "fag." That's all. And brings that can down right on the spine of the guy, who

just sort of shudders a bit, expelling air.

Clearly, LaBute does not follow the Mormon line about the showing of good. On the contrary, his work is built on the belief that great good can come from showing the bad.

I visited LaBute on the set of "Nurse Betty," which he describes as "a feel-good hit that includes scalping, love, a cross-country car chase, shoot-outs, comedy"—in other words, an entertainment, and perhaps a holiday from his usual despair. LaBute, dressed in a blue-and-black plaid shirt, jeans, sneakers, and a slicker with a packet of raisins tucked into the cuff, spent much of the first morning skulking around a crowded Pasadena bungalow, inspecting every cranny of a room where one of the film's heavies, played by Chris Rock, goes looking for Betty, the title character (Renée Zellweger). The film is essentially a chase movie, in which Betty, a wait-ress, sees her ne'er-do-well husband murdered for the cache of drugs he has hidden in her car; traumatized and deluded, she sets off for Los Angeles to marry her "fiancé," the doctor on her favorite soap opera. On the set, LaBute engages his cast as he does the world—with an almost presidential bonhomie, at once solicitous and standoffish. He speaks with the low-key collegial composure of someone who knows who he is—the boss. "Love that Tide!" he called to the set decorator, who was positioning the soap-powder box so that the camera would catch it in the corner of the frame. "Love that box of Tide!" The scene called for the actress Kathleen Wilhoite to hold a baby as she answered the front door; on this bright morning, the professional toddler, a hefty lump called Robert, was bawling himself red in the face. LaBute swooped up the child and cradled him in his thick arms, as adept at handling kids as adults. (He has an eleven-year-old daughter, Lily, and a seven-year-old son, Spencer.) "You'll have the baby in your arms. That'll give you an acting challenge," he said to Wilhoite. "It'll steal the scene," she said. LaBute shot her a grin as he walked away. "They often do," he said.

On the bungalow's front lawn, amid a scrum of technicians and prop hands, LaBute, an almost constant nosher, munched a few raisins. "My mom is very happy, because I'm doing more than she hoped for," he told me. "But she'd rather I was doing comedies. I told her, 'I just did, so wait till I do a drama.' "

Chris Rock ambled over, dressed like a Bible salesman, in a loose-fitting black suit. "He's great with scenery," Rock said. "He's the best hair director that ever lived." LaBute gave him an owlish look, greeted him as "Mr. Rock," and said they were nearly ready to shoot. "I don't smile in this movie. I brood," Rock said as he walked away. "Cheating America of the bullshit that is Chris Rock."

It is typical of LaBute that he would find a way to exploit Rock's edgy, darker essence rather than his show-biz surface, even in a commercial film. "Nurse Betty," written by John C. Richards and James Flamberg, is the first of a two-picture deal that LaBute cut with Propaganda Films (the company that joint-produced the four-million-dollar "Your Friends and Neighbors" last year). After he'd signed the contract, he had second thoughts and wanted to bolt; now he seemed to be contentedly and firmly at the helm. "There are a lot of firsts for me here," he said as the other children in the scene were being rounded up and given their orders. "First crane. First squib shot. First in all the things that you may not have dealt with—like anyone pulling a gun, let alone using it." To that list of firsts could be added: first big production (thirty million dollars), first seven-figure payday, first star-studded cast (Rock, Zellweger, Morgan Freeman), first happy ending, first film without his own narrative voice.

Even so, the Hollywood machine hasn't completely expunged LaBute's instinct for mischief, which became apparent a few hours later, when he was slumped in front of a monitor with two producers at his back worrying about the lack of coverage for an interracial sex scene. On the small screen, Rock was kneeling on a bed behind a white girl, pumping her for information while rogering her doggy style, as Jerry memorably does to Terri in "Your Friends and Neighbors." "This is why I wanted to do the script, " LaBute joked. In fact, he said, he shot the scene without coverage on purpose, so it could not be edited, in the hope of finessing his case against the inbred conservatism of the studio. "We talked about the sex," he explained. "Frontal would have been too intimate—he's getting information from the girl. It seemed less personal from behind. They have the same amount of clothes on—in fact, more than they had on in 'Your

Friends and Neighbors.' I think it comes down to the race thing. I really do."

After about ten minutes of calm discussion with the producers, LaBute accepted the postcoital option. "Just them in bed," he said. "Her sitting smoking. He's lying next to her, and they're talking." He shoved his fingers into a bag of Cheetos. "Let's do it!" he shouted to his assistant. "Light the bed. Let's look right down on them. And off we'll go. She'll blow a little smoke in his face."

The next day, the production caravan moved to a low-rent side street of downtown Los Angeles. "This is your 'I found the coke' scene. Your daddy will be proud of you," LaBute said to Rock. Rock started over toward his screen father, Morgan Freeman, who was sucking on a toothpick and looking like a Marlboro man, in cowboy boots and pressed jeans. By the time LaBute got the shot he was talking about, it was midday and a tent had been erected to protect the monitors from the glare of the sun. LaBute and his director of photography, Jean Yves Escoffier, watched the screens as Freeman and Rock, for about the tenth time, sauntered toward a parked LeSabre and pried its trunk open. "I shoulda been a film director when I was a kid," LaBute said, happy with the take. "Time would have gone by much quicker. Waiting for Christmas? Go make a movie."

LaBute, who has an encyclopedic knowledge of pop culture and can as easily imitate Don Knotts ("My body is a weapon") as discourse on Werner Herzog's "Stroszek," is a curious amalgam of theatrical influences. "What the fuck's her name? I mean, tits like that must have a name, correct?" has the vernacular wallop of a David Mamet line; actually, it is the self-incriminating telephone talk of Cary in "Your Friends and Neighbors." LaBute writes with the same linguistic cunning as Mamet and characterizes his admiration for the playwright as "beyond fan—stalker perhaps. Psychological stalker." He even managed to mount an expurgated version of Mamet's "Sexual Perversity in Chicago" during his undergraduate days, at Brigham Young University: "My posters were so rococo that the passer-by couldn't read what they said."

Where Mamet hears violence and evasion under conversational speech, LaBute hears a kind of moral and emotional entropy—what he calls "the chill factor"—under his characters' jabbering. "I tend to hear a false sense of warmth in the way we lead people in sentences," LaBute says. "'You know,' 'I mean,' 'Listen.' People are constantly trying to embellish what they say with this false sense of camaraderie—'I'm with you,' 'I'm with you on this.' A phrase that suddenly started coming up more and more and that I incorporated in 'Your Friends and Neighbors' was 'Is it me?' These men were constantly asking, without any sense of wanting to know the answer, 'Who's doing this?'"

In "Filthy Talk for Troubled Times" LaBute developed this idea by orchestrating a counterpoint of monologues in which people talk about wanting to connect while the form of the play insures that they aren't listening to each other. "Women. Fucking broads! . . .You can't fucking trust them," one drinker says to another. "Well . . . personally, I could never trust anything that bleeds for a week and doesn't die." The complete absence of empathy expressed by this vicious joke also finds a powerful metaphor at the end of "In the Company of Men," when the contrite Howard (Matt Malloy) goes in search of the female victim, Christine (Stacy Edwards), and finds her working in a bank. She wants no part of him or his apology; she leaves the bad feeling with him. "Listen," he says to her, then starts to shout when she doesn't acknowledge him. "Listen! Listen!! Listen!!! Listen!!!!" "It's so selfish," LaBute says of Howard's desire to have his impulse toward goodness acknowledged. "I think a lot of the characters I write, and certainly a lot of the male characters, are selfish. They just indulge themselves in taking care of their needs."

This sense of entitlement is the presenting symptom of most of LaBute's characters, and is part of what makes his work so distinctly contemporary. In addition to Mamet, he admires Wallace Shawn, whom he calls "the great chronicler of the ease with which we slowly tumble." "The difference between a perfectly decent person and a monster is just a few thoughts," Shawn writes in the appendix to his play "Aunt Dan and Lemon," which LaBute cites as an influence on his own modest proposals. Charles Metten, who taught directing at Brigham Young, calls LaBute "a young Ibsen," which is perhaps pitching it a bit high. But LaBute is an original voice, and the best new playwright to emerge in the past decade. He brings to his observations about human nature something that other contemporary American writers have not articulated with quite such single-minded authority: a sense of sin.

"The 'should's and 'have to's of Mormonism make Neil struggle with the sinful life," Metten says. "The Latter-Day Saints standards are so high. The humanness of Neil sends him in the other direction. He gets even in his writing." LaBute's plays, which percolate with corrosive skepticism, are, in fact, by-products of the righteous life. "The interesting thing about sin is that we've gotten a bit away from it," LaBute says. "There's a right and a wrong that goes beyond the daily practice of living, and I think we have gotten away from that idea, yet it sort of hangs over all of us." His stories show a sense of goodness being leached out of the lives of his characters and, more hilariously, out of their vocabulary. In "Your Friends and Neighbors," the subject comes up over a meal:

> BARRY: Do you think you're good?
> CARY: What, a good fuck?
> BARRY: No, "good." I'm asking you, do you think you're good?
> CARY: "Good," what do you mean, "good"? What kinda question is that?
> BARRY: I'm asking . . . I'm saying are you, you know, like, a "good person"?
> CARY: Hey, I'm eating lunch . . .

Later, when the thorny issue of salvation comes up—the question of whether they'll ultimately have to "pay" for their behavior, in Barry's weasel words—Cary says, "I mean, if there ends up being a God or something like that whole eternity thing out there, like, then, yeah, probably so. I dunno. We'll see. But until then, we're on my time, O.K.? The interim is mine." LaBute's characters are so lost to themselves, so separated from their souls, that they can't feel anything; they hurt people in *order* to feel something. The murderous mothers and fathers, the violent college boys, the conniving friends and rampant seducers in his work continually dramatize sin as the inability to imagine the suffering of others.

As a boy, LaBute often went to church and participated in Bible study, even though his parents didn't. He grew up with intimations of a faithless world—what he calls "a vague foreboding that something was not quite right." He explains, "I'm sure a lot of my love of stories—of watching film or theatre, imagining myself in some other context—came from the unsettling environment at home." When LaBute's producing partner, Stephen Pevner, called him at the Seattle Film Festival, after the initial success of "In the Company of Men," in 1997, Pevner remembers getting LaBute's soft-spoken mother, Marian, on the phone. "I said, 'It's taken so long. It must feel so good. He did it, he really did it!' She goes, 'I know. He captured his father perfectly.' I said, 'Well, I actually meant he did it. He pulled it off.' And she goes, 'I know what you meant.' "

"There's a great deal of my father in a lot of the characters that people find somewhat unseemly," LaBute says. Richard LaBute, who was ten years older than his wife, had wanted to be an airline pilot but ended up a truck driver; he specialized in long-distance hauling during Neil's childhood, which was spent mostly in Liberty Lake, Washington, outside Spokane. "As a kid, you get a sense of betrayal you can't put specifics to— a sense of women down the line is what one can make a leap to," LaBute says of his handsome father's long absences. (Richard and Marian were divorced about five years ago, after thirty-five years of marriage.) "My mother never talked about it. When I was old enough to talk about it, I really wasn't interested to find out the truth." He continues, "There must be something there that I don't necessarily want the answer to, because it helps fuel the writing."

Neil, the second child (his brother Richard, Jr., is a linguist and digital-processing executive in Minneapolis), was a bookish, sensitive, goofy-looking kid. Aaron Eckhart describes Neil's father as "a hard-ass" who was "always chipping at him." The family pattern, LaBute says, was to "spackle over problems" and "keep everything hidden—any kind of strife that would make my father angry. I can remember when he came home, a great sense of anticipation, because of not knowing what mood he'd come back in." His father's temper gave LaBute a sense of casual brutality and of "how much damage could be done with language." He goes on, "I can remember working with my father on a car. He'd gone inside. The only thing that really sets me off is inanimate objects, because there's no reasoning with them. I let out a tirade that would have made someone proud. I didn't realize he'd come back into the garage. He looked at me, and I got the sense of 'So this is part of the legacy I've left behind.' "

When LaBute gets angry, according to Eckhart, "he crawls inside himself." Pevner says, "If you're good to him, he's extremely good to you. If you're bad to him, forget it. What's worse than the wrath of God? You won't get anything. You will get nothing." LaBute doesn't like to be touched; he resists intimacy. "He doesn't want people to know too much," the actress Hilary Russell says. "He's the only friend of mine that I feel very close to but I don't know absolutely everything about. There's a lot of dark stuff, and he's trying to figure it all out." LaBute's cordiality and his mystery are confounding. It is as if, like his plays, the warmth of his surface disguises colder depths. "He's very hard to read," says Pevner, who has worked with LaBute for a decade and still doesn't know the exact address of his home, in a northern suburb of Chicago. "He likes ambiguity. He will end up doing something he doesn't want to do, simply not to have a confrontation. He articulates through his writing, and that's it."

LaBute's mother, a fervid Anglophile, encouraged her son's love of drama and film, but his father did not; from the age of ten, Neil waged a perpetual losing battle against his father about his being what he calls "an indentured servant" on a farm that his father operated as a sideline. To LaBute's knowledge, his father, whom he hears from infrequently, has never seen one of his plays or films. Charles Metten recalls sitting in his office at Brigham Young with LaBute, who was planning to write a play about fathers and sons for Metten to direct. "I asked, 'Will it be another "All My Sons"?' He said, 'No, it's gonna be better.' Then, for the first time in our friendship, he started to talk about his father. Tears welled up. He got very, very emotional. In fact, he left and went to the rest room."

Though LaBute was the president of his high-school class, he refused to attend Friday-night football games, because they coincided with the weekly changing of the feature at the local cinema. His yearbook is filled with pictures of him: in "You're a Good Man, Charlie Brown" (he played Snoopy), "Arsenic and Old Lace," and "Don't Drink the Water." At

Brigham Young, which he attended on a scholarship, LaBute continued to act, but he preferred the detachment of writing. He began providing monologues and scenes for friends going into the Irene Ryan Acting Competition, one of whom got to the finals. "I had a quick ability to write short, kind of pungent sketches and monologues," he says. "I had the hardest time writing anything of length, because I hated the idea of stopping. I loved to sit down and finish something. I was always writing short pieces. It was the opposite of writer's block." LaBute earned a B.A. in 1985; he married Gore, whom he had met at Brigham Young, and they moved to New York, hoping that he could parlay his sketch-writing skills into a berth on "Late Night with David Letterman" or "Saturday Night Live."

In his first, frustrating taste of the New York scene, LaBute's confidence was severely tested. A friend gave him the home telephone number of Lorne Michaels, "S.N.L."'s executive producer, and LaBute cold-called him. "'How did you get my number?'" LaBute remembers Michaels saying. "'Please don't call me here again. Send it in to the show.' That was the extent of my sketch-writing career. From then on, I started to say, 'Well, then, I'll just make it happen for myself as much as I can.' "

LaBute's early plays were the subject of scandal and concern at Brigham Young, where he worked toward a Ph.D. in the early nineties. "The faculty revered Neil, but they were also afraid of him," recalls Eckhart, who first performed LaBute's work as an undergraduate. "This material was absolutely subversive. They thought it was going to tear down the theatre department." The Mormon atmosphere "forced Neil to be more creative, because of the restrictions, the no-nos," Metten says. "Neil was in constant battle." For instance, in order to prevent the staging of "Lepers," which LaBute had rehearsed for three months, the administration locked up the theatre and even the lightboard; LaBute, who was able to get into the theatre only to give a final exam, cut short the exam and did his play. "There was a glee in him," says Tim Slover, who taught playwriting and in whose postgraduate course LaBute wrote "In the Company of Men." "He knew he was doing important work. But the glee was over the fact that this important moral work had surface features that appalled people."

In the larger world, LaBute's uncompromising scripts—which he typed all in lower case, so as not to impede the flow of his thought, and with no stage directions—were hard to sell. "There was a long period of writing plays and putting them away," says LaBute, who supported himself by teaching, and by working in a series of psychiatric hospitals and correctional institutions, where he was able to write late at night. Except for the productions he generated, mostly in university settings, his plays were not getting done. He was, he says, "torn by the hunger to get the work out there and have people see it."

"He wanted to be the greatest living playwright in America," Metten says of his student, whom he characterizes as "a pain in the butt because he was a genius." He adds, "When he would do his work, he knew it was darn good and that he would be ostracized from the regular community." LaBute's plays brought him into conflict not just with the community but with forces closer to home. At Brigham Young, his wife was conspicuously absent from his productions. "I came right out and asked 'Doesn't it hurt your feelings?' " Hilary Russell says. "He's like, 'You know, it did at first.' He just kind of hardens himself. She must know his work, and she's just avoiding it—she's going against every single Mormon standard in not supporting her husband." Although Lisa Gore is listed as a creative consultant on "In the Company of Men," there seems to have been serious disagreement on "Your Friends and Neighbors" up to the first day of filming. "There was a major issue of Lisa's being afraid he'd be excommunicated— I mean, in the Mormon church you're not supposed to even think impure thoughts," says Russell, who was on the set the first day, when LaBute got his wife's phone call. "She said, 'You can't make it. How can you make this film?' I knew something was wrong just by his eyes."

LaBute's exploration of self-aggrandizement is also, by inference, about self-sacrifice: it reflects in theatrical terms his own internal battle to be at once great and good. "There's the Church telling you, 'You can't make these films or you'll go to Hell,' " Eckhart says of LaBute. "And there are other ramifications. Neil's wife holds a position in the Church. You got the whole social thing. It's very acute. I think everything in his life, on a certain level, is telling him in some way to forsake his true love—his work."

Before he got the financing for "In the Company of Men," Eckhart remembers LaBute's saying, "I don't know if I can make a film. Who's going to trust me?" He was an unknown director, with an unknown script, unknown performers, and an unhappy ending. His father-in-law, an importer of industrial silks, declined to invest, but two of LaBute's former students stumped up their insurance payouts from a car accident. The actors got themselves to Fort Wayne, Indiana, where, in the mid-nineties, LaBute was teaching at St. Francis College; his next-door neighbor put them up. "We had a wonderful D.P. and sound guy, but, as far as everyone else, they were all volunteers from Fort Wayne—I mean, postal workers, college students, housewives," Stacy Edwards, who played the woman, says. "Neil was doing everything that normally would take at least six people to take care of."

LaBute shot "In the Company of Men" in eleven days, on twenty-five thousand dollars. Later, Sony added a quarter-million dollars in postproduction money to the film, and it grossed over five million dollars. "We knew through the entire shoot we really only had two takes per scene," Edwards says. "So you had to get it right." Eckhart recalls, "Stacy and I were sitting at that restaurant. It was six o'clock at night. We didn't close the restaurant down, because he had no money. Those customers are real, and they're kicking us out. So Neil comes up to me and says, 'Aaron, we've done it once, and it isn't right.' It was on my closeup and the last shot of the day. He says, 'Aaron, we've got one hundred feet of film left. We're getting kicked out of the restaurant.' He goes, 'Don't feel any pressure, but you have to get this one.' How many times did I hear that?"

There was no video playback, there were no dailies, and there was almost no movie when the lab gave LaBute three days to pay his bill or lose the film. But the end of the struggle came with a standing ovation at the Sundance Festival, where "In the Company of Men" won the 1997 Filmmakers Trophy. "In the middle of the screening, I turned to Matt Malloy and said, 'This thing is hot,' " Eckhart says. "I knew Neil felt that way. When we came out, it was right there on his face—'All right! This is going somewhere. I'm vindicated. Everything that I knew about myself has just happened.' He didn't say it. I saw it."

I last saw LaBute in Projection Room 7 of a squat building off Santa Monica Boulevard, where he was hunkered down in the far-right-hand corner of the first row of a screening room, watching seven hours of dailies. For this marathon, the members of his team were spread out behind him over five rows: they came and went, snoozed and talked as clapper board after clapper board announced a new take of shots 87 A through D. I sat directly behind LaBute, hoping he might talk to me during the process. He didn't. Instead, he worked away at a large bag of Doritos and a Pepsi as he watched a well-shot sequence that included a white Mercedes tearing up the ramp of a hospital emergency entrance and ramming an ambulance; an exchange of gunfire; flying bodies; breaking glass; and Nurse Betty, in her hospital disguise, pressed into real medical service by some gun-waving gangbangers who mistake her for the genuine article.

In the film, Nurse Betty is spellbound; and it struck me over the next hour that perhaps the purpose of this exercise for LaBute was to live, however briefly, in the exhilarating spell of the Hollywood system that had captivated him as an adolescent on those Friday nights. LaBute had accomplished the hardest thing: he had found both a style and an audience for his point of view. Now, for the moment at least, he was giving up the personal for the impersonal, the subversive for something that conformed more or less to the commercial formulas that his other movies shunned. "Nurse Betty," a will-she-or-won't-she saga, plays against LaBute's great strength, which is to force the audience to take a position rather than to abdicate thought for the sake of fun. I tried to see it through his eyes. Pevner had told me, "I think he wanted to acquire power—you know, psychological power, emotional power, financial power. To overcome his obstacles. I think he's truly a romantic figure."

In a way, a full-blown Hollywood movie could be seen as LaBute's victory lap—a little moment of vindictive triumph, to show the panjandrums of commerce who'd rejected his early work that he could succeed in this part of the business, too. In the past, he had access to nobody; now he was on the Rolodex of everyone in town. He was an artist with money chores to be done, and sometimes it was wise to give the piper a dance. There were historical precedents: Scorsese's "Cape Fear," Hitchcock's "Dial M for Murder," Huston's "Annie." Then again perhaps this dance was not for the piper at all but for the Mormon brethren, and maybe even for his wife, who wanted him to delight the world rather than disenchant it.

When LaBute and I talked again, a couple of weeks ago, he declared himself pleased with "Nurse Betty" and with the new bag of tricks he'd mastered. "It's sort of freeing," he said. I asked him if the film was LaButian, and, with typical LaButian ambivalence, he answered, "Yes— and no." He did see some thematic connections with his plays and his tougher work. "There is a series of mediocre-to-bad men and a woman scrambling to save themselves," he said. With LaBute, one way or another, salvation remains the issue.

BOB HOPE

THE C.E.O. OF COMEDY

Wᴴᴱɴ Bᴏʙ Hᴏᴘᴇ ʟᴏᴏᴋs ʙᴀᴄᴋ on the long lap of honor that is his life, he likes to tell a story about his vaudeville beginnings. In about 1928, not long after he'd started doing gags onstage, he was playing the Orpheum Theatre in Evansville, Indiana, and he noticed that his newly minted name had been wrongly billed as "Ben Hope, Comedian." In Hope's gruelling slog to stardom, which he didn't reach until he was in his late thirties, his name underwent a number of transformations. He entered the world, in 1903, as Leslie Townes Hope, but once he'd found the stage, as a song-and-dance man, the name changed from "Leslie" to the more masculine "Lester." When comedy gradually emerged as Hope's meal ticket, the name mutated again. Although his clippings have a few references to "Bill" and "Bobby," he settled on "Bob Hope"—not just because it read well on a marquee but because it had, he said, "more 'Hiya, fellas' in it." So when he saw the Orpheum's misprint the cocksure young comic buttonholed the theatre manager and upbraided him for the mistake. As Hope recalls their exchange, on an A&E Biography film, " 'What's your name?' the manager said. I said, '*Bob* Hope.' He said, 'Who knows?' "

Hope, who has a self-confessed "hatred of anonymity," kept a picture of the Evansville billing in his archive. "The fascinating thing to me is that he has a picture of it," his elder son, Tony, told me about his father, who stopped performing in 1995 and for the past few years has not been up to giving interviews. "He knew that in twenty years it would be a historic picture. That's his foresight. That's his drive. 'Everybody's gonna know who Bob Hope is.' " Hope is unique among the great entertainers of the century in having been at some point in his long, well-organized career No. 1 in radio, in film, and in television. "I've a terrible fear of being hijacked to a country where they've never heard of me," he joked in 1970. It was a nightmare that came to pass only once—when he visited Russia, in the late fifties. "I don't mind being killed, but ignored—never."

Since the nineteen-forties, the name "Bob Hope" has been part of the Western world's ozone. He has lived to see it not just in lights but in many other incarnations. There is the U.S.N.S. *Bob Hope*, the second-largest ship in the Navy; the C-17 jet fighter the *Spirit of Bob Hope*; G.I. Bob, a popular Hasbro doll; the Bob Hope/Chrysler Desert Golf Classic, in Palm Springs; Bob Hope High School for the physically handicapped, in Port Arthur, Texas; and the Hope Memorial Bridge, in Cleveland, Ohio (his father, who was a stonemason, worked on it). There are Bob Hope Theatres in Dallas and in Eltham, England, which was his birthplace; and a Bob Hope Street and Off-Ramp in Burbank, near NBC, where his sixty-year association with the network, which ended in 1997, has earned him a place in the "Guinness Book of World Records" for the longest contract with a single network. Hope's name has even been affixed to the planet's animal and plant life: the Bob Hope prize steer, the Bob Hope rose, the Bob Hope fern, which is green on top with black roots. "You've captured me completely," he wrote to the Chicago Horticultural Society, which cultivated the plant.

At ninety-five, Hope is nearly as old as the century, and he personifies its brash deliriums. His obsession with output, aggrandizement, and fame belongs to the modern era, particularly in this country. Hope, who joked in the late sixties that he left England when he was four "because I found out I could never be King," has established his own American kingdom. He still sends out six thousand Christmas cards a year. His 1998 press kit— "95 Years of Hope"—includes news of a congressional resolution making him an Honorary Veteran and of his receiving an honorary British knighthood; some publicity photographs; and a joke sheet about his getting old, which reads, in part, "It feels great to be 95. I mean, for those parts of me that still have feeling." Nowadays, Hope can't see very well and frequently refuses to wear a hearing aid ("They can hear what *I'm* saying," he says), but the celebrity machine he put in place more than half a century ago grinds efficiently on. Hope appears in another "Guinness Book of World Records" entry, as the world's "most decorated civilian." "I feel very humble," he said to President Kennedy when he was awarded a Congressional Gold Medal in 1963, "but I think I have the strength of character to fight it." His appetite for adulation remains unabashed; even in his dotage, he is still, as he famously sang, "Available":

> If you're handing out a plaque
> Or a special little statue
> I'll go home and pack
> And I'll soon be looking at you!

Just two years before a very young Hope arrived at Ellis Island, in 1908, dressed in two sets of clothes to save luggage, Henry Adams wrote in his autobiography, about the American century's new dynamism and prosperity, "All the new forces condensed into corporations were demanding a new type of man—a man with ten times the endurance, energy, will and mind of the old type." The great vaudeville clowns who preceded Hope— Chaplin, Buster Keaton, the Marx Brothers, Weber and Fields, Eugene and Willie Howard, Bobby Clark—acted out the deracinating momentum of the new century in their frenzy and their pratfalls. They were a noisy, rumpled, constitutionally unclubbable bunch. Their baggy excess and their dialects broadcast their separation from the mainstream: they were parodies of the new corporate energy.

Hope, on the other hand, personified it. He was a bright package of assimilated poise and pragmatism—the all-American average guy. There was no hint of the streets or the Old Country in his patter. "I simply can't tell a dialect joke," he says in his 1954 memoir, "Bob Hope's Own Story: Have Tux, Will Travel." In their manic bravado, the older generation of funnymen gave off a whiff of immigrant desperation and sadness at what had been left behind. Hope was all future. The wrinkles had been pressed out of his suits and out of his personality. He was an anxiety-free, up-to-the-minute, fast-talking go-getter on holiday. Dapper, streamlined, and cunning, Hope was the first corporate comedian. He gave what one NBC vice-president called "a lot of extra value for his money." He attended sales conventions, schmoozed the press, golfed with the corporate bigwigs. In his radio days, between 1938 and 1956, he was usually photographed behind an NBC mike; he found a way of linking the sponsors' brand names with his own ("This is Bob Pepsodent/Chrysler/Lever Brothers Hope"). Even in many of his seventy-odd films, Hope made sure that the jokes mythologized his corporate bosses. In "Road to Morocco" (1942), when he is perched on a camel behind Bing Crosby, singing the title song, it's Crosby who boasts "For any villains we may meet/We haven't any fear," and Hope who invokes the blessings of management: "Paramount will protect us/'Cause we're signed for five more years."

When the Old Guard clowns, like W. C. Fields and the Marx Brothers, were brought into the corporate fold, they fought with it continually or, like Keaton, were destroyed by it. Hope embraced the corporate idea and turned himself into a kind of comic franchise. "He discovered a formula for comedy that was better than what anyone else was doing, and he sought to expand it, not in depth, but in breadth," Tony Hope wrote me. "He put together a machine that spread the word to ninety per cent of the globe that when you said 'ad-lib' or 'standup' you meant Bob Hope, or a cheap imitation of him." As Hope said in the mid-fifties, "Between television, my daytime and nighttime radio shows, pictures, and personal appearances, I'm also working on a plan where, when you close your eyes, I appear on the inside of your eyelids." NBC, Paramount, the Academy of Motion Picture Arts and Sciences, and the United States military establishment were his co-producers, and those alliances made him a very rich man: conservative estimates of his wealth—at one time he owned a large portion of the San Fernando Valley, Malibu, and Palm Springs—are said to be between a hundred million and two hundred million dollars. (In 1983, *Forbes* put Hope's worth at more than two hundred million dollars, a figure he loudly disputed.) His product, like the corporations he served, was efficient, mass-produced, omnipresent, iconic. In his hands, laughter became an art of non-friction; his jokes went down as easily as Coca-Cola, and he, too, was the pause that refreshed.

Like any shrewd C.E.O., Hope believed in careful product planning. He employed as many as five press agents at a time, and he brought his particular combination of gall and good-enough looks onstage with a distinctive swagger: chest out, body pitched forward on the balls of his feet, hands cupped behind his swinging arms—as Jack Benny quipped, like a headwaiter trying to get a tip. "He came on as if he were carrying a great weight of almost civic dignity in front of him," Sir Laurence Olivier once told the BBC. "It's very amusing." Hope also established a kind of joke factory, which has remained intact from the late thirties until today. (Even now, he keeps a skeleton crew of two writers on retainer.) "I believe I was the first of the comedians to admit openly that I employed writers," Hope told William Faith in 1981, in "Bob Hope: A Life in Comedy," which is perhaps the best book about him. "In the early years of radio, comedians fostered the illusion that all of those funny sayings came right out of their own skulls."

In the course of the last half century, eighty-eight jokesmiths—sometimes as many as thirteen at a time—have been on Hope's payroll, and have provided him with upward of a million jokes. ("Hope?" Groucho Marx once said. "Hope is not a comedian. He just translates what others write for him.") "When you signed on for Bob Hope, you were at his beck and call seven days a week," I was told by Melville Shavelson, one of his first joke writers, who later went on to co-write two of Hope's strongest films, "Sorrowful Jones" and "The Seven Little Foys," which he also directed. Hope's reliance on writers became part of his shtick. "I keep an earthquake emergency kit in my house," he said. "It's filled with food, water, and a half a dozen writers." Among the writers, one of Hope's nicknames was Piggy. "Hope was a glutton," says Hal Kanter, who wrote not only jokes but also seven movies for Hope. " 'More, more, more. I want more jokes. I want more dates to play. I want more ice cream. I want more women. I want more applause.' " Hope was notorious for calling his jokesmiths at any time of the day or night. The writers' acronym for this sudden intrusion was "NAFT"—"need a few things." Larry Gelbart, who began writing for Hope in 1948, at the age of twenty, recalls one style of Hope phone call: " 'Oh, you didn't wake me, Bob.' Four-thirty in the morning. He'd say, 'Lar . . . ?' 'Yeah, Bob?' Then, silence, silence, silence. These extremely long pauses, which made you feel you oughta say something. He had this very funny way on the phone." In later years, when Hope was calling his writers he formed the habit of not identifying himself or saying "Hello" or "How ya doin'?" He'd just say, "Thrill me."

Jokes were not merely Hope's livelihood but a defining part of his identity. "Bob was a manufactured personality, constructed out of jokes," says Sherwood Schwartz, another of his early radio writers, who went on to create and produce "Gilligan's Island" and "The Brady Bunch." In time, Hope's writers were called upon to provide jokes even for his golf tournaments and his dinner parties. One recent writer, Martha Bolton, remembers a phone message from her boss: "Hi, this is Bob Hope. I'm trying to find my writers. Gene's off speaking somewhere. Mills is golfing. Si and Freddie are gone and just have their answering machine on. And you're probably out shopping. . . . Didn't I used to have a career?"

In May of this year, Hope announced the donation of his archive of jokes, radio broadcasts, video master tapes, film and radio scripts, photographs, and clippings books to the Library of Congress, along with three and a half million dollars to preserve the collection and to outfit a thirteen-hundred-square-foot room in the Jefferson Building which is to be called the Bob Hope Gallery of American Entertainment. Hope is careful about the company he keeps: his gallery will be next to the Gershwin Room. Until recently, a good portion of his memorabilia was collected in an outbuilding that served as the office for Hope and his staff. It sits about fifty paces from his Toluca Lake home—a six-and-three-quarter-acre former walnut grove, on the wrong side of the Hollywood Hills, which Hope bought in 1937 for about forty thousand dollars. He and his wife of sixty-four years, Dolores, with whom he has four adopted children, have turned it into a luxuriant oasis of rolling manicured lawns, dominated by a one-hole pitch-and-putt golf course whose sand trap and green are visible from Hope's three-room suite on the second floor. He spends much of his time there now, watching gigantic local crows mill around the orange-flagged pin.

On the surface, life at the Hopes' home goes on as usual. Gardeners primp the hibiscus and rake the leaves in the shadow of towering redwood and eucalyptus trees, which block out almost all of downtown Burbank, except for the logo of the Texaco Building, which brands part of their blue horizon above the tree line. Employees bustle from the house past a fountain filled with an exotic carrotwood tree and into the office; Hope's white German shepherds, Sno'el and Snowjob, Jr., prowl ten-foot-high hedges of blue-flowering plumbago which extend around the property and shut out the flat, blistering banality of the Valley streets. But over at the office, in the large mahogany study where Hope once met with his writers, an archivist has been at work since March cataloguing the trophies of Hope's lifetime in entertainment: three warehouses full of memorabilia, including fifty-four honorary degrees, five hundred keys to various cities, a golf club inscribed from Lana Turner, a piece of Queen Elizabeth's wedding cake, Eddy Foy's dance shoes, the propeller of an enemy plane signed by the soldiers who shot it down, and an open pack of Vietcong cigarettes and matches—the gift of a P.O.W., and one of Hope's most cherished mementos. For comedians like Hope, who have lived their lives largely in public, retirement is particularly poignant. Hope has not visited his old offices in a year, and his study has been denuded of its old sense of life and victory: the marlin over the fireplace is gone, the signed footballs from the N.F.L., the Big Ten, and the A.P. All-America teams are gone, and the four Emmy Awards have been packed away. In time, some of these artifacts will find their way to the Bob Hope Museum of Comedy, which will probably be built on a piece of property that Hope owns just opposite NBC.

In this divesting of corporate assets, the major one is the Joke File, which has been winnowed down to a select five hundred and twenty-eight thousand gags. This is Hope's treasury, and he has put a huge emotional and financial investment into it; appropriately, it's housed in an eight-by-five-foot Mosler bank vault. The archive comprises twelve four-drawer cabinets, five of them containing "keepers" that Hope has approved to be sent to Washington. It has a "Subject File for Gags," which begins with "Academy Awards, Advertising, Agriculture, Airplanes" and ends, twenty-eight pages later, with "War, Weather, Weddings, Women, Writers." Jokes are also cross-referenced within the categories. For instance, under "America" is printed: "Bicentennial, Constitution, historical American figures, progress over a hundred years, small towns, only in America, beginning. ALSO SEE HOPE SPECIAL ROUTINES (America Past, Present, Future)." Even though the contents are considered "Bob Hope jokes," he wrote very few of them: he edited them, gave voice to them, and paid tens of millions of dollars for them over the years. (Recently, the going rate has been between fifty and seventy-five dollars for an individual joke; his staff writers make between a hundred and fifty thousand and two hundred and fifty thousand dollars per year.) By contract, the jokes are Hope's intellectual property—an expression of his will, if not of his self. "The way I justify that in my own head is that the jokes are the result of a character that Hope created," says Gene Perret, who has written for Hope for nearly thirty years. "Many of the jokes that we do we wouldn't do if there were no Bob Hope."

The jokes have been retyped, without attribution, about seven to a page, onto quarto sheets of paper with the date, place, and subject in the upper left-hand corner. One picked at random from the "America" file reads:

> America. Honor America Day, 7/4/70
> Where else but in America could the Women's Liberation
> Movement take off their bras, then go on TV to complain
> about their lack of support.

From the outset, topicality was Hope's trademark. Many of the files are devoted to historical and show-biz figures. One file—an entire ream of jokes—is about Bing Crosby, his comic sidekick in the "Road" movies and the butt of a long-running public slinging match. ("I've been getting more exercise from my golf recently. I used to play a round with Crosby, now I just play around Crosby.") The files are also available on a computer database, so pages of jokes on a desired subject can be called up at the touch of a button. About certain recent historical figures, however, the system comes up curiously empty. There are no jokes in the file on Senator Joseph McCarthy, Malcolm X, or Martin Luther King, Jr., although Hope did joke about all three in their day, including one infamous gag at the 1968 Academy Awards ceremony, which had been delayed two days because of King's assassination: "About the delay . . . It didn't affect me, but it's been tough on the nominees. How would you like to spend two days in a crouch?"

In raising a laugh, Hope's jokes rarely raise ideas. Long before Vietnam, he was a kind of one-man pacification program who disabused both the public and himself of pain. "My youth was spent in a very tough

neighborhood in Cleveland, Ohio," he said in a TV monologue. "If you did-
n't get in three fights a day, you weren't trying." Jokes provided Hope, who
left school when he was nine, with an upbeat life script from which he
rarely deviated. "I don't make a hobby of mental turmoil," he wrote in
"Have Tux, Will Travel." "I don't think most people want that." Indeed,
what the public wants is forgetfulness, and Hope, whose sharp comic persona came into focus in the thirties, at a time when America's promise
seemed dim, lightened grave times. As one early radio broadcast intoned,
"Strike up the band! Bob Hope's the man / Who ties the cans to woe!"

Hope was the fifth of six boys, whose parents, even before they emigrat-
ed, had been floundering for a decade. William Henry Hope, called Harry,
had married Avis Townes, the daughter of a Welsh sea captain, in 1891.
Harry was a drinker and a gambler, who dreamed of becoming an archi-
tect; he shunted his ever-increasing family around England, seeking stone-
masonry work and a new beginning. The Hopes moved six times before
and three times after Leslie was born, and ended up in Bristol before leaving for America. (The family became United States citizens in 1920.) Avis
put all her energy into her family; while Harry tried his luck in Cleveland,
where his two brothers had put down roots, she was essentially a single
parent. "Believe me, Avis," her profligate husband wrote to her about life
in America, "when you get here, all you'll have to do is sit on the front
porch and chew gum."

But Harry's reports from the New World proved exaggerated. Steel,
not stone, was the material of the century's expansion, and Harry often
had no work. He drowned his disappointment in drink while Avis rented
out rooms in their house to make money. "I remember Dad saying, 'The
United States is a fine place for women and dogs. It's a poor place for horses and men,' " Hope wrote. "He had trouble adjusting himself to this country. I don't think he ever did." Hope was the family optimist, but, according to Leslie's sister-in-law Wynn Hope, who was the wife of his brother
Jim, Harry Hope was the family funnyman. "The father was the original
comedian," she once told Mel Shavelson. "He drank too much, and when
he didn't come home for dinner the boys would go around and they'd find
him entertaining in a bar. He had a wonderful sense of humor."

Over the years, as Harry continued to drink and grew increasingly pathetic and abusive, Avis turned to her boys for both financial and emotional support. She put them all on a pedestal; each son believed himself to be her favorite. ("Mother Had Hopes" is the piquant title of a memoir that Jim Hope wrote.) Avis took Leslie to see the legendary monologuist Frank Fay, who was one of the big comedy stars of his day, and who invented the profession of vaudeville master of ceremonies—a role that Hope later adopted. "He's not half as good as you," Avis said to her son loudly, forcing Hope to slump in his seat with embarrassment. But it was Avis's fierce faith in her son's ability which gave Hope the self-confidence that Fred Allen once observed he "reeked of," and which kept him, one way or another, on that pedestal.

Even when he was a kid, before the stage focussed Hope's enormous, restive energy, action was the magical antidote to whatever weighed him down. ("It's no coincidence that Bob Hope's name consists of two verbs," Larry Gelbart writes in his recent memoir, "Laughing Matters," about Hope's "incredible bursts of brio.") The boy, who was a chronic sleep-walker and lived with the unhappy daily spectacle of his father cowed by fear and regret, would later be dubbed Rapid Robert. He had big ambitions but no stomach for work. As a bakery delivery boy, he shook down customers for extra cash. He hustled prize money at local footraces with a series of underhanded strategies (jumping the gun, bumping opponents), and also flirted briefly with boxing. Calling himself Packy East, he won his first amateur bout by hitting his opponent while the fellow was looking to his corner for instructions. In his next—and last—fight, Hope was knocked out. "This fellow hit me so hard I bounced right into dancing school," he told the BBC in 1973. Hope studied dancing long enough to take over his instructor's class and teach it for a while. ("Leslie Hope Will Teach You How to Dance—Clog, Soft-Shoe, Waltz-Clog, Buck and Wing, and Eccentric," read some cards he had printed.) And dance was what put Hope onstage: he was hooked from the minute he got paid for the routine he'd worked up with his willowy blond girlfriend and first partner, Mildred Rosequist, in 1920. He wrote in "Have Tux, Will Travel," "We'd make seven or eight bucks and I split it with her." In fact, he chiselled her: according to Rosequist, he told her that their performances were for charity and pocketed the money.

Hope had larceny in his soul. As a teen-ager, he was jailed briefly for stealing tennis balls and racquets from a sporting-goods shop, according to Lawrence J. Quirk's recent biography. "Like most kids today or any day, I had to make my choice," Hope joked about his criminal record in a monologue for the Boys' Club, in 1967. "Was I going to go out and get a job and earn a living, or was I going to spend the rest of my life stealing? I decided to forget the job and stay with show business." To Hope, who referred to comedy as a "scam," laughter was another way of getting away with something. When he first began making good money on Rudy Vallee's "Fleischmann Yeast Hour," in 1930, Hope recalled, "I used to get the money and run around the corner and count it. . . . Like I was stealing it. And with my act I think mostly of theft." The shame and misery of Hope's childhood had robbed him of pleasure, ease, and a degree of playfulness; in a way, Hope "lifted" his father's sense of humor and reversed the vectors of their destinies. Harry, who worked in stone, had been overtaken by changing times, which made him obsolete; Hope, who worked in words, exploited changing times, which made him always up to date. In this psychological sleight of hand, lightness replaced gravity, profit replaced waste, and son replaced father as the family provider. As Hope's act evolved over the decades, it became the slickest of cultural hustles. "What I really am is a liar," Hope wrote in "Don't Shoot, It's Only Me," a book about his comedy. In myriad rascal roles (Turkey Jackson in "Road to Morocco," Painless Peter Potter in "The Paleface," the eponymous "Lemon Drop Kid"), or even as himself, in "Welcome to Britain," a 1943 instructional film for United States troops in England, wherein he explains English coinage to Burgess Meredith only to shortchange him, Hope enjoyed playing the impostor who admitted his larceny but still happily practiced it. Onscreen and off, he won the public's heart and picked its pocket at the same time.

Once, during a rehearsal for "Roberta," the 1933 musical that would make Hope a Broadway star, the show's composer, Jerome Kern, turned to him and asked, "How the hell did you get this ease on the stage?" Hope answered, "Mr. Kern, you don't know what I've been through." What

Hope had been through was thirteen years of vaudeville, which taught the lessons of free enterprise: thrift, self-reliance, perseverance, innovation, and ruthlessness. It was a paradigm of Darwinian struggle, in which only the fittest performers survived the schedule, the audiences, and one another. "You came out battling and you protected yourself at all times," Hope said of vaudeville. With so many partings, disappointments, ambitions, and tempers, vaudevillians, who worked and lived in close quarters on the road, learned to keep to themselves. Hope's guard was never down. To this day, he will frequently exclaim genially, "I'nnat great?" or "I'nnat something?" Steve Allen says, "You could have said, 'I'm having a heart attack,' and he'd say, 'I'nnat something?' To me that's not an appropriate response." But it's the vestige of an old vaudeville stratagem: a show of interest which belies self-involvement. Hope was always watching himself go by: detachment added to his glamour onstage and to his solitude off it. "I don't feel that I really know him," his elder daughter, Linda Hope, who has been her father's producer for more than a decade, told me. "That's a kind of sadness for me, because I would have liked to know him better." Linda's former husband, the writer Nathaniel Lande, says of Hope, "You never get into the inner space. Too threatening. Too vulnerable. I don't think anybody has ever gotten there. It's undiscovered." He adds, "And once you get there, there may be nothing there. We'll never know."

Hope was discovered in 1924 by the comedian Fatty Arbuckle, who got Hope into "tab shows"—mini-musicals in which Hope and his third dance partner, George Byrne, toured small-town America, first in "Hurley's Jolly Follies" and then in "Smiling Eyes" (both in 1925). "As far as stage presence and confidence, it did more for me than anything else," Hope said later. Afterward, billing themselves first as Dancing Demons and then as Dancemedians, Hope and Byrne worked their way up the food chain of variety entertainment, which included dancing with the Hilton Sisters, Siamese twins of some notoriety ("They're too much of a woman for me," Hope joked), and, in 1927, talking their way into a Broadway musical, "Sidewalks of New York." (This break turned into a bust when beefed-up production numbers by the show's stars made the pair's hoofing extraneous.) Before Broadway, Hope and Byrne had worked jokes in between dance; now they decided to work dance in between jokes:

HOPE: Where do the bugs go in the wintertime?
BYRNE: I don't know, you can search me.

The act bombed, and a William Morris agent told Hope bluntly, "You ought to go West, change your act, and get a new start." Working their way back to the Midwest, the disheartened team accepted an engagement on a bill in New Castle, Pennsylvania, where the manager asked Hope as a favor to come out after the last act and announce the next week's entertainment. One of the upcoming acts was a rube comic, whose stock-in-trade was tightfisted-farmer jokes. "Ladies and gentlemen," Hope declared, "next week Marshall Walker will be here with his Big Time Revue. Marshall is a Scotsman. I know him. He got married in the back yard so the chickens could get the rice." The audience roared; Hope's standup career had begun.

Within a few months, armed with a small derby, a big red bow tie, white cotton gloves, and a cigar, he was working solo in blackface for a lowly "rotary unit," which played a different theatre in Cleveland each night. "I scored well even if I was scoring in a minor league," Hope said. Four nights into the gig, he missed his trolley, and rushed to the theatre and onto the stage without makeup. "Don't ever put that cork on again. Your face is funny the way it is," the manager told him. This unwelcome news was Hope's first major comic discovery. "I'd thought my profile handsome in a dark, smoldering way, and discovering somebody thought it amusing was a shock," he said. Hope's lantern jaw and ski-jump nose—his slightly skewed good looks—made audiences more accepting of his brazenness. He soon got work in Chicago as an m.c. at the Stratford Theatre, where he stretched a two-week engagement into six months. "I worked fast, snappy, and impish," he said. Hope's jokes were not really trenchant, but his speed made up for it. By then he was earning three hundred dollars a week and was scrambling to find new material.

Although Hope's subsequent contracts with his writers would include paying them to come up with comic "poses," his easygoing manner was one pose he evolved on his own, in vaudeville—his "sneak attack," he called it. "I make a line seem like nothing. It's the opposite of hitting a joke too hard," he observed. In a way, Hope's self-expression was not in what he said but in how he said it. In "Roberta," for instance, he argued and finally won a battle with the librettist to change the segue into one of the show's best songs, "Smoke Gets in Your Eyes." Otto Harbach's book introduced the song with the line "There's an old Russian proverb—'When your heart's on fire, smoke gets in your eyes.' " Hope's contribution topped it with a laugh that caught the cultural mood of romantic disenchantment. "We have a proverb over here in America, too," he said. " 'Love is like hash. You have to have confidence in it to enjoy it.' " The wisecrack and others like it defined him as that comic cousin of the American booster: the card, a glad-handing showoff eager to disguise his depths. Hope's breeziness, which in later years he emphasized by walking onstage with a golf club, disguised the immodesty of his ego and the agility of his mind. When Hope was making his début as a solo performer in the revue "Ballyhoo of 1932," the curtain was late one night because the chorus girls weren't ready. In the midst of pandemonium, the producer Lee Shubert sent Hope out to calm the audience. "Ladies and gentlemen, this is the first time I've ever been on before the acrobats," Hope began. He waved to someone in the balcony and said, "Hello, Sam." He then explained, "That's one of our backers up there. He says he's not nervous, but I notice that he's buckled his safety belt." Hope stayed on for six minutes; by the time he was through, the producers had decided to let him warm up the audience every night.

On Broadway, Hope had some showstopping moments with classic songs—including Cole Porter's "It's De-Lovely," with Ethel Merman, in "Red, Hot and Blue!" (1936), and "I Can't Get Started," with Eve Arden, in "Ziegfeld Follies of 1936"—but not with classic comic material. "Bob Hope has a slick, humorous style of delivery which ought to put him in the front rank of talking bandmasters as soon as he gets something to say which does not bring the blush of shame to his cheeks," Robert Benchley wrote in The New Yorker about "Roberta." Hope's onstage ad-libbing generated more humor and attention than the show's lacklustre libretto. While singing a verse of "It's De-Lovely" in "Red, Hot and Blue!" Ethel Merman was not amused to discover Hope lounging at her feet; she told the producer, "If that so-called comedian ever behaves like that again I'll use my shoe to remodel his ski nose." Later, Merman said, "I'd rather bed with a porcupine than share the stage with that bastard."

By the mid-thirties, Hope had acquired a Pontiac with his name on it, a beautiful, devoted wife, and a high-powered agent, Louis Schurr. He had all the accoutrements of success except good material. One Broadway critic wrote, "Bob Hope has something, but you don't notice it if you're sitting five rows back"; even on radio, where he made frequent guest appearances, he was said by *Variety* in 1935 to be "easy to take, but hard to remember." But Hope made up in perspiration what he lacked in inspiration. "I used to do four shows a day in vaudeville, then drop into a night club," he said. "I might do thirty or forty minutes off the cuff. I thought nothing of working from twelve noon to one o'clock the next morning." He did benefits, he networked, he developed material. Hope was never anybody's first choice for the shows that became his triumphs. He was offered "Roberta" after William Gaxton turned it down; "The Big Broadcast of 1938," which gave Hope both his theme song, "Thanks for the Memory," and started his movie career, had been meant for Jack Benny; and "Road to Singapore," which was the first in a fabulous string of "Road" movies, had been offered to Burns and Allen and then to Fred MacMurray and Jack Oakie before the producers hit upon Hope and Crosby.

Hope did have one piece of luck: he came into his prime just as the talking pictures and radio were demanding the posture of ease—the illusion of authenticity which was Hope's biggest performing asset. Daniel Boorstin writes in "The Americans," about the emergence of mass media, "Naturalness itself was becoming a rare commodity which individual citizens were willing to pay for, while being (or at least seeming) natural became a special political talent." By 1941, when fewer than ten per cent of Americans were paying taxes on more than ten thousand dollars, Hope was earning about half a million dollars; both advertisers and statesmen were selling the system, and Hope's jokes, which were sharp but not barbed, created a sense of happy cohesion. (Not surprisingly, Hope was once asked to run as a Republican candidate for President.) "You have a nice show here," he told an audience in 1932, at a time when Hoover was using the motto "Prosperity's just around the corner," setting up the biggest topical laugh he ever got in vaudeville: "I was just standing out in front watching the other acts when a lady walked up to me in the lobby and said, 'Pardon me, young man, could you tell me where I could find the rest room?' and I said, 'It's just around the corner.' 'Don't give me that Hoover talk,' she said. 'I gotta go.' " Hope's gibes rarely drew blood. "I can't afford to go out and start knocking Democrats and knocking Republicans, because I'm usually selling a product everybody buys and I don't want to alienate any part of my audience," he said. In the end, he found that audience not on Broadway, where he was just a local star, but on radio, where, after 1938, he was a national figure. Radio also provided Hope with the one crucial ingredient missing from his rapid-fire stage patter: a comic character.

"We should take care to prevent your being a smart alec," Hope's agent Jimmy Saphier wrote in a prescient 1938 letter about Hope's upcoming Pepsodent radio show. "Let's try to build a lot of sympathy for your character, and have the rest of the cast bounce their jokes off you . . . as only sympathetic comedians have a chance for long life on the air." Unless Hope was carefully watched, his trademark brashness could seem like contempt. The character we know as Bob Hope grew over two years "like a weed," according to one of his writers. "We never told Bob this," Mel Shavelson says. "We took his own characteristics and exaggerated them. The woman chaser. The coward. The cheap guy. We just put them in. He thought he was playing a character. He was playing, really, the real Bob Hope." On the day Shavelson arrived in Hollywood from New York, he found himself an apartment and went to meet his new boss. "He asked me if I was married," Shavelson writes in an unpublished memoir, "How to Succeed in Hollywood Without Really Trying." "I said, 'Not yet,' and that seemed to please him. There was no one to share my apartment with me that lonely evening? . . . Then he said, 'You won't mind if I borrow the key? I'll leave it in the mailbox when I leave around midnight.' " Shavelson continues, "I never found out who she was. I had certainly found out who Bob was, though."

"He was a satyr," Hal Kanter says about Hope's not-so-well-kept secret. Hope's vanity was also transparent. "He never walked past the mirror without looking at himself or smoothing his hair," Frank Liberman, his publicist of forty-one years, says. Hope's parsimony, however, was more confounding. Although at the beginning he spent a third of his salary on writers, Hope was still capable of telling Larry Gelbart, "Ten o'clock. My house. Tomorrow morning. Bring your own orange juice." Hope liked to hustle his writers in pool, and also made bets on jokes that he didn't like but the writers did. "We never won, because he would kill the laugh in order to win the bet," Shavelson says. Even payday became a joke about Hope's ambivalence. In a North Hollywood house he once rented, there was a circular staircase. "Every week we'd gather at the bottom of the stairs," Shavelson recalls. "He would go up to his office, write out our checks, and make paper airplanes out of them. Then he'd yell out our names and throw them down. You had to jump up and catch it. He said he had to do it because it was the only exercise we got."

At the same time, Hope was a terrific audience for jokes and a fine editor of his writers' material. In the early days, according to Shavelson, "we'd meet at Hope's office at 9 P.M. Hope would never show until about ten, eleven o'clock. What we didn't realize for a long time was that it was Bob's excuse for getting out of the house. So when he'd finished with the girl, he'd show up at the meeting and we would have all the jokes ready for him." Shavelson adds, "Around one, when we'd all be starving, he'd send Sherwood Schwartz out for a quart of vanilla ice cream with pineapple syrup. Bob would go on with the meeting, eat the whole quart, never offer us anything." Each writer wrote an entire script every week and read it aloud for the others; by the process of elimination, the strongest jokes survived. To winnow them down, Hope marked them with a special code: 1 (titter), 2–3 (fair), check ("boff," as he called a big laugh), check with a line through it (super-boff), check with two lines through it (super-super-boff). He was always pushing for the big laughs. "We need a big kid at the back," he would prod his writers, meaning a strong comic finish. An hour-and-a-half script was compiled and previewed in front of a live Sunday audience; it was then cut down to a half-hour performing script for the Tuesday-night radio show.

The opening monologue—or "mono," as Hope always called it—was where his heart was. "He guarded the monologue like the Dead Sea Scrolls," Liberman says. No monologue was ever allowed to be mimeographed, carbon-copied, or included in any final script except Hope's own. In fact, in order to prevent the East Coast 10 P.M. audience from retelling Hope's "nifties" to West Coast friends in the three-hour time lag between performances, Hope often instructed his writers to do a second monologue for his California audience. Unlike his competitors, who were gentle (Jack Benny) or folksy (Fibber McGee and Molly) or droll (Fred Allen), Hope performed the monologues in a steamrolling, staccato style that owed its inspiration to the gossip columnist and radio powerhouse Walter Winchell, whom Hope always wanted to play in the movies. "Winchell went so fast you couldn't tell when he was lying," Shavelson says. Hope, who crammed as many as twenty-three jokes into a seven-minute riff, used wit instead of tidbits to achieve a similar kind of authority. He called débutantes "barebacks with greenbacks"; sailors were "wolves in ship's clothing"; a lorgnette was "a sneer on a stick." Among the news items that were the staples of the radio scripts was regular news about his career:

JANE RUSSELL: Bob, is it true . . . I hear "Paleface" got wonderful reviews.

BOB: I'll say. The critics raved about it. Walter Winchell gave it four orchids. Jimmy Fiddler gave it four bells. Whittaker Chambers gave it four pumpkins. (That's the last time I buy a joke from Alger Hiss.)

And Hope, who never worked dirty, had no qualms about working racy:

DOROTHY LAMOUR: Don't take me seriously, Bob. I was pulling your leg.

BOB: Listen, Dottie—You can pull my right leg and you can pull my left leg. But don't mess with Mr. In-Between.

"No one else came on and did that much material in that short a time," Larry Gelbart says. "It really was electric." He adds, "It was electronic vaudeville." The monologue was followed by skits and songs performed by regulars such as Jerry Colonna and by frequent visitors, like Doris Day and

Frances Langford; the show culminated in a sketch with the whole company. "But what it mostly was," Gelbart says, "was jokes, jokes, jokes."

By 1939, Hope was fourth among the radio comedians; by 1940, he was second; and when, by chance, on May 6, 1941, Hope grudgingly agreed to leave the studio and perform for soldiers at March Field, in California, he discovered the joys of a captive, entertainment-starved military audience: a constituency that vaulted him into first place and kept him there more or less for a lifetime. According to Milt Josefsberg, who wrote Jack Benny's signature gag ("Your money or your life"), the laughs in Hope's first broadcast to an all-female audience of Wacs "were so loud and long that the writers cut out seven minutes of script while the broadcast was in progress so the show would not run longer than the half-hour time period." From May of 1941 until June of 1948, Hope performed almost all of his four hundred radio programs at Navy, Army, or Air Force bases. Throughout the war and after it, Hope's work for the armed services far exceeded that of any other American entertainer, and it gave his comedy something that it would otherwise never have had: a mission. He'd found an audience that desperately needed laughter, and, Shavelson says, "he tailored his material to them." His entertaining of American troops was heroic and exhausting, and was also a brilliant and enduring advertisement for himself. He became the G.I.s' friend: Uncle Bob (the stand-in for Uncle Sam) was the man who would go to any lengths to bring jokes, girls, and the whiff of paternalistic American swagger to the homesick troops. "He has caught the soldier's imagination," John Steinbeck wrote in the New York *Herald Tribune*, in 1943. "It is interesting to see how he has become a symbol." Hope's troop shows created a reservoir of cultural good will which was invoked subliminally every time in the next half century when, before his entrance, the orchestra struck up "Thanks for the Memory." "I saw your sons and your husbands, your brothers and your sweethearts," he wrote in the preface to "I Never Left Home," an account of his Second World War barnstorming, whose dedication reads "B.H. to G.I." "I saw how they worked, played, fought, and lived. I saw some of them die." He added, "Dying is sometimes easier than living through it." On the page, the sentiment seems dreadful; on the stage, detachment played better. In

Tunisia, one disaffected member of the audience shouted, "Draft dodger! Why aren't you in uniform?" Hope shot back, "Don't you know there's a war on? A guy could get hurt!"

Hope's nonchalance broadcast to combat-weary soldiers the comforting notion that life wasn't always to be taken seriously. This message was brought home most sensationally in the hijinks of his motion pictures, especially the "Road" movies that he made starting in the forties, in which cowardice was lovable and danger was without consequences. "Hokum" was Bing Crosby's word for the loosey-goosey banter between him and Hope, which began when they shared a vaudeville bill at New York's Capitol Theatre, in 1932. Crosby was romantic and cavalier; Hope was impudent and driven. "They were a great team," says Norman Panama, who, with his partner, Melvin Frank, wrote many memorable Hollywood comedies, including Hope and Crosby's "Road to Utopia." "There was always something in front of Bob, whether it was a five-hundred-dollar suit or a three-hundred-dollar set of golf clubs. He used Crosby for protection, someone to share the responsibility for the laughs." Walter Winchell's ongoing mock war with the banana-nosed bandleader Ben Bernie had popularized the fashion of celebrity feuds; Jack Benny and Fred Allen, W. C. Fields and Charlie McCarthy, and Hope and Crosby—as Ski Snoot and Mattress Hip—soon followed suit. "There's nothing of the sacred clown in them, the Don Quixote, Sancho Panza thing—they're both Sancho Panza," the film critic Andrew Sarris says. "What they do is not sentimental. There are no tears, and there's no great joy, either. It's just efficient laughter."

The seven "Road" pictures built their parody of competitiveness into a lucrative running gag that played for more than twenty years, and continued until Crosby died of a heart attack on a Spanish golf course in 1977. Hope was so undone by Crosby's death that, for the first time in his life, he cancelled a performance. "I met him at the airport," Elliott Kozak, then Hope's manager, recalls. "I drove him home. He was a basket case. I'd never seen him cry." Kozak adds, "It wasn't because he was close. I believe that Bob felt, Well, if it happened to Bing, it could happen to me." But Hope and Crosby, who shared golf games and oil wells as well as films, rarely approached in private the rapport that their on-camera badinage suggested. "I don't think Bob ever called Bing just to say, 'Hey, how are you? How you feeling?' " Kozak says. Hope frowned on Bing's drinking; Bing looked askance at Hope's philandering. "Bing was a man with an education," says Hal Kanter, who wrote for both stars, separately and together. "He had a good vocabulary and spoke with good grammar. . . . He used to poke fun at Bob's lack of it. Bob, I think, resented it. He almost assiduously went around trying to improve himself." Kanter adds, "Whatever Bing had Bob wanted."

Among the other things that Hope envied were Bing's Academy Award for acting and his reputation as a romantic leading man. This offscreen ambivalence added emotional vigor to their amiable onscreen jousting, which, as Pauline Kael once wrote, "took the thud out of the dumb gags and topical jokes." Crosby recalled about their first movie, "Road to Singapore" (1940), "For a couple of days, when Hope and I tore freewheeling into a scene, ad-libbing and violating all the accepted rules of moviemaking, the director Victor Schertzinger stole bewildered looks at his script, then leafed rapidly through it, searching for the lines we were saying. 'Perhaps we'd better do it the way it's written, gentlemen,' he'd say reprovingly, but then he'd notice that the crew was laughing at our antics." At one point, Hope spotted one of the film's screenwriters, Don Hartman, and shouted, "If you recognize anything of yours, yell bingo!" But Norman Panama, who directed "Road to Hong Kong," says that Hope and Crosby's ad-libbing was a myth. "Bing never wanted anything changed. That's something everybody forgets. There were some ad-libs, but not nearly as much as the legend would have it."

On the set, and in public together, Hope and Crosby were always "the boys": their movies were really a sophisticated game of hide-and-seek with the occasional game of patty-cake thrown in each time the twosome combined to punch out the enemy. The "Road" movies also set the standard for the sexual fiasco that was Hope's lifetime cinematic stock-in-trade; in some instances, Hope's animal urges gave way simply to animals. In "Road to Bali" he's almost raped by a gorilla; in "Son of Paleface" he beds a horse. The fact that Hope almost never seemed to get the girl didn't spoil the happy ending for the audience; Hope always had himself.

Hope's character—the coward's coward—was balm to frayed wartime nerves, and a nice break from the usual strong, silent types. And yet release from the solemnity of self can't completely explain the depth to which Hope, both plus and minus Crosby, was absorbed by the culture. (Between 1941 and 1951, Hope was among Hollywood's ten biggest money-making stars, and in 1945, when Paramount announced there would be no more "Road" movies, it received seventy-five thousand letters protesting the decision, which it quickly rescinded.) In his many incarnations of braggadocio and cunning, Hope's character was a direct descendant of Sam Slick ("We are born in a hurry, educated at full speed, our spirit is at high pressure, and our life resembles a shooting star"). A kind of Yankee peddler, Hope sold himself in one implausible imposture after another: photographer as gumshoe ("My Favorite Brunette"), huckster dentist as Indian fighter ("The Paleface"), tailor as Casanova ("Casanova's Night Out").

In life, Hope could be every bit as sly as his persona. In the first flush of his film popularity, in 1940, he pressed Samuel Goldwyn to raise his salary from fifty to a hundred thousand dollars a picture. Goldwyn refused, but this didn't stop him from asking Hope, as a favor, to m.c. a gala première of "The Westerner," in Fort Worth. At the event, after a bevy of stars, including Gary Cooper, had been brought onstage, Hope called Goldwyn out and gave him a flattering introduction. Goldwyn returned the compliment. "I haven't made a comedy since Eddie Cantor left me," he said. "I never found a comedian who I thought could do as well—until now. I finally found one in Bob Hope." After the applause died down, Hope said, "That's very nice, Sam. Now let's talk money." Goldwyn was nonplussed. "Later," he whispered. "We'll talk later." "No, let's talk about it here," Hope said loudly. "These people won't mind. Let's get really comfortable. Why don't we just lie down and talk things over." With his audience howling with laughter in front of him, Goldwyn had no choice but to get down on the floor with Hope. "Now, Sam, about my salary," Hope persisted. Goldwyn reached for the mike, but Hope refused to hand it over, and finally Goldwyn whispered something in Hope's ear. Hope whispered something back, and they both got to their feet. "It's going to be a great pleasure to make a picture with Mr. Goldwyn," Hope told the audience.

He had his deal.

Although Hope won five "special" Academy Awards in his career, not one of them was for a specific acting role. "Welcome to the Academy Awards," he began the Oscar ceremony in 1968. "Or—as it's known at my house—Passover." When, in later years, Tony and Linda Hope suggested that they option John Osborne's "The Entertainer" as an Oscar-contending vehicle for their father, Hope demurred. "He always said he wanted an Academy Award for acting, but he also never wanted to get outside his persona," Tony Hope says. "He knew where his audience was, and he didn't want to risk it." Hope was wedded to the joke. And his habit of letting his joke writers gang-tackle scripts and turn them into a theatrical hodge-podge didn't help his artistic cause. In fact, Hope was at his tastiest when he danced. In a spoof of Al Jolson's Southern smarminess, "Apalachicola, Florida" ("Road to Rio"), or in his tap contest with Jimmy Cagney ("The Seven Little Foys"), something quirky, passionate, and personal came through which a lot of his critics felt was missing from his well-worked-out shtick.

But Hope's movie legacy lives on in the films of Woody Allen, who claims Hope as a seminal influence on his screen persona. "When my mother took me to see 'Road to Morocco,' I knew exactly what I wanted to do with my life," Allen says in the voice-over of his film homage to Hope, "My Favorite Comedian" (1979). Allen, a great writer of comic lines, admires Hope, a great reader of comic lines. "It's a delivery that's comparable to Groucho," Allen explained to me. "It's more realistic than Groucho, and so his range is much wider. Someone like Groucho, though he entertained, had a sense of deep surrealism or deep suffering. Hope's persona is glib. He's not concerned with suffering, but what he is concerned with is very, very amusing." The best comedy is about transgression; Hope's comedy was about conformity. He was a sheep in wolf's clothing—an image that Allen overhauled, adding angst and intellect to Hope's anachronistic glibness. But Allen's admiration of Hope's comedy is strictly in his films. "In other media, particularly television, he was not very good," Allen says of Hope's two hundred and eighty-four prime-time television shows, which began in 1950 and ended in 1997, and generally attracted a forty-per-cent share of the audience. "He was lazy, and nobody cared. He would come out and do these old-fashioned sketches, and after a while he was unashamedly reading from cards. It was just awful."

"When vaudeville died, television was the box they put it in," Hope joked a year before he went into TV. He turned television into his own personal vaudeville circuit. "Hope never developed a character in television, never," Larry Gelbart says. But, as America split over the Vietnam War, it was Hope himself, not his comic character, who played most dramatically in the nation. Until Vietnam, Hope had been a Cold War wit, whose jokes confirmed America's superiority. Russia? "Anybody without a stiff neck is a traitor." Africa? "Texas with Arabs." Korea? "Seoul has changed hands so many times the towels in the hotel are marked 'His,' 'Hers,' and 'Who's Sorry Now?' " Prodded by his liberal joke writers, Hope, to his credit, was one of the first comedians to take comic swipes at Senator Joseph McCarthy. "I have it on good authority that McCarthy is going to disclose the names of two million Communists," he said in a 1954 TV monologue. "He's just got his hands on the Moscow telephone directory." Hope's topical humor flattered as it teased, and this was the secret of his success as a court jester to eleven presidents. "He's been able to interject himself into the political arena without anybody getting mad at him," Gerald Ford told me. "He liked to sort of stick the needle in a little bit, but do it in a very nice way." (Hope said, "I love playing golf with Jerry Ford. If you beat him, he pardons you.")

In his compendium of presidential zingers, "Dear Prez, I Wanna Tell Ya!" (1996), Hope wrote, "Laughter is non-partisan." But laughter is never non-partisan: even embracing the status quo is a political position. The Vietnam War made this paradox—and Hope's deep-seated conservatism—transparent. He abandoned his posture of neutrality and began to take sides with his friends, who were known in other quarters as "the military-industrial complex." He lent his joke writers to Spiro Agnew and his presence to Richard Nixon, and his own jokes increasingly turned from saucy to sour: "Students are revolting all over the world. I don't know what they're revolting about, I just know that they're revolting." He tried to define a middle ground for himself. "I'm a hawkish dove," he said. "It's nothing like a pigeon, but if I have to lay an egg for my country I'll do it."

In Hope's role as G.I. Bob, it was business as usual. He continued to perform his troop shows, and his 1970 and 1971 Christmas specials from the war zone ranked among the all-time top thirty popular American TV programs and linked him inextricably in the public imagination to the Vietnam quagmire. "Hey, aren't you the guy who sponsored the Vietnam War?" a Van Nuys teen-ager asked Hope in the early seventies as he was buying an ice-cream cone.

In putting his comedy in the service of the state, Hope, who was dubbed "a Pentagon clown" by *Izvestia*, had become a controversial force of divisiveness instead of unity. One night in 1973 at the NBC studios, Hope slipped into the audience to watch "The Dean Martin Show," on which the comedian Don Rickles was appearing. The audience spotted Hope and started to applaud. Rickles waited for the applause to die down, and then said, "Well, the war must be over." The howls of laughter acknowledged Hope's dilemma. During the Vietnam War, Hope had found himself embattled and in the unusual position of occasionally being shouted down or at a loss for words. In 1970, at the Miss World contest, in London, he was interrupted by explosions and by the whirring of rattles in the audience, and hurled objects forced him to leave the stage briefly. According to General William Westmoreland, Hope did "more for the morale of the Armed Forces than any American that has ever lived." But his hard work received more of a mixed reception in the field than his publicity machine would admit. At Long Binh in 1971, Hope's show was met with banners that read "Peace Not Hope" and "The Vietnam War Is a Bob Hope Joke," and he enraged the soldiers when he said, "You're off the front page back home. The Vietnam War is now tucked away between 'Li'l Abner' and 'Chuckle a Day.' "At the end of that show, when a general presented Hope with a gift—a "Ho Chi Minh bicycle"—G.I.s walked out. Hope was unnerved. He shouted back at the hecklers, "In my heart, you're the guys that are against war because you're the guys that are helping to end it! You've all listened to that garbage of the other cats. . . . What have they ever done for the world? They talk a lot about the My Lai massacre . . . but that's a load of nothing, because they forget the good that we've done helping little kids and building orphanages."

In 1972, on a U.S.O. tour, Hope was billeted in Bangkok, for security reasons, and flown daily to different military installations in Vietnam. He joked, "When I came out of a temple recently, I found two Thai families in my shoes who refused to evacuate." The United States Ambassador to Thailand issued an official apology to the Thai government. "I get very little flak in the States, but when I do it makes good copy," Hope said, adding insult to injury. "For instance, the gay-lib movement made a big protest to NBC when I said in a show that their demonstrations were the only ones on earth led by a cop riding sidesaddle." Hope, who put such an emphasis on timing, seemed to have lost the pulse of his times. In fact, with twenty-five years of performing still left to him, he had lost something even more important: the allegiance of a younger generation.

These days, Hope pads about his rooms on the second floor of his Toluca Lake house, surrounded by autographed pictures of the war correspondent Ernie Pyle, F.D.R., General MacArthur, and the English Royal Family. "He's whistling all the time," Tony Hope says. "He's singing old songs to himself. The ones that come up most are the ones that he used to sing with my mother. He'll just sing his part to her if she's there, or without her being there." At dinnertime, Hope joins Dolores downstairs in the playroom, a large, informal second living room. They sit in the television alcove at a round maple table where Dolores likes to play gin rummy with friends. A framed sampler on the sideboard reads "O.K. So This Isn't Home Sweet Home—Adjust."

For sixty-four years, Dolores has had to do a lot of adjusting. "He's a rover by nature," Dolores told an interviewer in 1953. "The first year we were married, I saw so little of Bob that I wasn't sure we'd make a go of it. Now, of course, I've gotten accustomed to his being away, and I couldn't imagine life being any different." Her Catholicism and her family helped Dolores fill Hope's long absences. "There were times I wanted to pack it in," Dolores told the gossip columnist Cindy Adams; and times, too, when Hope did. "Marilyn Maxwell was really serious," Elliott Kozak says of the buxom blonde, who was known on the Paramount lot as Mrs. Hope in the early fifties. "Bob told me at one point he almost left Dolores for her."

But Bob and Dolores were a good partnership; they shared not only a sense of humor but an almost presidential faith in keeping up appearances. "There was a big social element to being successful as a standup comedian," Tony Hope says. "You had to have the right wife and the right kids . . . . You had to have the total image. And she created that for him." About her husband's notorious womanizing, Dolores told me, "It never bothered me, because I thought I was better-looking than anybody else."

Still, it was hard on her. "She longed for romance from this man, and he was cold as ice to her," says Kozak, who calls Hope "the most self-centered person" he has ever known. "We were in London one time," he recalls. "Bob, Dolores, and I were walking at night. All of a sudden, out of the clear blue sky, she pushed him up against the wall and said, 'Kiss me, Bob. Tell me you love me.' I was so embarrassed I didn't know what to say. I turned my back on it. . . . I never saw him go to her and give her a peck on the cheek. I was with him for twenty-five years." Hope was full of feeling for his public but undemonstrative in private. "MERRY CHRISTMAS. TRIP GREAT. FEEL FINE. LOVE BOB," he wired Dolores in 1965 from Vietnam.

Dolores and the children were extras in Hope's epic. Once, when Tony was around seven, he greeted his father as they sat down to breakfast at a Pebble Beach hotel by saying, "Good morning, Mr. Hope." The son had learned the lesson of the family well. "I wanted everybody to know who he was," Tony says. "Part of my obligation was to uphold the tradition—the image." It was hard for anyone in the family to get much of Bob Hope. "He cares more for the life of the audience than for the life around him," Linda Hope says. The children's memories are of Hope's going away: away to work, away on regular two-hour evening constitutionals, away to a war zone. "We spent a lot of time at Burbank Airport," Tony Hope says. "One time, as the plane was landing I was waving goodbye Daddy, not knowing whether he was coming or going."

Now Hope, who used to spend up to two hundred and fifty days each year on the road, is home to stay, and the household balance has undergone a subtle recalibration. In his heyday Hope told Tony, who was a high-school swimming champ, "I'm still the champion of this house." But, with nothing more to win, Hope's competitive drive is in abeyance. "He's so mellow, so benign," Linda Hope says. "I can hardly believe it." Their old friend Rosemary Clooney says, "He's very demonstrative with Dolores now." A few years ago, visiting Linda in Galway, Ireland, the Hopes were given Claddagh rings—bands with two hands and a heart in the middle—which are often used as wedding rings. "They have not had those rings off their hands," Linda says. "If the heart is facing out, it means that you're looking for the love of your life. If it's facing in, it means you've found the one. Dad keeps playing with it and ends up half the time turning it out, like he's looking for love. Mom keeps observing and saying, 'You've got your ring on backward, Bob.' "

As Hope has increasingly retired from public life, Dolores has come forward into it. In 1993, at the age of eighty-three, she resumed a singing career that had effectively stopped when Hope married her, in 1934. She has cut four albums, and last year sang with Clooney at New York's Rainbow and Stars. She offers an explanation for why she has waited so long to fulfill her own theatrical ambitions: "Bob has always said he never wanted me overexposed." But on her first album, "Now and Then" (1993), she sings a smoky-voiced "Come In from the Rain," which seems to comment directly on the man who now likes to come downstairs and listen to her rehearse. "Well, hello there / Good old friend of mine," the Carole Bayer Sager–Melissa Manchester tune begins, "You've been reaching for yourself / For such a long time." The song continues:

> It's a long road
> When you're all alone
> And a man like you
> Will always choose the long way home.
> There's no right or wrong
> I'm not here to blame
> I just want to be the one
> To keep you from the rain.

Hope is still evading what he calls "the big divot." When Dolores raises the issue of where they should be buried, he says, "Surprise me." These days, he's accompanied everywhere by his companion and aide, J. Paulin. They go for drives: he drops by the Lakeside Golf Club two minutes away from the house to play a few holes and have a brandy Alexander in the clubhouse. When he is down in Palm Springs, where he has a twenty-five-thousand-square-foot ultra-modern house on the top of a mountain, he will head out in the evening for the airport, where it's well lighted and empty. "All the rental-car people know him," Tony Hope told me. "He'll start working the airline terminal."

About a year ago, at a dinner party at Toluca Lake, Hope, who usually sits next to Dolores on such occasions, was sitting next to Tony and Tony's wife, Paula. "My mother blew him a kiss across the table and said, 'I miss you next to me,' " Tony says. "He turned to Paula and said, 'Sometimes I miss me, too.' "

But there are moments when the old Bob Hope shines through. At his ninety-fourth-birthday party, in May of last year, Rosemary Clooney sidled up to him and serenaded him with the usually unsung fourth chorus of "It's De-Lovely":

> He's appalling, he's appealing,
> He's a pollywog, he's a paragon,
> He's a Popeye, he's a panic, he's a pip,
> He's de-lovely.

Hope raised his eyes and grinned. "Fifteen curtain calls," he said.

INGMAR BERGMAN

THE DEMON LOVER

IN "THE HOUR OF THE WOLF," a film that is probably the darkest of Ingmar Bergman's journeys into his shadowy interior, the protagonist, an artist beset by night sweats, is fishing off a craggy promontory on an island where he has come to live. A pesky young boy materializes and by degrees invades the artist's tranquillity. They grapple; the boy scrambles onto the artist's back, tearing at his neck and trying to devour him. The artist smashes the boy against the cliff, then beats his head in with a rock, and finally, with a curious gentleness, lowers the vanquished demon of childhood into the sea. The scene, in its choreographed ferocity, is an allegory for Bergman's lifelong struggle to fend off the ghosts of his past, which he is determined to defeat, but with reverence.

The flat, windswept island in "The Hour of the Wolf" (1968) recalls Fårö, in the Baltic Sea, where Bergman, now eighty, spends most of his time. His single-story gray-brown house, which he built in 1966 for himself and Liv Ullmann, who was then his partner, sits unobtrusively on the island's isolated southeastern edge, hidden by a forest of scrub pines and overlooking shale beaches and the empty sea. The island—a two-hour hop by plane and ferry from Stockholm, where Bergman now ventures only in order to work—also provides the brooding setting for "The Passion of Anna" (1969), and its extremes match Bergman's roiling temperament. "I have such difficulty calming down—my stomach, my head, reality, everything. That is the reason I live in Fårö," he said this March, in Stockholm. "I have a feeling of complete balance. The sea, the house, the loneliness, the light. Everything is clearer. Much more precise. I have the feeling that I am living on a limit, and I'm crossing that limit sometimes." We were sitting in his small, soundproofed office at the Royal Dramatic Theatre, known as the Dramaten, where he was re-rehearsing Per Olov Enquist's "The Image Makers" for its American début. The play, which will appear at the Brooklyn Academy of Music, is a fictional account of the first screening of Victor Sjöström's silent film "The Phantom Carriage," for the Nobel Prize-winning Swedish novelist Selma Lagerlöf; her book about her alcoholic but idealized father was the basis for Sjöström's screenplay.

Bergman, who watches "The Phantom Carriage" once a year on Fårö, and who cast Sjöström memorably as the aging professor in "Wild Strawberries"(1957), also revisits his family in his work, but his method is the opposite of Lagerlöf's idealization. His films, which amount to a singular courageous act of emotional autobiography, explore ancient humiliations; his gift lies in his access to dark feelings and in his ability to call them out into the open, where they can be seen and acknowledged and finally understood. And though most of the Western world knows Bergman only as a filmmaker, his work in the theatre—from Shakespeare to Mishima—is of similar stature. With Enquist's play about Sjöström and Lagerlöf he dramatizes the struggle of all artists to impose their particular spirit on their material: in the act of reimagining their lives they somehow preserve and redeem both the inadequate parent and the memory of pain. This aesthetic transformation—the play calls it "resurrection"—is a game in which Bergman is without peer. While most people spend a lifetime building up defenses against the hurts of childhood, Bergman's defense is to embrace them. "I have always had the ability to attach my demons to my chariot," he writes in his 1990 book, "Images: My Life in Film." "And they have been forced to make themselves useful. At the same time they have still managed to keep on tormenting and embarrassing me in my private life."

When Bergman and I had last met, in 1996, during the opening in Stockholm of "The Bacchae," Bergman compared his theatre work to carpentry, and said he was eager to lay down his tools. He thought the play would be his farewell to the theatre. (He had bid adieu to filmmaking more than ten years earlier, after his Academy Award-winning "Fanny and Alexander.") He was looking forward to Fårö's solitude. He does not like noise—"Quiet" signs are posted around the Dramaten when he's at work.

He does not like lateness: he positions himself outside the rehearsal hall at ten each morning in case the cast wants to fraternize, and rehearsals begin promptly at ten-thirty; lunch is at twelve-forty-five; work finishes at three-thirty. He does not like meeting new people or people in large groups. He does not like surprises of any kind. "When I'm in Stockholm, I'm longing every day for that island—for the sea, for nature," he told me. "To listen to music. To write. To write without deadlines. When he was my age, my father—he was a clergyman—relearned Hebrew with a friend. They read Hebrew and wrote to each other in Hebrew. There are so many books I want to read. Difficult books. That's what I intend to do and what I'm longing for."

Bergman's retirement didn't last. "If I don't create, I don't exist," he told the Swedish press in 1976, when charges of tax fraud (from which he was completely exonerated in 1979) sent him into voluntary exile in Germany, where he stayed for several years. Since he was young, Bergman says, he has "created reality around me the way I wanted." He began as a boy, with puppets and magic-lantern shows, and has since contrived to be in rehearsal almost all his life. "Through my playing, I want to master my anxiety, relieve tension, and triumph over my deterioration," he writes in "Images." "I want to depict, finally, the joy that I carry within me in spite of everything, and which I so seldom and so feebly have given attention to in my work."

Indeed, when we think of Bergman's films, joy is not the first word that comes to mind: for most viewers, they call up an atmosphere of agitation, a tense balance between scrutiny and unknowing, a sense of the silence that rustles underneath personality. Yet through this mist of unhappiness another kind of joy is discernible—in the audacity of Bergman's camera, in the vigor of his argument against evasions of all kinds, and in the ruthless (and sometimes humorous) penetration into the contradictory drives of human nature. Before Bergman, film was mostly about what could be seen and depicted in the external world. Very little of important cinema was psychological: it was wars, chases, situation comedy. Bergman was the first filmmaker to build a whole œuvre through the exploration of the internal world—to make visible the invisible drama of the self. For future generations of filmmakers, he was a kind of bushwhacker, who found a way of embracing the Freudian legacy in cinematic terms and cut a path deep into the psyche—"the soul's battlefield," as Woody Allen calls Bergman's cinematic terrain.

In a career of nearly sixty years, Bergman has written some sixty films, most of which he directed; by the end of this year, he will have added another, "Faithless"—an account of his involvement in a love triangle, which Liv Ullmann is to direct. He has also mounted more than seventy plays; next February he will stage a new production of August Strindberg's "Ghost Sonata" at the Dramaten. When Bergman is in Stockholm, he lives in an apartment built on the spot where Strindberg lived, and the connection is more than spiritual:as Sweden's most expert storyteller, Bergman is Strindberg's heir. And anyone wishing to map the geography of Bergman's genius will find clues in the streets of Stockholm, where he grew up.

The Hedveg Eleanora Church is a high-domed ochre building on the fashionable east side of the city, where Bergman's father, Erik, served as minister for two decades, beginning in the mid-thirties, when Bergman was a teen-ager. The church stands just two blocks north of the Dramaten, where Bergman would eventually set up a kind of alternative ministry— first as the artistic director, for a few years in the mid-sixties, and later as a staff director and resident genius. It's startling that the church of Bergman's youth and the theatre of his adulthood should be so close together: a metaphor for the twinned inconsolability and solace with which his rebellious work always contends. Hedveg Eleanora is austere, monumental, and calm in the watery northern daylight; the Dramaten is an Art Nouveau promise of sumptuous pleasure: warm, noisy, bustling, bright.

But it was in Hedveg Eleanora that Bergman got his first extended lesson in masquerade. In the canopied gilt Baroque pulpit, which is thirty feet high and looms above the teal pews, Pastor Bergman, who was tall and handsome, cut an imposing figure; the young Bergman "never dared go to sleep when my father was preaching." "It was some sort of theatre," he recalls. "Fascinating and boring. The room had a magic, you know. It was always sold out. My father was a marvellous actor." Erik's performance of a righteous, receptive minister in public was entirely at odds with what the young Bergman saw at home—a "lamentable terrified wretch" full of "compressed hatred." The contradiction was the basis of Bergman's confounding sense of insecurity. "Offstage he was nervous, irritable, and depressive," Bergman writes of his father in his autobiography, "The Magic Lantern." "He worried about being inadequate, he agonized over his public appearances, kept writing and rewriting his sermons." Bergman adds, "He was always fretting and given to violent outbursts."

In the limestone solemnity of the church, Bergman senior spoke of good and evil and the promise of eternal life; his son was fascinated by something else. "Death was always present, because under the floor in the church there were graves," Bergman says. "I thought of the skeletons and the dead. Always in contact with the dead." It was not just the actual dead but the emotionally dead parts of his parents which Bergman was obsessed with. "You can't escape me," the ghost of the humorless, punitive Bishop says to his stepson Alexander, tripping the boy on his face at the end of "Fanny and Alexander" (1982). And Bergman never could escape. At nineteen, he had a sensational falling-out with his father. "The mountain of aggressions between us was so heavy and so terrible, I had to go my own way," he says. "I said to my father, 'If you hit me, I'll hit you.' He did, and I did it. I can still remember his face." The estrangement lasted some thirty years. "I look at him and think I ought to forget, but I don't forget," Bergman writes of his father in the autobiographical novel "Sunday's Children." "No, in fact, that's not true. I *wish* I could forget him." After Bergman's mother, Karin, died, in 1966, Bergman, then forty-eight, began visiting his eighty-three-year-old father every Saturday at four o'clock. "It was good to sit there with him," Bergman says. "We didn't talk about complicated things or the past. I think it was some sort of therapy for us both. When he died, we were friends."

Ingmar Bergman was interested not in saving souls but in baring them. Pastor Bergman invoked the Holy Spirit; his son made a spectacle of spirit and of his own version of the mysteries—what he called "the administration of the unspeakable." In his films and stage productions, Bergman always leaves room for the unknown, the intuitive, the invisible; he may have lost his faith in God but not his sense of the miraculous. He likes to recall a time when he and his father went to church, and the pastor, who was sick that day, told his parishioners that there would be no Communion. Erik Bergman went back to the sacristy, reëmerged in vestments, and assisted the pastor by offering Communion. Bergman used the moment as the ending of "Winter Light" (1963); it also provided him with, as he writes, "the codification of a rule I have always followed and was to follow from then on: *irrespective of everything, you will hold your communion.*" The theatre's communion is an altogether different kind; there are no sacraments, but in Bergman's profound dissection of character and feeling there is a sense of the sacramental.

The Dramaten is probably the best repertory theatre in the world. It currently employs three hundred and six people, including fifty actors, and this year, for the cost of about three Broadway musicals ($25 million), it mounted thirty-two productions, eighteen of which were new shows. Bergman saw his first play there in 1928, when he was ten. From the outset, it was a stimulating holiday from the deadly silence, evasions, and disciplined repressions of his family. "For me, the stage was a free zone, where everything was allowed," Bergman told me one afternoon as he took me to seat 675, in the second row of the upper circle, which is where he sat that first day, and where he still occasionally comes to sit and think about things after rehearsals or before an appointment. Dressed in his usual rehearsal mufti (a cardigan sweater, brown corduroy slacks, cashmere socks, white Reebok sneakers with a piece of black masking tape over the left toe), he eased his rangy, slightly stooped frame into the seat as stagehands loaded his production of Witold Gombrowicz's "Princess Ivona" onto the main stage.

"Oh my God, I love this house," he said, and immediately flashed back to his first visit. "I was alone. It was a matinée. A Sunday in March. My God, I'll never forget it. I was so excited I got a fever. So I had the enormous advantage of being ill on Monday, when there was some sort of math test at school. My mother had been a hospital nurse. You could never bluff her. I had a real fever, so I could stay at home. I was in bed the whole day. Not talking to anybody. Lying under the covers. Thinking of what I'd seen the day before."

Early in the the film version of "Sunday's Children" (1992), Bergman's towheaded proxy, Pu, sits with his playmates in the upstairs room of the blacksmith's house, where the blacksmith's bovine wife suckles a boy of five as well as her own infant. "Can I taste?" the dour Pu asks. The other children laugh. The woman says, "I don't mind, Pu, but you'll have to ask your grandmama or mum first." The easy access to emotion, attentiveness, embrace—all the coherence and pleasure that the breast symbolizes for a child—was never certain for Bergman.

"I was quite sure I had been an unwanted child, growing up out of a cold womb," Bergman writes. When Karin's account of her more than fifty-year marriage was found in a safe after her death, it left her husband devastated and Bergman vindicated in his childhood hunch about his mother's ambivalence toward him. Bergman ends his autobiography with an entry from his mother's diary written shortly after his birth, in 1918. She'd been married five years.

> Our son was born on Sunday morning on 14 July. He immediately contracted a high temperature and severe diarrhea. He looks like a tiny skeleton with a big fiery red nose. He stubbornly refuses to open his eyes. I had no milk after a few days because of my illness. Then he was baptized in an emergency here at the hospital. He is called Ernst Ingmar. Ma has taken him to Våroms, where she found a wet nurse. Ma is bitter about Erik's inability to solve our practical problems. Erik resents Ma's interference in our private life. I lie here helpless and miserable. Sometimes when I am alone, I cry. If the boy dies, Ma says she will look after Dag, and I am to take up my profession again. She wants Erik and me to separate as soon as possible. . . . I don't think I have the right to leave Erik. . . . I pray to God with no confidence. One will probably have to manage alone as best one can.

Ingmar was sandwiched between his bullying older brother, Dag, whose bed he once tried to set on fire, and his sister Margareta. Besides the children, Karin was saddled with her agitated husband and a full parish workload: she didn't have the emotional reserves to satisfy Ingmar's hectoring neediness. "Her reactions to me were incomprehensible," Bergman says. "She could be very warm and tender to me and very standoffish and cold."

Ingmar was frequently punished. When he wet his bed, which he did chronically, he was forced to wear a red skirt for the entire day; minor infractions of family rules meant that the child was temporarily "frozen out," meaning that "no one spoke or replied to you"; serious misdemeanors were met with thrashings, which were carried out with a carpetbeater in his father's study. "When the punishment quota had been established, a hard green cushion was fetched, trousers and underpants taken down, you prostrated yourself over the cushion, someone held firmly onto your neck and the strokes were administered," Bergman writes. "After the strokes had been administered, you had to kiss Father's hand, at which forgiveness was declared and the burden of sin fell away, deliverance and grace ensued."

Inevitably, in an environment ruled by caprice and control, Bergman became a showoff and a wily fabulist. "I was a talented liar," Bergman says. In "Fanny and Alexander" he repeats the true story of telling his school class that his mother had sold him to the circus. For the young Bergman, the unmooring anxiety was that he couldn't seem to hold his parents' attention—a distance emphasized by the fact that he was never allowed to address them with the intimate *du*. The excruciating frustration of not quite being able to reach a parent is a powerful mood in many of his films. In "The Silence" (1963) a boy languishes outside a hotel room where his mother has gone to bed with a stranger; in "Fanny and Alexander" brother and sister are locked away from the warmth of their mother in a drab room of the Bishop's house. These are chilling traces of Karin's iciness, which burned and numbed him at the same time.

"Already as a little boy, I had to figure out how to get my mother warm," Bergman recalls. "When I was five, I started to train myself to read my mother, her way of thinking and reacting. Then it went from my mother to the people surrounding me." This childhood maneuver became his greatest directorial asset. "He's a camera," the grande dame of the Swedish theatre, Anita Björk, says. "He looks at you and sees everything." Bergman's uncanny, prolonged cinematic scrutiny of the face—"No one draws so close to it as Bergman does," François Truffaut said—originates in a desire to get under Karin's skin.

From an early age, Bergman re-created in himself a kind of alternative mother—giving himself, in his fantasy-obsessed play, his own form of undivided attention. Bergman's puppets, toy theatres, and magic-lantern shows were worlds that he totally controlled and that were all-embracing reflections of him. In his films the consoling embrace is an iconic motif: in "Cries and Whispers" (1973), in which two sisters and a maid circle each other in a deathwatch over a third sister, the maid bares her breast and holds the dying Agnes to her; in "Sunday's Children," as Pu and his father find shelter from a rainstorm during a bicycle trip, the father wraps his jacket around his son's shivering shoulders.

These images resonate with Bergman's defining longing for what he calls "contact in the belly." "I wanted to touch," he says. "I had a very strong longing to touch other human beings. Still do." Bergman's hectic emotional life (he has had five wives, nine children, and mistresses in almost epic numbers) has been dominated by this ancient, unslakable emptiness and avidity. "He sought the mother," Liv Ullmann, who had a daughter with Bergman, writes about their five-year relationship in her own memoir, "Changing." "Arms that would open to him, warm and without complications."

Only Bergman's upper-class maternal grandmother, Anna Åkerblom, who had been a teacher, offered him unconditional acceptance. "To her I was not a child, I was a human being," Bergman says, recalling summers at her house in the country. "Every evening we'd sit down together on the same green sofa, perhaps for half an hour. We'd sit holding hands and we'd discuss things. Or she'd read something to me." Together, they went to the movies, they invented ghost stories, and, as he writes in "The Magic Lantern," they created their own crude cinematic scenarios: "One of us started by drawing a picture, then the other continued with the next picture, and thus the action developed. We drew 'actions' for several days. They could amount to forty or fifty pictures, and in between the pictures we wrote explanatory texts."

Bergman was the beneficiary of a focus that his grandmother had not been able to lavish on Karin, and that Karin, in turn, could not provide for her son. "Were we given masks instead of faces?" Bergman asks his mother in "The Magic Lantern." He answers his own question in "Persona" (1966), whose title has its root in the Latin for "mask." He separates the dead and the caring parts of his mother into two warring characters, who in the course of the drama merge, in a weird symbiosis, into one face. In the dreamlike prologue a bookish boy tries to touch the large fading image of a woman who looms and recedes at the same time; this turns out to be Alma (Bibi Andersson), who is a nurse, as Karin was—the bright, duty-bound, positive side of the mother. In the course of the film, Alma is infiltrated by the negativity of her patient, an actress called Elisabeth Vogler (Liv Ullmann), who rejects both speech and motherhood, and even goes as far as to rip up a picture of her son. "It's amusing to study her," Elisabeth writes in a letter about Alma, who has opened up to her over time, and who intercepts the letter. She feels betrayed, and her humiliation becomes an articulate, almost visionary energy, which she projects into the mute Elisabeth, conjuring her voice and speaking her story, which echoes the story of Karin and Ingmar:

> The child was sick. It cried unceasingly, day and night, I hated it, I was afraid, I had a bad conscience. . . . The little body had an incredible, violent love for his mother. I protect myself, defend myself desperately, because I know I cannot repay it. . . . And so I try and try. But it leads only to clumsy, cruel encounters between me and the boy. I can't, I can't, I'm cold and indifferent, and he looks at me and loves me and is so soft I want to hit him, because he won't leave me alone.

"Persona" puts the audience where the child in Bergman sits: full of contradictory feelings and images that are imminences of the betrayal of love and its even graver consequence, the loss of meaning. "The picture grows white, grey, the face is wiped out. Is transformed into Alma's face, starts to move, assumes strange contours," read the stage directions for the end of the film, which was originally called "Cinematography." "The words become meaningless, running and jumping, finally vanishing altogether.

The projector stops, the arc lamp is extinguished."

From the moment when the ten-year-old Bergman cranked his first projector and ran his first three-metre film loop through a magic lantern—lit by a paraffin lamp and throwing a trembly brown image on the whitewashed wall of his nursery wardrobe—the shadows on the wall, he says, "wanted to tell me something." He goes on, "It was a girl, a beautiful girl. She woke up. Stretched her arms out. Danced just one circle and went out. How I concentrated on this girl! Then I could move it the other way, so she came back!" The apparatus of film could retrieve or reverse the past; it could make the inert come to life; it could penetrate the senses and speak soul to soul with or without words. It was—and remains—a miraculous hedge against loss. Bergman says, "I still have the same feeling of fascination. It hasn't changed."

"Almost from the beginning, Ingmar knew exactly what he wanted," says Bergman's best friend, Erland Josephson, who starred in "Scenes from a Marriage" (1973), among many other Bergman projects. His performing partnership with the director dates from his student days, when the twenty-one-year-old Bergman cast him as Antonio in a university production of "The Merchant of Venice." "He was very strict and honest with the text, and very practical," Josephson says, adding, "He always knew that this is a profession for experienced people, and that he had to get experience as fast as possible." The Swedish painter Ann Romyn, who knew Bergman in his early professional years and found his energy "menacing," says, "He was a sort of sorcerer. He had powers, I would say. Imaginative powers. He could influence people."

In 1941, at the age of twenty-three, Bergman undertook for the first time to write uninterruptedly. The result in that first year was twelve stage plays and a libretto. One of the plays, "Kasper's Death," got him a job in the script department of Svensk Filmindustri, and there, from nine to five every day, he joined a "half-dozen slaves" trying to make screenplays from novels, stories, and scripts in need of doctoring. Soon the company was producing one of Bergman's original screenplays, "Torment" (1944)—an anguished Expressionist tale about a student who falls in love with a woman and finds out that he shares her with his sadistic, crypto-Nazi Latin instructor. The film's director was Alf Sjöberg, a grandee of the Dramaten, whose reputation for excellence would be surpassed in his life-time only by Bergman's own; he adopted the young author as a kind of protégé. When Sjöberg was otherwise engaged, Bergman even got to shoot the film's final exteriors, which represent his first professional footage. "I was more excited than I can describe," he wrote later. "The small film crew threatened to walk off the set and go home. I screamed and swore so loudly that people woke up and looked out their windows. It was four o'clock in the morning."

Over the next few years, Bergman made "Crisis" (1946), "It Rains on Our Love" (1946), "Port of Call" (1948), "Music in Darkness" (1948), "Prison" (1949), and "Thirst" (1949), all of which telegraphed in their titles a rebellious pessimism that shocked the Swedes. Except for "Music in Darkness," a story about a pianist blinded in military service, which was a box-office success, the films were generally not well received. "Bergman was treated like a subversive, blasphemous, and irritating schoolboy," Truffaut wrote in *Cahiers du Cinéma* in 1958. Nevertheless, Bergman was gathering support from the Swedish film industry. The producer Carl Anders Dymling allowed him to start from scratch on "Crisis" after three weeks of disastrous dailies. Victor Sjöström, then the artistic director of Svensk Filmindustri, taught him "about the power of the naked face and to be simple, direct, and tell a story," Bergman says. Sjöström also offered advice about the politics of persuasion both onscreen and off. "Don't keep having rows with everyone," he told Bergman. "They simply get angry and do a less good job. Don't turn everything into primary issues. The audience just groans." The film editor Oscar Rosander revealed "a fundamental truth—that editing occurs during filming itself, the rhythm created in the script." Several of Bergman's early scripts were co-authored, but increasingly he relied on his own narrative skills; he often writes his scripts in novel form before breaking them down into screenplays. "Ingmar had to do his own scripts simply because there were no novelists or playwrights who were any good in Sweden," Michael Meyer, the British translator and biographer of Strindberg and Ibsen, says. "They didn't have a Graham Greene."

At the same time that Bergman was directing films, he headed up a series of civic theatre companies—first at the Helsingborg City Theatre, where his appointment as artistic director, at twenty-six, made him the youngest in the nation's history. He continued this double duty throughout his career, and many of his early masterpieces ("Wild Strawberries," "The Seventh Seal," "Smiles of a Summer Night") were engineered in part to keep his theatre company together and working. By the early fifties, he had assimilated his influences (Cocteau, Anouilh, Hitchcock, classical theatre), and his films took an introspective turn: they moved from posing social problems to analyzing personal ones. When Bergman tried to dramatize the happiness of Swedish youth—in "Summer Interlude" (1951), "Summer with Monika" (1953), and, even tangentially, in the masterly "Wild Strawberries"—the films were strained, and Bergman understood why. "I myself never felt young, only immature," he wrote in "Images." "As a child, I never associated with other young people. I isolated myself from my peers and became a loner. When I had to formulate dialogue for my young characters, I reached for literary clichés and adopted a coquettish silliness."

Bergman was better at dramatizing his demons—what he calls the "heavy inheritance of universal terror" which permeated everything in his life. Liv Ullmann remembers a trip they took to Rome together, when he was "nervous of the plane and of everything." They stopped off in Copenhagen, and he needed to wash his hands, which meant leaving her, "the safe person," and taking the elevator down to the men's room. "After about ten minutes, I saw him come out of the lift. He had a proud little smile. He had done it!" She adds, "I still think of that little smile, which seemed to say 'Do you know what I've done all by myself?' He'd mastered his fear—and his fears are so everyday."

By his mid-thirties, Bergman had fresh anguish to add to his childhood material. His philandering was legendary: one revue song of the period went "I don't mind being wild and free / As long as Ingmar Bergman fancies me." Bibi Andersson, who took up with Bergman in the mid-fifties for a few years, says, "He was considered a rebel and a genius and brave and a little dangerous. He walked around with this beard and beret and boots. Too thin, too energetic, but wild. I thought he was the sexiest thing the world had created." She adds, "When he asked me to be with him, I thought to myself, I don't give a shit if I'm in love or not. I just want to be around this mind. I want to hear things. I want to learn things. My mother kicked me out." Andersson, who remains a close friend of Bergman's, sees him as "a very hysterical personality."

But Bergman was beginning to make something of his hysteria—something that, unlike his artless childhood outbursts, forced thoughtfulness from his audience about his mortified inner life. It was with "Sawdust and Tinsel" (1953) that he took his initial step into murky autobiographical terrain, and his soul-searching and his cinematic language brilliantly coalesced for the first time. In the character of Albert Johansson—a circus owner caught between his longing for a settled existence with the wife he has abandoned and his vagabond life with a circus bareback rider—Bergman created "a walking chaos of conflicting emotions" who was a simulacrum of his own erotic confusions. He had found his cinematic vein.

" 'Sawdust and Tinsel' was my first true picture," Bergman says. "You know, my lying went on for a long time. Suddenly I understood that I had to stop. I saw that the lies were some sort of filth on my pictures. . . . I had the conscious feeling 'Now, Ingmar, you must tell the truth every minute.' Then, in 1955, before 'Smiles of a Summer Night,' I was together with a girl. We were very much in love. I had to tell her the truth, and I did. 'I'm not going to marry you. I don't love you that way. I want to fuck you.' That was the beginning. Poor girl." Bergman's art now squarely acted out his anxiety, which he calls "my life's most faithful companion, inherited from both my parents, placed in the very center of my identity—my demon and my friend spurring me on." Erland Josephson says, "He is inconsolable, and he wants to be that—to be close to his own hurt parts." Out of this brokenness, Bergman generated a plethora of unsettling images: the clock with no hands ("Wild Strawberries"), the spectral dance of death ("The Seventh Seal"), the cuckolded clown bearing his naked wife over a rocky shore ("Sawdust and Tinsel"), and always the mysterious, protean illuminations of the human face.

Bergman's God-haunted stories gave an uncompromising form to the existentialist angst that was the intellectual vogue of nineteen-fifties Europe, sounding the rumble of loss under everything: love, sex, faith, identity. The films created a seismic disturbance when they were first shown, and nowhere more than in America, which embraced Bergman with an enthusiasm that Sweden never matched, perhaps in reaction to the insipidity of American entertainment in the postwar boom. Bergman was the antidote to the fluffy world of Doris Day, George Axelrod, and William Inge. " 'The Seventh Seal' and 'Wild Strawberries' came to New York," Woody Allen recalls. "I was stupefied. I was on the edge of my seat. They could've burned down the theatre, I wouldn't have known." Allen continues, "He's a great entertainer. This is what finally makes him great. It's not homework to go to his movies."

Not homework, perhaps, but sometimes hard work: "The Rite" (1969), about a trio of players being investigated by a judge, is, to all intents and purposes, incomprehensible. Occasionally, Bergman's stories collapse under the weight of their ambition to be at once in the avant-garde of cinema and of suffering. The suggestion of incest between sisters in "The Silence" seems arid; the schizophrenia in "Through a Glass Darkly" (1961) feels pat; the pessimism in "The Serpent's Egg" (1977), Bergman's study of twenties Berlin, verges on self-parody.

And Bergman, as the éminence grise of the art house, whose images are iconic and at times pretentious, is an easy target for parody. In "The Seventh Seal," for instance, Death arrives, in all his medieval regalia (white face, hooded cloak, scythe), and plays chess with the Knight. Woody Allen adored the scene, and sent up the figure in both film ("Love and Death") and fiction: in a piece called "Death Knocks," the Grim Reaper reappears for a game of gin rummy with a schlepper. Bergman himself is not above laughing at the solemnity of his cinematic idiom. For example, in "The Magician" (1958), when the ghost of an actor returns to haunt the mute impresario of a travelling magic show, he says, "I'm a ghost already. Actually better as such. I have become convincing, which I never was as an actor." Then there's the subversive joy of Bergman's Uncle Carl, his mother's soft-headed inventor brother, who turns up as a character in "Fanny and Alexander" and astonishes the kids by blowing out candles with his farts.

Although his movies are complex, Bergman usually manages to make his ideas clear and exciting for an audience. His startling dramatic fillips reveal a story's pulse—as, for instance, in "Cries and Whispers," where Agnes dies twice, to allow Bergman to expose her sisters' cold hearts. "If you find the rhythm, the heartbeat of the play, or if you can make it in the film, it is much easier for an audience to live with the story and accept it," he says. "The wonderful thing about Ibsen or Strindberg or Shakespeare or Euripides is there is a drive, a rhythm. You feel, My God, I can listen to this. It's a fantastic feeling. It's breathing."

The oxygen of Bergman's own seductive intelligence is most apparent in his work with actors. He is very selective about whom he collaborates with, and careful about choosing roles that will exploit an actor's particular qualities. "Without that actor, he's not interested," says the choreographer Donya Feuer, who has worked with Bergman since 1964. Bergman's explosive intensity and his acute attentiveness put actors in a powerful creative force field. "It's very much in the way he looks at you," Feuer says. "There's something so naked, so exposed, so vulnerable, so available to him all the time, no matter what he's doing, and that availability, I think, is part of his talent. . . . He really listens. He's not listening to what he wants to hear. He's listening to what he's hearing, and understanding it, not criticizing it."

Bergman, who is deaf in his left ear but claims that with his right ear he can "hear like a three-year-old child," explains, "If I listen to them, they not only listen to themselves, they also listen to each other. And, if I do speak, it's important to say the precise word and not to start a discussion. That is the worst thing you can do as a director. Don't discuss. Just say the right word at the right moment. If it's planned, it will be unspontaneous and make the actors suspicious. That was a great difficulty when I worked in Germany for six years. I had to translate. My intuition told me the right thing in Swedish, but in the time it took to translate the word, the moment had passed."

When Bergman walks into a rehearsal, he is meticulously prepared. "I read and reread and reread the play," he says. "The writing and the blocking take me four pages a day, every day except Sundays." On the rehearsal floor, Bergman works very close to his actors. "He's sitting on your shoulder all the time," Elin Klinga, one of Bergman's recent acting discoveries, says. He can be seen consistently right up under his actors' chins in a television documentary about the making of "In the Presence of a Clown," Bergman's superb TV play, in which Uncle Carl leaves a sanitarium to take his newest brainstorm—a "living talking picture" about the last days of Schubert—on the road. At one point, Bergman smooths Erland Josephson's furrowed brow. "Don't wrinkle so much," he says. In the theatre, Bergman doesn't sit and watch from the auditorium until it's time for technical rehearsals. According to his son Mats, an actor at the Dramaten (he was a memorably lubricious fop in Bergman's version of "The Misanthrope"), when his father is displeased with what he's watching "he looks at you but not very long, a very short glimpse, and then he looks at something else." It's easier to tell when he's pleased. "He's shouting, screaming, laughing 'Good!' Like a cheerleader."

Sometimes, in the hubbub of blocking and in order to cut through conversation, Bergman will grab actors and walk them through a particular movement to show what he has in mind. "When he grabs your arm to lead you around, it's very frustrating," Bibi Andersson says. "You feel how he trembles. If you feel your arm resist in any way, he feels that. It's like taking your pulse. He takes you literally by the wrist." She continues, "I bridled at that until I realized that he doesn't do it to be in charge of me—he does it to sense if I'm with him."

"When I work, it's not important what I'm saying, it's the contact," Bergman says, and he recalls that the talented, taciturn Ingrid Thulin once said, "Ingmar, when you talk to me I never understand what you say. But when you don't talk to me I understand completely what you mean." Bergman goes on, "A good actor is very physical. I can talk to his body, and I know before he knows if his body-mind accepts or doesn't accept what I want. I feel it in my body." He adds, "To force an actor to do something is silly. You can convince him, you can talk to him. Then we have the opening, and he makes what you want him to make. Then, five days after the opening, he starts to change a little of what I've said to him. Then suddenly there are ten actors who start to change a little of what the director has told them. There is no rhythm anymore. There is no performance anymore....So it's a good idea to have the actor feel good about the blocking, the thinking, the rhythm. Then we will make a common creation."

Bergman has a special empathy for his actresses, from whom he's been able to coax, in Truffaut's words, "dormant genius": Maj-Britt Nilsson, Harriet Andersson, Eva Dahlbeck, Gunnel Lindblom, Ingrid Thulin, Bibi Andersson, Liv Ullmann. (To this film list should be added Bergman's stage collaborations with Lena Endre, Marie Richardson, Pernilla August, and Elin Klinga.) Bibi Andersson compares him to Strindberg, who "needed women to feed him. When they couldn't inspire him, it was over. That's similar to Bergman. In his younger years, he had women. Now he has actresses. He still loves to create around an actress." And the actresses all have to grapple with Bergman's desire to decipher and to possess them. "He wants to be the only one for you," Klinga says. "He told Anita Björk and me when we were working with another director, 'I'm very jealous.' And he was. We hugged him and said, 'We're yours.' That's like a twelve-year-old boy again." As Bibi Andersson puts it, "He really wants to get under your skin." She adds, "He also feels penetrated." In this exchange of energy, there is a significant erotic charge. The reciprocated gaze—the thing that so bedevilled Bergman as a child—is what gives him his power as a director. "You feel absolutely recognized," Ullmann says. "I have the feeling of finally being seen, and because I'm being seen I blush more. I come out with words in a way I never knew I would. I dare to laugh, which I always thought was very difficult. I dare to cry."

For Bergman, rehearsals impose an exacting discipline, not only on the actors but on his own explosive emotions. It's a situation in which, as Erland Josephson has written, Bergman is "overpoweringly self-assured in his efforts to overpower insecurity; full of empathy in order to keep his impatience under control; full of impatience in order to keep his empathy under control." Bergman says, "If I'm in the rehearsal in my own private turmoil—either fury or love—then I can't hear the actors, I can only hear myself. When I go into the rehearsal room or into the film studio, I must switch. I am the director."

As much as possible, Bergman leaves nothing to chance. "Everything must be predictable and predicted," Josephson says. "The only thing allowed to surprise Bergman and others is Bergman himself." He hates "tumult, aggression, or emotional outbursts," but he has been prone to all three. "No one could be as angry as Ingmar," Ullmann writes in "Changing." Once, on Fårö, she remembers questioning something he did. Bergman flew into a rage. "He ran after me. I knew I was going to die," Ullmann says. "I went into the bathroom. I locked myself in. Then suddenly he kicked right through the door. His slippers landed on me. He started to laugh. I came out because he thought it was so comical. We made it up immediately." She adds, "If you disagree, he feels he's not loved. I think he feels that to be loved he must be loved unconditionally." In his early days as a director, Bergman threw chairs as easily as tantrums; even now he still believes in the occasional well-planned "pedagogic outburst."

"Sometimes when he's at his most angry and controlling—he can be really tough to work with, because he wants everything his way—deep down you can be very moved," Ullmann says. "He is protecting that one place where he feels safe: his creativity. The director. The writer. The master of it all." When Bergman's control is challenged, onstage or off, life can get complicated. In 1995, Bergman cancelled what was to be his farewell production in America, the New York engagement of his glorious version of "The Misanthrope." The Stockholm production, which ranks among my top ten productions in a lifetime of theatregoing, was the best Molière I've ever seen—a court world turned into a den of gorgeous and predatory animals. It ran for a hundred performances, and caused an unholy row within the Dramaten and in the Swedish press. "He came, he saw, he cut them to bits," declared the *Expressen* when Bergman came in from Fårö to see the production again before rehearsing it for the New York trip and found certain "deviations" from the interpretation he'd initially agreed on with the cast. "If I think I am being betrayed, I am quick to betray," Bergman writes in "The Magic Lantern." "If I feel cut off, I cut off." Bergman felt he couldn't trust even a re-rehearsed production to be performed without more surprises. So he withdrew his imprimatur and prevented his beautiful production from travelling. Lars Löfgren, then the head of the Dramaten, tried to reason with Bergman. "I said, 'You're a staff director. You're supposed to be here to work,' " Löfgren recalls. " 'If the production is not good at the moment, it has *been* good, and it must be rehearsed, because we're going to New York with it. I want you back with me.' He said, 'You don't respect my artistic work.' I said, 'Of course I do.

That's why I want you back.' He didn't come."

Though Bergman characterized the incident as "a sneeze in eternity," it ended his long friendship with Löfgren. Bergman regards such shows of aggression as occasionally necessary, even if he feels repentant about them afterward. "I discovered early into our rehearsals that to be understanding and to offer a sympathetic ear did not work," he writes of directing Ingrid Bergman in "Autumn Sonata." The actress, in the role of a concert pianist who gave everything to her art and nothing to her children, had worked out her intonations and gestures before she arrived at the read-through; in the manner of an American film star, she also objected to some of Bergman's lines. "When it was over and we were alone, Ingmar said, 'I can't go through with this,' " says Ullmann, who co-starred in the film, and who had rarely seen the director "really, really down." "She'd stop every other sentence and say, 'Is she going to say something like this? I can't say something like this.' " Ullmann continues, "You know, none of us had ever criticized anything Ingmar wrote." Ingrid Bergman bridled at the dialogue for a scene in which Ullmann, who plays the daughter, delivers a tearful, corrosive diatribe against her. "Help me!" are the words that the script called for the mother to come back with. As Ullmann recalls, "She said, 'I'm not saying that. I want to slap her face.' Ingmar got so shocked. They walked out of the studio, and we heard them shouting out in the corridor. Terrible. We looked at each other and thought, This is the end." Finally, the actress spoke the words, but on the screen her eyes tell a different, indignant story. Out of the tension between her and Bergman she'd made something that even he was amazed by.

"We have to have direct contact with the childish," Bergman says. "Actors who don't have direct contact with their childhood are not good actors. They are boring intellectual actors." But the very childishness that is the wellspring of Bergman's genius is also the source of his occasional capricious cruelty. After Josephson went to Paris for a weekend while in rehearsal for a Bergman show, he and Bergman stopped talking for about a year. "Ingmar didn't like it," Josephson explains. "I didn't miss any rehearsals, but he was angry because I took the risk. I was out of his control for a weekend. He started talking about my face, my chins. It was terribly aggressive. He has a talent for knowing where to put the knife."

Humiliation may be Bergman's theme, but it can also be his practice, as Sir Laurence Olivier discovered when Bergman directed a 1970 National Theatre production of Michael Meyer's version of "Hedda Gabler," with Maggie Smith. Olivier—whom Bergman always referred to in private as "Lord Olivier"—was then the National's artistic director. Meyer recalls sitting with Olivier and watching Bergman work with the actors: "Suddenly Larry said, 'Oh, Ingmar?' So Ingmar, who hasn't been interrupted, I think, in about forty years, turned around and said, 'Yes, Larry.' Larry said, 'I'm only suggesting this and you may think this is absolute rubbish . . . ' And then there was a ghastly hush at this really sort of very melodramatic suggestion. Ingmar said with a pause-no one knows the value of a pause better than Ingmar Bergman—'Perhaps, we'll see,' and went on directing." Meyer continues, "In the afternoon, Larry made some equally fatuous suggestions. This time, Ingmar didn't even turn around. He just paused for I should think a full minute with his back to Larry and then said, 'Yes,' and went on directing." The next day, Olivier was absent from rehearsals. Some weeks later, after a ponderous dress rehearsal, Bergman asked everyone up to Maggie Smith's dressing room "to thank us all personally." Meyer continues, "We all trooped up there. And when Larry naturally enough came up, Ingmar publicly and very rudely excluded him from the meeting. This was the unforgivable thing, to humiliate him in that way."

When Bergman left Sweden in 1976 to live in Germany, he wrote a long letter to his countrymen, published in the *Expressen*, which concluded on a supercilious note: "I quote Strindberg, when he went mad, 'Watch out, you bastards, I'll see you in my next play.' " But the Bergman who returned to Sweden in the early eighties was not the same man. "It was like night and day. There was an enormous humility," Donya Feuer says. "I think he suddenly felt he had nothing to protect. He was open to what was going on with other people. He was more considerate of everyone." Part of this transformation was the influence of his fourth wife, Ingrid von Rosen, whom he married in 1971 and with whom he lived happily until her death, from cancer, in 1995. "I had contact with reality through Ingrid," Bergman says. Feuer explains, "She managed everything—telephone calls, letters. She was the only one who could read his handwriting and type out the scripts. . . . She was very upper class, very well educated, and very refined. She never competed with his professional work. She was responsible for bringing all the children together."

For Bergman's sixtieth birthday, in 1978, all nine of his children gathered at Fårö for the first time. From that moment, Bergman, who is referred to jokingly within the family as the Big Gorilla, became an unlikely but beloved patriarch. "He was nonexistent as a father—except now, when the children are grown," Liv Ullmann says. "They idolize him. I think he's been very lucky with the mothers, because I, at least, have never bad-mouthed him. I must say there were years when Linn didn't see him." When Linn, their daughter, was about seven and was keeping her mother company in the dressing room, Ullmann remembers Bergman's encountering her for the first time in four years. " 'Oh, Linn,' he said, and swung her around in his arms for half a minute. Then he said, 'You know, Linn, Daddy has work, too. He has other things to do.' And then he left the room. That was it."

Bergman now has more contact with his children, some of whom are in the arts. Linn is a novelist; Eva runs the Backa Theatre, in Göteborg; Daniel directed "Sunday's Children." But, even though Bergman has renovated a few buildings on his Fårö property as a summer enclave for his children, it's not easy to get near him. "They have dinner once, maybe, if at all," Ullmann says. "Then they fight to sit at his side. Sometimes he comes by for coffee. They never know when, and it's an honor. Then he has his cinema. He invites some to the cinema in the afternoon, others in the evening."

When Ullmann shuts her eyes and thinks of Bergman, she sees, she says, "this man who sits in a chair with this smile—a kind of half smile—and very, very lonely, feeling he is a stranger." She adds, "He is connected to his creativity, but not necessarily to the world." The isolation that defines Bergman is part of what animates the uncanny atmosphere in his work and activates his unconscious. He claims that there are two ghosts—a judge and a cobbler—who occupy his Fårö outbuildings, and who appear only at night. "I have heard voices," he says. "Once I saw my mother. I was sitting looking out at the sea. Then suddenly I felt that somebody was standing behind me. I looked, and she was there. Very beautiful and very young."

For more than half a century now, Bergman has traded in the mysteries with the sure knowledge "that there are a lot of realities in our reality." He says, "We don't know anything about those realities. The musicians and the prophets and the saints have given us some messages—have given us intimations of the ineffable." Bergman can hear it at the end of Beethoven's Ninth Symphony. "The chorus is going higher and higher, and suddenly is silent," he says. "Then you hear four or five bars, and you have a feeling that reality has opened up. Beethoven, who was deaf, had heard something that never had been written before." Part of Bergman's gift to his century has been to make visible the mystery he sees around him—to glimpse the eternal in the stage-managed transcendence of play. "Anything can happen, anything is possible and likely," the Grandmother says to Alexander, reading from Strindberg's "A Dream Play," in the last beat of "Fanny and Alexander." "Against a faint background of reality, imagination spins and weaves new patterns."

"Ingmar got the life he wanted," Erland Josephson says. "He is the protagonist of his own life. It's a drama. He's creating that drama all the time. Now we have to discuss how to end the drama—some philosophy for leaving the stage." Josephson continues, "We've promised if we get senile to say to each other, 'No, that's enough.' " For the moment, it's not. Bergman's strategy seems close to Edmund Wilson's stoic dictum: "Keep going; never stoop; sit tight; / Read something luminous at night."

"I'm my own god, I supply my own angels and demons," a Bergman character says in "The Rite"; Bergman is also his own clown. A few months ago, he walked into the office of one of the Dramaten's dramaturges, Ulla Åberg, and pinned on her bulletin board a color photograph of himself with a clown's red nose. The image is apt. Bergman, like Uncle Carl in "In the Presence of a Clown," is capering with the absurd: defying death in his art and watching oblivion loom ever closer in his life. But mortality is the one thing Bergman can't redeem through imagination. "I couldn't manipulate being born," he says. "When Ingrid came home and told me she had cancer, I knew the whole time that it was hopeless, but Ingrid didn't know. That was the second time I saw reality. It was impossible to manipulate that." Bergman is curious about the third time he'll come up against that intractable reality. "I'm an old man. I am close to the great mystery," he says. "I am not afraid of it. I am fascinated, not afraid."

A few years ago, when Lars Löfgren was still head of the Dramaten, he and Bergman walked past the greenroom, a spacious place full of oil paintings of the theatre's old luminaries and big pieces of well-upholstered furniture, which give it the cozy feel of a gentlemen's club. The greenroom door was open, so Bergman walked in. Nobody was there. Löfgren recalls, " 'Listen!' Bergman said. I couldn't hear a thing. 'What is it?' I said. Bergman said, 'They're all here.' 'What do you mean?' 'The actors,' Bergman said. 'They're not finished with the theatre.' " Löfgren continues, "He looked around the room and turned to me and very lovingly said, 'One day, we will be with them.' "

MIKE NICHOLS

MAKING IT REAL

ONCE, IN THE EARLY SEVEN-
ties, Mike Nichols was sitting in a commercial jet as it took off from J.F.K.
Moments after it was airborne, the plane went into what Nichols recalls
as "an unnervingly steep bank. Everybody looked at each other. Nobody
knew what it meant." The pilot came on the intercom. "We are experiencing—" he began in his best "Right Stuff" drawl. Then, suddenly, he said,
"Just a minute!" The mike went dead. In the long silence that followed, the
people on the airplane started to panic. A woman a few rows in front of
Nichols turned around and looked squarely at him. "What do we do now,
Mr. Success?" she said.

Nichols, who has a sharp American wit but courtly European manners, bit his tongue. "All those 'Mr. Success' years would have been hard
to explain to anybody if I tried," Nichols, now sixty-eight, says. "What I
really wanted to say to that envious woman was 'Don't worry. There's still
nothing happening inside me. I'm not experiencing success or anything
much.'"

But feelings aren't facts. From the moment Nichols made his name, in
the late fifties, as the lanky deadpan half of the comedy team Nichols and
May, he took up residence in success. As early as 1961, a letter addressed
to "Famous Actor, Mike Nichols, U.S.A." reached him. And, by the seventies, Nichols represented the high-water mark in not just one but three
areas of American entertainment. As a comedian, he improvised routines
with Elaine May which are among the treasures of American humor; as a
stage director, beginning in the early sixties, he had a string of commercial hits that made him the most successful Broadway director since
George Abbott; as a film director, he made the bold, intelligent "Who's
Afraid of Virginia Woolf?" (1966) and "The Graduate" (1967). The latter,

for which he won an Academy Award and which both summed up and influenced his generation, got him off the Hollywood blocks perhaps faster than any director since Orson Welles.

Nichols has made seventeen films in the last three decades. Success, however, as Winston Churchill said, is never final. On May 3, 1999—just one day short of sixty years since Nichols, then Michael Igor Peschkowsky, the son of a White Russian émigré and a German beauty, arrived in New York by boat from Germany—he found himself at one of those occasions he likes to call a "ratfuck," at Lincoln Center's Avery Fisher Hall, where more than three thousand citizens had gathered to celebrate his lifetime achievement in film. The first part of the evening was a cinematic homage. Just before it began, Nichols and his wife, Diane Sawyer—the most observed of all observers—took their seats in the front row of a box just beside the stage and surveyed the illustrious guests below, among them Richard Avedon, Steve Martin, Itzhak Perlman, Stephen Sondheim, Caroline Kennedy Schlossberg, and Barbara Walters. Nichols assumed the runic crooked smile Elizabeth Taylor describes as "that smile that tilts up at one end, that you can read so much into—a shared joke, a certain skepticism." Then, one by one, various grandees of American popular culture—Meryl Streep, Paul Simon, Elaine May, Harrison Ford, Buck Henry, Nora Ephron, Candice Bergen, Art Garfunkel, Matthew Broderick, Nathan Lane—filed into the box, too, and flanked the evening's sovereigns. They were part of Nichols's story; later in the ceremony, in their encomiums from the stage, they would individually swear allegiance to him like courtiers to a king—which, in a way, he is.

"He knows that all the Versailles stuff is bullshit," says the screenwriter Buck Henry, a close friend who has scripted three of Nichols's films, including "The Graduate." "He knows when his ass is being kissed, and he knows when it isn't, although it is most of the time. He casts a baleful eye on all of it, but in his heart he wants it and needs it." In its deluxe panoply, the Lincoln Center extravaganza fulfilled one of Nichols's lifelong fantasies. "He's on an island that belongs to him, manned on the turrets by men with machine guns," another close friend, Richard Avedon, explains. "People can only get in with a passport, and then only his friends." The need for a seamless armor is the legacy of Nichols's friendless, despairing refugee childhood. When he arrived from Berlin, at the age of seven, he was totally bald; he'd been permanently denuded of all body hair at the age of four, a reaction to a defective whooping-cough vaccine. He knew just two English sentences—"I do not speak English" and "Please do not kiss me." He'd lost his homeland, his language, his class pedigree, and, by the age of twelve, he would also lose his father. "I was a zero," Nichols says now. He adds, "In every way that mattered, I was powerless." Nichols sought something to counteract his paralyzing sense of inadequacy and to disarm a world that he saw, and still sees, as predatory and cruel. "The most useful thing is if your enemy doesn't know he's your enemy," Nichols told me, setting out the rule of dissimulation by which, over the years, he has kept the world in his thrall. "Never let people see what you want, because they will not let you have it. Never let anybody see what you feel, because it gives them too much power. You're probably better off not showing weakness whenever you can avoid it, because they'll go for you." With its aspects of detachment, generosity, and control, the imperial posture has served him well.

On the night of Nichols's gala, Elaine May couldn't resist a wink at his jerry-built crown. "So he's witty, he's brilliant, he's articulate, he's on time, he's prepared, and he writes," she said. "But is he perfect? He knows that you can't really be liked or loved if you're perfect. You have to have just enough flaws. And he does. Just the right perfect flaws to be absolutely endearing. And my three minutes are up, but if I had another four seconds I'd tell you every one of those flaws."

Nichols is a purveyor of aplomb, a rare commodity these days. He lives like a pasha and long ago took up the kingly pastime of breeding Arabian horses. (In 1972, he had the national-champion stallion and mare, Elkin and Elkana.) Over the years, Nichols, who calls himself "a Dionysian who gets tired easily," has also been romantically linked to a variety of goddesses—goddesses of literature (Robert Graves's Black Goddess, Margot Callas, who was Nichols's second wife), goddesses of glamour (Suzy Parker), activism (Gloria Steinem), society (Jackie Onassis), and the media (Sawyer, who became the fourth Mrs. Nichols, in 1988). Well before Nichols grew into his grandiosity, his hauteur had him typecast in college plays as the Dauphin and the emperor. With his long Russian nose, he emits a kind of mandarin snottiness—what Woody Allen calls "his superb contumely," adding, "It's supercilious in the way we all wish we had the genius for. He's a nice version of George Sanders in 'All About Eve.' " At a dinner party in the sixties, Nichols corrected Norman Mailer, who had declared that his favorite line of poetry was Dylan Thomas's "Do not go quietly into that good night." "Actually, it's 'gentle,' " Nichols said. " 'Quietly' wouldn't scan, would it?" Mailer rounded on Nichols, calling him a "royal baby," a put-down that Nichols thought was "pretty good." (In jollier circumstances, Sawyer has been known to refer to her husband as "His Royal Cuteness.")

At the finale of the gala, Nichols had planned to go onstage and say to the assembled, "Well, that's all very well and good, but what about my humanity? What about my *fucking* humanity?" But Art Garfunkel scuppered the joke by speaking earnestly to that very point. So when Nichols stepped before his audience—a tall man with big, gnarly hands and an indulged belly that precedes him by some inches—he resorted to another gripe. "Where the hell is Dustin Hoffman?" Nichols said. "He was nothing when I found him." His straight face caught the audience off guard and made the joke ambiguous. "It's like the monster not showing up at the tribute for Dr. Frankenstein," he continued. "Actually, I suspect that his not showing up is related to my not going to his A.F.I. tribute, although that was all the way across the country. . . . Well, it's all blood under the bridge now."

But blood has a way of sticking to things; even the solvent of Nichols's wit can't wipe out certain dark spots. In his movie career, things have not all gone Nichols's way. There was a string of flops in the mid-seventies: "Catch-22" (1970), "The Day of the Dolphin" (1973), "The Fortune" (1975), and "Bogart Slept Here," which Nichols closed down in production; there followed a seven-year hiatus before his next film, the excellent "Silkwood" (1983). Some of his later movies—"Heartburn" (1986), "Regarding Henry" (1991), "Wolf" (1994)—were more or less rumbled by the critics. In 1995, after Nichols had shown the final cut of "The Birdcage" (which went on to gross more than a hundred and eighty million dollars worldwide) to his editing team on Martha's Vineyard, he sat down with them for a celebratory meal. "I was very emotional and very angry. I couldn't speak all through lunch," Nichols told a friend. "The film was so good, so strong. I realized I'd had no inkling of my anger at the people who had written me off. My reaction, instantaneously, was 'Fuck you, bastards. You thought I couldn't do this anymore. Well, look at this.' "

So, here at his retrospective, Nichols both masked and displayed his vindictive triumph. As a parting shot, he announced that he was leaving the next day for Los Angeles, to go into preproduction on his new film—a comedy called "What Planet Are You From?" And he left the audience with a slightly altered version of W. H. Auden's acid envoi—a ruler's deadpan rebuke to those young upstarts "who think they could do it better" and who might dismiss the proceedings as merely "geezer aggrandizement":

> Death takes the innocent young,
> As poets have frequently sung,
> The rolling-in-money,
> The screamingly funny,
> And even the very well-hung.

In mid-July, I caught up with Nichols in his current kingdom, Sound Stage 15, at Culver Studios, in Culver City, where a broken ankle and crutches—the result of a spill on the set—in no way impeded his show of good spirits. "Life is difficult and fucked up and complicated," Nichols says. "The cutting room isn't." At the studio, his power is absolute. "I really need to control it. Every aspect of it, every nuance of the reading. How long every second of every shot is," he says. "Partly because that's the job, and partly because I just have to. I'm happy when I'm controlling it and uncomfortable when I'm not and crazed when it's out of control."

On the set, Nichols's wit serves him well both as a social lubricant and as an equalizer. In conversation, he lays out his colorful word hoard like a vender at a bazaar—a delightful abundance of erudition, playfulness, and surprise, which helps take the odor off his Eeyore-like nature. His voice, which is nasal and comes from the back of his throat, can wring all sorts of sardonic music from the sounds of words. "A retreat? How *moving*. It's not a sweat lodge, is it?" he says, taking a call on his portable phone as the crew prepares for a scene with Garry Shandling and Ben Kingsley. "Come and see me. We can have a *tiny* retreat in my trailer."

While the shot is being set up, Nichols hobbles away toward his trailer, which is parked opposite the sound stage; the makeup man standing at the shadowy threshold of the building cautions Nichols about the ledge he's standing on. "Thank you, Roy," Nichols says. "Where were you when I fell in that hole?" Among the myriad problems facing Nichols on this particular cerulean day, as he clambers up the steps to his trailer, is what to get the cast as an end-of-production present. "My assistant came up with a silver—what do you call it—vibrator," he says. "I'm not sure. Maybe if it has *Ars Gratia Artis* on it." Inside, the trailer is dominated by photos of his handsome children—Daisy, thirty-five, who dubs movies into French; Max, twenty-five, who is a record-company A. & R. man; and Jenny, twenty-three, a student at Brown—and by food (See's Candies, jelly beans, nuts, chocolate-chip cookies). Nichols, who has never met a calorie he didn't like, is, as Candice Bergen says, "a poster child for unhealthy living." Because he's currently immobilized and can't climb up onto the space-station set, a gizmo called a "god box" has been installed in his trailer, just opposite the sofa. A microphone allows Nichols to talk directly to his players as he watches them. "It's annoying," he says. "It's like wearing a condom. You're there and you're not there."

"What Planet Are You From?" is about an alien, played by Shandling, who, as part of a plan to dominate the universe, is sent to earth to impregnate as many women as possible and take over the planet from within. Nichols inspects a replay of the just completed scene in which Ben Kingsley, the leader of Shandling's planet, taps him for the procreative mission. "The success of our planet's domination of the universe rests in your hands," Kingsley says, in his gravest British Received Pronunciation. "Now, if you'll come this way we'll arrange your transfer and attach your penis." A big, chesty laugh rumbles through Nichols's body. "Kingsley was put on earth to say that line," he says, and laughs some more. Nichols has as many kinds of laughs as he does ironic inflections, but his high-pitched Big Laugh is like no other. His eyes widen, his body stiffens, his pale skin reddens as hilarity crashes over him. In that moment of wipeout, all of Nichols's power, self-consciousness, and royal command vanish into childish delight. This wheezy, teary collapse has been captured on record

("Nichols and May at Work"); and anyone who has been in its force field knows the strength of its infectiousness. "It's incredible when you get it," Neil Simon told me. "It inspires you to show him more material to get it again."

In the next shot, which is the movie's finale, Shandling goes into a righteous harangue—"Why are we taking over earth? Is that what it's about? More, more, more?"—and Nichols stops him in mid-flow. "It's a moment from an operetta," he says. "We don't want that gesture. It's too Jewish." Speech, like the portrayal of a character, is in the details; Nichols watches over it with vigilance. "I constantly have to edit the things I want to say," he adds. "Shambling and I get into this kidding thing, but then it gets a little bit out of hand." "He's called 'Shambling,' is he?" I ask. Nichols fixes me with a lidded glance. "Well, now and then," he says. Nichols continues, "He's playing the game of student with the master, which is partly meant to disarm me. He's not without self-knowledge. He knows how to use me to make certain things happen to him in scenes. The game is useful to us both."

But the previous week, for what Nichols said was the first time in his directing career, he had screamed at his star, who is also the film's co-author. Nichols knows that he can be withering. There was a moment during the filming of "The Day of the Dolphin" when Nichols saw himself becoming a tyrannical bastard. "I remember that I told the D.P."—director of photography—"toward the end that I was not proud of the way I had treated the guys and I wanted to apologize," he says. "And he—a very mild man—said, 'It's too late for that.' It took my breath away. It made me realize that I had to put the brakes on completely. Because nobody can fight back, the director has an absolute obligation to treat people decently." By his own admission, he had gone "totally nuts" at Shandling, in an outburst that sent people scurrying off the set. He explains, "Garry came in and didn't know the scene, although he'd written it. Annette Bening, of course, knew it perfectly. After it was over, I said something to her about her character." Bening plays a ditzy recovering alcoholic, with no knack for picking Mr. Right. "Garry said, 'I think she should be kooky.' I said, 'You do? Her clothes are kooky, the set is kooky, her lines are kooky—you want her to *act* kooky, too?' I said, 'Why don't you come in prepared and do your own work?' "

"It was mean," Bening told me. "He was attacking Garry inappropriately. It was really out of line." Shandling apologized for being unprepared, and Bening then met with Nichols in his trailer to defend Shandling's right to have a creative conversation, a point that Nichols conceded when he, in turn, apologized to Shandling. In Nichols's remorse, Bening saw a "fierce superego." "He's not as generous to himself as he deserves to be," she says. "He's got a voice in him that's very harsh, and unnecessarily so." In his surprising anger—he now says he was "much angrier than seemed warranted"—Nichols saw "the dim racial memory of rage," that little boy in himself who is still angry and whom he constantly struggles to keep down. "He's the one," Nichols says. "He's somewhere saying, 'Don't fuck with me.' And I can't stop him."

"All the shit was in the beginning," Nichols says of his life. Hitler—or his voice, broadcast from speakers on dockside lampposts—literally saw Nichols and his three-year-old brother, Robert, off to America in 1939. Nichols remembers not being allowed to board the *Bremen*, which was leaving from Hamburg, until the traffic-stopping speech was finished. The brothers, each with ten marks in a purse around his neck, made the journey alone across the Atlantic. Their mother, Brigitte, was ill and stayed behind for a year and a half before rejoining the family; their doctor father, Paul, who had left Russia for Germany after the revolution in 1917, had gone ahead to New York in 1938, just before the Nazi takeover, to set up a practice on the prosperous Upper West Side. On their first night off the ship, Nichols remembers seeing Hebrew writing on a delicatessen and asking his father in German, "Is that allowed?" He also remembers watching his brother throw a tantrum while his father "pretended to call the police on the pay phone to deal with him." "He had no experience as a father," Nichols says. "He had no idea what to do." Paul saw his boys only intermittently during their first year in America. He placed them with an English family, some patients of his who agreed to care for them while he was establishing himself. "They were awful," Nichols says. "They would kiss their own children good night, then shake our hands. We'd get a spoonful of milk of magnesia and go to bed." Things didn't improve much when the Peschkowsky family was reunited. "My parents fought all the time," Nichols recalls. "They would have divorced if my father hadn't died—something that my mother immediately forgot." Much later, Nichols learned that his father "was impotent with her and not with many other women." Both parents had a series of lovers. "There were always other people, in Germany and here," he says. "It was just the way things were."

Nichols felt "landlocked" in the family, trapped in the battle between his warring parents. A lot of the contention was about him. "I wouldn't go to school. I wouldn't get up in the morning. I answered back," Nichols says. He "had a mouth," which made both his schoolmates and his family wary of him. "My father wasn't too crazy about me," Nichols says. "I loved him anyway. One of the things I regretted for a long time was that he died before he could see that he would be proud of me. I was actually more what he wished for than he thought." He adds, "He could rage." (Nichols still remembers his father, in the heat of an unhappy family moment, saying to him and his brother, "I'll be glad to get rid of you two.") "But he also told funny stories, and he used to dance for us in his underwear. He did routines at parties that people loved to hear." In later life, Nichols was told by the impresario Sol Hurok, who had been one of Paul's patients, "You're not as funny as your father." And it's through his father that Nichols feels he understands the stoic bravado of Chekhov's characters. "He was the Russian as entertainer," he says. "What I loved [my father] for—even when he wasn't noticeably loving me—was that he had great vitality and joy of life." Paul never let his darkness show in public. "I feel linked to him in many ways, and that's one of them," Nichols says.

By contrast, Brigitte, who was thirty-four when her husband died, at the age of forty-four, became "a nightmare of accusation," someone who collected injustices. "She was one of those people who would hold you responsible for everything that happened to her and how bad she felt now," Nichols says. He would try to kid her out of her misery. "Everything wounded her," he says. "She was always wounded to the quick. 'I raised you so you could say that to me? Thank you very much, I deserve that.' It went on for hours, days."

Brigitte, who had no profession, no money, no proper English, and only a few friends, would go to the Stanwood Cafeteria, on Broadway, and sit alone for hours. Over the years, she worked in a bakery, a bookshop, even set up a translation agency to support her boys. But after Paul was gone they found themselves plummeting well below the level of middle-class gentility to which they had been accustomed. Although Nichols blocked out the degree of their humiliating poverty, his brother subse-quently reminded him of "bug-infested apartments" and of their mother "giving up to the point where she didn't do the laundry. We weren't clean." "She always had some mysterious illness," Nichols adds. When he went home after school to their drab rooms at 155 West Seventy-first Street— "one of those tiny apartment houses with podiatrists on the first floor"— he frequently found Brigitte propped up on her living-room sofa bed (the boys shared the bedroom) with a table of pills, "maybe a hundred and fifty bottles of medication, and the phone, on which she always was."

In time, Nichols discovered that he could make people laugh by telling stories about his mother. In fact, Nichols and May's definitive sketch, "Mother and Son" ("Someday . . . you'll have children of your own. And, honey, when you do, I only pray that they make you suffer the way you're making me. [*Sobs.*] That's all I pray, Arthur. That's a mother's prayer") was inspired by one of Brigitte's lethal phone calls. As Nichols recalls, it went, " 'Hello, Michael, this is your mother. Do you remember me?' I said, 'Mom, can I call you right back?' Literally. And I called Elaine." He and May were playing at the Blue Angel then. "I said, 'I have a piece for us.' I told her the line. She said, 'We'll do it tonight.' And we did it pretty much the way it is now. She had the identical mother."

Before he found a way to make light of his difficulties, Nichols was swamped by them. From his first day at the Dalton School, on the Upper East Side, the clouds of exclusion and isolation glowered over him. "The kid was as far outside as an outsider can get," says Buck Henry, who was in his class. "He was Igor Peschkowsky when he was at Dalton. He did not speak English. He wore a cap all the time." Nichols says, "I remember being on the school bus in New York and saying, 'What means 'emer-gency'?" By the time he reached high school (the progressive school Walden, from which he graduated in 1948), Nichols had mastered English, had a make-do wig, and had learned the idiom and style of his peers, but his assessment of himself during these "searing, painful years" was that he was "the most popular of the unpopular kids." "That was cast in bronze, that's where I was chained in the galaxy forever," he says. "I thought about revenge a lot in those days."

A lazy and lacklustre student, Nichols had a quick mind and a formidable intellectual inheritance. (His maternal grandmother, Hedwig Lachmann, did the translation of Oscar Wilde's "Salomé" that Richard Strauss used for his opera; his grandfather Gustav Landauer, among whose best friends were Martin Buber and B. Traven, was a writer turned activist, who was a leader of the German Social Democratic Party, and whose brutal execution by the Nazis had been the reason for the family's exodus.) Nichols filled his solitude with activities that took him out of himself and into exotic other worlds. At sixteen, he went with a date to the second night of Elia Kazan's production of "A Streetcar Named Desire." "We just sat there," Nichols says. "We didn't talk. We couldn't believe there was such a thing." He adds, "I just wanted to be around theatre." He also read voraciously (all of Eugene O'Neill by the age of fourteen, James Joyce's "Ulysses," E. M. Forster's "A Passage to India"); he was a constant moviegoer; he hung out in Central Park and at the Claremont Riding Academy. "I got to exercise people's horses; sometimes, when people were thrown off, I would catch the horses on the bridle path and ride them back." Animals calmed Nichols; unlike his classmates, they were responsive, unself-conscious, and unable to pass judgment. "The refugee ear is a sort of seismograph for how one is doing," Nichols says. At high school, he explains, "I *heard* what they thought of me—'nebbish,' 'poor boy'—and what they thought of each other. A thousand tiny victories and defeats in an ordinary conversation. I didn't know what to do with it."

To this day, even though Nichols wears a wig, the intrusive, objectifying eyes of others continue to be a threat. "Staring is something that still makes me absolutely nuts," he says. He thinks of the public as "something to be controlled and tamed." "The first person to come up to me at a party is in danger to this day," Nichols says. "My reflex is to attack the first couple of people. I can't stop. Diane is right there, taking off the edges, fixing it. By the third or fourth person, I can be friendly." To Nichols, the audience has always personified Them—the annihilating mob of his childhood, whom he characterizes as "the beast" with "too much power." He says, "I

was so impaled on what people thought. I had to train myself away from
that. I never had a friend from the time I came to this country until I got
to the University of Chicago. I was seventeen."

He ended up there by a fluke: it was one of the only schools in
America that didn't require the College Boards, and Nichols hadn't taken
them. "Once I got there, I had a very specific and powerful sense of 'Oh
my God, look, there are others like me. There are other weirdos.' " The
publisher Aaron Asher, who shared college digs with Nichols, says, "We
were all freaks. We were way ahead of the country. There was sex. There
was dope. There was a subculture." Asher was just one of Nichols's new
friends, who were "refugees or first-generation Jewish intellectual guys."
When Nichols mentioned to Asher that his grandmother had written the
libretto for Strauss's "Salome," Asher joked, "Oh, really? Was she Hugo von
Hofmannsthal?" Nichols says, "I was looking at somebody who knew who
Hofmannsthal was and that he wrote libretti for Strauss. No such thing had
ever happened to me before."

The first person Nichols met at registration was Susan Sontag; they
struck up a lifelong friendship. "I thought he was terrific," Sontag says. "I
adored him from the start. He was totally alive and incredibly verbal. We
talked about books, about feelings, about how to get free of our pasts.
Because we were interested in theatre, we were interested in observing
people. I would happily have become his girlfriend physically, except I was
intimidated by the hair problem and felt he was untouchable." (Thirty
years later, Sontag confessed to Nichols that she couldn't accept the scars
from her mastectomy: "I have this thing, and every time I take a bath I'm
horrified." He said, "Susan, now you know how I have felt all my life.")
Asher characterizes Nichols's look as "something out of a German
Expressionist movie," but says that, "despite the strangeness of his appearance, he did very well with the girls. He was courtly, and he was well read,
which got you a long way at that university."

Nichols, who had begun therapy, was also deeply depressed. "I would
spend long times in my room and just not come out," he says. "Sometimes
I would step over all the dishes and the Franco-American spaghetti cans
and hang out with some friends, then go back to my lair." Nichols d.j.'ed
a popular show of classical music and chat at WFMT, but his depression

almost cost him the job. "He was funny and knowledgeable but totally unreliable," says Asher, whose cousin owned the station. "They fired him a number of times."

"I couldn't be a *person* that many hours a day," Nichols explains. "I needed—still need—a lot of time lying on the bed absolutely blank, the way I assume a dog is in front of the fire. A persona takes energy. I just needed a rest from it. Not to be anything in relation to anyone else."

When Nichols did emerge from seclusion, he worked up his losses into a kind of legend. According to one of his theatrical cohorts, quoted in Janet Coleman's "The Compass," Nichols behaved like "a princeling deprived of his rightful fortune." Nichols was so poor that he took to eating the leftovers from the coffee shop where the director Paul Sills was then a waiter. "He rattled his tin cup," Nichols's friend Hayward Ehrlich, now an associate professor of English at Rutgers, says. "When Mike appeared, you knew that he needed a cup of coffee or a sandwich or something. It became his way of relating to people, to have them sort of help him out of his impoverishment. I think Mike loved to magnify his sense of adversity so that in some way he could triumph over it."

Much to Nichols's surprise, during his sophomore year he found himself "near the center of the in-group" and "a minor celebrity." The theatrical talent pool at the University of Chicago was extraordinary: Sills, Ed Asner, Severn Darden, Anthony Holland, Zohra Lampert, Barbara Harris, Gene Troobnick. Nichols directed his first play, Yeats's "Purgatory," with Asner, and he performed in a number of plays, among them "Androcles and the Lion," "St. Joan," and "La Ronde." He played Jean the valet in a production of Strindberg's "Miss Julie," directed by Sills. "He wasn't the working-class man and couldn't come close to it," Sills says now. Nichols agrees; it was, he says, a "pathetic, awful production." He remembers "this evil, hostile girl in the front row staring at me throughout the performance. I was about four feet away from her and she stared at me all through it, and I knew she knew it was shit, and there was no way I could let her know that I knew." A few days later, the show mysteriously got a rave review in the Chicago *Daily News*. Nichols recalls rushing up to Sills on the street with the paper; Sills was with the girl who had unsettled Nichols from the audience. He scoured the review, while the girl read over his

shoulder. "Ha!" she said, and walked away. Nichols, who was already toy-
ing with the notion of a theatrical career, had just met his future: Elaine
May.

Some weeks later, on his way back from his disk-jockey gig, in the spring
of 1954, Nichols caught sight of May in the waiting room of the Illinois
Central's Randolph Street Station.

Their friendship began with an improvisation. "May I sit down?" he
asked. In a thick Russian accent, May replied, "If you *veesh*." "Off she went,"
Nichols says. "She started us on that." They played out the scene, which
Nichols characterized as "half spy, half pickup," all the way home. "I think
I went home with her and she made me her specialty, which was ham-
burger with cream cheese and ketchup—the only thing she cooked,"
Nichols recalls. "She didn't know conventional dishes. She was utterly a
rebel. That was part of the fun of it."

May was also a femme fatale. "Everybody wanted Elaine, and the people who got her couldn't keep her," Nichols says. But, even at their first
meeting, which led to a brief romance, he remembers feeling that "we
were safe from everyone else when we were with each other. And also safe
from each other." He goes on, "I knew somehow that she would not do to
me the things she'd done to other guys. I knew she wouldn't lose interest
and move on. I knew instantly that everything that happened to us was
ours."

May's life had been as painful and complex as Nichols's. "It's almost
hard to convey how neurotic we were," Nichols says. Although she had
dropped out of high school at fourteen—the only thing she enjoyed there
was diagramming sentences—May was, as Edmund Wilson noted in his
diary when he fell under her dark-eyed spell in the late fifties, "something
of a genius." She had grown up in a nomadic acting family, spending a good
part of her childhood playing a little boy named Bennie in a travelling
Yiddish theatre run by her father, Jack Berlin. According to her second
husband, Sheldon Harnick, who wrote the lyrics for "Fiddler on the
Roof," the death of May's beloved father when she was ten left her to a
future of apprehensive relations with men. She was married for the first
time at sixteen; by eighteen she had a child, Jeannie Berlin, who was about

four years old when Nichols met May and was being raised in Los Angeles by May's mother. By the time she reached Chicago, May had studied acting, performed a hillbilly act under the name Elly May, and written advertising copy. May, who saw herself primarily as a writer, was unofficially auditing courses at the University of Chicago and trying to develop a screen treatment of Plato's Symposium. (She once convinced a philosophy class that everyone in the Symposium was drunk and that that was the point of Plato's discourse.) "The only safe thing is to take a chance," May always told Nichols, who was ravished by her daring and her quirkiness.

Nichols and May had talent, but, more important, they had chemistry. They were quick; they were guarded; they were crazy. They were also "insanely judgmental" snobs, bound together, Nichols says, "by tremendous hostility to everyone else but never to each other." (May once said, according to Nichols, "that if somebody told her that I had burned down her house with her whole family in it, she would say, 'Oh, I must ask Michael why he did that.' ") "I feel in opposition to almost everything," May, who no longer gives interviews, said in a Profile of the duo published in *The New Yorker* in 1961. Like Nichols, she used wit as a pesticide, and her juicy good looks were a particularly disconcerting contrast to her sharp tongue. Once, Nichols recalls, when two men followed her down the street making kissing sounds, May turned on them and said, "What's the matter? Tired of each other?" "Fuck you!" one of them shouted at her. May turned and faced the guy. "With what?" she said.

Nichols dropped out of college in 1953, and, in 1954, he decamped to New York to study the Method with Lee Strasberg. "I have decided that if I don't make it as a nervous young man," he wrote to a Chicago friend, "I will wait and become like Robert Morley, who is clearly the funniest man in the world." But in 1955, with no prospect of work, he returned to Chicago with the promise of twenty-eight dollars a week as part of a new company called the Compass Players, of which Sills and May were founding members. The goal of the Compass, which would evolve into Chicago's legendary Second City, was to do away with conventional plays and make theatre by improvisational means. "I was terrified of improvising," Nichols says. "I didn't even know what it was. I hated it, and I was very bad at it." Nichols cried in his scenes for months "because that's what

I thought I'd learned from Strasberg. Paul and Elaine kept me going. The fact of Elaine—her presence—kept me doing it."

In the first successful scene they did together, Nichols played a riding instructor, and May his pupil. "We both realized as we got into the middle of the scene that I would get to stand in the middle of the stage and watch her cantering as both horse and rider around me." During the scene, a member of the cast ran into the bar where the other actors were congregated, shouting, "Come quick! Mike has a character!" Nichols reflects, "What is implied in that story—and it was true for the first time in my life—is affection. They had some affection for me. I began to understand that I could be kidded, and people could be fond of me, and that this would all be a pleasurable thing."

As intellectual high-wire acts go, there is no riskier or more astounding enterprise than going out in front of an audience and creating something out of nothing. "You're showing off how smart you are, how good you are," Buck Henry says. "You have the pleasure of having not only performed it but written it at the same time." Improvisation—a process, Nichols says, that "absorbs you, creates you, and saves you"—allowed the actors to stay on the edge of emotion and character without connecting deeply to their interior lives, and this suited both Nichols's and May's private natures. "I would never have been a performer without her, and I don't think she would have without me," Nichols says. "Elaine and I are, in some weird way, each other's unconscious." Nichols made the shapes; May filled them in. "She was shockingly, endlessly inventive. She could go on and on—I couldn't," Nichols says. "I did my jokes, and then I was through."

Within the Compass Players, May could be funny with several different actors, but Nichols could be funny only with her. "I never did a good scene of any kind with anybody else," Nichols told Jeff Sweet, in "Something Wonderful Right Away," an oral history of the Compass Players. "For me, it depended on a certain connection with Elaine and a certain mad gleam in either her or my eyes when we knew something was starting." The mad gleam meant, as he explained to me, "Oh, fuck, I know where you're going. That's a great idea you've just had, and when you get there I'll be ready." That focus—reminiscent of a parent's empowering gaze—was inspiring. "We had to figure out something or we would disappear, each of us," Nichols adds. (He would later find a similar containing attentiveness in Diane Sawyer. "All of her is available all the time," he says.) With May, Nichols could drop his mask. "*I* interested me when I was with her," he says. "It wasn't only that she was so great but that when I was with her I became something more than I had been."

Onstage, in their own version of Truth or Dare, Nichols and May kept upping the ante on each other. Once, in an improv about an egotistical d.j. and a starlet called Barbara Musk, Nichols quizzed May about her next movie. "My latest motion picture is . . . called 'Two Gals in Paris.' It is the life story of Gertrude Stein," May said. "What do you play in the picture, sweetheart?" Nichols asked. "Well, I was really just lucky enough to get the part of Gertrude Stein," she said. "I had heard that Gertrude Stein was going to be played by Spencer Tracy," Nichols said, maneuvering her into a tight corner. "Only as a child," May shot back. When the conversation got on to the soundtrack of the movie, May said that she'd recorded the title song. Nichols promptly asked her to sing it. On the spot, May ad-libbed an entire song, which ended:

> There was dashing Dmitri, elusive Ivan
> And Alyosha with the laughing eyes.
> Then came the dawn
> The brothers were gone
> I just can't forget those wonderful guys.

The University of Chicago proved the perfect place for nurturing their particular ironic and informed voices. "It was the most referential community that I think ever existed in this country," says Nichols, who improvised entire scenes in the style of writers suggested by the audience. "At the Compass, we could drop 'Dostoyevsky' as a name and get a laugh. We were living in the context in which the referential joke was just the highest currency." They were also coming of age in a "safer, quieter place" than New York. "Chicago is not a city of fashion, nor is it full of pride and excitement over its art," Nichols says. "They were very calm about Compass. They came. They laughed. They went home."

Nichols and May were beginning to find resources in themselves that they hadn't known they had, including the ability to make anger work for them. "Rage is the best engine, of course, if you have a tremendous gift to employ it properly," Nichols wrote to a friend. Once, when Nichols was performing a sketch about pretentious snobs at a private party, the actor playing the effete host offered to put on a record. "Would you like to hear 'The Four Seasons'?" he asked. "Perhaps just 'Winter,'" Nichols replied. "To freeze his ass was a pleasure," says Nichols, who found that with jokes he could "cow the shit" out of the public. "When a joke comes to you, it feels like it's been sent by God." He adds, "What it is, really, is discovering your unconscious."

There were other discoveries. When Nichols was onstage, even the "curse" of imagining what others thought of him became an asset: "I could hear what the other actors were thinking, where they were going, what the audience was thinking." Nichols also learned "the Aristotelian things" about the building of a scene—conflict, theme, resolution. He and May found ways to "grab the opposite." "There had to be a core to a scene," Nichols told Jeff Sweet. "It didn't matter how clever the lines were. If they weren't hung on a situation, you were only as good as your last line. . . . But if you could grab a situation, whether it was a seduction or a conflict or a fight, once you had that spine, then things could come out of it." And when the jokes were found, Nichols husbanded them. "If there was a laugh to be gotten and Elaine didn't set up the feed line, Mike would work with her until she did," another Compass member, the comedian Shelley Berman, said. "He did everything but lasso her." For a while, according to Janet Coleman, Nichols and May worked with Berman, a trio that May suggested they call "Two Cocksuckers and Elaine." "I actually liked Shelley," Nichols said. "But one day he came offstage and said, 'Hey, guys, Mike had three scenes in that set, and I only had two.' It was a whole new idea in Eden to count. The group was finished in six months."

Nichols and May themselves nearly foundered in 1958, when they were working in St. Louis, where a new Compass Players venue had been launched. Nichols had recently married the Chicago TV personality and singer Pat Scot ("Isn't it a beautiful first wedding?" May said at the ceremony), who joined him on weekends. During the week, on a strictly platonic basis, Nichols and May shared a room, which she vacated when Scot arrived. On those days, May stayed with another company member, Del Close. Nichols was jealous of Close, not for romantic reasons but because May was so much a part of his identity that he couldn't share her. "I persecuted the shit out of Del," Nichols says. "Nothing could stop me. Elaine finally said to the producer, 'I can't stand it anymore—you've got to fire Michael.' " Nichols was summarily fired.

Some weeks later, from New York, where he had gone with Scot (though, as May had predicted, the marriage didn't last much longer), Nichols called to ask May if she'd like to audition with him for the New York agent Jack Rollins. Rollins handled such cabaret talent as Harry Belafonte and Woody Allen. "They were immediately astounding. They were complete," Rollins says, of the first time he set eyes on the team, at his office in the Pierre Hotel. "He is Mr. Practical. She is insanely creative. But Mike is the one that made the act live in this world." By the following Tuesday, Nichols and May were playing the Village Vanguard. "A couple of weeks later, we were on 'Steve Allen,' " Nichols says. "Then we were on 'Omnibus,' and we were very famous. The whole thing took about two months." After the "Omnibus" show, Nichols remembers calling May at 4 A.M. to say, "What do we do now?"

As McCarthyism, the Cold War, and racial unrest made their generation anxious, Nichols and May struck a new disenchanted chord in American life. "Nobody was doing any humor about post-Korean War young people, that urban generation," says the cartoonist and playwright Jules Feiffer, who, when he first heard them, "didn't dare laugh, because I was afraid of missing something." He adds, "Humor was Bob Hope still. When I saw Mike and Elaine, suddenly you felt not just that this is funny but that this is true." Woody Allen, who wanted to write for Nichols and May, says that comedians like them "were touching on some kind of truth—truth of character, social truth, truth of wit. And, suddenly, part of that whole new sense of truth was that they wrote their own material." With Nichols and May, Jewish angst, Freud, literacy, irony, and sex were ushered into the discourse of mainstream comedy. They, along with Mort Sahl, Jonathan Winters, and, later, Lenny Bruce and Woody Allen, were the renegades who led comedy away from the ersatz to the authentic. "The nice thing is to make an audience laugh and laugh and laugh and shudder later," May said. The frisson was the shock of recognition. Nichols and May had the uncanny ability at once to comment on character and to fill it from within. "They were like music," Steve Martin says, referring to the swift intimacy of their overlapping rhythms, the deft interplay of May's soft, breathless voice and the reedy clarity of Nichols's sound. For instance, in their sendup of public outrage over Charles Van Doren and the "Twenty-One" scandal:

> NICHOLS: Thank heaven for the investigation.
> MAY: Oh, yes.
> NICHOLS: When I feel worst I say to myself, "At least the government has taken a firm stand."
> MAY: Oh, yes. Well, they can't fool around with this the way they did with integration.
> NICHOLS: No.
> MAY: This is a . . .
> NICHOLS: . . . moral issue.
> MAY: Yes.
> NICHOLS: A moral issue.
> MAY: *Yes! Yes!* It is a moral issue.
> NICHOLS: A moral issue.
> MAY: And to me that is so much more interesting than a *real* issue.

"Smart is not necessarily funny," Martin says. "You can go through a whole evening of smart and have laughed completely perfunctorily." But Nichols and May could be approached from either a dopey or a smart place. For example, their classic sketch about two teen-agers smoking and making out in the front seat of a car contained two pieces of inspired physical business: May in the middle of a passionate kiss opening her mouth to breathe and emitting a puff of smoke (a joke Nichols later used in "The Graduate"), and the clinching lovers trying to pass a cigarette from one trapped hand to another.

However, sometimes smart alone could bring down the house. Nichols began his sendup of Tennessee Williams—a high-pitched, hard-drinking Southern playwright called Alabama Glass—with the playwright explaining his newest work to the audience. "Before the action of the play *begins*," Nichols drawled, "Nanette's husband, Raoul, has committed *suicide* on bein' unjustly accused of *not* bein' homosexual."

"Most of the time, people thought we were making fun of others when we were making fun of ourselves," Nichols says. "Pretentiousness. Snobbiness. Horniness. Elaine was parodying her mother, as I was mine, and a certain girlishness, flirtatiousness in herself." He adds, "It was utterly freeing." And redeeming. In the teen-ager sketch, for instance, Nichols and May were sending up the cheerleader and the football star, those high-school paragons they never were but now got to play. "We *were* those people, and it healed something, weird as it sounds," Nichols says. Onstage with May, Nichols felt, "I could be anybody I needed to be. I used to have a mental image of cracking a whip when I was talking to the audience. I could control them with jokes." Offstage, the person he presented as Mike Nichols was another version of his stage persona—witty and apparently able to handle everything. "'We'd like to say a few words about adultery— it's coming back.' That's who I was." He adds, "You start imitating somebody who is calm about all that. You imitate it long enough, and it becomes true."

But, while his public persona stanched old anxieties, success brought new ones. May cared more about process, Nichols more about results. "She was always brave," he says of her desire to improvise. "But I became more and more afraid. I wasn't happy with getting paid a fortune for something and not having tried it out in advance." By the late fifties, Nichols was earning more than half a million dollars a year. He adds, "The audience didn't give a shit whether you were improvising or not. They'd come to see good comedy."

The team's creative differences came to a head in their brilliant Broadway show, "An Evening with Mike Nichols and Elaine May" (1960), which I saw during its yearlong run. "We were irreproachable," Nichols says. "We never got a negative review. We never had an empty seat. Everybody loved us. Everybody felt they had discovered us." But discovery—the fearless adventure of creating in the moment—was gradually being leached out of their performances by the repetition of set routines. May grew increasingly unhappy. "Sometimes she'd be late. What is so difficult? Two hours out of twenty-four. It's a perfect job. It wasn't that way for her," Nichols says. "We had huge fights about it. I never could understand why she found it so difficult."

The most stunning moment of the evening—a kind of augury of their collapse—was a sketch called "Pirandello," a twenty-minute exercise in which Nichols and May began as two little kids, playing at insulting each other like Mom and Dad, then became Mom and Dad yelling at each other, and then turned into a pair of actors having trouble with each other onstage. Suddenly, in a terrifying shift, Nichols and May were in the middle of some ugly private squabble. At one point, in what Buck Henry characterizes as "a moment of unbelievably intense embarrassment for everyone," Nichols turned to the audience and said, "My partner and I . . ." May said, "Well, screw this," and started to walk offstage. Nichols grabbed at her, ripping May's blouse as she pulled away. She started to cry. "Michael, what do you think you're doing?" she said. "I'm doing 'Pirandello,' " Nichols said. Breaking into smiles, they took their bows. But at one performance Nichols and May actually came to blows: Nichols hit her back and forth across the face, May clawed at his chest until it bled, and the curtain had to be brought down. "We cried together. It didn't happen again," he says. "I think, in many ways, I persecuted her. I went on at her, 'This is too slow, this has to go faster.' "

The end was slow in coming. In October, 1962, Nichols took the lead in May's play "A Matter of Position," which opened in Philadelphia. "It was sort of about me, which she never quite admitted," Nichols says. But, with him on the stage and May in the audience, the balance of their relationship irrevocably shifted. "Suddenly, Elaine was not next to me, doing it with me, but out there judging me," Nichols says. "It was horrendous." The play itself added to the atmosphere of fiasco. As the Philadelphia *Sunday Bulletin* wrote, "Those members of the audience who had not already beat a hasty retreat before the final curtain, as many did, were left with a sensation of numbness that was too far down to be attributed to heartburn." Nichols and May were no longer two against the world. May was looking for a replacement for Nichols, and Nichols was saying to people, "Get her to cut the play or I'm leaving." The play died in Philadelphia; and, although they didn't exactly speak the words, so did their friendship. "It was cataclysmic," Nichols says.

"Mike was in a state of deep depression," says Robby Lantz, Nichols's theatrical agent at the time. "He really wasn't functioning. He went to bed. Period." Nichols was now half of a comedy team. He had lost his best friend, his livelihood, and the scaffolding of his identity. "Mike has no tolerance for failure," says a former collaborator who tried to rally him after May's departure. "I didn't know what I was or who I was," Nichols explains. His predicament was summed up one afternoon on Park Avenue by Leonard Bernstein, a member of the deluxe set he'd become part of. Bernstein put his arm around Nichols. "Oh, Mikey," he said, "you're so good. I don't know at what, but you're so good."

What Nichols was good at, it turned out, was something that his acting classes with Strasberg, his improvising, and his comedy act with May had all been a preparation for: directing. In 1962, in New Jersey, he'd directed a collection of Jules Feiffer cartoon sketches, "The World of Jules Feiffer," with music by Stephen Sondheim. "It was clear to me that he was extraordinary," Feiffer says. But it was not clear to the producing fraternity or to Nichols. As an apprenticeship, Lantz sent him on what Nichols calls "the lamest possible job," to direct Wilde's "The Importance of Being Earnest" and play the Dauphin in Shaw's "St. Joan," at a Vancouver theatre festival. "Every night at midnight he called and said, 'Get me out of this. I don't want to do this,' " Lantz recalls. "I said, 'This is precisely what the doctor ordered.' " And so it proved. The Broadway producer Arnold Saint-Subber was shopping for a director for Neil Simon's "Nobody Loves Me." Although Saint-Subber didn't have enough confidence to guarantee the tyro director the Broadway show, he was prepared to let Nichols try out the play in Bucks County, Pennsylvania. Nichols had only seven days to mount "Nobody Loves Me," which was later retitled "Barefoot in the Park."

After the first reading at Saint-Subber's house, when none of the actors laughed, the notoriously nervous Simon, known as Doc because of his ability to swiftly rewrite a line and make brilliant comic fixes, wanted to call off the play. Nichols was unruffled. "The play was so light, so sweet, so funny, that my job was to make it real," says Nichols, who impressed Simon with his extraordinary calmness. "I was absolutely confident about what everything should be and where everybody should be." Nichols told his talented cast—Robert Redford, Elizabeth Ashley, Mildred Natwick, Kurt Kasznar—to treat the play as if it were "King Lear." "Let's do it as though we don't know what's going to happen," Nichols remembers telling the cast. "Let's not let them know it's funny."

But it was Simon who didn't know that his play was funny. At the first Bucks County rehearsal, he sat outside the rehearsal hall. "Suddenly, I heard a roar," Simon says. " 'Thank God, they must be up to a good part.' I went inside. It was Mike telling them a story during the break. Then we went back to the play—no more laughs."

"Doc said, 'Let's call it off. This is not a play. I never thought it was a play,' " Nichols recalls. "I said, 'Let's decide after the first preview. Let's just see how it is with an audience.' Of course, they yelled and screamed and fell out of their chairs. Doc never worried again." Nichols adds, "I had instant maturity."

This marked the beginning of what is probably the most successful commercial partnership in twentieth-century American theatre. "We were obsessed in the same way," Nichols says of Simon. "I could wake him up at two in the morning and say, 'I've figured out what's wrong with the third act,' and he would curse me and then come down and meet me in the lobby to listen to it. It was the joy of discovering things together."

As a comedian, Nichols had watched himself become what he calls "a show-biz baby." "I was narcissistic," he says. "I would get mad. I bitched about our billing. I did all the things I dislike. Comedy is the only work in the world in which the work and the reward are simultaneous. Comedians get it on the spot. They get the laugh. It's very corrupting to your character." But as a director Nichols got to play adult instead of baby. "There was something about serving something that wasn't me," Nichols says. Within fifteen minutes of starting rehearsal for "Barefoot in the Park," he had a life-changing revelation: the experience of taking care of others made him feel taken care of. "I had a sense of enormous relief and joy that I had found a process that both gave me my father back and allowed me to be my father and the group's father," he says.

Nichols's love for his actors was palpable; he created a protective environment for them. "They're giving everyone the right to assess, evaluate, criticize everything about them—their noses, their asses, their intelligence, their worthiness or lack of worthiness," he says. "They're really out there." Nichols was a shrewd father—clever about wielding his authority and about maintaining boundaries. During "Barefoot in the Park," Redford came to Nichols in a quandary: he was being upstaged by the showy Elizabeth Ashley. "I can't bear it," he told Nichols. "Every night when I kiss Ashley, she kicks her leg up behind her. I feel like I've been used. I'm embarrassed." "Why don't you do it, too?" Nichols suggested. Redford did as he was told and got a huge laugh; Ashley promptly stopped her upstaging.

Some of Nichols's charges could be notoriously bumptious. Sometimes he tamed them with his high-definition humor. Once, during a heated rehearsal of "The Odd Couple," Walter Matthau looked out at Nichols in the auditorium and said, "Mike, can I have my cock back now?" "Props!" Nichols said. With other wayward actors, like George C. Scott, he knew when to be politic. During the rehearsals of "Plaza Suite," Scott disappeared for three days. "We're in the middle of a scene, and George walks in. Collar up—it's winter—hands in coat pockets. He's just standing there looking at us," Simon recalls. "I look at Mike, and I'm anxious to hear what he's gonna say. Mike said, 'Hi, George. We're on Act II, page twenty-one.' " On the other hand, Nichols could be strict about certain kinds of behavior. At an early rehearsal of "The Prisoner of Second Avenue," the cast, which included Peter Falk and Lee Grant, was blocking a scene on the stage of the Plymouth Theatre. "One of the actresses said, 'Mike, if she stands over there, I don't think this part of the house is gonna see me,' " Simon recalls. "Mike turned and whispered to the producer, 'Fire her.' "

Nichols's authority rested, in large part, on his unique understanding of the audience. Onstage, and later in film, his work sought—some would say too eagerly—to speak to the audience in a popular way. At its best, this sensibility produced "The Odd Couple," one of the century's classic comedies. At its most indulgent, it allowed Robin Williams, as Estragon in

"Waiting for Godot" (1988), to break the play's artifice of isolation and ad-lib with the paying customers. "The experience of living in front of the audience for all those years in Chicago did something to me," Nichols says. "It gave me some closeness to them, some trust." His sensitivity to audi-ence reaction was the issue in a dramatic falling-out he had with David Rabe, whose play "Streamers" was probably Nichols's greatest artistic tri-umph—a beautifully staged and terrifying barracks tale of homosexual baiting. When it came to Rabe's next play, the powerful "Hurlyburly," Nichols explains, "I was desperate for him to cut. I kept saying, 'I won't do this to the audience.' I could not get him to see the show from the audi-ence; he only saw it from the light booth." Rabe, who finally went mute in protest ("He couldn't reach me. I was not listening," Rabe told me), stayed with the show until it opened but spoke hardly a word to Nichols. Nichols won the argument and the cut play was a success, but it cost him their rela-tionship.

Improvisation had given Nichols another invaluable directorial impulse: "To damn well pick something that would happen in the scene—an Event." As Nichols explains it, the Event in any scene subliminally seeks an agreement with the audience on the human experience. "While you're expressing what happens, you're also saying underneath, 'Do we share this? Are you like me in any way? Oh, look, you are. You laughed!' " The building of this agreement through observation and detailed comic busi-ness was Nichols's signature: Art Carney, in "The Odd Couple," suddenly single and so nervous on his first date that when he lights the woman's cig-arette he closes his Zippo on it; the newlywed Elizabeth Ashley, in "Barefoot in the Park," who knows nothing about housekeeping, holding a match to a log in the fireplace, or slamming from room to room in a pas-sionate argument with her husband while simultaneously undressing.

Nichols has a gift for making things real. During the tryouts for "Barefoot in the Park," he and Simon stood at the back of the theatre watch-ing a scene in which the bride, after a week of marriage, screams that she wants a divorce. "I said to Mike, 'I don't think we should be watching this,' " Simon recalls. "He said, 'Why not?' I said, 'It's too personal, what they're doing on the stage.' And Mike says, 'Good, I'm glad you like it.' "

Between 1963 and 1984, Nichols chalked up about a dozen Broadway hits in a row, half of them with Simon. "Over and over again, he'd say when everybody was getting nervous, 'It's only a play. They're not going to be waiting for you in front of your house with torches,'" recalls Simon, whose hit play "The Sunshine Boys" was a script that he had abandoned until Nichols encouraged him to complete it. But one thing about theatre did make Nichols nervous: seeing his stage business and his contributions to scripts go into movie versions without remuneration. He was the first director to demand, and get, a share of the author's royalties, which, when added to his director's royalty and his piece of the subsidiary rights, quickly made Nichols a very rich man. (According to his accountant, if all his stock and film income were lost, he could still "live comfortably" on his production royalties.) "I wasn't pleased with giving it to him, but I can't argue with it," Simon says. "I would rather have him do it and have the play be great. I never worked with anyone in my life—nor will I ever work with anyone—as good as Mike Nichols. And, when you talk about percentages, what Mike asked for was more than made up for by what I made on 'The Sunshine Boys.'"

Money played a large part in how Nichols measured his achievement. "He always pushed with agents—I speak for us all: more money, more power, more billing," Robby Lantz says. "Eventually, the demands became cruel. Artists in the theatre should not take from each other things that are not necessary." But Nichols, who had almost been wiped out in his first show-biz incarnation, was building an unassailable second career. "The butterflies in my stomach won't stop fluttering until I have thirty million dollars," the producer Lewis Allen overheard Nichols telling Lillian Hellman. "He's ruthless when he wants to be, or sometimes maybe even when he doesn't want to be," Lantz says. "He doesn't let anything stand in his way."

Nichols was also avid for artistic excellence, which he needed power to protect. He learned this lesson in his first taste of Hollywood, in the mid-sixties. Elizabeth Taylor had chosen Nichols to direct her in "Who's Afraid of Virginia Woolf?," even though she had never seen or read the play: she trusted, she said, Nichols's sense of the tragic, which she'd intuited from their friendship. And it was Taylor whom Nichols invoked when Jack

Warner, reversing production plans, insisted on shooting in color. As Nichols recalls, "I said, 'Mr. Warner, it's impossible for several reasons. The sets are built. Elizabeth's thirty-three years old—her makeup will never withstand color. How can she go from thirty-three to fifty-six and have us believe the makeup in color?'" But Warner insisted. The screenwriter and the producer, Ernest Lehman, whom Nichols sardonically nicknamed Slugger, said nothing. "Well, O.K., I'll tell you what," Nichols told him. "You make it in color. I'll go home. I like it at home." Warner immediately conceded: "All right, black-and-white," he said. "After that, he treated me very kindly," Nichols says. "Until he threw me off the picture at the end. When it was mixing time, he saved time and trouble and just had his crew mix it."

But even here Nichols had unexpected leverage. Each night from the set, the editor, Sam O'Steen, would play him the sound mix over the phone and Nichols would give him notes on what to change. Finally, Nichols got word to Warner that he wanted to cut a deal. Warner was worried that the film, which was about adultery, drunkenness, and brutal family battles, would not be approved by the powerful Catholic Legion of Decency. In exchange for being allowed back on the set, Nichols came up with a plan to deliver the Legion: "When the Monsignor sees the picture, Jackie Kennedy will sit behind him. When it's over, she will say, 'How Jack would have loved it!' " Jackie Kennedy did as her friend asked; Warner got the Legion's blessing; and Nichols duly finished his film, the first film ever for which all of the four leading players were nominated for Oscars.

Nichols, whose film technique is not showy, is a director's director. "He tends to get actors to give him their finest hours," Steven Spielberg says, citing Kathy Bates's long monologue in "Primary Colors." For Nichols, who himself gave a tour-de-force performance in Wallace Shawn's "The Designated Mourner," at London's Royal National Theatre in 1996, the director's job is to help the actors turn psychology into behavior. When Nichols talks to actors and to students at the New Actors Workshop, which he founded with Paul Sills and George Morrison, in 1988, he is generally oblique, offering up examples from his own life to clarify a theatrical moment. "You kind of just free-associate all day long," says the writer-director Nora Ephron, who worked with Nichols on

"Silkwood" and "Heartburn." "Then suddenly you get something that actually is good enough to find its way into the thing you're working on." The veteran director Billy Wilder says, "Mike's scenes have a kind of inner content, which the audience feels and follows. He's very lucid." "What you're looking for every day is one little surprise," Nichols told Charlie Rose about directing. "It's like seeding a cloud and hoping it will rain."

The process requires patience, luck, and a gentle touch. Once, during the casting of "Carnal Knowledge," Jules Feiffer, who wrote the script, told Nichols that he was worried about putting the twenty-three-year-old Candice Bergen in the lead. "Can she act?" Feiffer asked. "Mike said, 'She'll act for me.' And she did." In his recent biography of Edward Albee, Mel Gussow quotes Richard Burton (who played the harried professor in "Who's Afraid of Virginia Woolf?") on Nichols. "He appears to defer to you, then in the end he gets exactly what he wants. He conspires with you rather than directs you, to get your best," Burton said.

Nichols's goal is to match the actor to the part. "If I can cast the right people and figure out the things they should be doing in the scene, they don't have to do anything but show up," Nichols says. "Nobody has to act." Over the years, Nichols has made some particularly daring, less than obvious choices—Art Garfunkel in "Carnal Knowledge," Adrian Lester in "Primary Colors," Hank Azaria in "The Birdcage"—but the outstanding example of inspired casting is Dustin Hoffman in "The Graduate," since Hoffman was both unknown and physically wrong for the preppy Benjamin Braddock, a Wasp college athlete who has an affair with one of his parents' friends. "There is no piece of casting in the twentieth century that I know of that is more courageous than putting me in that part," says Hoffman, who considers the film "the most perfect movie I've ever been part of," adding "I was a paralyzed person. I had come from a paralyzed background—the suffocation of that family. I was not acting."

What Nichols saw in Hoffman—"a dark, Jewish, anomalous presence"—was, of course, himself. Through improvisation, Nichols had learned to "treat yourself as a metaphor"; Hoffman gave him the same opportunity in film. "If the metaphor is powerful, it's always underneath you and you're always surfing it. You're always serving it," says Nichols. Even Hoffman's whimper, Nichols says, "was my little whimper when Jack

Warner would tell a joke—in fact, people had to tell me to try not to whimper when he told jokes, that he would notice." Hoffman remembers Nichols taking him aside when he was listless in front of the cameras, a couple of months into the shooting, and saying, "This is the only time you'll ever get a chance to do this scene. It's going to be up there for the rest of your life." Hoffman adds, "He really meant it. It makes me cry, because he had that kind of passion, and it had that importance. I've never forgotten it. Mike worked like a surgeon every second."

Steven Spielberg calls "The Graduate" "a visual watershed," and invokes the moment when Benjamin races home ahead of Mrs. Robinson to tell her daughter Elaine, whom he loves, about his affair with her mother. "All of a sudden, the mother appears in the door behind Elaine, Elaine turns, and the focus racks to the mom. But when Elaine turns back the focus stays—Elaine is actually out of focus—and very slowly comes back until she is sharp and she realizes that Benjamin and her mother have been shtupping. I had never seen long lenses used that way to illuminate a character moment."

In Spielberg's encyclopedic appreciation of Nichols's cinematic innovations, he lists the handheld camera in "Who's Afraid of Virginia Woolf?," which "further complicated" the anxiety and turned the couple's war into "a dance"; the "brilliant use of light" in "Day of the Dolphin," when the aquarium lights are turned on and a dead body is discovered floating inside the tank; the way Nichols built, bit by bit, the paranoia and terror in "Silkwood," which was, for Spielberg, "one of the most frightening and suspenseful things I had ever seen in a movie"; the long opening shot in "Carnal Knowledge," at the college party, and the way he "made love to Ann-Margret through the lighting." That controversial film, which Nichols considers his darkest, was a coruscating look at predatory sexual chauvinism and at women's suffering, themes that resonated with Nichols's own life at the time. "He was not nice to his girls," says a close friend of those middle years, when Nichols was married to his third wife, the Anglo-Irish novelist Annabel Davis-Goff, who is the mother of two of his children, Max and Jenny. (He had split up with Margot Callas in 1964.) "He was a terrible household tyrant."

"Carnal Knowledge" dramatized this tyranny. The night before Nichols was to shoot the crucial scene—the bedroom fracas between Jonathan (Jack Nicholson) and the depressed Bobbie (Ann-Margret), in which Jonathan goes berserk trying to force Bobbie out of his house and calls her "a ball-busting, castrating, son-of-a-cunt bitch!"—Feiffer sat with Nichols as Nichols explained why the scene had to go. "It's just so ugly, it's so awful, people are gonna hate it, and they're gonna hate the movie," Feiffer remembers him saying. "We went for a bite," Feiffer adds. "I just sat in the car listening to him go over and over why he couldn't shoot it. Finally, he just looked at me and said, 'No, we've got to do it, because it's true.' "

But after the box-office failures of both "Carnal Knowledge" and the ambitious but misguided "Catch-22"—a story whose surreality was not Nichols's strong suit—Nichols began, by his own admission, to lose his way. Once, during this period, he sat idling in his Rolls-Royce at a Beverly Hills traffic light when a pimp in a flashy car pulled up beside him. "That's a Silver Cloud," the pimp said. "And you, man, are the silver lining." And so it had seemed, until, after his third miscue, with "Bogart Slept Here," it wasn't. Nichols told the world that he'd lost his appetite for making movies, but what he'd lost was a vital sense of connection to what he was doing and what he wanted to say. "Usually it happens right away, when I'm reading a script—I see a moment, and I know what that moment is, and it's my hook into the whole thing," Nichols says. In the years between closing down "Bogart Slept Here," in 1975, and starting "Silkwood," in 1983, those moments of compelling inspiration eluded him. In the interim, besides developing a film version of "A Chorus Line" (which he subsequently abandoned), he produced the musical "Annie" and the one-woman Broadway show that launched Whoopi Goldberg's career.

Then, sometime in the middle of the eighties, visions of an altogether different kind appeared to Nichols: for about six months, he experienced a Halcion-induced psychotic breakdown. He became delusional—he was convinced, for example, that he had lost all his money, and that he'd turned from being "the hero of the story" into the villain. "Because I'd lost the money, I was the bad guy. I'd brought shame and unhappiness to my family," he says. "It was a horrible feeling of abject despair and self-loathing." He was wide-eyed and gaunt. Nothing seemed to help. He called Buck Henry to ask if he'd give him enough sleeping pills to end his life if it was absolutely necessary. "Of course, I said I would," Henry says. "I was lying." At one low point, Nichols sat with the producer John Calley, now the head of Sony Pictures, and tallied up his assets item by item on a foolscap pad. Calley says, "I'd add the numbers up and at the bottom it would have thirteen million six, and I'd say, 'Do you see thirteen six?' He'd say, 'Yes.' I'd say, 'Now, can you accept that?' He'd say, 'The only thing I could accept would be you telling me that when I go into debtors' prison you will take care of the children.' " (Max was then eleven and Jenny was nine.) By the time Halcion was identified as the chemical source of his problem and Nichols stopped taking it, he had learned, he says, "what people are like when you're not so shiny and you don't have your powers." (His marriage to Davis-Goff broke up shortly thereafter.)

His collapse proved cautionary, and his subsequent movies, from Neil Simon's "Biloxi Blues" and "Working Girl" to "Primary Colors" and "The Birdcage," were an aggressive reassertion of his commercial shine. With the exception of "Primary Colors," a subtle dissection of power and marriage, the films are crowd-pleasing fables. Nichols's impulse was clearly to build himself as solidly as possible into the Hollywood system. "Every development executive, every studio president, has a list of directors," Spielberg says, "and Mike has never been off the A-list." This puts Nichols's survival at the top of the Hollywood tree at thirty-four years and counting—longer than such legends as Preston Sturges, Billy Wilder, John Huston, and Frank Capra. Spielberg adds, "You want him because you know that he's going to tell the story better than it was told in the screenplay you bought. You're going to be getting basically two scripts for the price of one." Nichols knows the value of stories like "The Remains of the Day," "All the Pretty Horses," and "The Reader"; they are works he has produced, or will produce, but wasn't interested in directing. He loved the intellectual showboating of Stoppard's "Arcadia," a play about chaos theory, and wanted to make it into a film, but he couldn't make the numbers work. "You don't want to take advantage of your friends and say, 'Would you mind doing this at a quarter of your price?' " he says.

"If movies hadn't changed so radically, what Mike would have been, perhaps should have been," Jules Feiffer says, "is the successor to a director like George Cukor—working in romantic comedy with urbane wit and style. But those times passed. So he had to shuffle around to find something to replace that." In choosing his projects, Nichols needs to feel, he says, that "only I can do this." When he picked "What Planet Are You From?," he thought, Yes, this is for me. I know what to do with it. Nichols's next film, starring Robin Williams and with a script by Elaine May, will be a remake of the classic Ealing comedy "Kind Hearts and Coronets." "I can only follow my excitement," Nichols says. "Sometimes I wish it were more highminded, and sometimes I'm glad that it's not. I have no choice either way. I don't think 'The Graduate' and 'Carnal Knowledge' were any different from what I'm doing now." But the fact remains that the early pictures said new things in an ironic, challenging way, and the later work ruffles no feathers.

In any case, Nichols's asking price for mainstream movies has gone up: he now gets about seven and a half million dollars just for taking on a film, plus approximately twelve per cent of the gross. "So it's hard for him to say no," John Calley says. Some of his friends wish he would. "He knows I don't like a lot of the stuff he does. I think it's beneath him," Buck Henry says. "He should be doing more 'Hurlyburly's." But Nichols, who has heard the arguments, is unmoved. "All movies are pure process," he says. "A commercial movie isn't less process than an art movie. You can't make your decisions about a film on the basis of 'Is it important enough? Is it serious enough?' It's either alive or it's not for me. If it's alive, I want to do it." He adds, "If you're funny, and you stay funny, I think that's already doing pretty good."

In the pale-gray calm of his midtown editing suite, Nichols sits behind his editor, Richie Marks, who works away at an Avid console, tweaking the finale of "What Planet Are You From?" on a triptych of screens. Bening and Shandling—the earthling and the reconstructed alien—stand facing each other to reaffirm their marital vows. Bening is saying, "Harold, meeting you has taught me the universe is one big screwed-up place where everyone's just trying to work out their problems, but I'm honored to work them out with you, because . . . I think . . . I love you." When the lights come on, Nichols says, "I have this experience over and over. I make a movie because it draws me, and when I get it all finished I think, Christ, look, it's about me." The alien, who comes to earth merely to exploit women, has been humanized by love—and he becomes, as Nichols points out, "simultaneously the leader of his planet." In Nichols's eyes, his marriage to Diane Sawyer has wrought the same miracle. "True love made Pinocchio a real boy," Nichols said in a TV interview. "We all sort of feel like we're contraptions, like we pasted ourselves together—a little bit from here, a little bit from there-and then, if you're very lucky, along comes someone who loves you the right way, and then you're real."

"Mike spent many years without happiness. I mean, there were dark years where it wasn't quite working in relationships," Calley says. "He was in them but they weren't giving him a lot of joy. With Diane, he doesn't have to pretend not to be who he is to make a partner comfortable." Intimacy requires equality; and Sawyer, who has her own constituency, checkbook, and clout, is in every way an equal to Nichols, whom she first met while waiting to board a Concorde flight from Paris. Even today, if asked to shut her eyes and picture him, Sawyer sees Nichols as she did that first day: "All that light in his eyes and some sort of invitation. He's just full of invitation. It's like, 'Let's be young together. Let's see things for the first time and tell each other the absolute truth, want to?' " After their chance meeting, Sawyer approached Nichols for a TV interview: "I just had this idea of wild intelligence and that there'd be some surprise there," she says. The surprise was, she says, "that there was no end to the surprises."

Nichols and Sawyer live on the seventh floor of a handsome Fifth Avenue apartment building with a view of the Metropolitan Museum of Art from their library. Most of Nichols's art collection was sold off at bargain-basement prices in his Halcion panic; at one point he owned six paintings by Balthus, including the infamous "The Guitar Lesson," which hung over his bed. ("I had to get rid of it," he says. "It pissed off too many women.") But there is still a Stubbs, a Fischl, and a beautiful Morandi study of bottles whose hard-won peace echoes the current mood of its owner. He is on record as saying that the best definition of happiness appears in Tom Stoppard's "The Real Thing." "Happiness is equilibrium," the main character says. "Shift your weight." "It's good, and it's true," Nichols continues Stoppard's thought. "You have to stay light on your feet and remember what's important and what's not." These days, Nichols teaches; he attends meetings of Friends In Deed, an outreach charity for people with AIDS and other life-threatening diseases, which he founded with the actress Cynthia O'Neal; and he keeps up a proliferating E-mail correspondence. He visits his horses, and he even cooks now: his specialties include lemon pasta, risotto with smoked mozzarella, and sour-cream-peach ice cream. Sawyer leaves notes on the floor beside their bed when she slips off to the network every day at 4 A.M. to anchor "Good Morning America"; before going back to sleep, according to Sawyer, Nichols "opens one eye and says, 'Tell it like it is.' "

On the chaise longue in the bedroom is an embroidered pillow with words that play on a line from one of Nichols's favorite movies, "Lawrence of Arabia," in which an Arab tells Lawrence to abandon a straggler in his party. "It is written," the Arab says. The cushion gives Lawrence's answer: "Nothing Is Written." It seems an apt motto for Nichols's journey. Nichols, who keeps no diaries and few mementos of his extraordinary life, is still all future. "He can go on and on until he chooses not to go on anymore," Spielberg says of Nichols's moviemaking career. But the greatest of Nichols's mises en scène is himself: he has created a person who lives well in the world.

At the end of our time together, he sat back on the sofa and declared himself pleased with the conversation. "I do well with the fundamentally inconsolable," I said. The words seemed to surprise Nichols and to press him back in his seat. His eyes fluttered shut for a moment, then opened. "We get a lot done, you know," he said.

BERT LAHR

THE LION AND ME

ON NOVEMBER 6TH, 1998, twenty-six years after "The Wizard of Oz" was last released and on the eve of its sixtieth anniversary, a spiffy, digitally remastered print of the film arrived in eighteen hundred movie theatres throughout the land. With a rub rub here and a rub rub there, "The Wizard of Oz," which never looked bad, has been made to look even better. Dorothy's ruby slippers are rubier. Emerald City is greener. Kansas, a rumpled and grainy black-and-white world, has been restored to a buff, sepia Midwestern blandness. And, since everything that rises nowadays in America ends up in a licensing agreement, new Oz merchandise will shower the planet like manna from hog heaven.

The last time I watched "The Wizard of Oz" from start to finish was in 1962, at home, with my family. My father, Bert Lahr, who played the Cowardly Lion, was sixty-seven. I was twenty-one; my sister, Jane, was nineteen. My mother, Mildred, who never disclosed her age, was permanently thirty-nine. By then, as a way of getting to know the friendly absence who answered to the name of Dad, I was writing a biography—it was published, in 1969, as "Notes on a Cowardly Lion"—and I used any occasion with him as field work. This was the first time we'd sat down together as a family to watch the film, but not the first time a Lahr had been secretly under surveillance while viewing it. The family album had infra-red photographs of Jane and me in the mid-forties—Jane in a pinafore, me in short pants—slumped in a darkened movie house as part of a row of well-dressed, bug-eyed kids. Jane, who was five, is scrunched in the back of her seat in a state of high anxiety about the witch's monkey henchmen. I'm trying to be a laid-back big brother: my face shows nothing, but my hands are firmly clutching the armrests.

Recently, Jane told me that for weeks afterward she'd had nightmares about lions, but what had amazed her most then was the movie's shift from black-and-white to Technicolor, not the fact that Dad was up onscreen in a lion's suit. Once, around that time, while waiting up till dawn for my parents to return from a costume party, I heard laughter and then a thud in the hall; I tiptoed out to discover Dad dressed in a skirt and bonnet as Whistler's Mother, passed out on the floor. That was shocking. Dad dressed as a lion in a show was what he did for a living, and was no big deal. Our small, sunless Fifth Avenue apartment was full of Dad's disguises, which he'd first used onstage and in which he now occasionally appeared on TV. The closet contained a woodsman's props (axe, jodhpurs, and boots); a policeman's suit and baton; a New York Giants baseball outfit, with cap and cleats. The drawers of an apothecary's cabinet, which served as a wall-length bedroom bureau, held his toupées, starting pistol, monocle, putty noses, and makeup. In the living room, Dad was Louis XV, complete with sceptre and periwig, in a huge oil painting made from a poster for Cole Porter's "Du Barry Was a Lady" (1939); in the bedroom, he was a grimacing tramp in Richard Avedon's heartbreaking photograph of him praying, as Estragon, in "Waiting for Godot" (1956).

Over the decades, the popular memory of these wonderful stage performances has faded; the Cowardly Lion remains the enduring posthumous monument to Dad's comic genius. While we were growing up, there was not one Oz image or memento of any kind in the apartment. (Later, at Sotheby's, Dad acquired a first edition of L. Frank Baum's "The Wonderful Wizard of Oz.") The film had not yet become a cult. Occasionally, a taxi-driver or a passerby would spot Dad in the street and call out, "Put 'em up, put 'em *uuuhp!*" Dad would smile and tip his tweed cap, but the film's popularity didn't seem to mean as much to him as it did to other people.

As we grew older and more curious, Mom had to prod Dad out of his habitual solitude to divulge tidbits of information to us. So, as we assumed our ritual positions around the TV—Mom propped up with bolsters on the bed, Jane sprawled on the floor with our Scotch terrier, Merlin, me on the chaise longue, Dad at his desk—the accumulated knowledge we brought to the movie was limited to a few hard-won facts. To wit: Dad had held out for twenty-five hundred dollars a week with a five-week guarantee, which turned into a twenty-six-week bonanza because of the technical complexities of the production numbers; in the scene where the Lion and Dorothy fall asleep in the poppy field and wake to find it snowing, the director, Victor Fleming, had asked for a laugh and Dad had come up with "Unusual weather we're havin', ain't it?"; his makeup took two hours a day to apply and was so complicated that he had to have lunch through a straw; he wore football shoulder pads under his twenty-five-pound lion suit; and his tail, which had a fishing line attached to it, was wagged back and forth by a stagehand with a fishing rod who was positioned above him on a catwalk. It was only memories of the Munchkins, a rabble of a hundred and twenty-four midgets assembled from around the world, that seemed to delight Dad and bring a shine to his eyes. "I remember one day when we were supposed to shoot a scene with the witch's monkeys," he told me. "The head of the group was a little man who called himself the Count. He was never sober. When the call came, everybody was looking for the Count. We could not start without him. And then, a little ways offstage, we heard what sounded like a whine coming from the men's room." He went on, "They found the Count. He got plastered during lunch, and fell in the latrine and couldn't get himself out."

Dad, in his blue Sulka bathrobe, with the sash tied under his belly, was watching the show from his Victorian mahogany desk, which was positioned strategically at a right angle to the TV. Here, with his back to the room, he sat in a Colonial maple chair—the throne from which, with the minutest physical adjustment, he could watch the TV, work his crossword puzzles, and listen to the radio all at the same time. Except to eat, Dad hardly ever moved from this spot. He was almost permanently rooted to the desk, which had a pea-green leatherette top and held a large Funk & Wagnall's dictionary, a magnifying glass, a commemorative bronze medal from President Eisenhower's Inauguration (which he'd attended), various scripts, and the radio. On that afternoon, long before Dorothy had gone over the rainbow and into Technicolor, Dad had donned his radio earphones and tuned in the Giants' game. "Bert!" Mom said. "Bert!" But Dad didn't answer.

This was typical. At dinner, after he finished eating, Dad would some-times wander away from the table without so much as a fare-thee-well; at Christmas, for which he never bought presents, the memories of his unhappy childhood made the ritual exchange of gifts almost unbearable, so he'd slip back to his desk as soon as possible. Now, just as his ravishing Technicolor performance was about to begin, he'd drifted off again, retreating into that private space.

That was irrefutably him up there, disguised in a lion's suit, telling us in the semaphore of his outlandishness what he was feeling in the silence of his bedroom. It was confusing, and more disturbing than I realized then, to see Dad so powerful onscreen and so paralyzed off it. "Yeah, it's sad believe me missy / When you're born to be a sissy / Without the vim and *voive*," Dad sang, in words so perfectly fitting his own intonation and idiom that it almost seemed he was making them up. In a sense, the song *was* him; it was written to the specifications of his paradoxical nature by E. Y. (Yip) Harburg and Harold Arlen, who had already provided him with some of his best material, in "Life Begins at 8:40" (1934) and "The Show Is On" (1936).

"I got to the point where I could do him," Arlen told me. And Harburg, who once said that he could "say something in Bert's voice that I couldn't with my own," saw social pathos in Dad's clowning. "I accepted Bert and wanted him for the part because the role was one of the things 'The Wizard of Oz' stands for: the search for some basic human necessi-ty," he said. "Call it anxiety; call it neurosis. We're in a world we don't understand. When the Cowardly Lion admits that he lacks courage, every-body's heart is out to him. He must be somebody who embodies all this pathos, sweetness, and yet puts on the comic bravura." He added, "Bert had that quality to such a wonderful degree. It was in his face. It was in his talk. It was in himself."

When the song began onscreen, Dad swivelled around in his chair to watch himself; once the song was over, he stepped forward and switched over to football.

"Dad!" we cried.

"Watch it in Jane's room," he said.

"Is it gonna kill you, Bert?"

Dad's beaky profile turned toward Mom; his face was a fist of irrita-
tion. "Look, Mildred, I see things," he said. "Things I coulda . . . I'm older
now. There's stuff I coulda done better." Mother rolled her eyes toward the
ceiling. I returned us to Oz. Dad pulled the headphones up from around
his neck and went back to the hand of solitaire he'd started. His performance was enough for the world; it wasn't enough for him.

Onscreen, the Lion was panic-stricken but fun; his despair was delightful. ("But I could show my prowess / Be a lion, not a mouesse / If I only
had the *noive*.") The Lion had words for what was going on inside him; he
asked for help and got it. At home, there were no words or even tears, just
the thick fog of some ontological anxiety, which seemed to have settled
permanently around Dad and was palpable, impenetrable—it lifted only
occasionally, for a few brilliant moments. "I do believe in spooks. I do. I
do. I do" is the Cowardly Lion's mantra as the foursome approach the
Wicked Witch's aerie. In life, Dad was constantly spooked, and his fear
took the form of morbid worry. It wasn't so much a state of mind as a con-
tinent over which Dad was the bewildered sovereign. Onstage, Dad gave
his fear a sound—"*Gnong, gnong, gnong!*" It was a primitive, hilarious yaw-
ping, which seemed to sum up all his wide-eyed loss and confusion.
Offstage, there was no defining it. The clinical words wheeled out these
days for his symptoms—"manic depressive," "bipolar"—can't convey the
sensual, dramatic, almost reverent power of the moroseness that Dad
could bring with him into a room, or the crazy joy he could manufacture
out of it onstage. It was awful and laughable at the same time. We could-
n't fathom it; instead, we learned to live with it and to treat him with
amused affection. He was our beloved grump. He was perpetually distracted from others, and, despite his ability to tease the last scintilla of
laughter from a role, he had no idea how to brighten his own day. "I listened to the audience, and they told me where the joke was," he told me
backstage at S. J. Perelman's "The Beauty Part" (1962) after he'd got a
howl from a line that had no apparent comic payoff. Why couldn't he listen as closely to us?

When you kissed Dad on the top of his bald head—it smelled deli-
ciously like the inside of a baseball glove—he didn't turn around; when

you talked to him, he didn't always answer; sometimes he even forgot our names. That was the bittersweet comedy of his self-absorption. But the Lion confessed his fears, he looked people in the eye, he was easy to touch (even Dorothy, in their first fierce encounter, puts a hand on him); he joined arms with the others and skipped off down the Yellow Brick Road. At the finale, their victory was a triumph of collaboration. In private, as even our little family get together made apparent, Dad never collaborated; he never reached out (in all the years I went off to camp or college, he wrote me only one letter, and it was dictated); he never elaborated on what weighed him down and kept us under wraps. But there was a gentleness to his bewilderment, which made both the audience and the family want to embrace him. His laughter was a comfort to the world; in his world, which was rarely humorous, we comforted him. All the family forces were marshalled to keep Dad's demons at bay and "to be happy," an instruction that translated into specific behavior that would generate no worries—good humor, loyalty, gratitude, obedience, and looking good.

If Dad had had a tail, he would have twisted it just as the Lion did; instead, he had to make do with his buttons and with the cellophane from his cigarette packs, which he perpetually rolled between his fingers. What was Dad afraid of? We never knew exactly. Things were mentioned: work, money, Communists, cholesterol, garlic, the "Big C." Even a fly intruding into his airspace could bring a sudden whirlwind of worry as he tried to stalk the pest with a flyswatter. "The son of a bitch has been hit before," he would say, lashing at the fly and missing. Dad's global anxiety seeped into the foundation of all our lives; it was hard to see, and, when it was finally identified, it had to be fortified against. One of the most efficient ways to do this was to treat Dad as a metaphor—a sort of work of art, whose extraordinary and articulate performing self was what we took to heart instead of the deflated private person who seemed always at a loss. Any lessons Dad taught about excellence, courage, perseverance, discipline, and integrity we got from his stage persona. His best self—the one that was fearless, resourceful, and generous, and that told the truth—was what he saved for the public, which included us; otherwise, as every relative of a star knows, the family had to make do with what was left over. Even at the end of our Oz viewing, Dad brushed aside our praise, which seemed only to increase his anxiety. As he shuffled into the kitchen to get some ice cream, he glanced over at Mom. "If I'd made a hit as a *human being*, then perhaps I'd be sailing in films now," he said.

When "The Wizard of Oz" opened in New York, on August 17, 1939, fifteen thousand people were lined up outside the Capitol Theatre by 8 A.M. Dad's photograph was in the window of Lindy's, across the street, and the *Times* declared his roar "one of the laughingest sounds since the talkies came in." "Believe me it was a tonic for my inferiority complex which is so readily developed in Hollywood," Dad wrote to Mildred, who would become Mrs. Lahr in 1940. As an animal, in closeup, and eight times as large as life, Dad, with his broad, burlesque energy, was acceptable; there was no place for his baggy looks and his clowning, eccentric mannerisms in talking pictures except on the periphery of romantic stories. Despite his huge success, Metro soon dropped his option. He signed for a Broadway musical, "Du Barry Was a Lady." "Well, how many lion parts are there," Dad said as he departed from Hollywood.

Over the years, especially after my son was born, in 1976, I'd catch glimpses of Dad as the Lion, but, perhaps out of some residual loyalty to his bias, I could never sit through the film. The hubbub around the movie irritated me, because the other accomplishments of the performers were swept away in the wake of its unique and spectacular success. I think Dad knew that he was a hostage to technology: a Broadway star whose legend would go largely unrecorded while, by the luck of a new medium, performers who couldn't get work on Broadway would be preserved and perpetuated in the culture. Nowadays, the general public doesn't know about the likes of Florenz Ziegfeld, Abe Burrows, Ethel Merman, Bea Lillie, Billy Rose, Walter Winchell, Clifton Webb, and Nancy Walker, whose stories intersected with Dad's.

What lives on is the Cowardly Lion. When I watch him now, I don't see just the Lion; I see the echoes—the little touches and moves—of those long-forgotten sensational stage performances that Dad condensed into his evergreen role. His floppy consonants, slurred vowels, malapropisms, and baritone vibrato all derived from the collection of sophisticated operatic sendups he'd developed first for Harburg and Arlen's "Things" (from

"Life Begins at 8:40") and "Song of the Woodman" (from "The Show Is On"), to be perfected in "If I Were King of the Forest":

> Each rabbit would show respect to me,
> The chipmunks genuflect to me,
> Tho' my tail would lash
> I would show compash
> For ev'ry underling
> If I, if I were king.
> Just king.

The Cowardly Lion's boxing bravado ("I'll fight you both together if you want! I'll fight you with one paw tied behind my back! I'll fight you standin' on one foot! I'll fight you wit' my eyes closed!") and his woozy body language (the shoulder rolls, the elbows akimbo, the bobbing head) were grafted onto the Lion from Dad's portrayal of the punch-drunk sparring partner Gink Schiner, in his first Broadway hit, "Hold Everything" (1928). And when the Wizard awards the Cowardly Lion his medal for courage, even Dad's vaudeville act, "What's the Idea" (1922–25), came into play: he swaggered like the policeman he had impersonated while trying to both arrest and impress the hoochy-coochy dancer Nellie Bean. "Read what my medal says—'Courage,' " the Lion says. "Ain't it de truth. Ain't it de *trooth*."

In later years, one of the many canards that grew up about the film was that there was a feud between the old pros and the young Judy Garland—that they had tried to upstage her and push her off the Yellow Brick Road. "How could that be?" my godfather, Jack Haley, who played the Tin Man, told me. "When we go off to see the Wizard, we're locked arm in arm, and every shot is a long shot. How can you push someone out of the picture with a long shot?" Although Garland wasn't pushed out, her "Over the Rainbow," which became the anthem of a generation, was almost cut from the movie three times. According to Dad, Harburg hadn't liked the original tune, which he found too symphonic and heroic. Years later, when I was working on a book about Harburg's lyrics, Arlen explained the deadlock, which Ira Gershwin had finally been called in to arbitrate. "I got sick to my stomach," Arlen told me. "I knew Ira didn't like ballads. He only liked things with a twinkle. Ira came over, listened, and said, 'That's a good melody.' I knew the heat was off. Yip tried out a few musical notions and came up with the lyric." Another of their favorite numbers, written for "Oz," was one called "The Jitter Bug," in which bugs bite the travellers, who begin to dance with the trees and flowers. It was cut for reasons of pace and of balance, and though it gave Dad a big dance number, he never expressed regret over the loss of the material. What he remembered was the hard work and the offscreen hacking around. "Smith's premium ham!" the old pros yelled at one another before takes. "Vic Fleming had never experienced guys like us," Dad told me. "Some legitimate directors can't imagine anybody thinking about something else and when he yells 'Shoot!' just going in and playing." He went on, "We'd kid around up to the last minute and go on. You could see he got mad and red-faced. Some actors try and get into the mood. They'll put themselves into the character. I never did that. I'm not that—let's say—dedicated."

Dad died on December 4, 1967, the day I finished my book about him. He had never read any part of it. I saw him again in a dream on January 25, 1977. I'd been arguing about comedy with the distinguished English actor Jonathan Pryce, and had stepped out of his dressing room to cool off, and there was Dad in the corridor. "He was wearing his blue jacket with padded shoulders," I wrote in my diary. "He smelled of cologne, and he felt soft when I hugged him. I said, 'I love you.' I can't remember if he answered. But it felt completely real, with all the details of his presence—smell, feel, look, silence—very clear. I woke up sobbing." I added, "When will we meet again?"

So far, he has not reappeared in my dreams; but, in another sense, as the reissue of "The Wizard of Oz" only underscores, he has never really gone away. He's a Christmas ornament, a pen, a watch, a beanbag toy, a bracelet charm, a snow globe, a light sculpture, a bedroom-wall decoration. (Neiman Marcus's Christmas catalogue includes Dad in "The Wizard of Oz" bedroom—"the ultimate child's bedroom"—which, at a hundred and fifty thousand dollars, is more than twice as much as he was paid for the movie.) In the space of only two days this fall, on the merchandise channel QVC, a new offering of Oz paraphernalia sold about a million and a half dollars, which seems to prove the claim on the Warner Bros. fact sheet that " 'The Wizard of Oz' has Universal Awareness." I should be outraged by all this, I suppose, since Dad's estate gets no money. I should deplore the trivialization of him as an artist and bemoan the pagan impulse to make household gods of mortal endeavor. (When Dad took up painting, in his last years, and realized that there was a market for Cowardly Lion artifacts, even he got the franchise itch, and stopped doing flowers and vegetables in order to churn out lions, which he signed and sold to friends.) But, if I'm honest with myself, these tchotchkes comfort me. They are totems of Dad's legacy of joy, and of his enduring life in the century's collective imagination.

I'm an orphan now, but I'm full of gratitude for the world that made me. I get letters from older readers who knew my parents, and who tell me in passing how proud Dad was of Jane and me. It's nice to know. I think Dad loved us, but it was in the nature of his way of loving that the knowledge is not bone deep. So the marketed trinkets work for me like Mexican *milagros*—talismans that are extensions of prayer and are tacked by the prayerful onto crosses in thanks for the miracle of survival. I'm pushing sixty now, but I find that the conversation with one's parents doesn't end with the grave. I want Dad back to finish the discussion—to answer some questions, to talk theatre, to see me now. Almost anywhere in the city these days, I can turn the corner and run into him. I stroll past a novelty store on Lexington Avenue, and there's Dad as a cookie jar. I steal a peek at the computer of a young woman in the Public Library, and, by God, there he is as a desktop image. I go to buy some wrapping paper at the stationery store, and his face stares at me from the greeting-card rack. "Hiya, Pop," I find myself saying, and continue on my way.

MILDRED LAHR

THOROUGHLY MODERN MILLIE

My MOTHER, WHO WAS
known to the world for over fifty years as Mrs. Bert Lahr, died at the age
of eighty-eight last December. Her first name was Mildred, but in her
declining years my sister, Jane, and I called her Millie, a diminutive she'd
detested in her prime but came to enjoy in old age, since it summoned up
the carefree, gallant part of her—the part that had caused her to douse
herself for years with only one fragrance, "Joy," and to insist on having her
ashes dropped in the foothills of Reno. There, in 1937, on a dude ranch,
she spent what she said were the happiest six months of her life, while she
was in the process of getting divorced from her first husband but was not
yet married to my father.

Millie was a former Ziegfeld girl, who invented a world for her great
blond beauty to inhabit—a world of happy times. "I had fun," she'd say,
reviewing her life, and she did. El Morocco, the Stork Club, the Colony
Club. Havana, Palm Beach, Palm Springs, Beverly Hills. She was born on
Valentine's Day in Cincinnati, in 1907, the second of four children of
Helen and Edgar Schroeder—a hairdresser and an engineer. But she was
abandoned, first by her father, who left the family when she was small, and
then by her mother, who couldn't afford to keep her. So "fun," when she
finally achieved it in adulthood, was a hard-won destiny—a kind of trophy
for her willpower. Even in doddering old age, when she was reduced to
shrugs and scrambled simple sentences, Millie made a show of frivolity.
She'd stand by the elevator outside her fourteenth-floor midtown apartment and ask me, "Wanna dance?" And we did, on the hallway's stale rus-
set carpet. She'd laugh and laugh, and to see Mom laugh was the best. At
those times, she seemed to ask nothing of the world except that it make
her smile. Later, when she had trouble getting out of her armchair, she'd

ask her caretakers to pull her to her feet and dance with her, to the music on her cassette player, which sat on a lacquered black table beside her. She loved Satchmo and Ella Fitzgerald, especially when they sang Cole Porter. Mom and Dad had lived on the same floor of the Waldorf Towers as Porter in 1940, when they were first married and Dad was starring with Ethel Merman in Porter's "Du Barry Was a Lady." Armstrong, Fitzgerald, Frank Sinatra, Duke Ellington, Benny Goodman: the people Millie liked to dance to in the solitude of her room were people she'd met in public when the whole world seemed to find its way to her table.

"I can tell you for sure—it's a *bitch* getting old," she wrote me in 1981, when she was seventy-four. "I had four calls yesterday and everyone talked about their problems—I decided to listen and say *nothing*. I loathe those *types* of calls. Nuff of that." Beauty is the promise of happiness, and to the end of her days Millie lived by beauty's harsh discipline. Life's blemishes had to be hidden away at all costs. At eighty-eight, she still had ten different Estée Lauder lipsticks in her bathroom, and she refused to go out without gloves to hide the liver spots on her hands, which betrayed the age she could no longer remember. Often, when Jane and I took her to dinner, strangers would approach the table to compliment Millie on her beauty, and though she was by then too deaf and confused to understand much, she would hold her head high as Florenz Ziegfeld had taught her and flash her iconic smile. "The Ziegfeld strut," as it was called, was a way of behaving in the proximity of the paying customers to create a sense of aloofness and decorum—to appear at once unattainable and irresistible— and Millie carried it off. She liked to be entertained but didn't entertain; she liked to be fed but wouldn't feed; she liked to be kissed but didn't embrace. Her stock phrase, repeated throughout my childhood, was "Does a mother have to ask for a kiss?" It was almost a command—as if affection were the duty we children owed someone so perfectly formed and so perfectly placed as she. When she was being regal, it was fun to tease her: her backbone would stiffen, and her chin would rise, but her eyes would be shining as she said, "It ain't funny, McGee"—or, even better, brandishing the back of her hand, "You fresh mutt." And once Mom's mask of stature dropped, she showed off a spirited impertinence—when, for example, Dad chased her, nude and squealing, into the bathroom with his Polaroid camera ("Bert, don't you dare!"), or when he tried to goad her into an argument about the roast beef ("You call this meat? This is petrified wood!") so that the tape recorder he'd hidden under the dinner table could capture her curses.

Even in her heyday, my mother didn't say much or have much to say, and her reticence about herself magnified the illusion of her never being at a loss. In almost all the family photos through the decades, she is perfectly composed: feet arranged in third position, teeth gleaming between full lips turned up at the corners from forming the word "Yippee!" Beauty was her capital, and she invested it shrewdly. "She never opened flowers unless there was jewelry in them," said Eve Bealey, another Ziegfeld girl, who roomed with Millie at the St. Regis Hotel when they were chorines together. Mom's looks got her groped under the table by Ernest Hemingway on a yacht in Bimini ("He got a fork in his hand for his trouble," she said) and earned her a marriage proposal from Winthrop Rockefeller. She never lost faith in her incandescence. "I was the prettiest woman in the room," she startled me by saying once in the late seventies, as we emerged from a party of younger folks. She liked to recall a night in the early thirties when, in evening clothes, she and Dad strolled home from Tavern on the Green across the Sheep Meadow in Central Park. A group of dispossessed men warming themselves over a garbage-can fire waved to her and Dad as they passed. "Weren't they angry at the sight of you?" I asked. "No," Millie said. "We gave them hope."

Millie's glamour clearly gave *her* hope. "To get her picture in the papers is the more or less harmless ambition of many a girl who leads a remote and routine existence in a factory or in a general or department store or even on a farm," Ziegfeld wrote in the *Ladies' Home Journal* in 1923, when Millie was a teen-ager. "If her worth and beauty were only known! Or if, like Cinderella, she could only get to the party somehow!" Millie got to the party by the end of the twenties, but her teen-age years, she wrote in "Grandmother Remembers," a fill-in book she started but never completed for Jane's daughter Maya, were "miserable." Millie refused to discuss her past in detail, but the outline of her story was grim enough. She had been fobbed off by her mother onto nuns in a convent, then forced to live with strict grandparents, who, she claimed, treated her like a servant. Her education had been uneven. Once, sitting in a West Side restaurant on a summer afternoon in the late seventies, she told me, "I remember, when I was in the convent, going off by myself and sitting on a hill and wondering if anybody would come to get me. They didn't." Tears streamed down her cheeks as she continued, "I never told your father any of this. I wanted to forget about it. Anyway, he never asked." She said she escaped from the convent with a girlfriend by climbing down a ladder of knotted sheets. It was not the first or the last of Millie's attempts to escape Cincinnati and her circumstances. When she was about ten, her mother was hoping to have her adopted by the formidable and childless Washington grande dame Alice Roosevelt Longworth: the Longworths were a Cincinnati family, and this was before Mrs. Longworth finally had a child of her own, in 1925. In a special photograph that was sent to Mrs. Longworth, Millie is a picture of Edwardian sobriety and industry: high-buttoned shoes, hair held together by a white bow, hands resting on an open book, modest smile calibrated to show character but not eagerness. My mother kept that photograph, along with tattered press clippings and other snapshots of the past, which she would rarely discuss, in a box under her bed. In her story, only Mrs. Longworth's pregnancy prevented Mom from becoming a Roosevelt (though Mom would have been seventeen by then and thus hardly a candidate for adoption). Instead, in time, she aligned herself with the democracy's substitute for aristocracy: celebrity.

Millie, who was intellectually uncertain about so many things, spoke with absolute authority about the imperialism of fame: she once upbraided me for letting my friends call me Lahrheim, which was Dad's original name. (He changed it by deed poll in 1939.) "Your name is Lahr," Millie insisted over tea. "Face it, Mom," I said. "You were married to one of the great Jewish entertainers." Millie folded her napkin carefully in front of her and fixed me with a look. "John, your father was not Jewish," she said. "He was a star."

When Millie engineered her getaway from Cincinnati, it was not as a prim image of Edwardian propriety but as a semi-nude totem of the Jazz Age, modelling the symbols of American womanhood's new mobility—knee-length skirts, skimpy swimsuits, ankle bracelets, and cars. My favorite picture in the box under the bed shows Millie in the Miss Cincinnati contest, on a sweltering Midwestern afternoon: with hands on hips, she struts by the side of a municipal swimming pool, towering above the heads of an ogling, mostly male crowd and the coatless judges, who sprawl on chairs. I can tell by the pitch of Millie's smile that she's relaxed and confident in this arena. Here, at least, she has no responsibility but to be, and she has the world positioned exactly as she liked it: at arm's length and at total attention.

"A very excited young lady arrived in New York today," said a Pathé press release dated July 18, 1929. "She is Miss Mildred Schroeder who was declared the winner of the 'Pathé Pretties' beauty show for which she was awarded a cash prize, a trip to New York with all expenses paid, and a role in George Le Maire's new comedy 'Barbers' College.' " Millie was twenty-two when she got to Manhattan. She quickly discovered that with the thrill of new possibilities came new terrors. "If you only had one good dress and one pair of shoes, a spot on the dress or the heel breaking was a disaster—a real disaster," she told me. "You didn't want to feel ever again that life was so precarious." But she was lucky. Earl Carroll almost immediately put her on Broadway in the chorus of his "Vanities," and she followed that with a part in "Fine and Dandy" (1930). She then appeared in "George White's Scandals of 1931," which is where Dad first saw her. They met officially four months later, at a penthouse party given by George White, where Millie's sincerity and her nervousness (she was twisting a handkerchief) attracted the sensationally nervous comedian.

Around that time, Millie had her horoscope done. The typed, thirty-four-page booklet was still in her desk when she died. "You are not only a child of DESTINY, but also one of OPPORTUNITY," the closing pages read. Although Bert Lahr was nearly forty—his wife and former vaudeville partner, Mercedes, was in a mental home, and their son, Herbert, was farmed out to an aunt in Arizona—Millie, always a curious mixture of propriety and pragmatism, seized her moment. "I never believed in marrying an actor," Millie told me when I wrote "Notes on a Cowardly Lion." "I thought that one should marry a businessman. I found Bert so different from my picture of an actor. He was a shy person, and that, I think, attract-

ed me. I think he gave me his number, and I think I called him." They
became inseparable. Millie's smile worked its charm; and Dad found it
hard to begrudge Millie anything. He set her up in an apartment at 25
Central Park West with a maid aptly named Peace Determination. In
1936, when Dad claimed he couldn't get a divorce from Mercedes, Millie
gave him six weeks and then sent him a wire: "WAS MARRIED TODAY SATUR-
DAY TO MR JOSEPH ROBINSON ATTORNEY WE ARE ABOUT TO SET SAIL ON OUR
HONEYMOON SOON WILL BE AT SEA AND BERT I LOVE YOU AND HAVE A GREAT
ADMIRATION FOR YOU AS ONE MIGHT HAVE FOR A FATHER NOT A HUSBAND SO
ON THE SPUR OF THE MOMENT DECIDED TO GET MARRIED."

Millie and Robinson had a nine-day honeymoon in Cuba. When she
returned, Dad was suicidal, and pressure from the theatrical community
was enormous. There were private detectives, threatened lawsuits, fierce
confrontations—and after six weeks Millie caved in. "I could not find happiness with you," she wrote to "Robby," and proceeded to divorce him;
Dad, whom the press branded a "love thief," eventually obtained one of the
first divorces in New York State on the ground of incurable mental illness.
Over their twenty-seven-year marriage, Millie often regretted her decision out loud to us, although the scandalous breakup with Robinson was
not mentioned until I began research for Dad's biography, in the mid-sixties. "You *can* love two men at the same time," Millie told Susan Shamroy,
a young actress who roomed with her for a while after Dad died, in 1967.
She had kept her love letters to Robinson, which he had returned to her,
in the top drawer of her writing desk; when I re-read them now, they give
off the gushing Pollyanna scent of Mom in the thirties, when she once
inscribed a photo to a girlfriend, "Oodles of love Woogie Woogie."

Another thing Millie's horoscope said was "You have extraordinary
power to control the insane or those who are psychically out of balance."
Certainly my chronically insecure father was emotionally off kilter. Both
he and Millie, in their own ways, were inconsolable, but because Dad
acted out his sadness both on and off the stage Millie was free to accentu-
ate the positive. In taking care of Dad, Millie hid her own depression from
herself. She was his "Miss Pep"; he was her powerful protector. And almost
overnight Millie found herself at the big table of American life. You can
hear her wonder at it all in a telegram she sent to her mother in 1932:

"MOTHER DARLING AT LAST I GAZED ON THE CAPITOL STOP WASHINGTON IS A
BEAUTIFUL PLACE STOP CAME ON HERE FOR BERT'S OPENING IT WAS THE BIGGEST
HIT EVER KNOWN IN ZIEGFELD'S LAST TEN SHOWS." Soon thereafter, when Sam
Goldwyn asked Millie and her showgirl friend Lucille Ball to come to
Hollywood, Dad begged her to stay in the East, and Millie agreed. She
wanted family and security above all else. While she sometimes acted with
Dad in vaudeville in the off-season or on the occasional one-reeler, the
production to which she gave herself wholly was the management of his
comic genius. She was the sounding board, the butler, the babe, the keeper
of the scrapbook and the flame. She got Dad to make regular contact with his
first wife and their son; she encouraged him to début "Waiting for Godot"
on Broadway; she remembered people's names, which Dad habitually forgot. She created a climate of buoyancy around Dad's gloomy, impossible
self-involvement and connected him to the real world; he, in turn, connected her to fame's adolescent fantasy of having everything all the time.

Millie knew most of the movers and shakers of her era, but she
showed little curiosity about them. It was enough that Hemingway had
made a pass at her (she didn't need to read his books); that she had dined
with the phobic Howard Hughes, who met her at the door with shoebox-
es on his feet (she didn't need to know the story of his fortune); that she
cruised the city after closing time in Walter Winchell's car as he followed
the fires and gangland rubouts that came over his police radio (she didn't
really need to know about Manhattan, whose myth she and Dad were
helping to make). The only history that absorbed Millie was her own.
(When I called her on July 12, 1991, to tell her I'd turned fifty, she said,
"How old am I?") Although she had a reputation for liveliness, she was
curiously passive. She knew how to be admired but not how to be intimate. She seemed to vaguely understand this problem, although she never
discussed it. On her dresser mirror she'd taped a poem by Max Dunaway
called "Love":

> Be it! don't just say it.
> Live it! don't just pray it.
> Do it! don't forget it.
> Give it! don't just get it.

Mom took almost girlish delight in being swept up in the slipstream of provided pleasures. When Jane and I were growing up, in the forties and fifties, these diversions seemed to be non-stop. I remember, most nights, waiting up for Mom and Dad on the threshold of our room, touching Jane's head for "lucky sweat" to keep me safe from the awful things moving behind the curtain. (To call them "monsters" now is to trivialize the enormity of annihilation that lurked there.) The clock in the hall would strike three, then four, and sometimes five as I waited for the elevator door to clang open. When it did, I'd bolt back into bed and pretend to be asleep. Millie—always only Millie—would come in, the sound of her rustling dress preceding her, smelling of perfume and gin as she bent over to kiss us. To this day, neither Jane nor I can stand the smell of gin: the whiff of abandonment. When I confronted Mom about this in adulthood, she was nonplussed. "Your dad wanted me with him," she said. "That was the deal." The price the famous pay for their success is other people—and in this case, that meant Jane and me. We came to see ourselves as the parents who raised *them*. Certainly, Millie never lost her childish expectation of being cared for and entertained. To the end of her days, she loved the New York skyline, the hubbub of headwaiters, the excitement of a curtain going up; and even when she was well beyond partying her first words of greeting were usually "Where are we going?"

Over the years, the lid that Millie put on her story occasionally shifted, and things leaked out. The most sensational revelation came in the early eighties, on Shelter Island, where Millie and my own family were staying with different households. Our hostess was in the throes of a volatile love affair, and when I took her with me to pick up Millie, who was invited to dinner, we got on to the sour subject of romance.

"There's nothing wrong with romance," Millie piped up from the back seat.

"Yeah, sure. You were only married to the most unromantic man in the world."

"Who said anything about your father?" Millie said.

I checked Millie in my rearview mirror. "What do you mean?"

"After your last novel, John," Millie said, "do you think I'm going to tell you anything?"

I pulled over on the shoulder. "I'm not moving until you tell me what you mean."

Millie's hand played across her pearl choker. Her chin assumed the Ziegfeld tilt. "I'm going to say two words, John. And that's the end of it." She paused. We waited. "Joseph Cotten," she said.

In the decade or so that remained of her life, she could not be drawn out on the subject of Cotten, except to say, "He was a very nice man." But last year, as Mom was having her hair washed in the hospital by her hairdresser, Helen Sigiel, whom she had been going to every Friday at 3 P.M. since 1939, Helen told me, "I remember once she came in and said, 'Helen, make me look beautiful. I've got a big date.' I thought she meant your father. But it was Joseph Cotten." At the mention of Cotten, Millie looked up and smiled. Later, after Millie's funeral, Helen had more to say: "Mrs. Lahr said your father was a very selfish lover—sort of left her in the lurch, so she just met others. She went out with Joseph Cotten for a long time." Helen thought of Millie as brave, and I think she was. "She got out of life what she wanted. She just went out and got it," Helen said. Millie, who had fought so hard for a family ("You had 'em, Mildred," said Dad, who didn't want more children, "you raise 'em"), was fiercely protective of her children and of her happiness. Her close girlfriends knew of her flirtations (three more longtime relationships, including one with the actor Dean Jagger, emerged after her death), but with her children, even after we'd had our own marital chaos, Millie stayed *shtum*. Until this year, Jane could never admit to me that at the age of fifteen she and her best friend had stumbled on Mom at P. J. Clarke's having a double date with one of our fun-loving "aunts." "We'd get dressed up, and we'd go and sit and have Bacardi cocktails and pretend to be our mothers," Jane recalls. "We're in there on our regular weekend jaunt and I look up and there, at a table, is Mom and Aunt Louise with maybe three guys. They were animated, having a great time, giggling. Then I suddenly got the picture that this went on all along. We kind of snuck out. They didn't see that we'd seen them. I was devastated. I went home and cried." But in the last year of Mom's life Jane noticed that, in her babble, Mom was wrestling with the high times of her past. Once, Mom told Jane she'd had a dream about Dad, and she started to cry. "He was really very good to me. I miss him," she said, and added, "But I loved the boys."

Dad was present at our conception but was otherwise engaged. He was a friendly absence, whose support was primarily financial, but it took guile to pick his deep pockets, and Millie, who was ashamed of her lack of learning, was determined that her kids be sent to the best schools: Riverdale, Dalton, Yale, Oxford, the Slade School of Fine Art. All Dad's fee-saving suggestions were pooh-poohed by her. "John's not going to Notre Dame!" I remember her insisting when Dad announced that he'd secured my admission to the Blue and Gold after bending an elbow with the university's president at the Stork Club. "He's applying to Williams, where Foxy Sondheim's son Stephen goes," Millie told him. She had great powers of denial and therefore of idealization. "She wanted Shirley Temple," Jane says. "She got Eloise." Still, in public anyway, we were presented as pint-size bundles of abundance, who proved that the system and the family worked. Jane, who was born with a wandering eye, became perfect after an operation at the age of five; I was—well, if not the perfect son, then the perfect date. By the age of ten, I was lighting ladies' cigarettes, holding the chairs of the women next to me, tipping the hat-check girl.

Dad made his decisions unilaterally and often against Millie's vested interest. In 1943, for instance, he put the Beverly Hills house they'd built up for sale while Millie was giving birth to Jane; he didn't even consult her. He did tell her, however, as soon as she came to after her Caesarean section. But Millie's credo, and the only advice she ever gave me, was "Don't let anything get in your way." In her heyday, she was not beyond "fainting" to keep Dad's attention on her, rather than on his "Hot-Cha!" co-star, Lupe Velez, who fancied Dad and infamously wore no underwear; nor was she beyond throwing her golf clubs out the car window when Dad, a one-handicap golfer, refused to play with her. Sometimes her tantrums backfired. I remember being awakened in the late fifties by a furious row and Mom's sensational curse "Oh, Bert, go shit in a hat!" I rushed to their locked bedroom door and peeked through the keyhole. In his blue-and-red Sulka bathrobe, with the sash knotted under his beer belly, Dad was standing toe to toe with Millie, who was right up under his gherkin nose.

Suddenly, Dad popped Millie one, and she dropped out of my field of vision. Dad didn't. He backpedalled to his corner, like the middleweights he liked to watch on television. He stood there bouncing on his toes and waiting for Millie to get to her feet so he could finish her off. She was down for the count.

Millie's blows tended to be indirect. She had learned from decades of living with a tyrannical star how to kill with kindness and how to deliver a full-court press of guilt. "Be careful," she said to me when I left for London in 1970—a move that she never understood or accepted. "You're the only man I have left." The subtext of Millie's lament was: I behave perfectly, I make very few demands, I hold everything in, and what do I get? This theme was spelled out when a *New Yorker* reader sent me a letter from Millie, written in 1971, that read, in part, "You never come out ahead with children no matter how hard you try. So my honest advice is to think of *yourself*—I never did and find with all the love and background I gave John and Jane, I am still very much out of their lives. C'est la vie." When taken to task for this sort of behavior, as Millie was once by my exasperated ex-wife ("You manipulated Bert! You manipulated John! You're a terrible manipulative woman!"), Millie rose grandly above the indictment. The next week, however, she took me aside. "I've looked 'manipulative' up in the dictionary, John," she said. "And I am none of those things. And what's more, you better be nice to me, because I'm not going to be around that long."

She equated the spilling of emotion with bad form, so when she got angry she would usually get very quiet. She'd say, "I'm off him!" (Or "them!" or "you!") And she was—off into some unreachable, unknowable zone of her interior. To a child, it was like death; it was scary to see her vanish before your eyes. Once, in the late forties, on the luxury train to Las Vegas, where Dad was to play the Thunderbird Hotel, they got into a bad argument in our couchette, and Millie went into one of her silences. The tension was miserable. I went into the bathroom, and came out holding my penis. "All right, you guys," I said, doing my Edward G. Robinson. "Drop the gun!" And they did—they laughed. That's how I got interested in jokes; jokes were mind-to-mind resuscitation. I learned to keep a wary eye on Mom for signs of her disappearing act, and I became expert at consolation. But sometimes you couldn't hug or joke Millie back to life.

Once, after our parents had gone without speaking to each other for forty-eight hours, Jane and I sent them a telegram that read, "TALK."

Mom and Dad managed to stay together for a lifetime, but there were occasional dramatic U-turns. In June, 1965, when I was cramming for my final exams at Oxford, there was a knock at my door. I opened it, and Mom was standing before me in open-toed shoes and her mink stole. "I've left your father," she said. Dad's first wife, Mercedes, had just died, and he'd stayed up for three nights mourning her. They'd argued; Mom walked out. After a few weeks of sulking in her tent—or rather in mine—she returned to Dad, but the issue was more definitively resolved years later, literally from beyond the grave, when a famous British medium put Millie in touch with Dad. "I asked him if he had seen Mercedes, his first wife, who has been dead for some time," Millie is quoted as saying in "Ena Twigg: Medium" (1973), in a case history called "The Return of Bert Lahr." "And Bert said No, and anyway, he told me, I was the one, I was his love. He said he'll be waiting for me when I take my step." Incidentally, Dad also delivered his editorial complaints about my nearly four-hundred-page biography of him. "He said he thought it could have been longer," Millie said.

Millie never married after Dad died, but she had offers. "I never wanted to cook for a man again," Millie said; she had never willingly applied heat to food in any case. She had a hard time mourning Dad, perhaps because in her conscious devotion she'd unconsciously wished him dead for so long. She moved out of our sunless Fifth Avenue apartment and into her sunless midtown apartment. She rarely entertained. She'd nod to people in her building, but she kept her distance. "First thing you know, they're inviting you to drinks, then you've got to invite them back," she said. She had her independence, her children, her name. She enjoyed being Mrs. Bert Lahr, which could still get her a good table at Sardi's and the occasional big welcome from maître d's at the expensive watering holes around town, which she could hardly afford now. Gradually, she cobbled together a quiet new life for herself: she got a job as a librarian at the Christian Science Reading Room, on Fifth Avenue at Forty-eighth Street; she went to concerts with her friends from work. When Dad was alive, she'd loved the nights; now she loved the mornings. "Darlings, I haven't any news," she wrote, signing off a letter in 1978. "Tomorrow at 5:45 A.M. will be here too soon, when I arise and pray for all of you and get dressed and stand on the corner for the bus. N.Y. is very quiet and rather interesting at that hour."

It was a brave fight for a personal, not a public, identity; and, despite Mom's earlier protests to us about how she'd got a "bad deal" from us kids, it was a journey that she had to make alone. In her old age, she seemed to me more vulnerable, more valiant, and more fun, despite her unnerving habit of wearing my high-school ring on her wedding finger and introducing me as "my hus—my son, John." She was no longer the Look Police, correcting our hair, our clothes, our methods of child-rearing. (She had once taken exception to my playing so much with my infant son, Chris. "You know, he'll never remember," she said.) As an octogenarian, she sailed into life with abandon. "I don't care," she'd say with a saucy roll of her shoulder when asked where she wanted to go; or she'd wait while something she couldn't hear or understand was painstakingly explained to her and then say, "Exactly." She remembered no names, she paid no bills, she knew no directions. Although she stopped reading, she continued up to the end to work the "à la carte" side of the menu like a champ. In the end, the big spender and the notorious demander of service had her American Express card cut before her eyes in Bloomingdale's after five months' worth of bills had gone unpaid, but she felt not a twinge of humiliation. On the other hand, she had her victories. "I live there," she'd say triumphantly when I dropped her at home after a trip to the movies, as if she'd discovered the wheel instead of her apartment building.

At the end of her life, Millie was a wave and a smile—almost heroic. She had a showgirl's sure knowledge of how to make an entrance and an exit, and she saved her most eloquent words for last. At the hospital one afternoon, she got particularly agitated and adamant. "You don't believe me," she said. "There's been an announcement. This house is closing. Now and forever. You're always so sure of yourself, John. I'm telling you, this house is closing." Although she lived three more weeks, on a respirator, she never spoke again.

The day after Mom died, Jane and I went to her apartment. Before she'd gone into the hospital for the last time, she had said she wanted to give me something. "What would that be?" I asked. "My blue dress," she said. I loved that answer, but I would have preferred answers of a different kind—something that would help me better understand her and how we got to be who we are. Still, I suspected that she had left something for us in the apartment. On big solo journeys, like one she took to Europe in the late fifties, Millie had handed us letters containing avowals of her love before taking off, and when I opened her desk drawer I felt even more certain of my hunch. There, positioned so we couldn't miss it, was an envelope with "My Will—This is For John and Jane" written on it in Millie's well-formed extrovert's hand.

But then we pulled her old box of photos out from under her bed, and while Jane picked through them I made a beeline for a massive mahogany chest, which, when we were growing up, had stretched the length of our parents' bedroom wall, with enough bookshelves at either side for the World Book Encyclopedia, Dad's complete edition of Samuel Pepys's diaries, and his scrapbooks. In the middle of this towering construction were five rows of small drawers, each the size of a Stilton cheese and with its own elegant china knob. In those days, the drawers were filled with mysterious things: Dad's wig, a policeman's badge, a starting pistol, his stage monocles and false mustaches, papers concerning his change of name. And in 1970, when Mom moved to her one-bedroom, the chest moved with her and came to rest in the living room.

I had to push past Millie's walker and her wheelchair to get close to it. Maybe what I'd find wasn't a letter to us. Maybe it was letters to Millie from her mother. Or love letters from Joseph Cotten. Maybe it was a childhood diary. Or something from Dad that would shed light on their thirty-six-year association. I opened the drawers slowly, starting at the bottom and moving upward from left to right. At one point, I had to clamber onto the ledge of the chest to reach the drawers at the very top, near where Mom and Dad had once hidden their dog-eared copy of "From Here to Eternity." It felt like holding on to a rock face. I tilted each high drawer out as far as I could, and then, on tiptoe, strained to feel into every corner. The drawers were all empty.

INDEX

A NOTE ON THE AUTHOR

John Lahr has been writing about theater and popular culture for *The New Yorker* since 1992. He is the author of sixteen books, among them *Notes on a Cowardly Lion: The Biography of Bert Lahr* and *Prick Up Your Ears: The Biography of Joe Orton*, which was made into a film. He has twice won the George Jean Nathan Award for Dramatic Criticism. John Lahr divides his time between London and New York.